# READING COUNTRY MUSIC

# READING COUNTRY MUSIC

Steel Guitars, Opry Stars,

and Honky-Tonk Bars

*Cecelia Tichi, Editor*

DUKE UNIVERSITY PRESS   Durham and London   1998

© 1998 Duke University Press
All rights reserved
Printed in the United States
of America on acid-free paper ♾
Typeset in Berkeley Book by
Tseng Information Systems, Inc.
Library of Congress Cataloging-
in-Publication Data appear on
the last printed page of this book.

The text of this book originally was
published without the index and essays
by Herbert, Kreyling, Lang, Lanham,
Neal, and Rumble as volume 94, no. 1
(1995) of the *South Atlantic Quarterly*.

# Contents

# Acknowledgments

Publication of *Reading Country Music* has been aided greatly by the generosity of the Country Music Foundation, in particular the Director, William Ivey, and the Registrar of Collections, Mark Medley. I am thankful as well to David Sanjek of the Broadcast Music Incorporated (BMI) Archives for assisting with photo requests.

At Duke University Press, Reynolds Smith, Executive Editor, has been ever encouraging and helpful, while the copyeditor, Bob Mirandon, worked meticulously for the benefit of the entire book. Pam Morrison guided the production with patience and firmness. The assistance of the press staff has helped us all become better readers of country music.

# Introduction

Cecelia Tichi

"Country music is our heritage," Chet Atkins said in one interview. "They oughta teach it in the schools." If "Mister Guitar" has a point, then *Reading Country Music* advances one genre of American music toward the forum of education, broadly conceived, at this cultural studies moment. Atkins's pronouns are in some sense disconcerting. The *we/us* in "our heritage" will strike some as overdetermined, proprietary, and univocal, and the pedagogical "they" as problematic in its authoritarian overtones and disavowal of certain folks (*them*). But Atkins essentially makes the point that country music is a genre indigenous to the United States, that it bears historical weight and ought to be accorded legitimacy and serious attention by educators.

Why so little attention thus far? Folklorists aside, the cultures of country music and of the academy seem mutually exclusive. Country music is a latecomer to the latter, arguably because of its association with a social sector that the intelligentsia has been reluctant, even loath, to engage, namely, lower-class Southern whites. There is a mandarin streak in the academy that militates against certain areas of study even in the late twentieth century. Black blues, jazz, rhythm & blues have all proved exotically attractive to white intellectuals as expressions of a distinctly "other" culture. Rock & roll has proved alluring for its expression of young rebellious anger, sexuality, social alienation. But, on the whole, academics have shunned a music linked to white poverty ("white trash") and racial prejudice, as if scholars might be demeaned or found guilty by association.

Country music's self-representations have also perhaps played a part in leading potential commentators to overlook it. Its down-to-earth images of untutored simplicity have seemed at best like vestiges of a bygone rural romanticism now reduced to hay bale fetishism. In part, country music artists abet the image of country music as unskilled. The late Bill Monroe, often called the father of bluegrass music, said, for example, "I never wrote a tune in my life. All that music's in the air around you all the time. I was just the first one to reach up and pull it out." Perhaps we should be paying closer attention to what country-folk songwriter and performer Iris DeMent says about the songwriter's and the artist's struggle with their work as a kind of sweat equity: "Sweet is the melody, *so hard to come by*" (my italics).

Does it take media popularity to attract analytical attention? Probably. By 1994, there were nearly 2,500 country music radio stations in the United States, and between 1990 and 1993, country music record sales increased from $664 million to $1.7 billion. In any given week, according to industry figures, 72 percent of the American public listens to country music on the radio, a figure that is already approaching market saturation as country music looks to Europe and Asia for new markets, concert venues, consumer groups. So the moment is right for *Reading Country Music*.

As its editor, my goal for this volume is quite simple: that any reader's relation to country music change markedly as a result of reading even one of the essays included here. Front-to-back reading is not presumed. An analogy from the visual arts may be useful: a placard in the Baltimore Art Museum quotes the painter Grace Hartigan as saying that she wishes a viewer of her lush, tropically colorful canvases to enter and exit through many pathways. So in *Reading Country Music: Steel Guitars, Opry Stars, and Honky-Tonk Bars,* a reader can chart her or his own course. From one essay to another, connections will suggest themselves, complexities will build.

Not surprisingly, most of the contributors to this volume are based in the geographic areas most closely identified with the history and commercial vitality of country music. Some are lifelong scholars of this music who generously agreed to contribute new work undertaken especially for this volume. Others, equally generous, agreed to extend their disciplinary concerns (e.g., in literature or fine arts) into the realm of country and bluegrass music. The editor and contributors alike owe thanks to Candice Ward, managing editor of *SAQ,* for her guiding hand and her eager enrollment in a "speed readin'" course in country music. Our thanks go as well to Robert K. Oermann, who generously provided many photographs from his personal collection, and to the Country Music Foundation, particularly its director, William Ivey, and its photoarchivist, Chris Skinker, for waiving photograph permission fees and otherwise assisting several contributors so that *Reading Country Music* could be enhanced by images from the CMF archives. Our thanks as well to the BMI Archive, especially David Sanjek.

This volume is noteworthy in another way, too. As any scholar writing on the subject of copyrighted popular music knows, music publishers are notoriously unwilling to grant permission for quotation of lyrics without requiring payment of prohibitively expensive fees. (The Graceland Estate warns that even the name "Elvis" is copyrighted and subject to legal action if used without permission.) "Free speech isn't free," goes a bitter joke. Yet free speech is abrogated when scholarly interpretive arguments must, in effect, exclude the primary evidence on which they are based, or at least must reduce that evidence to the secondary status of paraphrase, description, characterization. The good news is that the principle of fair use is being upheld here, and these scholars supported in their necessary quotation of relevant song lyrics. Now you can start reading country music because they were free to pursue their business of writin' about it.

# Sing Me a Song about Ramblin' Man

*Visions and Revisions of Hank Williams*

*in Country Music*

 **Christopher Metress**

To get there you take I-65 straight south out of Nashville. The ride is good and gentle, and before you know it you're crossing the Tennessee River into the Heart of Dixie and you're starting to see more frequent signs for Birmingham, the only city that stands between you and Montgomery. After you pass through the Magic City, skirting it to the right, the land starts to flatten out as red iron mountains give way to rich black soil. In just over an hour, you will see Montgomery on the horizon. Stay on I-65 until you near the center of the city. You will exit here and work your way carefully through the streets, following the map on the passenger's seat beside you until you find the road with seven bridges.

Oakwood Cemetery Annex is tucked away in a modest section of the city, only a few blocks from the state capitol building. When you get there it's not hard to find his grave, for it's marked by an upright slab nearly twice the size of a man. Made of Vermont granite, it shines like marble in the afternoon sun. At the top of the slab you find the opening notes of "I Saw the Light." Below this and to the left, a bronze plaque shows him smiling and playing his guitar, and beside it, etched into the granite, sunshine pours through a thicket of layered clouds. A little further down, just above eye level, the name "Hank Williams" is cut deep and thick and clean into the memorial stone.[1]

Resting at the base of this slab is an exact replica of Hank's hat, surrounded by small granite squares where someone has chiseled the front-page sheet music to some of Hank's greatest songs. A few feet in front of all this lies a flat slab that marks the grave itself. The whole area is framed by a rectangular

border of stone, and inside this frame stand two urns for decoration and two benches for rest. The grave is not busy at this time of day. A few wrappers and cigarette butts on the artificial turf around the plot let you know that others were here not long ago, but in the quiet of this particular afternoon you rest awhile on one of the benches and spend a few moments listening to the clouds move soundless as smoke overhead.

When it's time to go you might decide to walk out the way you came in. But you shouldn't. If you do, if you leave the grave the same way you approached it, you will miss something very important. So, instead of retracing your steps, you get off the bench and walk straight toward the upright slab. Take it in one last time—the deep cut of his name, his sharp face molded in bronze, the clouds and sunshine etched into the granite like some fragile but palpable hope. Now move past the slab. Here, standing in the shadows at the back of the slender marker, you will find a poem entitled "Thank You, Darling." Unlike the lyrics and notes carved into the front of the stone, these words will be unfamiliar:

> Thank you for all the love you gave me
> There could be one no stronger
> Thank you for the many beautiful songs
> They will live long and longer
>
> Thank you for being a wonderful father to Lycrecia
> She loves you more than you knew
> Thank you for our precious son
> And thank God he looks so much like you
>
> And now I can say:
> There are no words in the dictionary
> That can express my love for you
> > Someday beyond the blue

The poem is signed "Audrey Williams."

At first, what is happening on the backside of Hank Williams's gravestone seems quite clear: Audrey Williams, the grieving widow, is paying her final tribute to her husband. But something makes you uncomfortable. Is it the disjunction between the simple lyrics chiseled on the front of the slab and the discordant poetry cut into its back? Perhaps, yet there is something so touching in what you've just read: the widow fighting through her pain to write a final song for her songwriting husband. Still, something bothers you. It's only after you've listened a little longer to the silence overhead that you remember Audrey Williams wasn't Hank's widow.

Now you begin to understand what's really happening here on the shadowy side of Hank's grave. Everything about the gravesite centers on Hank, or so it first appears. The marker has his name on it, those are his lyrics etched in stone, that's his image cast in bronze. They've let his name, his face, and his words speak for themselves. When you look behind the grave, however, you see that Hank hasn't had the final say. Hank's a legend, after all, and legends become legends because we don't let them have the last word. Rather, after they are gone we continue to speak for them, creating them, if not in our own image, then at least in an image that serves our own purposes. And that's what's happening here in Montgomery. Miz Audrey is staking her claim, making Hank Williams *her* Hank Williams because she knows that another Williams, Billie Jean, is out there trying to stake *her* own claim. When Miz Audrey writes,

"Thank you for our precious son / And thank God he looks so much like you," you can almost hear the satisfaction, the legacy and the claims of inheritance that are asserted in those lines. The Hank Williams buried here isn't just any Hank Williams but *her* Hank Williams.

In 1975 Moe Bandy released a song by Paul Kraft entitled "Hank Williams You Wrote My Life." As true as these words are to many country music fans, they may blind us to another important fact: just as Hank Williams wrote our lives, we have written his. Audrey Williams's poem at the gravesite in Montgomery was not the first attempt to take hold of Hank's life and inscribe it in a certain way. And it definitely wasn't the last. For instance, in 1953, the year Hank Williams died, every major recording studio in Nashville released a song about him, sixteen tributes in all.[2] The first to be released was Jack Cardwell's "Death of Hank Williams." A Montgomery disc jockey and singer for King

Records, Cardwell knew Hank in his pre-*Opry* days. When he heard of Hank's death on New Year's Eve, he wrote a song about it that very night. A week later, on 8 January, King Records released "The Death of Hank Williams." It went as high as #2 on the charts, kept out of the top spot by one of Hank's own songs, "Your Cheatin' Heart." With more than 107,000 singles sold, "The Death of Hank Williams" may have been the most successful of all these tribute records, but it really wasn't that much different from the rest. Beginning with a peaceful image of Hank lying in the back of his car, "in a deep and dreamless sleep" from which he never awakens, Cardwell's song tries to reassure us that Hank Williams has "gone to a better land."

When listened to one after another, the sixteen tribute songs of 1953 construct a highly specific image of Hank Williams. A little more than a year before his death, remember, Hank had left Nashville in disgrace. In the tribute songs, however, there is little, if any, mention of the Hank Williams who got himself fired from the *Opry* for repeatedly embarrassing the Nashville establishment with his drunkenness and unreliability. Yes, Arthur Smith sings, in his "In Memory of Hank Williams," about how, "like all of us Hank had his faults," but those faults are not specified in any of the tributes. What we get, rather, is a kind of hagiography, a portrait of Hank Williams as a country music saint who has gone peacefully to his just reward.[3] In "Hank Williams Meets Jimmie Rodgers," for instance, the Virginia Rounders sing of a "great meeting in Heaven" between the two kings of country music. In this song, Hank doesn't so much die as "answer his Maker's call" to perform with the angels. Jimmie Rodgers tells Hank that he and the angels needed some help in their "heavenly band," so they decided to call for the best singer on earth. In the end, we are assured that

> The voices of Rodgers and Williams,
> The greatest this world's ever known,
> Will blend up yonder forever
> Around that heavenly throne.

As if their point had not been made well enough in this song, the Virginia Rounders also released "There's a New Star in Hillbilly Heaven," in which they speculate that the angels called for Hank Williams because they needed "someone to write them new songs."

Jimmie Skinner's "Singing Teacher in Heaven" and Johnny Ryon's "That Heaven Bound Train" each maintains this comforting portrait of a singer called home to "his Maker." Skinner assures us that Hank has "traveled on to a house of gold" where "the saints of God abed." For Ryon, Hank "is riding to glory on that Heaven bound train," where he will find angels to sing "the many songs that [he] will bring." Moreover, both Skinner and Ryon imagine moments when they will join Hank in some unbroken circle in the sky. Ryon sings of how "someday we all will be with him again" when we are called upon to ride "that Heaven bound train," while Skinner prays for a reunion with Hank on the day when he himself must "join the heavenly choir."

In "Hank, It Will Never Be the Same Without You," Williams's good friend Ernest Tubb sings of how, from the start, Hank's life was full of "misery." But that misery doesn't matter now because, in his death, Hank has finally achieved that goal he struggled "so bravely for" in life: "eternal happiness." A similar sentiment is found in Jimmie Logsdon's "Hank Williams Sings the Blues No More," in which we are assured that Hank has now found "a new singing place / Where the sun shines on his face." In "The Last Letter," Jimmy Swan offers the most explicit assurance that the Ramblin' Man has indeed achieved eternal peace when he sings of how he dreamed one night of meeting Hank Williams in heaven. Swan's dream centers on an image of Hank holding tightly to a "little white Bible."

Many of these first tribute songs were written by artists who knew Hank well, so we certainly can't fault them for being sentimental portraits of a good friend. But as Hank Williams, Jr., said on one of his early albums: "In January of 1953, my father stopped being a man and became a legend."[4] These tribute songs initiated the construction of that legend. The man who died alone in the backseat of a car because his heart finally failed him after so many years of heavy drinking had now simply passed away in a "deep and dreamless sleep." This long night's sleep, more of a summons from heaven than an actual death, had finally allowed the Ramblin' Man to gain his rightful rest. Moreover, the man who had been fired from the *Opry* two years before no longer existed. Instead, Hank now sings forever with the angels in some kind of *Grand Ole Opry* in the sky, and we too will sing with him "someday beyond the blue." Hindsight has allowed Hank Jr. to understand exactly what was going on in 1953. In *Living Proof,* his 1979 autobiography, he wrote: "While [Daddy] was alive, he was despised and envied; after he died, he was some kind of saint. And that's exactly how Nashville decided to treat Daddy—country music's first authentic saint."[5]

Nashville may have needed a saint, but Miz Audrey simply needed a husband. If the tribute songs served to smooth over the divorce between Hank and Nashville, Miz Audrey's songs served to smooth over her divorce from him. In a series of records released during the first two years after his death, Audrey Williams had her chance to write Hank's life the way she wanted it to be read.

Fighting for custody of his memory as well as his estate, she was not only billing herself as "The One and Only Audrey (Mrs. Hank) Williams," she was singing about herself that way as well. On one of her early records, she tapped into the heaven imagery of the tribute songs, and just as the Nashville musicians imagined a reunion with Hank in the great beyond, Miz Audrey imagined a heavenly reprise of her wedded bliss with Hank on earth. "Are you writing songs for me up in Heaven?" she asks Hank. "So when I meet you beyond the blue, / You'll say 'Come here and listen to me,' / Then I'll smile and listen just as we used to do." In another song, entitled "My Life with You," she sings of how she and Hank first met and of how, when they were later married, she wept with happiness. She notes, however, that their "happiness didn't last long" because people started "wagging their tongues," and in the next stanza, she describes their divorce in a way that, well, makes it seem like they never got divorced:

> Along about then, everything went wrong,
> Little did we know it wouldn't be long
> 'Til you'd be in Heaven no more to be blue,
> It's hard to go on without my life with you.

When she wasn't writing her own songs about Hank, Miz Audrey was recording songs that carefully wrote her back into Hank's life. In Lycrecia Williams's 1989 memoir, *Still in Love with You: The Story of Hank and Audrey Williams,* she recalled one of her mother's Decca recording sessions in August of 1953:

> Still backed by the Drifting Cowboys, but short one guitar player, [Mother] recorded three emotional numbers that day. First was a recitation of Daddy's "To My Pal Bocephus," a poem filled with a father's hopes and concerns for his baby son. She read the words just as Daddy would have done, without changing the wording for the speaker as a "man" and a "father." Her second number, "I Forgot More Than You'll Ever Know About Him," a current hit . . . for the Davis Sisters, was so appropriate to her feelings about Billie Jean's claims to Daddy that it might have been written just for her. For the last song, Mother rewrote the lyrics to Daddy's "Ramblin' Man" to express some of her own thoughts:
>
> > Some folks might say that I didn't care,
> > But wherever you went I was always there.
> > When I get lonely, at your grave I'll stand.
> > So I'll be near my ramblin' man.
> > I still love you honey and I can't understand
> > I am a ramblin' gal that lost her ramblin' man.[6]

As Chet Flippo argued in *Your Cheatin' Heart: A Biography of Hank Williams,* those who knew Hank "revise[d] his history to sweeten their own."[7] And this, of course, was what Audrey Williams did when she decided to revise Hank's music—in revising "Ramblin' Man," she was revising *the* Ramblin' Man and sweetening her life with him. The two bitter divorces and the long separations never really happened because, in truth, wherever Hank Williams went, she was "always there."

As much as Miz Audrey was rewriting in song her husband's problematic past, she was also writing in life her son's promising future. Whereas other artists could only pen or perform tributes to Hank, Audrey Williams could turn her son into a living, singing tribute. And this she did. Although it was to a son named Randall Hank Williams that Audrey gave birth on 26 May 1949, she raised him as "Hank Williams, Jr." The boy's renaming was only the beginning. In his autobiography, Hank Jr. recalled those early years of careful refashioning: "Mother used to coach me in things Daddy said and then I'd go on stage and the audience would go crazy. They'd say I sounded just like ole Hank, and I guess I did."[8]

By age eleven, young Hank sounded enough like "ole Hank" to take the *Opry* stage and sing a few of his father's songs. Four years later, in 1964, he appeared on the *Ed Sullivan Show* and sang "Long Gone Lonesome Blues," a cover of his father's #1 hit from 1950. Peaking at #5, the song gave fifteen-year-old Hank Jr. his first chart record. When he tried to follow up later in the year with two singles of his own songs, he reached no higher than #42 on the charts. To the young Hank Williams, the message couldn't have been clearer: "There'd be the people [at my concerts] who came looking for my daddy, who wanted to hear nothing but 'I'm So Lonesome I Could Cry' and 'Jambalaya and a crawfish pie-a and a me-o-my-o,' and would be bitterly disappointed when they found only me."[9]

Hank Jr. didn't break into the top ten with one of his own songs until "Standing in the Shadows" was released in 1966. While this wasn't a cover of one of his father's earlier hits, it was nevertheless a song about his father. In "Standing in the Shadows," Hank Jr. maintains that he's "just doin' the best [he] can," but that "it's hard" when you have to stand in the shadow "of a very great man." He recognizes the burden of his father's legacy, but he also makes it quite clear that he's happy to bear that burden because it allows his father's music to "live on and on and on." When he followed up "Standing in the Shadows" with "I Can't Take It No Longer"—another one of his own songs—Hank Jr. failed again to reach the top of the charts. His next single, "I'm in No Condition," peaked at #60 and was followed by "Nobody's Child," which managed to climb to #46.

Hank's 1968 album, *My Songs,* produced only one chart single, "I Wouldn't Change a Thing About You (But Your Name)," which hit #31. The success of "Long Gone Lonesome Blues" and "Standing in the Shadows," coupled with the failure of every other song up to that point, made something else quite clear to Hank Jr.: if he sang his father's songs, or sang about how willing he was to carry on his father's legacy, he'd be accepted; if not, he'd flounder at the bottom of the charts. It's no wonder, then, that early in his career he released such albums as *Hank Williams, Jr. Sings the Songs of Hank Williams* and *Songs My Father Left Me: The Poems of Hank Williams Set to Music and Sung by Hank Williams, Jr.*

In the late 1960s and early 1970s, Hank Jr. the performer remained faithful to the country-music-saint image of his father created by the tribute records and by his mother. In recalling those years, however, Hank Jr. admitted knowing that this image wouldn't last: "Essentially, what was happening [in the late 1960s] was that one myth of Hank Williams was getting ready to overtake the other. . . . While *Opry* folks were still praising Daddy's name . . . [a group of] young singers and songwriters had adopted a live fast, die young, and leave a beautiful corpse posture, and they talked about the way that Hank did it." [10] Unfortunately, what was happening in country music—a shift from one Hank Williams myth to another, and from the sweet, respectable arrangements of the "Nashville Sound" to the hard-driving honky tonk tunes of the "Outlaw" movement—was also being played out in Hank's personal life. In *Living Proof,* he wrote: "The years all run together—'71, '72, '73, '74. An endless nightmare of bars and shows, of sick mornings and stoned nights and big chunks of time where there are no memories. Of Jim Beam and cheery, multicolored pills, and strange girls with vacant eyes." As a result, "people were starting to come to my shows to see if I would fall off stage. . . . For a measly five bucks you could step right up and see whether the son of the greatest country artist of all time could get through his set without dropping a guitar or forgetting the words to 'Cold, Cold Heart.'" [11]

It was during these tough years that Hank Jr. began to question in song the myth of Hank Williams. "Standing in the Shadows" pictures Hank Sr. as "a very great man," and that's all that is said; when Hank Jr. claims that "there'll never be another Hank Williams," we know he's thinking of the Hank Williams who's singing with Jimmie Rodgers in heaven. At one point in the song, Hank Jr. sings about how, when he is performing in concert, he will occasionally look up toward the ceiling to ask his father how he's doing, to receive, as it were, his father's heavenly blessing. But in "Hank," a 1973 release, Bocephus sings about a more complex Hank Williams: "They say Hank was a mighty heavy drinker, I don't know. / They say Hank was a mighty heavy thinker, I reckon that's so." The song continues in this vein, with Hank Jr. telling us first what "they say" and then whether he agrees or disagrees with that. For instance, when "they say" that whiskey wrecked his father's health, Hank disagrees, but when "they say" his father sang a "real good song," Hank agrees. If "Standing in the Shadows" expressed his certainty that there would "never be another Hank Williams," in "Hank" he's not certain how many Hank Williamses there were. What Hank Jr. is sure of, however, is that what "they say" must be confronted and, perhaps more importantly, contested.

Feeling trapped by the legacy of his father's music, Hank Jr. was saved by it, ironically enough. One afternoon in 1974, when Hank Jr. was racing his Ford truck along I–65 at a hundred-plus miles per hour, he finally had to pull off the road for gas in Clarksville, Tennessee. The first pump he found was at a general store that doubled as a local bar. He went into the store, ordered a shot of Jim Beam, and headed for the jukebox. "I walked over to that jukebox like I owned the place," Hank Jr. remembered. "I dropped my quarter down the slot and started looking. What I found was my ghost, my inspiration, my daddy, this time in the form of Linda Ronstadt singing 'I Can't Help It If I'm Still In Love With You.'" His own marriage having just recently collapsed, Hank Jr. broke into tears at the jukebox: "It was like Daddy reachin' out across the years, telling me he understood." [12]

Feeling "touched by some kind of c & w muse," Hank Jr. staggered back to his truck and in ten minutes wrote the lyrics to "Stoned at the Jukebox." [13] On one level, this song is about the breakup of his marriage. But on another level, it's about his coming to terms with his father's legacy. In "Stoned at the Jukebox," Hank Jr. not only recognizes his father's music for what it really is, "hurtin' music," but he also recognizes that, having been haunted by this hurtin' music all his life, he has begun to live it out. One myth of Hank Williams was indeed giving way to another—Hank Jr. was becoming the Hank Williams that everyone talked about but no one dared to sing about.

After "Stoned at the Jukebox," he made a real effort to turn his life around, to get out from under the shadow of what "they" kept saying about his father. The first step was to get out of Nashville, which he did in 1974 when he moved to Cullman, Alabama. The second step was to put together a new album, which he also did, in 1975. *Hank Williams Junior and Friends* seemed to make good on his promise to himself to start over again, to make "*my* music, not Daddy's, not Mother's or anybody else's. . . . Music for 1974 instead of 1953." [14] Marking a new direction all right, this album included "Living Proof," a cut that Hank Jr. considered "the most important song I've ever written," a song that "was going to be the exclamation point at the end of the old Hank Williams Junior." [15] In

"Living Proof," Hank Jr. laments having been "living for more than one man" all of his life and swears that he doesn't want to pay the price his father paid. Whereas in 1966 the Hank Jr. of "Standing in the Shadows" had been glad to bear the burden and keep his father's music living "on and on and on" for the old "fans and friends," by 1975 the Hank Jr. of "Living Proof" was vowing to "quit singing all them sad songs." When he asks at the end of the song why he has to be "the living proof" of his father's legend, we see that he's no longer willing to stand in that shadow. Moreover, as he sings elsewhere in the same song, he doesn't want to be a legend either—he "just want[s] to be a man."

But as important as this song was, "Living Proof" did not really represent "the exclamation point" that Hank Jr. hoped it would be. Yes, he turned his life around in the mid-1970s, as he swore that he would not become the "Living Proof" of the "Williams Curse." But, contrary to his vow, Hank Jr. did not "quit singing all them sad songs." Nor did he stop singing about the Ramblin' Man who wrote those sad songs.[16] The change was not that Hank Jr. put his father behind him. Rather, what changed was Hank's attitude toward his father and the myths that "they," the Nashville establishment, had created about him.

Early in his career he knew that Nashville had made his father into "country music's first authentic saint." He knew as well that he himself was "the chosen one," designated to walk in the shadow of that saint.[17] In his teens and twenties, Hank Jr. played the role perfectly, practicing the patter and giving back to Nashville the ghost it wanted to see and hear. But when he started popping pills and drinking booze and running around all over town, Nashville turned on him, and it did so by using his father against him. Music City had Hank Jr. in a double bind: On the one hand, he was expected to be the model son of the "Singing Teacher in Heaven." Then, when he proved to be no son of a saint, Nashville sighed with resignation: What else could they expect from a (Hank) Williams? The first one had let them down, and the second one was sinking even lower. Whichever vision of Hank Sr. they held up before him—country music saint or irredeemable sinner—Hank Jr. couldn't win. He was shadowed by a myth that the *Opry,* not the Son of Ramblin' Man, controlled.

But by 1976 he had figured out a way to beat the myth. According to Hank Jr., after "Living Proof" was released, "ole Hank's reincarnation had finally hung up his guitar, and Hank Williams Junior had a story to tell."[18] But in the story Hank Jr. told about himself, his father was still a major character, if not the hero. Before 1975, Hank Jr. had let everyone else tell him who his father was and what his father's life meant. As long as he listened to others' stories, he was stuck with the role of either the son of a saint or the son of a cheatin', boozin', no-account failure. But after 1975, Hank Jr. hung up the two-hat legend of

Hank Sr. that Nashville had fashioned and started writing his own version of his father's life. What he linked up with was a third myth of Hank Williams — not the saint, not the sinful failure, but "the most wanted outlaw in the land."

In a steady series of revisionist songs, including "Feelin' Better," "Family Tradition," and "The Conversation," Hank Jr. took his lead from singer-songwriters like Kris Kristofferson and Waylon Jennings.[19] The Outlaw movement that began in the late 1960s and peaked in the mid-1970s had created an antiestablishment Hank Williams long before his son ever embraced that vision. While Hank Jr. was still trying to sort through all the things that "they" kept saying about his father, Kris Kristofferson began to tell Nashville that Hank Williams was an Outlaw, and, if "they" didn't like this image of Hank, well, "they" could kiss his ass. At the same time, Waylon Jennings was proudly proclaiming, "I'm A Ramblin' Man," thus offering himself up as the Second Coming of the original Outlaw. Moreover, Jennings had surveyed the Nashville music scene and wondered aloud, "Are You Sure Hank Done It This Way?" Seeing nothing in Nashville but "rhinestone suits and new shiny cars," Waylon concluded that country music needed to change. The change, of course, would come from the Outlaws themselves — as the ones who were out there speeding their young lives away, they were the rightful heirs to the Hank Williams legacy. In the early 1970s, the Outlaws were trying to tell Nashville that it no longer understood what country music was all about, and the best way to accomplish this was to show Nashville that it had never really understood what Hank Williams was all about.

In "Feelin' Better," his 1977 follow-up to "Living Proof," Hank Jr. acknowledges his debt to the Outlaws, singing about how he had to get out of Nashville because the folks there "wouldn't let me sing nothing but them sad old songs." Thanks to "Waylon and Toy [Caldwell] and all the boys," however, he could sing his own stuff now, a kind of Southern country rock less suited to Nashville than to "Macon and Muscle Shoals." But in this new stage of his career, he was not just singing his own music; he was also writing his own version of his father's life. Nowhere was this done more forcefully, or more skillfully, than in two songs from 1979: the top-ten hit "Family Tradition" and the Waylon Jennings duet "The Conversation."

In "Family Tradition," Hank Jr. admits that he's changed direction in the last few years, and that in doing so he has broken with the Nashville tradition. But then he asks Nashville to think about his "unique position." If he drinks, smokes dope, lives a hard and tragic honky tonk life that runs counter to the Nashville tradition, well, that's just his "family tradition" after all. With this song, then, Hank Jr. was able to turn the tables on Nashville and the dictates of its tortuous logic: be like who we say your father was (the country music saint), but not too much like who we say your father also was (the irresponsible failure)—or we'll run you out of town for not being the living proof of your father that we want, and need, you to be. In "Family Tradition," Hank Jr. created his own kind of tortuous logic and then turned it on Nashville: Yes, he admitted, there's a Nashville family tradition. Fine. But there's also a Williams family tradition. And his family tradition isn't like their family tradition, and he's the one named Williams here. So, if "you stop and think it over," the Nashville tradition and the Williams tradition are nothing alike. In 1952, Music City may have kicked Hank Williams out of the family, but, in 1979, his son was returning the boot.

In the opening stanza of "Family Tradition," Hank Jr. sings about how, lately, some of his Nashville "kinfolk have disowned a few others and me." Then, teaming up in "The Conversation" with one of those disowned others—Waylon Jennings—Hank Jr. took back the family inheritance. In fact, what Hank Jr. and Waylon did in this song was akin to what Audrey Williams had done in Oakwood Cemetery Annex back in the 1950s—staking a claim to Hank Williams. First, these two disowned Outlaws set out to take control over what was said about Hank Williams. At the beginning of the song, they agree not to "talk about the habits / Just the music and the man." Next, having set the agenda, they set about exposing the hypocrisy of those who have staked false claims to Hank's memory. In their refrain, they both sing:

> Back then they called him crazy,
> Nowadays they call him a saint.
> Now the ones that called him crazy then
> Are still ridin' on his name.

The final revisionary step, of course, is to stake their own claim to Hank, to "write"—and thus "ride"—on his name. So when Waylon asks Hank Jr. whether his father would approve of the Outlaws if he were alive today, Hank assures Waylon that the original Ramblin' Man would be "right here by our side." The early tribute singers placed themselves beside Hank Williams in heaven; Miz Audrey claimed the same place with him "beyond the blue," where she would join Hank and he'd "say 'Come here and listen to me.'" Now, here were Hank Jr. and Outlaw Waylon claiming that the Ramblin' Man would "be the first one on [their] bus and ready to ride." "The Conversation," which begins with Waylon's invitation, "Hank, let's talk about your daddy," drives straight toward its calculated, revisionist conclusion, in which both voices are joined in proclaiming, "You know when we get right down to it, / He's still the most wanted outlaw in the land!"

Hank Jr., Waylon, and others continued to promote this outlaw image of Hank Williams well into the next decade, while some, like Charley Pride, in his 1980 release "I Got a Little Bit of Hank in Me," were reasserting the more sanitized, saintly vision of the Ramblin' Man.[20] In the 1980s and 1990s, however, yet another image of Hank Williams emerged, one that is best illustrated by two Top 10 songs: David Allan Coe's "The Ride" (1983) and Alan Jackson's "Midnight in Montgomery" (1992). In neither song is Hank portrayed as a saint or an outlaw, nor is he put on a heaven-bound train or the Outlaws' bus. Instead, the Ramblin' Man has become a weary ghost who cannot ride with either gang.[21]

"The Ride" (written by J. B. Detterline and Gary Gentry) sets out to revise every tribute song ever written about Hank by turning the "Singing Teacher in Heaven" into the tormented ghost of I–65. As Coe's recording of the song opens, he is making the same trek to Nashville that Hank made twenty years before. Thumbing his way north from Montgomery, he is offered a ride by a stranger in an "antique Cadillac." The Hank who had appeared to Jimmy Swan in a dream, holding a "little white Bible" in heaven, now appears as a "ghost white pale," "half drunk and hollow-eyed" stranger. No longer harmonizing with the angels in heaven, Hank is back on earth dispensing hard and bitter truths. In the song's haunting refrain, Hank warns the singer, "If you're big star bound, let me tell you it's a long hard ride." In the final stanza, Hank stops the car just south of Nashville and begins to cry: his passenger must get out here because Hank is going back to Alabama. We're not told why Hank Williams won't drive on into Music City. In an Outlaw song, he would probably be rejecting Nashville. Hank's tears in "The Ride," however, suggest not a defiance of Nashville, but a longing for home and, perhaps, acceptance. Envisioned in this song as a lonesome exile, Hank is doomed to ride the highway between Montgomery and Nashville, never finding rest, never gaining peace, never getting home. "The Ride" revises Hank Williams with its own hard and bitter truth: No matter how much we'd like to believe otherwise, Hank never got on Johnny Ryon's (or Cal Shrum's) "Heaven Bound Train," never found the "eternal happiness" that Ernest Tubb envisioned. Nor did he ever board the Outlaw's bus with Waylon and Hank Jr. The bitter truth? Hank Williams's life was a long hard ride, and so was his death.

At the beginning of "Midnight in Montgomery," Alan Jackson is headed in the opposite direction from Coe—or so it first appears. Riding south on I–65, Jackson is not "big star bound," he's already a big star (witness the Silver Eagle). On his way from Nashville to Mobile for a "big New Year's Eve show," Jackson stops for just a moment in Montgomery to pay homage to Hank Williams. He is surprised when a "drunk man in a cowboy hat," with "haunted, haunted

eyes," appears. This ghostly Hank has little to say to Jackson except to thank him for caring enough to visit. When Hank quickly disappears, Jackson wonders whether he was "ever really there." Still uncertain, Jackson reboards his bus, leaving Hank behind. If the implication of "The Ride" is that Hank must drive eternally up and down I–65, then Jackson's song implies that Hank can't ever get on I–65, or any other road, for that matter, neither heading for Provo on the Outlaws' bus nor bound for glory on a celestial train. Moreover, while the refrain of Jackson's song assures us that Hank will always be "singing there" in Montgomery, he won't be performing the way he did in the previous tribute songs. During the 1950s, Hank was said to be singing in the heavenly choir, while in the 1970s, he was still touring, in spirit at least, with the Outlaws. But Jackson's song leaves Hank to sing alone, at "midnight in Montgomery," with a "smell of whiskey in the air." Like Coe's "hollow-eyed" highwayman Jackson's "haunted"-eyed ghost stands side-by-side with no one, and no one stands side-by-side with him.

The developing visions of Hank Williams that I have mapped out here, from heavenly saint to defiant Outlaw to lonely ghost, should by no means suggest that every country artist has accepted this development, that Hank Williams's presence is now only that of a haunted, and haunting, apparition in country music. In "Me & Hank & Jumpin' Jack Flash," a song released in 1992, the same year as "Midnight in Montgomery," Marty Stuart dreams of a visit with Hank Williams in "hillbilly heaven." Stuart's Hank is still putting on concerts and giving his blessing to the truly authentic country singers (like Stuart himself). In fact, Stuart adds his own little twist to the narrative I've been tracing here when he implies that his entire album, *This One's Gonna Hurt You,* is actually a revelation from Hank himself—that Hank, not Marty, wrote all the songs.[22] Hank seems, to Marty Stuart at least, to still be the great "singing teacher in heaven."

In his biography of Hank Williams, however, Chet Flippo argues that this great singing teacher

> never really got it straight in his mind whether he was writing for Saturday night . . . or whether he was writing for Sunday morning. . . . He kept writing both kinds of songs and could never get it entirely straight in his own mind just where he belonged. He wanted to have Saturday night, drink it up and have a good time, but then he'd start to feel guilty and want to go back to Sunday morning and the sunlight and the white church and innocence.[23]

I think that much the same can be said for us. Just as Hank Williams struggled to figure out "where he belonged," we too have struggled to figure out what place he holds in country music. As soon as we have chiseled one version of Hank Williams's life we feel guilty, knowing that our song tells us more about ourselves than about the man. So we chisel another version. And then another. And yet another. Our own restlessness and uncertainty keep us on the road, on a constant journey between Nashville and Montgomery, between Music City and Hank's city, in search of an answer. But perhaps in the end there is no answer except this one: Hiram "Hank" Williams died on 1 January 1953, and, whether we want to admit it or not, we've all been writing on his back ever since.[24]

NOTES

1   Those who have been to the grave in recent years will be aware of how, in the spirit of this essay, I have revised the scene (as indicated by my last photograph). My apologies to Miz Audrey.

2   Here is a complete list of those 1953 songs (for recording information, see Selected Discography): "The Death of Hank Williams" (Jack Cardwell); "Hank, It Will Never Be the Same Without You" (Ernest Tubb); "Hank's Song" (Ferlin Husky); "Hank Williams Meets Jimmie Rodgers" (The Virginia Rounders); "Hank Williams Sings the Blues No More" (Jimmie Logsdon); "Hank Williams Will Live Forever" (Johnny and Jack); "(I Would Have Liked to Have Been) Hank's Little Flower

Girl" (Little Barbara); "In Memory of Hank Williams" (Arthur Smith); "The Last Letter" (Jimmy Swan); "The Life of Hank Williams" (Hawkshaw Hawkins); "Singing Teacher in Heaven" (Jimmie Skinner); "That Heaven Bound Train" (Johnny Ryon; Cal Shrum); "There's a New Star in Hillbilly Heaven" (The Virginia Rounders); "Tribute to Hank Williams" (Joe Rumore); "A Tribute to Hank Williams, My Buddy" (Luke McDaniel).

3   The one exception is Ferlin Husky's "Hank's Song."

4   See Hank Williams, Jr., *Insights Into Hank Williams* (MGM Records, 1974).

5   Hank Williams, Jr. (with Michael Bane), *Living Proof: An Autobiography* (New York, 1979), 64.

6   Lycrecia Williams, *Still in Love with You: The Story of Hank and Audrey Williams* (Nashville, 1989), 125.

7   Chet Flippo, *Your Cheatin' Heart: A Biography of Hank Williams* (New York, 1981), 240.

8   H. Williams, *Living Proof,* 37.

9   Ibid., 17.

10   Ibid., 129.

11   Ibid., 161, 163–64.

12   Ibid., 165.

13   Ibid., 166.

14   Ibid., 168.

15   Ibid., 181.

16   In 1979, for instance, Peter Guralnick wrote, "It is no accident . . . that [Hank Williams, Sr.] continues to be a dominant presence in [Hank Jr.'s] themes if not in his music or his writing, which is far more particular, or confessional anyway, than anything his father ever wrote. On *The New South* alone there are four songs that refer directly or indirectly to Hank Williams, and it seems an irony that Hank Junior will never escape, that the more he tries to pull away the more he will be reminded of his father's name." See his *Lost Highway: Journeys and Arrivals of American Musicians* (Boston, 1979), 230.

17   H. Williams, *Living Proof,* 24.

18   Ibid., 190.

19   These three songs, of course, do not represent a complete list of Hank Jr.'s revisionist songs, for example, "The Ballad of Hank Williams" or "A Whole Lotta Hank" (see Selected Discography). Note as well that Hank Sr. often appears in songs that are not devoted entirely to him. On *The New South,* for instance, several songs (e.g., "Montgomery in the Rain" and "The Blues Man") make reference to Hank Sr.

20   Hank Jr.'s 1983 release "A Whole Lotta Hank" seems to have been written in rebuttal to Pride's assertion that "I Got a Little Bit of Hank in Me." In "A Whole Lotta Hank," Hank Jr. is once again reclaiming his inheritance from those who would appropriate, and define, it for themselves.

21   For another song that manifests this third vision, see Robin and Linda Williams's

"Rollin' and Ramblin' (The Death of Hank Williams)," on their 1988 album, *All Broken Hearts Are the Same* (see also Emmylou Harris's version of this song on her 1990 album, *Brand New Dance*).

22  The opening song on the album, "Me & Hank & Jumpin' Jack Flash," ends with the suggestion that the next song was sung by Hank Williams during Stuart's dream. The third cut no longer plays with this suggestion—or so it appears. But the last song on side two is followed by fifteen seconds of silence, after which Stuart is heard to say, "And that's when I woke up," thus suggesting that the entire album was sung by Hank during Stuart's dream.

23  Flippo, *Your Cheatin' Heart,* 49.

24  Considerations of space and thesis have precluded discussion of every song ever written about Hank Williams. The following list, by no means definitive, covers songs not mentioned elsewhere in this essay and is intended to aid other scholars (for recording information, see Selected Discography): "The Car Hank Died In" (The Austin Lounge Lizards); "From Hank to Hendrix" (Neil Young); "The Ghost of Hank Williams" (The Kentucky HeadHunters); "Hank" (Jerry Bergonzi; Treat Her Right); "Hank Drank" (Bobby Lee Springfield); "Hank and George, Lefty and Me" (Tommy Cash); "Hank and Lefty Raised My Country Soul" (Stoney Edwards); "Hank, You Still Make Me Cry" (Boxcar Willie); "Hank Williams from His Grave" (Paleface); "Hank Williams Led a Happy Life" (The Geezinslaw Brothers); "Hank Williams's Guitar" (Freddy Hart); "Has Anybody Here Seen Hank?" (The Water-boys); "I Feel Like Hank Williams Tonight" (Jerry Jeff Walker); "I Remember Hank" (Lenny Breau); "I Think I Been Talkin' to Hank" (Mark Chestnutt); "The Night Hank Williams Came to Town" (Johnny Cash); "Wailin' with Hank" (Art Farmer Quintet); "When He Was Young, He Was Billed as the Next Hank Williams" (Jerry Farden).

# Blue Moon of Kentucky Rising

# Over the Mystery Train

*The Complex Construction of Country Music*

 **David Sanjek**

> Somebody told me when I came to Nashville
> Son you finally got it made
> Old Hank made it here
> We're all sure that you will
> But I don't think Hank done it this way
> Naw, I don't think Hank done it this way.
> — Waylon Jennings, "Are You Sure Hank Done It
> This Way?" (© 1975 Songs of Polygram International,
> Inc. Used by permission; all rights reserved)

In one of his most celebrated and often anthologized poems, Wallace Stevens placed a jar in Tennessee, causing the "slovenly wilderness" about it to assume shape and form; that receptacle then "took dominion everywhere" and was "like nothing else in Tennessee."[1] The Country Music Association (CMA), founded in 1957, has had a similar effect on country music. Like Stevens's jar, it has achieved dominion as the principal professional organization of the country music industry. The CMA elects members to the Country Hall of Fame; selects the winners of its prestigious annual awards, which are conferred in a televised ceremony; and astutely promotes the image of Nashville, Tennessee, as the center and source of all that is quintessential to the genre. Despite the counterefforts of the Academy of Country Music (ACM) in California, which was formed in 1965 to break up the CMA monopoly on country music and to gain more attention for the virtually ignored efforts of West Coast country performers, Nashville remains the center in the public consciousness.[2] For all intents and purposes, Nashville is "Music City, USA," which is identified by the vast majority of the public with country music itself—despite the fact that the city did not become a major recording center until the early 1950s and that few practitioners of country music have been native Tennesseans. (In truth, Texas can probably claim to have spawned more country artists than any other state.)

Furthermore, the city has always been less than wholeheartedly enthusiastic about being the home of the country music industry. As a character in Lee Smith's splendid novel about a country music dynasty, *The Devil's Dream*, observes, "Nashville itself has kind of a split personality—there's the folks in the music business, and then there's these old families with big homes and a lot of money they've had for generations."[3] Even the *Grand Ole Opry*, one of America's secular shrines, was ignored by the city fathers in its early days, as was the music performed by its members. It took the major local newspaper, the *Tennessean*, two years even to acknowledge the *Opry*'s existence, mentioning it for the first time in 1927.[4] Shortly thereafter, when the *Tennessean* began to include record reviews, those of country artists betrayed more than a touch of condescension; as Charles K. Wolfe has observed, "They are nearly always placed last and at times are quite critical."[5] Clearly, Nashville was willing to profit from country music, but that did not mean its citizens had to like these musicians or welcome them into their homes, except perhaps over the radio or on the phonograph.

Each time I travel the streets of "Music Row," the section of Nashville that houses the music publishers, record companies, and recording studios, I'm reminded of the complex, often ambiguous nature of country music and of its promoters' habitual efforts to erase, or at least cover up, its contradictions. The neighborhood superficially resembles a suburban development. Tree-lined avenues and well-kept lawns present a façade that, despite the occasional business sign, seems altogether domestic, while behind the doors deals are hammered out, demo tapes are circulated, and an endless series of three-hour sessions continues to build up the country music repertoire. Music Row's resemblance to a stage set should not lead one to assume that country music is made by sleight of hand, but rather that a complex and ingenious mythology underlies the industry's public testimony to the "simplicity," "authenticity," and "reality" of the music it markets.

The fact that advocates of country music continue to employ these terms, which thoughtful partisans of most other forms of indigenous American music have either long since abandoned or at least called into question, should come as no surprise. For there is still a widely held conviction that something in country music is irreducible, some essence that only a select body of artists can access. Jimmie Rodgers, the Carter Family, Roy Acuff, Bill Monroe, Bob Wills, Ernest Tubb, Hank Williams, Lefty Frizzell, Johnny Cash, Patsy Cline, George Jones, Buck Owens, Merle Haggard, and Willie Nelson, to name but a few of the most illustrious country artists, constitute an unimpeachable pantheon to whom contemporary performers turn for inspiration and from whom audiences seek affirmation of their own feelings and beliefs. As "Bad" Blake, the fictional down-and-out country star in Thomas Cobb's novel *Crazy Heart,* says about the music,

> Well, mostly it's supposed to be about people, what they are, what they feel. It's not just some cute saying laid over a nice, tight hook. Music today, you listen to it, say "that's clever," and you forget it. I get the feeling it doesn't have anything to do with anyone. At least no one I know, or would want to know.[6]

The cleverness that Blake abhors never speaks to or about "people who aren't real special, who are never going to be. They grow up, slip around, and they die. And the music is the glamour of that kind of life." [7] "Slip around" alludes to Floyd Tillman's 1949 honky tonk classic "Slippin' Around" and, like the expression "getting by," suggests entanglements of everyday life from which Blake's "people who aren't real special" hope to be released by their favorite country artists. It is this kind of audience and this public function that Waylon Jennings apparently feared he had either abandoned or abused when he doubted that "Hank" had "done it this way." While any number of country songs have taken up the theme of cheating on a spouse or lover, Waylon's song raises the question of country music performers' cheating their audiences or themselves.

The possibility of breaking a covenant between singer and society, or of failing to maintain the standards set by country's pantheon, bedevils many contemporary performers as well as fans both within and outside the genre. In a recent issue of the alternative music journal *Option,* rarely a forum for discussions of country, several rock artists, including John Doe (of the defunct L.A. punk band X) and Al Jourgensen (of the industrial rock band Ministry and its offshoot The Revolting Cocks), express their love of country music and their belief that it must be considered a forerunner of rock & roll, but that what is currently emerging from Nashville doesn't deserve to be called "country." [8] Strange bedfellows, perhaps, but admonitions against country's abandoning its "roots" have been heard since the first documented recording, fiddler A. C. "Eck" Robertson's "Sallie Gooden," was released by RCA Victor in 1922. In *The Devil's Dream,* Smith describes the sense of desecration felt by some rural musicians when they first offered up their music for sale. Smith's fictional family participates in the famous Bristol Sessions (the weeklong 1927 field recording sessions during which producer Ralph Peer discovered Jimmie Rodgers and the Carter Family), and one member, Lucie Queen, fearing "that they have just given up something precious by singing these songs here to these strangers, . . . feels a sudden sense of loss."[9] However, the sense that something precious was being sold off is itself an element of the mythic country music "tradition." As Bill C. Malone, country's preeminent historian, has noted:

> If Southern white folk music was neither pure white nor "Anglo" in origin or manifestations, neither was it exclusively rural or noncommercial. Folk isolation was never complete. . . . Southern pockets of rural folk culture . . . have never been completely immune to the forces of technological or social change.[10]

Nevertheless, the rhetoric of "desecration" and "abandonment" persists. Throughout country's history, misguided or otherwise inappropriate efforts to protect the music from one or another group of barbarians at its gates eventually gave way to what some might call progress, others merely the transformation, for better or worse, of public tastes. The resistance for many years of the *Grand Ole Opry* management to the use of electric instruments, let alone drums (the first drums had to be played behind a curtain), or its frowning upon the on-stage cigar smoking of western swing bandleader Bob Wills, was not qualitatively different from Charlie Rich's televised burning of the envelope in which John Denver was identified as the CMA's 1975 Entertainer of the Year, the award that Rich had received the year before. Each gesture of resistance—the *Opry*'s to drums and on-stage smoking, Rich's to what John Denver represented in music—was generated by the feeling that some covenant had been broken, some inviolable rule overturned or ignored. What might be more productively examined, however, is the affective dimension of these gestures, their signification of a set of values and practices whose origins were never exclusively musical. The social practice of the consumption of popular music has always been a complex phenomenon. George Lipsitz has observed that

> as one would expect from any practice so laden with emotional investment and so central to the invention of one's own identity, the use of music becomes conflated by . . . individuals with other important issues: how they make meaningful connections with others, how they monitor and remake themselves, how they remake the past, and how they dream of something better for the future.[11]

It is necessary, therefore, to investigate in more depth how country music has constructed itself, to step behind the façade erected by the CMA or the front doors of Music Row, and, like Waylon Jennings, to ask whether Hank Williams could have "done it" in the hat-act, hunk scene of Nashville today.

The substance of country music, not to mention its interfusion with other vernacular forms of American popular music, routinely exceeds precise generic definitions of or theoretical assumptions about the boundaries between regions, races, or aesthetic regimes. My title embodies some of that complexity as it refers simultaneously to the careers of Elvis Presley, Bill Monroe, and Junior Parker. On the flip side of Elvis's first Sun Records release, he covered Monroe's bluegrass classic "Blue Moon of Kentucky," revving up its rhythmic intensity so effectively that Monroe, pleased with the transformation, henceforth always played it in a similarly hell-bent manner. Shortly thereafter, Presley released his rerecording of Junior Parker's "Mystery Train." (Parker was another Sun Records artist, a black blues singer whose career would stretch into the 1970s.) The fact that Presley routinely borrowed from any number of musical genres, not to mention that his work has itself been tagged with any number of generic labels—pop, rock, gospel, country, and rhythm & blues amongst them—should remind us of the porousness not only of American music, but also of American culture.

The degree to which all forms of American culture, musical and otherwise, constitute a complex and considerable amalgamation of elements varies, but might be employed nonetheless to attain those significant ends of which Lipsitz writes. Definitive answers to such questions would require a longer work than this one, but some provisional conclusions may be drawn from an examination of the following four factors: (1) the virtually invisible role of the instrumentalist in the documented history of country music; (2) the presence of African-American elements in a music referred to by some as the "white man's blues"; (3) the haphazard, if not criminally neglected, public documentation of country music's history; and (4) the need for a language of analysis as rich as country music itself. When John Morthland writes that "the saccharine, homogenized, overproduced songs full of glib generalities I hear most often on the radio today have little to do with the rowdy good spirits, hard truths, and high, lonesome cries that first drew me to the music," we need to respond by asking where the songs that drew Morthland to country come from: Did they arise, as does all American popular music, from what Tony Russell calls "omniracial media"? Why are many of them unavailable to the public, and why have they been replaced by a "saccharine, homogenized" music? And, finally, why is their analysis, like the worst of country music, rife with "glib generalities"? In the process of raising such questions, we may recognize or rediscover, in the words of Nick Tosches, "what a crazy bastard thing country music is."[12]

A NUMBER OF YEARS AGO, when I first attended the *Grand Ole Opry*, then still at the Ryman Auditorium, I noticed a peculiar phenomenon: each time a musician initiated an instrumental break, the announcer would egg the audience on to applaud even before the solo had been completed. Such behavior seemed antithetical to the reverential response of most jazz audiences; even rock fans, for all their enthusiasm, usually hang on every note of a live performance. Although I realize how singer- and lyric-centered country music is, the dismissive response at the Ryman to the contribution of the instrumentalists was striking nonetheless. It was as if the musicians were dispensable, even interchangeable, props whose sole purpose was to enhance the vocalist as the object of audience admiration.

A recent review by Morthland reminded me that, my experience at the Ryman notwithstanding, the history of recorded country music recognizes the contribution of instrumentalists to the signature sounds of individual artists or recording centers. The subject of Morthland's review, the contemporary artist Junior Brown of Austin, Texas (inventor of and performer on the "guit-steel," a combination steel and electric guitar), is contextualized as follows:

> Junior is the ultimate country fan, turned into the ultimate country artist. As a guitarist, he echoes everyone from Billy Byrd (Ernest Tubb's main man) to Don Rich (ditto to Buck Owens) to the dead-string of Luther Perkins (early Johnny Cash) to '50s West Coast session man Joe Maphis to Little Jimmy Dickens. Much of this gets filtered through Duane Eddy and surf twang and the improvisations and distortions of Hendrix. On the other half of the guit-steel, he's incorporated lap-steel styles from the Hawaiian-influenced Leon McAuliffe (of Bob Wills' Texas Playboys of the 1930s), the explosively bluesy Bob Dunn (of Milton Brown's Brownies) and Don Helms (of Hank Williams' Drifting Cowboys), as well as pedal steel from the drooping shroud of Bud Isaacs (Webb Pierce's sideman, who created the instrument), the jabs and roundhouses of '60s sidemen Lloyd Green and Little Roy Wiggins, and the double-whammy note-bending of John Hughey, Conway Twitty's top soloist.[13]

Morthland's inventory illustrates not only the rich and substantial ancestry of country instrumentation, but also the degree to which none of the famous solo artists he cites (Ernest Tubb, Bob Wills, Hank Williams, or Buck Owens) would have been as individually recognizable or as popular without the contributions of their sidemen. Inopportune applause may have drowned out the musicians I heard that night at the Ryman, but the recorded legacy of country's sidemen still keeps their music well within earshot. Nevertheless, while current recordings routinely list sidemen, for many years the instrumentalists were not identified and were recognizable only to the cognoscenti or to diligent discographers. Furthermore, gaining access to landmark or representative recordings by prominent country musicians remains difficult, although the recent release of two country volumes in the *Guitar Player Presents Legends of Guitar* series is a step in the right direction.[14] In addition to nearly all the individuals mentioned by Morthland, the country volumes include several tracks by the master of country finger-picking, Merle Travis, and the original 1948 recording of "Guitar Boogie" by Arthur Smith, a cut whose riffs remain common parlance for any self-respecting country picker.[15]

What makes the routine ignoring of sidemen so peculiar is the fact that so many of the major transformations in the country music canon have been inaugurated by instrumentalists, principal among them the "countrypolitan" sound (also known as "country pop") and the "Nashville Sound," pioneered by guitarist and RCA Records producer Chet Atkins in the mid-1950s. The Nashville Sound emerged from jam sessions by studio musicians at the Carousel Club in Printer's Alley, that notorious strip of downtown Nashville adjacent to the Ryman Auditorium, where the *Opry* crowd's bar, Tootsie's Orchid Lounge, could also be found. Together with Atkins, bassist Bob Moore, guitarists Hank "Sugarfoot" Garland and Grady Martin, pianist Floyd Cramer, drummer Buddy Harmon, and saxophonist Boots Randolph developed a style described by Morthland (who notes the absence of a fiddler or steel guitar player in the mix) as possessing "a relaxed flow to it, a soft and loose beat that was a little like jazz; it swung, but ever so gingerly."[16] Praised by many as the salvation of country at a time when rock & roll was ascendant, but damned by others as insufferably bland, the style developed by Atkins's ensemble achieved hegemony over the country music recording industry for more than a decade. Few could break their hold on session work, and fewer still their influence on how country was supposed to sound. As Bill Ivey and Douglas B. Green observed, "That so few talented people could take control of the sound of a major segment of American popular music is remarkable to say the least. It also shows just how small, in relative terms, the country music industry of the late 1950s and early 1960s really was."[17] It should be added, however, that while these musicians are thought to have constituted one of country's first "house bands," that "first" should really be credited to those musicians among Red Foley's accompanists—Zeke Turner (electric guitar), Jerry Byrd (steel guitar), Louis Innis (rhythm guitar), and Tommy Jackson (fiddle)—who played on the vast majority of country recordings (and on recordings in other genres, too) produced by Cincinnati-based King Records, starting in 1948. Nevertheless, Atkins and his associates constituted a force to be reckoned with, whether as an aesthetic adversary to be challenged or as a model to be emulated.

Any number of reasons might be offered for the failure to adequately recognize the major role of instrumentalists in country music's development. Even the CMA has been guilty of overlooking country's best musicians (i.e., by repeatedly selecting in years past Danny Davis and the Nashville Brass, a rural clone of Herb Alpert and the Tijuana Brass, for its Country Instrumental Group of the Year award). Some conjecture that an inbred sobriety, born of country music's religious roots, is the source of the genre's antipathy to technical flash or displays of virtuosity. Robert Cantwell has wondered if the absence of drums, for example, "does not ultimately go back to the slave owner's fear of the African talking drum and its power to transmit insurrection." [18] Rural Protestant sects typically regarded musical instruments as the devil's tools; in *The Devil's Dream,* Smith's preacher exhorts his congregation to abandon such worldliness: "No choir, no hymnbooks, no organ, no piano—no instruments of any kind. *Christ don't have no truck with the things of this world.*" [19] The temptation to indulge in "the things of this world" implied by such proscriptions against music, among other pleasures, recalls W. J. Cash's argument in his 1941 classic, *The Mind of the South,* that the Southern personality was vexed by two diverging "streams": hedonism and religiosity. Only by a fierce effort of the will could the Southerner unite "the two incompatible tendencies in his single person, without ever allowing them to come into open and decisive contention." [20] Thirty years later, Greil Marcus hears that same conflict in the rhythms of rock & roll, with its boastful energies representing a resurgence of the forces of vitality that the Southern mind fought to repress. Country music, according to Marcus, offered a form of individual expression and access to a shared sense of community, but those bonds often proved to be emotionally and aesthetically restrictive; such a musical community could be beautiful, but "it is not hard to see how it could be intolerable. All that hedonism was dragged down in country music; a deep sense of fear and resignation confined it, as perhaps it almost had to, in a land overshadowed by fundamentalist religion, where original sin was just another name for the facts of life." [21]

It may well be that the struggle to suppress country music, this "deep sense of fear and resignation" by which it was constrained, provoked the eruption of country's deviant offspring, rockabilly, and caused so many to rail against it as a threat to their livelihoods, if not to their souls. Rockabilly, in the words of

Malone, "gave vent to impulses that had long been imbedded, if often dormant, in Southern culture—a hell-for-leather hedonism, a swaggering masculinity, or, in the case of the women, an uncharacteristic aggressiveness, and, strangely, a visceral emotionalism among both men and women that seemed as reflective of the church as of the beer joints."[22] That "visceral emotionalism" is, in effect, curtailed when instrumental virtuosity is discouraged or goes unrecognized in country music. Perhaps what I observed that evening at the Ryman was a secular version of the preacher's control over his congregation: the assembly was permitted to enjoy the thrill of music's power to lead one into excess and prideful virtuosity—but not for long. The current abandonment of extended instrumental breaks in contemporary country music (When was the last time you heard a steel guitar on a Top 10 single?) is more the result of demographic factors than of aesthetic or cultural ones; marketing surveys indicate that much of the country music audience, especially women, do not like the sound. Nevertheless, its absence should remind us that the pleasure of the text includes its aural component.

◆⟡

On the same side of the railroad track
Where people have nothing to lose
I'm the son of a gambler whose luck never came
And a white man singing the blues.
—Merle Haggard, "White Man Singing the Blues"

IN THE FIRST VERSE of "White Man Singing the Blues," the chorus of which is my epigraph, Merle Haggard eloquently articulates his affiliation, and that of country music, with African-American culture:

The old man paid no mind to color
'Cause he knew that I'd been down and out
Old Joe said that I was a soul brother
From things I'd been singing out
He liked how I played my old guitar
He sat down beside me to sing
Together we hummed out an old-timey blues.

"Old Joe," the aging musician to whom he refers, represents all those figures who, like Bill Monroe's Uncle Pen, served as repositories of musical knowledge and tradition for so many country artists, although in this case cultural transmission crosses racial as well as generational lines. The words of this song might surprise those who identify both Haggard and country music in general with the most retrograde of sensibilities. For some people, I imagine, Haggard will always be identified with the ideological small-mindedness of "Okie From Muskogee," while others will never get beyond the kind of attitude toward country music that Richard Goldstein articulated in 1974: "I can never encounter a white southerner without feeling a murderousness pass between us."[23] These sensibilities also seemed to inform two pioneering works on country music that were published in 1970: John Grissim's *Country Music: White Man's Blues* and Paul Hemphill's *Nashville Sound: Bright Lights and Country Music*. Grissim declared that the music embodies "an unspoken reaffirmation of the values which seemed to work so nicely in simpler, less dangerous times," while for Hemphill "country music has always been the soul music of the white South": "If one would preserve the rural musical styles, he must also preserve the culture that gave rise to them, a society characterized by cultural isolation, racism, poverty, ignorance, and religious fundamentalism."[24]

An inability to question such cultural prejudices fuels many people's ignorance of and antipathy to the music. As Malone has observed, "The stereotyping from which country music has always suffered had its roots in the twin set of prejudices that Americans have harbored at least since the Civil War, concerning their rural origins and the place of the South in mainstream American culture."[25]

Nevertheless, the cross-fertilization between country and African American music has by now been amply demonstrated. Tony Russell's groundbreaking study *Blacks, Whites, and Blues,* which was published the same year that Grissim's and Hemphill's books appeared, documented that cross-fertilization:

> The black man's contribution to the body of world folk music is nowadays widely recognized, but too often it is thought to stop at the blues, jazz and spirituals: the black people's most personal creations. It is nearly as important to see that white country music in America would not have its present form if it were not for black workmanship. Indeed, the only way to understand fully the various folk musics of America is to see them as units in a whole; as traditions with, to be sure, a certain degree of independence, but possessing an overall unity.[26]

Cultural autonomy remains a relative phenomenon; to refuse to see beyond it interferes with the possibility of observing "more margins between cultures, more degrees of freedom, more stylistic hybrids, more places to go, more peoples to see, more discoveries of all the different ways there are to be human, and a much deeper comprehension of human purposes on this planet."[27] Such an all-encompassing point of view may, however, conflict with sensitivity to the integrity of cultures other than one's own. Reductionism or, even worse, cultural imperialism can be avoided, though, if we recognize that all transcendent realms of authenticity are fictions and that any given cultural identity will retain a mixed, relational dimension. According to James Clifford, one of the principal exponents of contemporary ethnographic critique, "Intervening in an interconnected world, one is always, to varying degrees, 'inauthentic': caught between cultures, implicated in others"; as a consequence, "if authenticity is relational, there can be no essence except as a political, cultural invention, a local tactic."[28]

Such a relational authenticity is precisely what Russell documented in country music prior to the late 1930s, when "the bearers of tradition," both black and white, were "not purists, but eclectics."[29] Those artists who produced what we have come to call "white country blues"—Jimmie Rodgers, Riley Puckett, Frank Hutchison, Cliff Carlisle, Emmett Miller, Tom Darby, and Jimmie Tarlton, principal among them—grew up and became musically proficient within racially mixed communities. Ledgers from rural stores of the 1920s and 1930s indicate that recordings of country blues performed by African Americans sold as well as the fiddle music or hillbilly songs recorded by whites, thereby demonstrating the influence of what Cantwell has designated the "aural tradition"—the "convergence of individual enterprise, folk tradition, commercial expedience, audial technology, and social cohesion."[30] While record companies routinely applied the name "blues" to all manner of music, one can discern the skilled instrumental work and lyrics as well as the vocal techniques of rural black blues in the earliest recordings of country music. Even such a seemingly white subgenre as cowboy music has antecedents in the African-American tradition. When Jess Morris recorded the earliest known variant of the cowboy classic "Old Paint" for John A. Lomax and the Library of Congress in the mid-1940s, he reported that he had learned it from a black man who worked for his father.[31]

Country music performed by both blacks and whites of the 1940s was promoted by entrepreneurs, who could profit by marketing the music of either group to consumers from either group. Small, independent record companies aided the development and dissemination of both African-American and white country music. *Grand Ole Opry* announcer Jim Bulleit founded Bullet Records in 1945 and released the first Nashville studio recording that was produced neither as a portion of a field recording nor in the studios of wsm, the *Opry*'s flagship station.[32] Bullet Records artists included both country and blues musicians: Johnnie Lee Wills, brother of western swing pioneer Bob Wills, scored his biggest hit, "Rag Mop" (1950), with the label, and Ray Price's first record, "Jealous Lies" (1950), was also a Bullet release. Bullet recordings by prominent black artists included "Nashville Jumps" (1946) by Cecil Gant, whose moody ballad "I Wonder" (1945) was one of the first rhythm & blues sides to cross over to the pop charts. Recordings by other black musicians were also distributed by Bullet, for the label carried releases by Sam Phillips's Sun Records in its early days, when blues, not rock & roll, dominated Sun's catalog.

The most substantial and influential instance of country music's multiracial promotion by the recording industry was that of the Cincinnati-based King Records.[33] Founded by Syd Nathan in 1943, initially as a means of providing country music to the rural immigrant clientele of Nathan's local record store, King Records soon recognized an equally exploitable market in Cincinnati's black community. Both rhythm & blues and country artists found their way to the King studios. A significant number of them were produced by, and in some instances wrote songs with, one of the few black Artists and Repertoire (A&R) men in the entire recording industry, Henry Glover.[34] Furthermore, largely in order to fully exploit company-held copyrights, Nathan had Glover produce versions of the same songs by *both* white country and black rhythm & blues artists; indeed, even the bands on a number of these recordings were racially mixed. Glover explained his strategy this way: "You couldn't sell Wynonie Harris to white folk, and black folk weren't buying Hank Penny. But black folk might buy Wynonie Harris doing a country tune."[35] Examples of this musical and racial cross-fertilization include versions of "Well Oh Well" by country pianist Moon Mullican and black bandleader Tiny Bradshaw; "Why Don't You Haul Off and Love Me" by country harmonica player and vocalist Wayne Raney and rhythm & blues singer "Bullmoose" Jackson; and "Finger Poppin' Time" performed by rhythm & blues ensemble Hank Ballard and the Midnighters as well as by bluegrass pioneers the Stanley Brothers. The most telling example of an "omni-racial" King Records release was the country classic "Blues Stay Away From Me." Released in 1948 by a prominent country duo, the Delmore Brothers, accompanied by Wayne Raney, the song's melody had originated in a chart, "Boarding House Blues," written by Glover for the black rhythm & blues-affiliated Lucky Millinder Band. Glover taught it to the Delmores and Raney, who then came up with the lyrics. The resulting song, which is credited to all four, remains a country standard to this day.

A more recent and much publicized manifestation of generic and racial cross-fertilization in American music was the 1994 release *Rhythm, Country & Blues*. Coproduced by country executive Tony Brown and rock producer Don Was (their teamwork itself a collaboration between two, supposedly antithetical communities), the recording consists of duets performed by country and rhythm & blues singers, with the songs likewise selected from the repertoire's of both genres. The work was featured on (and thus obviously promoted by) PBS, which aired an hour-long documentary on the recording's production, a rare instance of *either* of these genres of American vernacular music receiving the imprimatur of that most august of institutions, the Public Broadcasting System. *Rhythm, Country & Blues* itself remains more interesting or successful in theory than in practice. To my ears, the duet format lends itself not so much to collaboration on as to cohabitation of a particular piece of music, and, in a number of cases, the artists might as well be living in segregated neighborhoods. Alternating the verses also tends to separate the styles from one another, and when the voices (and genres) intersect on choruses, the result, while sometimes sympathetic, is too frequently synthetic. One splendid and touching exception is the rendition by Sam Moore (of Sam & Dave) and the late Conway Twitty of Tony Joe White's "Rainy Night in Georgia." Moore exhorts Twitty to attack the final chorus with the full range of his deep baritone, which is reminiscent of Brook Benton's classic interpretation of the song as well as that of White himself. The resulting laughter and the simpatico style of Moore and Twitty together create an impression of mutual admiration and regard, not a PR act for the cameras or the recording tape.

The hype accompanying the project proves less easy to swallow. Some have noted the fact that the recording on which country and rhythm & blues purportedly merged was produced by MCA, but this is hardly surprising given that the label's list is strongest in these genres and that this recording constitutes part of the publicity machinery for some of MCA's younger country artists on the release (specifically, Vince Gill, Trisha Yearwood, Clint Black, and Reba McEntire).[36] At the same time, the choice of artists illustrates the way in which each genre is viewed as a commercial commodity: virtually every country performer here is one with current chart credibility, while almost all of the R&B artists are past their greatest period of chart success. One must wince, too, at some of the hyperbole in James Hunter's liner notes. It may make for good copy to refer to the merging of the two traditions as "a great, even radical idea," but that language rings false to anyone with more than a dim memory of the music's past. For instance, the career of African-American soul singer Joe Tex comes to mind: his development was guided by Buddy Killen, one of country's most successful publishers; nearly all of his releases were recorded in either Nashville or Memphis, with country sidemen; and, in 1968, he recorded an entire album of country covers, *Soul Country,* for Atlantic Records. Finally, the "radical" nature of this project is undermined by Hunter's description of the two genres as forms of performance in which "everyday people cope with their problems. They never back away from the lavish vocal gesture or the plain emotional facts." Somehow, I thought we had gone beyond such discourse and become aware of the fact that both genres are too complex for appeals to emotionalism or homespun authenticity to adequately address their substance.

These examples ought to lay to rest the misguided perception of country music as racially exclusive. They should also counter such glib characterizations of it as those made by *The Nation's* Gene Santoro, ordinarily a prescient critic of American popular music, who described the music as rhythmically stiff and weighed down by regressive nostalgia.[37] More to the point, the intersecting traditions of black and white country music could be analyzed as paralleling that coexistence of hedonism and religiosity in white Southern culture observed by Cash. These conflicting drives might also be viewed as analogues of the double consciousness that W. E. B. Du Bois saw as endemic to the African-American experience. In any case, demonizing either a segment of the American population or the culture it produces leads to the kind of insularity and resistance to innovation or change that Robert Altman suggested in the lyrics of the song with which he concluded his 1975 film, *Nashville:* "You may say that I ain't free / But it don't worry me."[38] What we might hear instead in the best of country music is what Marcus heard in the Sun recordings of Elvis Presley: "This is a rhythm of acceptance and rebellion, lust and quietude, triviality and distinction. It can dramatize the rhythm of our lives well enough."[39]

ON A RECENT TRIP to Nashville, I caught a cab from Music Row to the rundown neighborhood of the Ryman Auditorium (reopened in June 1994, as a museum and performance site, after a multimillion-dollar renovation), Tootsie's Orchid Lounge, Printer's Alley, and the original Ernest Tubb Record Shop. In years past, an invitation to perform at the Record Shop meant nearly as much to a fledgling country artist as being booked to appear on the *Opry* itself. (A scene in the 1980 Loretta Lynn "biopic," *Coal Miner's Daughter,* commemorates just such a Record Shop performance and contains what was probably the last film appearance by Tubb, who died four years later.) When my late-middle-aged cabdriver heard where I wanted to go, he began naming his favorite country singers and complaining about how hard it was to find their "records" (showing his age by that now-outmoded terminology).

Had the driver tried to find these at the Tubb store, chances are that he would have been out of luck. The bins for the most part contain only very current recordings, with a mere smattering of older vinyl records, apparently stocked for the sake of older customers like my driver. Ernest Tubb has been dead for ten years, and the artists of his generation, as well as those who preceded them, might just as well have never recorded for all the record labels have done to keep their work, specifically their *original* recordings, in print. The truth of the matter is that virtually no other genre of American music has been as shabbily treated as country in terms of its maintenance as living history. Try to find recordings by the artists who are enshrined in the Country Music Hall of Fame; with luck, you'll be able to locate a "Greatest Hits" package by most of them, but many of their major releases remain out of print or have been replaced by lower-quality rerecordings, a sadly common practice in the country music industry, where producers apparently assume that the public cannot tell the difference or doesn't care. Should a consumer like my cabdriver be lucky enough to find a vinyl original, the price would probably induce sticker shock.

The listings in Morthland's *Best of Country Music* or in the 1989/90 *Country Music Catalog* printed by the California-based Roots & Rhythm distribution service make the paucity of available material strikingly clear. And it is not just a matter of being unable to locate a copy of Tubb's original "Walking the Floor Over You"; try to find a Webb Pierce or Eddy Arnold album, let alone one by a less well-known artist like Stoney Edwards or Gary Stewart. The willingness of the present-day country music community to jettison the steel guitar parallels its indifference to keeping the music of the past available to contemporary consumers. One wonders if, in the ongoing process of country's development and continual redefinition, the ineffable "something" that made the music unique and irreducible has disappeared altogether. Uncomfortable as I am with referring to ineffable qualities and unwilling to adopt the rhetoric of "authenticity" wholesale, it remains indisputable that the price of seeking the recorded origins/original recordings of country music is too high. One should not need to spend so much time and money on recordings that ought to be as accessible as those of any other musical genre. Without such access to country music of the past, how is one to ascertain whether or not contemporary artists have returned to country's "roots," much less what those roots are and where they lie?

Of course, it would be an exaggeration to imply that nothing but material by the latest Top 40 wunderkinder can be purchased. While the number of country music boxed sets or multiple-CD packages cannot compete with the production of jazz, blues, or rock, efforts are being made to bring material from the industry's backlists to the marketplace. At the same time, such efforts are more often than not made by foreign rather than domestic record companies. Since 1975, the German Bear Family label has provided an invaluable service to country music aficionados (and those of other genres, too) by their efforts to market exhaustive inventories of recorded works by major artists. Their country catalog lists comprehensive boxed sets of recordings by Johnny Cash, Bill

Monroe, Marty Robbins, Kitty Wells, Hank Snow, Ernest Tubb, Flatt & Scruggs, Jimmie Rodgers, and the Louvin Brothers. However, their premiere achievement to date is a 12-CD set of all of Lefty Frizzell's recordings (entitled *Life's Like Poetry;* see Selected Discography), packaged with a 152-page, LP-sized booklet, one of the most extensive CD reissues in any genre of music and probably the most comprehensive reissue of any country artist's recordings. Overkill to some and invaluable cultural artifact to others, the Frizzell project and others by this company are documenting American music on a scale that few U.S. labels apparently consider either commercially viable or financially feasible.

On the other hand, there are pitfalls to the canon-making endeavors of a company like Bear Family Records (or of the U.S. firm Rhino or of British reissue labels like Ace, Charley, Krazy Kat, or See For Miles), let alone the more limited but exemplary efforts of the Country Music Foundation. Mark Fenster, one of today's most adept academic analysts of country music, has warned against

> the construction of the subject of the box set (whether it is an artist, record label, or a genre) as an object of desire, study, and collection; the categorization and control of the proliferating and ever-expanding tests of popular music history; and the experience of listening within the ongoing flow of everyday life. The boxed set does not answer or "box in" these issues; rather, it marks the incomplete and impossible attempt to construct the "collected" artist, the categorized history, and the enraptured listener.[40]

Fenster critiques the manner in which boxed sets become legitimations of an artist, genre, or label through the construction of a "narrative of greatness."[41] Inherent to that process is the misguided assumption that any such enterprise could wholly encompass the entire extent of knowledge or understanding of a given subject. We have to remember that merely reissuing country's backlisted recordings does not in itself clarify the music's form or function; reissues provide crucial material for study, not clear expositions of country music's prior construction or consumption. Furthermore, the boxed set represents "the transformation and control of history within material goods and property—history can be sold, history can be owned"—an apt but ironic assertion in light of the country music industry's apparent inclination to own pieces of recorded history but not to sell them.[42] (My Nashville cabdriver was most interested in finding tracks by Jim Reeves. I wonder how satisfied he is by the recent RCA two-CD set of Reeves's recordings—or if he has the equipment to play it.) The virtual disappearance of a significant number of recorded works by American musicians exemplifies that old "tree falling in the woods" conundrum from

Philosophy 101: if a recording is made but cannot be heard, it effectively does not exist.

I RECENTLY INTERVIEWED Harlan Howard, one of country's preeminent songwriters. Of the many interesting comments he made, I was particularly struck by his observation that lyrics constitute the heart of country music and that, while many composers can write a serviceable melody, very few can compose cogent lyrics. In the case of those who write about country music, it seems equally true that not many produce prose that "sings" in a manner commensurate with their subject. Nor have the venues available to these writers encouraged much artistry—most being little better than flack sheets. For example, the long-established *Music City News,* once part-owned by country singer Faron Young, paints a rosy picture of the industry and helps to sell its products. Nevertheless, there are some exceptions to these hack publications: *Country Music* magazine, a showcase for some of today's best music journalists, publishes articles on the current scene and record reviews that hold the work of today's country artists to high standards, which (alas) they seldom meet, let alone exceed; the *Journal of Country Music,* published by the Country Music Foundation, is another exemplary publication—one recent issue (14:2, 1992) tackled the rarely addressed subject of African-American country artists; and, for individuals committed to the music's past, the *Journal* of the American Academy for the Preservation of Old-Time Country Music has proved a valuable resource, with its biographical profiles on various country music pioneers and its regular feature, "Recommended Recordings," which, incidentally, attests to the paucity of reissues. While fanzines have proliferated for all popular musical genres, I have come across only two country 'zines: *Twangin'* and *The Feedlot.* (The latter's masthead identifies it in boldface as "The Journal of Real Country Music.")[43] On the other hand, the principal mass-market music periodicals— *Rolling Stone* and *Spin*—and the magazines that cater to a culture-consuming crowd—*Details* and *Interview*—devote very little space to country music. I would not be at all surprised to discover that the number of country artists featured on the cover of *Rolling Stone,* for example, is still in the single digits.

With regard to the academics and professional music critics who write about country, we can round up the usual suspects: Rich Kienzle, Bill C. Malone, Charles K. Wolfe, Ivan Tribe, John Morthland, and Nick Tosches are among the handful of writers who comprise country's literati. Their work has unquestionably contributed to the documentation and analysis of the music's history, especially the categorization of its subgenres and the evaluation of its recordings. But a certain spark often seems to be missing: Where is the writer who can describe country music with the virtuosity that Whitney Balliett has brought to jazz in the pages of the *New Yorker*? Will anyone ever contextualize country music in the web of American culture as deftly as Albert Murray did with jazz in *Stomping the Blues* (1976) or Greil Marcus with rock in *Mystery Train* (1975)? The business of American popular music as a whole has received scant attention from scholars and journalists alike, with country being no exception; even the study of individual record labels and their management that Nelson George wrote about Berry Gordy's Motown; Charlie Gillett, about Atlantic Records; or Peter Guralnick, about the Southern Soul labels, has no equivalent in the field of country music.[44] There is not even an adequate discography, essential to any genre of music scholarship, for country: pre–World War II country music will finally receive its due, however, when Tony Russell's long-awaited accounting of the period's releases is published. While academics and others writing on country have begun to document the names, dates, and places in its history, then, all too many other questions or points of reference still await their attention.

Part of the problem may be that most Western scholarship (and journalism, too, for that matter) on popular culture, musical and otherwise, tends to treat the subject in an unnecessarily narrow or myopic manner. As Ralph Ellison asked over thirty years ago, "Who knows very much of what jazz is really about? Or how shall we ever know until we are willing to confront anything and everything which it sweeps across our path?"[45] In a similar manner, Charles Keil, a (white) musicologist and scholar of African-American music, critiques his own methodology, and that of many of his peers and successors, in his "Postscripts" to the 1993 reprint of his now-classic 1966 study of Chicago, *Urban Blues:*

> White writers on the blues tend to be folklorizing, documenting, defining, and social scientific; let's get it down. Black writers are more inclined to celebrate blues as a core metaphor in process, the center of a worldview that incorporates jazz, literature, aesthetics, philosophy, criticism, and political strategy. In other words, they want to build on it.[46]

Who has attempted to define country music's "worldview," or, even better, attempted such an analysis from the kind of cross-disciplinary perspective that Keil advocates? No names come to mind. Some should.

To be fair, any attempt to construct such a comprehensive analysis must overcome a number of obstacles, not the least of which is the unavailability of archival recordings. But even keeping up with the wide range of current material requires more time, energy, and money than most of us have to spend. The rapidly proliferating number of country radio stations, however welcome, is not necessarily helpful, for, like most media formats, country music programming is dictated by the market, that is, radio station owners and programmers, aiming to sell advertising time, play it safe, aesthetically and otherwise. But that is only the tip of the proverbial iceberg. For all the pronouncements about how "hot" country has become, "the genre," as James Hunter observes, "unlike rock or R&B, has yet to break apart into different taste sectors that can always sustain themselves financially within the big picture." [47] And for all the visibility of Garth Brooks or Billy Ray Cyrus, a good deal of country music is not considered mainstream, but rather what the industry tends to label (and often to ghettoize as) "alternative," or, to use rock critic Robert Christgau's term, "semi-popular" music. Few country divisions of major record companies have a department, or even an individual, to handle such material. If an artist's style is not intrinsically radio-friendly, he or she might as well throw in the towel; as singer/songwriter Matraca Berg caustically observed about the response to her recent release *The Speed Of Grace:* "In Nashville, people listen to my new record and say, 'Boy, that's not a country record.' People outside say, 'Well, that's kind of a country record.' Call it a purgatory record." [48]

If any uncategorizable piece of country music is to be thus condemned, then so will be most female country artists. Patsy, Loretta, Tammy, Dolly, and Wynonna notwithstanding, the genre is still a virtual "boys' club." As Mark Schone recently reported, in 1991 thirty-six female country artists received contracts, while male artists picked up three times more than that, and, of releases that charted, only 12 percent were by women, the lowest percentage since the 1960s. Furthermore, this situation persists despite the fact (as indicated by a recent Record Industry Association of America [RIAA] survey) that half of all country releases are purchased by women (with an even higher figure of 70 percent if purchases over the last thirty years are counted). [49] Female empowerment seems not to be on Nashville's agenda, and "D.I.V.O.R.C.E." is out of the question; as long as record company management remains in its present state, all that female performers can do is stand by their men. For, despite the long history of women's substantial contributions to the genre, these have only recently been documented in a major scholarly work: Mary A. Bufwack and Robert K. Oermann's *Finding Her Voice: The Saga of Women in Country Music.*[50] One can only wonder, given this degree of terra incognita, how much of country music overall may have escaped us and whether even the best histories of the genre are incomplete or marred by bias, willful and otherwise. Furthermore, can we really hope to capture the whole picture by merely adding more facts to our store of knowledge, or (at the risk of what might seem romantic language) will something irreducible in country music be overlooked in our quest for "just the facts"?

In answer to that question, I can only quote from and applaud David Whisnant's remarks on the occasion of the installation of the Jonathan Edwards Memorial Foundation Collection at the University of North Carolina, Chapel Hill. In noting the importance of the collection's material on American vernacular music, including country, Whisnant declared, "We have remained too content with first-documentation of detail, with a rather indulgent musical hero-worship, with a hesitancy about close reading of the social texts that parallel the stylistic ones, with a necessary but still in some ways obfuscatory defensiveness and defiant celebration." Whisnant went on to say that we still need to address "questions of stigmatization and delegitimation vs. legitimation and revitalization; of cultural assimilation and acculturation vs. cultural survival and organic transformation; of the utility of contending world views and value systems; of the progressive and regressive roles of culture in broader social and political transformation."[51] The extent of the work that still needed to be done led Whisnant to conclude with a measured and resonant critique of cultural studies:

> What this leads me to observe is that we have for decades been doing a work (and in many respects doing it very well) the larger significance and potential of which we have not yet fully grasped: it is the work of cultural resistance against those central forces of all mass cultures which aim (or *function,* whether they consciously aim or not) to contain, to divide and shame, to push beyond the margin and into the ghetto, to homogenize and delegitimate, to render politically sterile and inert.
>
> As we turn inward we will begin to admit that although it is in some senses an act of defiance and resistance to sing, play, or record *any* song from any alternative, marginalized, delegitimized tradition, no matter how sexist, racist, or politically reactionary the song may be, it is not defiant or resistant *enough.*[52]

The present moment in country music's history seems ripe for rising to Whisnant's challenge, especially his call for resistance to the forces of mass culture—in this case, the recording industry's control over and suppression of country music. In a recent editorial in *Rolling Stone,* Anthony DeCurtis asserted that the current popularity of Garth Brooks (and of country music generally) among middle-aged consumers, of which I count myself one, must be accounted for in more than solely musical terms.[53] Having raised that question, however, he did not then fully answer it. Yes, members of my generation (at least as it is chronologically defined) do find much current popular music loud, abrasive, and confrontational, as DeCurtis suggests, but why, then, don't they/we object to these qualities in the country music of Brooks and other performers? One answer to this question brings us back to Waylon Jennings and answers *his* question, with which we began. To those who would criticize Garth Brooks for not being Hank Williams, we might reply, with Robert Christgau, "I don't give a fuck how Hank woulda done it. Hank died too young to suit me."[54]

NOTES

1   Wallace Stevens, "Anecdote of the Jar," *The Palm at the End of the Mind* (New York, 1972), 46.

2   For two useful articles on West Coast country, see Rick Mitchell, "The Bakersfield Sound: Roots and Revival," *Musician* (July 1989): 52–56, 58, 60, 62, 118; and "California Country," *Request* (May 1993): 32, 34, 36–37. Neither article, in my view, goes into enough detail on either the rich legacy of California western swing or the country recordings made under Ken Nelson's supervision at Capitol Records.

3   Lee Smith, *The Devil's Dream* (New York, 1993), 276.

4   See Charles K. Wolfe, *The Grand Ole Opry: The Early Years 1925–35* (London, 1975), 22.

5   Ibid., 36.

6   Thomas Cobb, *Crazy Heart* (New York, 1987), 53.

7   Ibid., 70.

8   See Mark Kemp, "Searching For A Rainbow: Country Without Borders," *Option* 53 (November/December 1993): 90–97.

9   Smith, *Devil's Dream*, 124.

10  Bill C. Malone, *Country Music U.S.A.*, rev. ed. (Austin, 1985 [1968]), 5.

11  George Lipsitz, Foreword to Susan Crafts, Daniel Cavicchi, Charles Keil, and the Music in Daily Life Project, *My Music* (Hanover, NH, 1993), xii–xiii.

12  John Morthland, *The Best of Country Music* (Garden City, 1980), xv–xvi; Tony Russell, *Blacks, Whites, and Blues* (New York, 1970), 30; Nick Tosches, *Country: Living Legends and Dying Metaphors in America's Biggest Music,* rev. ed. (New York, 1985 [1977]), 5.

13  John Morthland, "Outta Nowhere," *L.A. Weekly,* 10–16 September 1993, 45.

14  See Selected Discography. The liner notes are by Rich Kienzle, one of country music's most prolific and knowledgeable scholars; see also his *Great Guitarists: The Most Influential Players in Country, Jazz, Blues, and Rock* (New York, 1986); "Steel," *Country Music* (January 1976): 37–38, 61–62; "Electric Guitar in Country Music," *Guitar Player* (November 1979): 30–41; "Hank Garland," *Guitar Player* (January 1981): 76–86; "The Forgotten Hank Garland," *Journal of Country Music* 9 (1982): 28–32, 41–46; "Grady Martin: Unsung & Unforgettable," *Journal of Country Music* 10 (1985): 54–60. See also Debbie Hollay's chronicle of the career of Ernest Tubb's most famous accompanist, "Billy Byrd: The Jazzman Who Wore Cowboy Boots," *Journal of Country Music* 12 (1987): 43–47; and James Sallis, on Hank Garland, in

*The Guitar Players: One Instrument and Its Masters in American Music* (Lincoln, NE, 1994 [1982]).

15  For an analysis of Smith's "Guitar Boogie," see Jim Dawson and Steve Propes, *What Was the First Rock 'n' Roll Record?* (Boston, 1992), 45–47.

16  Morthland, *Best of Country Music,* 282.

17  Bill Ivey and Douglas B. Green, "The Nashville Sound," in *The Illustrated History of Country Music* (Garden City, NY, 1980), 244.

18  Robert Cantwell, *Bluegrass Breakdown: The Making of the Old Southern Sound* (New York, 1982), 97.

19  Smith, *Devil's Dream,* 39; her emphases.

20  W. J. Cash, *The Mind of the South* (New York, 1991 [1941]), 58.

21  Greil Marcus, *Mystery Train: Images of America in Rock 'n' Roll Music,* 3d ed. (New York, 1990 [1975]), 133.

22  Malone, *Country Music U.S.A.,* 250.

23  As quoted in James C. Cobb, "Country Music and the 'Southernization' of America," in *All That Glitters: Country Music in America,* ed. George Lewis (Bowling Green, 1993), 83. (Goldstein's comment originally appeared in "My Country Music Problem—And Yours," *Mademoiselle* [June 1973].)

24  John Grissim, *Country Music: White Man's Blues* (New York, 1970), 9; Paul Hemphill, *The Nashville Sound: Bright Lights and Country Music* (New York, 1970), 12, 242.

25  Bill C. Malone, *Smithsonian Collection of Classic Country Music* (Washington, DC, 1981), 5.

26  Russell, *Blacks, Whites, and Blues,* 10.

27  Charles Keil, "Postscripts," in *Urban Blues* (Chicago, 1993 [1966]), 230.

28  James Clifford, *The Predicament of Culture: 20th Century Ethnography, Literature, and Art* (Cambridge, MA, 1988), 11, 12.

29  Russell, *Blacks, Whites, and Blues,* 26.

30  Cantwell, *Bluegrass Breakdown,* 145.

31  See Morthland, *Best of Country Music,* 99.

32  See Martin Hawkins, "Bullet Records: A Shot in the Dark," *Journal of Country Music* 8 (1981): 33–40. Country material from Bullet is included on Redita 108, *Boogie With A Bullet,* and two volumes (27 and 28) of the Dutch Collector Records' series *Boppin' Hillbilly,* while blues material can be found on Krazy Kat 783, *Nashville Jumps: R&B From Bullet 1946–53.*

33  See David Sanjek, "Plug It Again, Syd: King Records and the Construction of Crossover," forthcoming in the proceedings of the 1993 International Association for the Study of Popular Music conference, Stockton, CA.

34  John Rumble, "Roots of Rock and Roll: Henry Glover at King Records," *Journal of Country Music* 14 (1992): 30–42.

35  Ibid., 36.

36  For this interesting observation (plus others on the presence of African Americans

in country music), see Keith Moerer, "Black Cowboys and Country Soul: Who Says Honky-Tonk and R&B Don't Mix?" *Request* (April 1994): 36–37, 68–72, 74.

37　See Gene Santoro, "Country Comforts," *The Nation,* 8 April 1991, 458.

38　Joan Tewksbury, *Nashville* (New York, 1976); lyrics by Keith Carradine.

39　Marcus, *Mystery Train,* 173.

40　Mark Fenster, "Boxing In, Opening Out: The Boxed Set and the Politics of Musical Production and Consumption," *Stanford Humanities Review* 3 (Autumn 1993): 146.

41　Ibid., 146.

42　Ibid., 148.

43　*Twangin'* is available from editor/publisher Cheryl Cline at 2230 Huron Drive, Concord, CA 94519; *The Feedlot* from Lee Nichols, 2101 Chicon Street, Austin, TX 78722–2430. Perhaps not coincidentally, both fanzines are published in major sites of country music production that the hegemony of Nashville tends to obscure.

44　See Nelson George, *Where Did Our Love Go? The Rise and Fall of the Motown Sound* (New York, 1985); Charlie Gillett, *Making Tracks: Atlantic Records and the Growth of a Multi-Billion Dollar Industry* (New York, 1974); Peter Guralnick, *Sweet Soul Music: R&B and the Southern Dream of Freedom* (New York, 1986).

45　Ralph Ellison, *Shadow and Act* (New York, 1972 [1962]), 224–25.

46　Keil, "Postscripts," 236–37.

47　James Hunter, "Is Country Music Too Big for Radio?" *Musician* (March 1994): 38.

48　Ibid., 43.

49　Mark Schone, "Nashville's 12 Percent," *L.A. Weekly,* 11–17 September 1992, 43.

50　Mary A. Bufwack and Robert K. Oermann, *Finding Her Voice: The Saga of Women in Country Music* (New York, 1993).

51　David Whisnant, "Turning Inward and Outward: Retrospective and Prospective Considerations in the Recording of Vernacular Music in the South," in *Sounds of the South,* ed. Daniel Paterson (Chapel Hill, 1991), 177, 178.

52　Ibid., 179–80.

53　Anthony DeCurtis, "Opinion," *Rolling Stone* (November 1992): 23.

54　Robert Christgau, "Garth's World," *Village Voice,* 10 November 1992, 73.

# Bloody Daggers and Lonesome Graveyards

*The Gothic and Country Music*

**Teresa Goddu**

CECELIA TICHI: But you're talking about country. . . . I mean, I've heard some of those traditional old songs you have called Appalachian dead-baby songs. So you're suggesting that country had to move well out of that old sentimental, old-time formula, that it just wouldn't work for contemporary country music?

RODNEY CROWELL: Well, that stuff is almost like Edgar Allan Poe. It's like, my thirteen-year-old daughter, for me to get her to understand a song like "Little Rosewood Casket." . . . [Sings] "There's a little rosewood casket / Laying on a marble slab." Just real Gothic.

. . . . .

CECELIA TICHI: That's interesting, the Gothic. Bluegrass seems to get away with that still. I don't mean *get away with,* I mean, it's part of that genre. And when you enter into the bluegrass world, then it's okay. But not in country as a whole, not rock-age country.[1]

I begin with this conversation between Cecelia Tichi and Rodney Crowell not only because it served as the genesis for this article, but also because it situates the gothic in relationship to country music in several important ways. First, it connects *country music* to the *gothic,* two terms that are rarely conjoined. Country music often conjures up images of home and heartbreak, but rarely the haunted houses or beating hearts of Edgar Allan Poe. Second, it situates the gothic within a specific line of country music: bluegrass. Associated with traditional, old-time country music and filled with stories of violent murder, unatoned sin, and ghostly visitations, bluegrass is permitted the morbidity and excess that mainstream country cannot "get away with." Tichi's point—that bluegrass's more marginal status allows it a range of meaning no longer available to "rock-age country"—suggests that the gothic mode is not only repressed in mainstream country music, but also that it reemerges in bluegrass, the genre associated with country's roots and self-consciously constructed as its past.

In its effort to appeal to a national audience, the "new" country music tries to exorcise its gothic elements by disassociating itself from particular regional stereotypes, many of which are associated with the gothic: horror, violence, perverted sexuality, the grotesque. Moreover, new country reconfigures the gender dynamic that bluegrass sets into play, a dynamic that serves as bluegrass's central trope for the gothic's transgression of social norms. Despite its attempted transformations, however, "hot, new country" continues to be haunted by that "old-time formula."

COUNTRY MUSIC'S PRESENT STATUS as a national draw has much to do with current attempts to redefine the South—what John Egerton has termed the "Americanization of Dixie" or the "Southernization of America."[2] As seen in the political rise of Jimmy Carter and Bill Clinton to the presidency, the "new South" is able to go national. But while the "new South" can represent the nation, the "old South," which was often depicted in oppositional and gothic terms, was the regional representative of everything the nation was *not*. Having come to be associated with the excessive and the transgressive—from its climate, which was seen to be excessively warm to its perceived transgressions of social and sexual norms (i.e., slavery and incest)—the South was seen as a savage place rife with violence and perversion. The new South, no longer the benighted backwoods of the nation, now belongs to the suburban sunbelt. Perceived as having overcome much of what made it distinctive—economic impoverishment, educational ignorance, religious fundamentalism, racial intolerance, violence—either by "catching up" with the nation economically or by exporting its "vices" of violence and racism to the rest of the nation, the new South has managed to revamp its negative image and, in so doing, to move, at least momentarily, from the margin toward the national center. However, like Carter, who was haunted by the hillbilly image of his brother, and Clinton, who continues to be suspected of sexual excess and corruption, the new South still bears traces of its older, negative image.

The packaging of country music in the 1990s has participated in the regional redefinition of the South. Country, long caricatured as hillbilly music, is now selling the nation an idealized image of America by mass marketing more wholesome images of the South: rural nostalgia, conservative politics, and traditional values. From Barbara Mandrell's Sunsweet Prune ads to Ross Perot's use of Patsy Cline songs in the 1992 presidential election, country music has been making a comeback on the basis of a clean image and family values. In doing so, its appeal has broadened, and new constituencies have been attracted. As Richard Peterson and Paul DiMaggio have argued, country music is no longer a Southern phenomenon; instead, it now plays to a national audience of the religiously and politically conservative working class.[3] In an age dominated by heavy metal and rap, country music, according to *Rolling Stone,* is also attracting baby boomers as it recycles the soft rock of the seventies.[4] In his 1992 review of Garth Brooks, Anthony DeCurtis argued that country music had "become the refuge of older rock and roll fans who [were] put off by the anger, abrasiveness, and decibel level of the music favored by listeners in their teens and twenties: rap, alternative and metal. At the same time, Brooks . . . won over a younger generation of country fans by spiking his music with a rock and roll kick."[5] Turning away from the urban sounds of hard rock and its more demonized counterparts—heavy metal and rap—much of the American listening public seems to be drawn to the softer twang of country music. Indeed, from Brooks's virtual rock & roll stage shows to the Super Bowl XXVIII halftime show called "Rockin' Country Sunday," country music appears to be offering the excitement of rock without the hard edge. Moreover, given the way that "hot" has become a distinctive marker of the younger generation of country stars, applied equally to Billy Ray Cyrus (country's own Chippendale dancer) and to the summer 1993 and 1994 syndicated television show *Hot Country Nights,* country music also seems to have (safe) sex appeal. Like Branson, Missouri, a replica of Las Vegas with all the glitter but no gambling, country music has apparently retained just enough of the South's "wild" or uncivilized image to make itself marketable, but has packaged it in such a way that it no longer poses a threat. While Garth Brooks may sing, as in his recent television concert "This Is Garth Brooks, Too," of a love that is "yearning" to get "out of control" ("Standing Outside the Fire"), the fire that erupts as he sings is a carefully controlled stage effect. What used to be truly scary about the South is now, it would seem, sexy but safe.

This transformation of the South's image from "devilish" to "down-home," as Jack Kirby labels it, has a long and varied history.[6] Country music's new wave of popularity in the 1970s was accompanied by a move toward home and hearth. *Glen Campbell's Goodtime Hour, The Porter Wagoner Show,* and *Hee Haw* were TV series that aired concurrently with *The Beverly Hillbillies, The Andy Griffith Show,* and *The Waltons.* Country's hillbilly image was no longer seen as threatening, but as comforting and even comic—with the benighted backwoods populated by rustic folks and ridiculous rednecks. When Richard

Nixon opened Opryland in 1974, he underscored the national image of country music, which, he told the crowd, "talks about family. It talks about religion. And it . . . makes America a better country."[7]

This is not to say, however, that country music did not continue to be associated with its devilish side, as the Nixon/Opryland connection might suggest. In the 1970s, such artists as Willie Nelson, Waylon Jennings, Johnny Cash, Hank Williams, Jr., and Merle Haggard built their images on the American outlaw tradition. Tanya Tucker established herself then as the young singer of such gothic hits as "Delta Dawn" (1972), "Blood Red and Going Down" (1973), and "Would You Lay With Me (In A Field of Stone)" (1974). Moreover, *Newsweek*'s cover story on country music (18 June 1973), which featured a cover photo of Loretta Lynn and was sandwiched between accounts of Watergate and the corruption scandal at Columbia Records, revealed country's continued affiliations with the demonic. Country music in the 1970s was likewise tied to a national feeling of defeat and disillusionment.[8] Robert Altman's *Nashville* (1975), which made the South a backdrop for the nation's corruption, reinforced this association by making a fiddle case the repository of violence.[9] Moreover, perhaps the best-known film of Southern haunting and violence, *Deliverance* (1972), which, when read as a Vietnam-era film adaptation of James Dickey's novel, also refracts the nation's violence through the South, was one of the first mainstream films to use a country music sound track. Like *Bonnie and Clyde* (1967), in which Flatt & Scruggs's "Foggy Mountain Breakdown" had been used to underscore its scenes of lawlessness, *Deliverance* employed the "Dueling Banjos" theme not only to haunt the movie's journey into the heart of darkness, but also to emblematize the film's central dualisms in its opening scene. The musical duel between the Atlanta businessman, Drew (Ronnie Cox), and the banjo-picking idiot savant, who is portrayed as a grotesque figure straight out of a Flannery O'Connor story, sets up the oppositions that the film will explore and collapse: city/country, civilized/wild, moderation/excess, effeminacy/masculinity. In the 1970s, then, the devilish, perverted image of the South persisted in both mainstream country music and bluegrass.

By contrast, country music's current range of images seems—at least so far—more limited. This constricted range is reflected more generally by the relatively sanitized media images of the South. The violent hillbilly world of *Deliverance*, for instance, has been transformed in the 1990s into the upper-middle-class, stylized world of another film adaptation of a novel, Pat Conroy's *Prince of Tides*. While a brutal rape scene is at the center of both films, *The Prince of Tides* moderates the horror of emasculation by containing it in a flashback to a childhood trauma revealed by Tom Wingo within the safety of a therapist's office—and the comforting arms of his soon-to-be lover, Dr. Lowenstein. This strategy of narrative containment through mediation characterizes the film as a whole. Framed by Tom's prologue and epilogue and intermittently narrated via his voice-overs, *The Prince of Tides* casts Tom as the viewer's guide through his violent world. *Deliverance,* on the other hand, requires its audience to experience the horror without any mediation or frame: the viewer does not know who will survive the rape. The 1991 *Prince of Tides* turns *Deliverance's* 1972 tale of self-dissolution into a story of self-healing: no longer emasculated, Tom can go home to his wife and daughters after being sexually regenerated by his affair with Lowenstein. Where *Deliverance* depicted the horror as uncontainable and unforgettable, with Ed (Jon Voight) still haunted by nightmares at the end of the movie (despite being told by his wife to "go back to sleep"), *The Prince of Tides* affirms the exorcising power of therapy. A healing narrative of return (Tom reconciles himself to his past as he returns to the South), *The Prince of Tides* domesticates *Deliverance's* narrative of fear and flight ("Don't ever come back here," says one of the townspeople, chillingly, to the men).

The sound tracks to these films underscore their differing messages: the threatening chords of *Deliverance's* bluegrass track are replaced by a swelling, sentimental orchestral score in *The Prince of Tides.* Moreover, instead of serving as an indicator of the threatening redneck, the fiddle in *The Prince of Tides* comes to symbolize Southern masculine pride. In the scene where Tom and Lowenstein's husband (a famous violinist) confront each other, the latter insults Tom by "dumbing down" his Stradivarius, turning it into a fiddle and playing "Dixie." Tom retaliates by playing the "dumb Southerner": holding the Stradivarius over the balcony, he threatens to drop it into the street below until Lowenstein's husband apologizes (as ordered by the "Southern gentleman") to *her.* Like the banjo in *Deliverance,* the fiddle in *The Prince of Tides* operates as a class marker; both instruments also signify how class intersects with region. But instead of serving as at least a temporary point of identification between two men of different classes and regions, as the banjo does in *Deliverance,* the violin/fiddle in *The Prince of Tides* marks and maintains the irreconcilable differences between them. Where *Deliverance* had threatened to collapse the opposition between new and old South, *The Prince of Tides* endeavored to regenerate the South without disturbing the North.

This move toward narrative containment of what might remain threatening about the South dominates current media images of the region. From such TV series and films as *Evening Shade* and *I'll Fly Away,* both of which end with moralizing voice-overs, to *Fried Green Tomatoes,* which contains its depictions of racial violence and potentially threatening lesbianism by means of its "new

Woman" and "new South" framing tale, the devilish, "perverted" image of the old South is moderated and mediated through the South's "quaint" penchant for storytelling. The more recent television representation of the South in the weekly drama *Christy* continues this trend. Based on Catherine Marshall's best-selling 1967 novel about her mother's life as a schoolteacher in Appalachia, *Christy* (which stars Kelly Martin of *Life Goes On*) conveys a domesticated image of the South. Set in an early twentieth-century "wild, far-off place," as the opening credits tell us, *Christy* is displaced both in time and in space. The narrative frame of each episode further contains and distances the South: Cutter Gap may be a world full of feuding and violence, but Christy's reassuring voice will guide us through it. Moreover, through her "civilizing" influence, Cutter Gap slowly improves with each episode: Ruby Mae learns to bathe; a child's failing eyesight is restored; and Dr. MacNeill's science begins to make inroads on backwoods superstition, while Miss Alice's Quaker tolerance remains steadfast despite the fatalism of this Calvinist community. Even when "gothic" moments occur (as when Dr. MacNeill's wife returns from the dead to haunt his budding romance with Christy), they are quickly dispelled: the sexual excesses of Dr. MacNeill, who has one too many love interests, is easily resolved when Margaret leaves Cutter Gap as abruptly as she had arrived, her tuberculosis a sign that her real death is assured. Despite its scripted warnings about cultural chauvinism, the show makes its loyalties clear. Each episode teaches Christy the same lesson: her attempt to "civilize" Cutter Gap is praiseworthy; she need only learn about mountain culture in order to understand how to change it. Unlike the novel, which opens with Marshall and her mother returning to Cutter Gap, where they find everything in ruins and question the high price of progress, the television series constantly assures us that progress—however slow and slight—is always positive. The South can be civilized, its violence and wildness contained.

The same message would seem to be conveyed by country music's image in the 1990s. Violence still erupts, but it is well-contained now by the music's image of sexual and social order. In order to understand how this domestication was accomplished, it is crucial to understand "new country's" relationship to its older counterpart, bluegrass. It is through its connections to bluegrass, in which a broad range of gothic associations still persist, that mainstream country's hauntings—and exorcisms—become more visible. Steeped in blood and gore, bluegrass pierces the listener with its "high, lonesome" sound and its chilling stories of violent murder and unatoned sin. Filled with ghosts, dark and dreary woods, and little lonesome graveyards, it remains the locus of death and dread in country music. To read country music without considering bluegrass is to miss its long and continuing gothic tradition.

BLUEGRASS'S ALIGNMENT with the gothic is rooted in the British ballad and broadside traditions. Evolving out of "the reservoir of folksongs, ballads, dances, and instrumental pieces brought to North America by Anglo-Celtic immigrants," hillbilly music (and its closest offspring, bluegrass) built its own repertoire of traditional ballads.[10] The British ballad "The Oxford Girl" was transposed into an American ballad, "The Knoxville Girl." While the translation from British to American form often elided the supernatural aspects of the original and, due to the influence of Christian fundamentalism, often added a "moral," many gothic elements remained, especially in songs based on supernatural or religious narratives.[11] Not only are many of its themes gothic, but the bluegrass sound has been described in gothic terms as well: "hauntingly beautiful" is the phrase used repeatedly about the "high, lonesome" sound of bluegrass vocalization. Characterized by high-pitched singing with great vocal tension and a driving pace, bluegrass is "wrought out of high energies and powerful tensions." [12] These tensions and the strict conventions that performers must observe ally bluegrass with the sublime: "The aims of bluegrass harmony singing and of bluegrass lead singing are really one aim. Both strive for that moment of consummate intensity at which conflict and pain, and the consciousness of them, have transcended themselves." [13] Depicting the extremity of human experience within a tightly controlled form built on opposition and tension, bluegrass demonstrates its gothic antecedents both thematically and formally.

The landscape of the music reinforces its connection to the gothic. Like the landscape in a Cormac McCarthy novel, the world depicted by bluegrass is one of dreadful beauty, marked by blood-stained spots and haunted by the walking dead. From the dreary, funereal landscape of a song like the Louvin Brothers' "In the Pines," where a man "moans" for his lost love, to the misty mountains and deep canyons of "The Brown Mountain Light," where an old slave comes back from the grave to search for his master, bluegrass depicts a fallen world of darkness and doom. Whether peopled by Satan or a clutch of ghosts, whether set in a graveyard or a deserted cabin, the bluegrass song is invariably preoccupied with death and destruction: Ralph Stanley's "Old Man Death" describes the singer's fear of the Grim Reaper and of shivering in the "cold, cold ground," while in A. P. Carter's "Answer to Weeping Willow" a man yearns to join his dead lover by laying himself "down in death" next to her, and the speaker in Roy Acuff's "Lonely Mound of Clay," refusing to leave his lover's grave, finally joins her beneath the ground.

Even bluegrass love songs are about death. Indeed, a link between love and death is the focus of an entire subgenre of songs about men killing their lovers. Bluegrass takes an omnipresent theme in country music, such as unrequited love, and ratchets it up a notch, often making what is merely melancholy downright morbid. As Kenneth Tunnell notes, bluegrass songs are filled with violence:

> A content analysis of bluegrass murder ballads reveals three distinct patterns. First, in almost every case, the murder occurs between acquaintances and nearly always where a man kills a woman. Second, the woman's death is nearly always a violent one where her body is cruelly disposed of (viz., thrown into a body of water). Third, the murders depicted in song are characterized by either a lack of explanation for the violent acts or an explanation based on the man's jealousy and desire to possess the woman.[14]

Showing sex to be anything but safe, love in these songs becomes just another type of death. Southern novelist Lee Smith underscores this connection in *The Devil's Dream*: "I did not even want her to love him," says Lizzie Bailey, "because the very notion of love terrified me, bringing to mind all the old ballads, which show love as a kind of sickness, or a temptation unto death, a temptation which destroys women, even as it destroyed Mamma. To me, 'falling in love' was like falling in death."[15] The erotic longing for death that characterizes so many bluegrass songs is heightened; instead of being the only way to join a dead lover, death comes to symbolize the actual consummation of love.

This image of terrifying love can be found in such classics as "Banks of the Ohio," "The Knoxville Girl," "Poor Ellen Smith," "Down in the Willow Garden" ("Rose Connelly"), "Little Glass of Wine," "Pretty Polly," and "Young Freda Bolt."[16] One song title, "The Fatal Wedding," sums up the plot of all these songs. In many traditional bluegrass songs, a man kills his lover/fiancée for no clear reason, then confesses to the murder and goes to prison. In "The Knoxville Girl," for instance, the speaker takes an evening walk with his lover. A mile from town, without any warning, he picks up a stick and "knock[s] that fair girl down." The more she cries for mercy, the more he beats her, until the ground flows with her blood. Unsatisfied, he drags her "round and round" by "her golden curls" before finally "throwing her in the river / that flows through Knoxville town." The only hint of an explanation is given in the refrain:

Go down, go down, you Knoxville girl
with the *dark* and *roving* eyes
Go down, go down, you Knoxville girl,
you can never be my bride (emphases added).

The song ends with his having visions of hell and being imprisoned because he "murdered that Knoxville girl, the girl [he] loved so well."

This plot line is repeated in several other songs. After asking his love to take a walk in order to talk about their wedding day, the speaker in "Banks of the Ohio," for example, holds "a knife close to her breast" and pushes her into the river to drown. Watching "her as she float[s] down," he cries "My God, what have I done? I murdered the only woman I loved / Because she would not be my bride." The next morning the sheriff knocks on his door and asks him to go down to the "banks of the Ohio." In "Down in the Willow Garden" this familiar plot of love, murder, and imprisonment is enacted with an especially gruesome murder. Here, the speaker first poisons his lover's wine, then "draws" a saber through her and, as if that were not enough, throws her into the river as well. At the song's end, he is headed for the scaffold, knowing that the devil is waiting for him.

These narratives usually consist of two parts: the murder and the punishment. In each song, the murder enacts a ritual misogyny. The woman who begins as the innocent "true love" is quickly transformed into a femme fatale who must be both possessed and punished. The possessiveness seems unmotivated since the woman is almost always pictured as willing to marry the man. Nevertheless, the discussion of marriage always seems to precipitate the murder. Indeed, as Ralph Stanley remarked at the 1994 Summer Lights Festival in Nashville, marriage is a type of murder: "If you get murdered, you go real quick," but "if you get married, you sort of ooze out." The unexplained relationship between the discussion of marriage and the act of murder is constitutive of the violence in these songs. No explanation for the murder seems needed, nor is one typically offered. When a reason is given, it is often merely implied, with the woman murdered either because she will not become the man's wife or because she has already sullied that role by her sexuality. In "Banks of the Ohio," "she would not be [his] bride," whereas in "Little Glass of Wine" the woman asks to "stay single just one more year." The "Knoxville girl" is killed because of her "dark and roving eye," while the implication in "Down in the Willow Garden" is that the murder is financially motivated: "My father often told me that money would set me free / If I would murder that dear little girl / Whose name was Rose Connelly." The disjuncture between the male speaker's opening protestations of love for a woman and his sudden murder of her points toward the unarticulated subject that drives all of these songs: the threat of female sexuality. The woman is seen as a sexual transgressor either by wanting to remain single, hence nonmonogamous, or by already being pregnant. By emphasizing that the woman is "unprepared to die" ("The Knoxville Girl"), the songs further underscore women's sexuality as sin. Murder offers the perfect, if strictly individual, solution to the problem of female sexuality: male possession via punishment.

The song "Pretty Polly" typifies this subgenre: "Willie" (the stock name of the man in most of these songs) entices his lover into experiencing "pleasures" before marriage. When "Polly" regrets having been led astray, Willie tells her that her fears are "about right" and that he "dug on [her] grave the best part of last night." In response to her plea, "Please let me be a single girl if I can't be your wife," he stabs her in the heart. The murder both enacts Willie's "pleasure" and eliminates the threat of Polly's sexuality. As in "Poor Ellen Smith," where Ellen is found "shot through the heart, lying cold on the ground / Her clothes . . . all scattered and thrown on the ground," the murder is described as a rape. The phallic power exhibited in these murderous acts paradoxically represents both male dominance and lack of control. The excessiveness and obsessive repetition of this violence enacts a hypercontrol that actually signifies a loss of control. Repetition, the hallmark of the ballad form, authorizes this obsessive misogyny by ritualizing it; however, it also signifies the continuous effort needed to contain female sexuality. By enforcing women's chastity, the grave, it would appear, becomes the only (safe) sexual venue for men.

A song like "Barbara Allen" emblematizes this point: William has taken to his bed, dying for the love of Barbara Allen, who rejects him because of an imagined slight. When she does finally go to him, it is too late—he is already dead. Her punishment for being so "hard-hearted" is to die as well, the next day. In death, however, William gets the upper hand:

> Out of his grave grew a red, red rose
> And out of hers a briar
> They grew and grew in the old churchyard
> Till they couldn't grow no higher,
> They lapped and tied in a true love's knot.
> The rose ran around the briar.[17]

Here, William's (cultivated) rose totally encompasses Barbara's (wild) briar; true love becomes a knot that secures the man's control over the woman, who is strangled in his cold embrace. Like Tanya Tucker's "Would You Lay With Me

(In A Field of Stone)," in which a woman tests her lover's affections by asking him whether he would die for her if her "needs were strong," "Barbara Allen" begins with woman's power over man, but ends, as all these songs do, with female sexuality neutralized or domesticated by death.

This fear of and extreme response to female sexuality is further illuminated in two other songs, "Katie Dear" and "The Little Girl and the Dreadful Snake," both of which describe young women approaching sexual maturity. In "Katie Dear," it is her parents, not Katie's lover, Willie, who represent the threat of death for female sexuality, with their silver and gold daggers by their bedsides. When Willie wants to ask for Katie's hand in marriage, she tells him that "there's no use in askin'" because her parents, who are in their rooms "taking rest," have daggers there with which to "slay the one [she] love[s] the best." Whether read as an actual incest narrative or not, this song denies Katie an adult or independent sexuality. The only viable solution is death: while Willie claims that if Katie's parents say no, "we'll run away," he ends up killing himself with the golden dagger, an act that Katie quickly copies. In order to be with the one that she "love[s] the best," Katie must die with him. This resistance to the sexual maturing of girls is also apparent in "The Little Girl and the Dreadful Snake," where a little girl gets lost in the dark woods and screams for her father when she sees an "awful dreadful snake." The father finds her too late and realizes that she will "have" to die. After asking her father to kill the snake and to tell her mother goodbye, the little girl dies. The last stanza concludes with an injunction against parents' letting their children stray from home, or their guidance. Once again, female sexuality is life-threatening: the little girl *must* die; her impurity must be punished. In all of these songs, a woman who becomes sexual cannot stay alive. As for love, it "is a violation which leads to further violations and punishments."[18]

While love literally violates and kills women, it only punishes men: women always go to the grave, but men may go to prison, the scaffold, or hell. Moreover, male punishment is often mediated by the ballad structure, with retribution promised but often suspended or deferred. "Pretty Polly," for instance, ends by declaring that Willie's "soul will go to hell," but we are not witness to his spiritual torture as we were to Polly's murder. Even when punishment is not suspended, it serves to contain the more extreme elements of the story. At the end of "Little Glass of Wine," the poisoning is almost forgotten as the lovers die together with their arms around each other. The final lines — "Oh, God, oh God, ain't this a pity / That the both true lovers are bound to die" — naturalize the murder, sentimentalizing both deaths as part of a romantic story of star-crossed lovers and true love gone awry.

Some ballads make the premeditated act of murder palatable by turning it into a moral or theological lesson. "Poor Ellen Smith" concludes with the speaker's stating that even though his "days in this prison are ending at last," he will never be "free from the sins of [his] past." Here, punishment is moralized so as to explain away and give closure to the horror and incomprehensibility of the murder. Once it has been situated in the more expected pattern of sin and redemption, the murder becomes less incoherent and begins to make more sense. A similar resolution occurs in the Carter Family song "Young Freda Bolt." Once again a fair young maiden is invited on an evening walk to discuss marriage with her sweetheart. And once again she is cruelly assaulted (smashed by a stone this time) and left to die in "agony." Instead of revealing what becomes of her killer, the final stanza eulogizes Freda: God hears her cry and sends a band of angels to bear her spirit to the other world. The moral is that heaven—not death—is the outcome of murder. What begins as a typical love-and-murder ballad ends as a hymn of salvation. The murderer becomes just another lost soul, while the way the woman met her death becomes inconsequential as it is subsumed by the song's larger lesson of sin and redemption. The moral exorcises the horror.

Indeed, these violent songs are often part of a repertoire that also includes hymns and gospel songs. According to some estimates, about 30 percent of any bluegrass band's repertoire consists of gospel songs; in countering songs of faithless love with songs of steadfast faith, such repertoires turn the sexual battleground into a moral or spiritual one. Bluegrass may open the door to extreme desires, but, as Robert Cantwell has noted, bluegrass also makes it "the business of morality to subdue or of religion to harness" them.[19] For instance, during a 1994 show by the Nashville Bluegrass Band at Nashville's Station Inn, "Who's Knocking at My Door," a song that stages the moral that what we "sow" we must "reap" by evil's knocking at a sinner's door, was immediately followed by the gospel hymn "Teach Me, Jesus, How to Pray." The religious impulse in bluegrass music, then, tends to offset and moderate its gothic horrors. An audience can vicariously enjoy the thrills and chills of the songs while also being taught a moral lesson, as Satan and the Pearly Gates are alternated in the bluegrass repertoire or program.

Yet even though the religious themes of bluegrass can often be made to rationalize more gothic elements, the gothic is not so easily contained. Not only do the morals seem tacked on and insufficient to explain away the horrors perpetrated in many songs, but the religion offered is of little comfort. As Catherine Marshall puts it in *Christy*, the highlander's faith is "a belief to make the heart quake, not to comfort it."[20] Songs of salvation and redemption also have their demonic counterparts in songs of haunting and damnation. One such ballad,

"The Ghost of Eli Renfro," gives a different twist to the murder song. After killing his wife with a "long sharp bowie knife," Eli is put to death by hanging. Unwilling to accept his sinfulness and to ask for redemption, Eli instead puts a curse on the town. Now, when the moon is full, Eli can be heard dragging his chains and moaning the names of people. The narrator, who quakes at hearing this story, decides to leave town so that Eli will never call his name. Unlike the songs where the horror is neutralized by a just punishment or a moralized ending, "Eli Renfro" sustains its horror. Eli remains unrepentant; his sins are not exorcised, but passed on through a curse. The violence of this song is not safely contained; instead, it is contagious. Like the obsessively reproduced plot of all of these songs, violence breeds more violence—and more songs.

Given that these gothic horrors continue to resurge in the music, despite efforts to contain them, one might well ask how bluegrass continues to "get away with" its gothic image. There are several explanations. First, bluegrass's more marginal status allows it to access a broader range of themes. Relegated to special programs on the radio, but wearing its limited commercial appeal as a badge of pride, bluegrass constructs itself as an "outsider" and hence does not have to follow the rules that constrain mainstream country music. Even more importantly, bluegrass "gets away with" being gothic by virtue of its self-construction as a music securely located in the distant past. This self-conscious image is apparent in the recent movie *High Lonesome* (1993), which recounts the history of bluegrass. Its central figure is Bill Monroe, the "father of bluegrass," who is filmed returning to and being interviewed in his old Kentucky home, now in ruins. Through Monroe, the avuncular figure who surveys the ruins and recounts stories from his childhood, the movie associates bluegrass with what is long gone. One almost expects to hear the bluegrass classic "Log Cabin in the Lane," which describes a decayed log cabin as the speaker's only remaining friend, playing in the background. When Monroe mournfully states that there is no longer "any home to go home to," the movie plays off a nostalgic sense of the past; throughout, Monroe represents the old-time traditions that bluegrass still aims to preserve. His image, like so many that bluegrass cultivates, projects the music as the last vestige of the authentic and the real. But, as Cantwell points out, "Hillbilly music has never been anything but entrepreneurial and commercial, prospering in the one commodity which in America is ever in short supply—the past."[21] Given the image of bluegrass, however, even an informed viewer or listener would find it hard to believe that the genre was less than half a century old (Monroe created the form in the late 1930s and developed it, along with others, in the 1940s, but it did not become a distinctly named genre until the 1950s). While bluegrass may appear to be caught in a time warp, it is anything but static. With a third generation of performers now coming into their own (e.g., Alison Krauss, Laurie Lewis, Sam Bush, Tony Rice, Tim O'Brien, and Kathy Chiavola), bluegrass continues to evolve, often fusing with other musical forms (classical, jazz, the blues). Its orientation toward the past is more image than reality, yet it is an image that serves bluegrass well, allowing it to "get away with" more than mainstream country music can. The nostalgic image of the past that bluegrass propagates can easily accommodate songs of doom and dread. While bluegrass may be best known for its songs of home and salvation, performers still sing about violent death. The Nashville Bluegrass Band's 1993 release of "Open Pit Mine," in which a man kills his wife and her lover, then buries them "deep" in the open pit mine, is one such example. Securely fixed in the past, bluegrass songs of violence pose no threat to the present.

Or do they? Despite its "cleaned-up" image, "new country" continues to be haunted by bluegrass. The oppositions between new country and old bluegrass—present versus past, the domesticated versus the devilish South—may appear fixed, but in fact they are continually blurring and collapsing. However strongly associated with the past and an old, devilish image, bluegrass continues to flourish in the new South nonetheless. A matter of style rather than period, traditional bluegrass operates in the same chronological plane as mainstream country music. One can listen to bluegrass every Tuesday night at the Ryman Auditorium, and to the hot new country stars the rest of the week. As concurrent musical genres, bluegrass and mainstream country not only share the present moment, but also the past of their distinct tradition. The violent excesses of bluegrass classics are the roots of country music as well. While the new country of the 1990s may attempt to suppress its devilish heritage, it continues to evince traces of the gothic that still dominates bluegrass.

GOTHIC ELEMENTS in mainstream country music have long reflected its "dark side," Southern Gothic tradition.[22] Artists of the 1990s continue to mine the gothic vein in such songs as Garth Brooks's "We Bury the Hatchet," where a couple continues to dig up old hurts because they bury the hatchet with the handle "sticking out," or Randy Travis's "Before You Kill Us All," which compares a woman's walking out on a man (even though he is in the wrong) to murder (if she does not come back, she will "kill" him). Here, gothic metaphors are used to describe love that has gone wrong, but traditional bluegrass plots of deathly love can also still be found in the new country music. Marty Brown's eerie love song "She's Gone" is one such example. Claiming that Brown invokes the ghost of Hank Williams and that "She's Gone" is "a proper descendant of such great country-music spine-chillers as Dill and Wilkin's 'Long Black Veil,'"

*People* magazine recently announced that "nobody else in Nashville today is writing anything as unabashedly gothic."[23] Told from the point of view of a man weeping over his lover's grave, "She's Gone" falls into the long line of bluegrass songs in which a lover yearns for death as a way to be reunited with a lost love. Standing at midnight in a graveyard, alone and scared, the speaker moans the same refrain over and over again: "She's gone." With his lengthened vowels and high-pitched wail, Brown reproduces the "high, lonesome" sound of bluegrass. Moreover, his use of sound effects—blowing through tubes and hoses to enhance the eeriness and repeating certain chords on a synthesizer to produce a sound of relentless doom—further exaggerates the song's tone of dread. "She's Gone" ends with a shotgun blast as the speaker kills himself. Once again, the price of true love is death.

However, the darkness of "She's Gone" is contained by its penultimate position on the album, which concludes with "Wild Kentucky Skies," the album's title song. By ending with a song about a man returning to his lover and walking side by side with her in the "sunshine," Brown not only negates the gloom of "She's Gone," but also revises its power dynamic by projecting the despair onto the woman: she becomes the one who has been weeping, while he is the one who was (temporarily) lost. Just as its soothing violin strings ease the listener out of the dread heard in "She's Gone," "Wild Kentucky Skies" translates the threatening female power that can make a man kill himself into the traditional plot of weeping womanhood. "She's Gone" encodes the gothic elements of the bluegrass tradition, while the album's concluding song endorses its sentimentality.

This revisionary mode seems to be the typical means for incorporating the gothic in the new country music. Even though new country tends to "clean up" the bluegrass plot, giving it a more acceptable veneer, the same old story continues to surface. If women are no longer knifed for no apparent reason, the violence inherent in male love for women continues to haunt these songs nevertheless. The same ritual misogyny can be heard in the new country music, but in a kinder and gentler form. Randy Travis's "Before You Kill Us All" video, for instance, is a cartoon, with female independence—her walking out is refigured as "man" slaughter—neutralized via Garfield images. Garth Brooks's "Papa Loved Mama," which describes a man ramming his rig into a motel room in order to kill his cheating wife and her lover, is another instance of the face-lift that the new country music has given to bluegrass misogyny. Even so, Mama still ends up in the "graveyard," and Papa in the "pen." Instead of rationalizing the murder through a moral, this song deflects the violence by distancing it in the accounts of an eyewitness, the motel clerk, and of a newspaper. Papa is actually last seen warming up his diesel, which makes an "eerie" sound. The aftermath (the rig buried in the motel room) is revealed in the newspaper account and that of the clerk (instead of braking, Papa had increased his speed as he approached the motel). By distancing the violence, the song softens its blow. Moreover, by replacing the traditional murder weapon—a simple knife or poison—with a tractor trailer, the song renders the violence cartoonish, even funny. Humor deflects horror, and Brooks's song can participate in the ritual misogyny of gothic bluegrass without being held accountable for it.

Even when that misogyny is overt, as in Johnny Cash's recent single, "Delia's Gone," it is still easy to get away with. By resurrecting this old folk/blues song about a man who murders his lover over and over again in lieu of marrying her, Cash is banking on the bluegrass plot's appealing to a new generation of listeners. The "new" Cash is merely a recycled image of his former self, the singer who built a career on such haunting bluegrass ballads as "The Long Black Veil." "Delia's Gone," a song about a "devilish" woman who needs to be destroyed, makes no attempt to obscure its antifeminist message. While Delia's power is obvious from the many "rounds" it takes to kill her—"Delia's gone, one more round, Delia's gone"—the song nevertheless celebrates the man's excessive violence (he kills her twice with a submachine gun). As *Pulse!* described one performance, the crowd cheered at some "of the song's more hard-boiled lines." Once again, violence against women is neutralized through humor, with the song's speaker described as a "psychopath-with-a-funny-bone."[24] Moreover, when Cash performed "Delia's Gone" on *The Late Show with David Letterman* (10 June 1994), Letterman, who seemed unsure of how to respond to the song, made a quick recovery by quipping, "I don't mind telling you I was frightened." Even with only a slight face-lift, it would seem that the gothic bluegrass plot can still go country.

The history of Garth Brooks's video of "The Thunder Rolls," however, has revealed the point at which the bluegrass plot becomes unacceptable. Through its dark and stormy landscape as well as its narrative of an unfaithful man returning home to his wife and their love growing "cold," "The Thunder Rolls" draws on gothic bluegrass. However, this time the plot is reversed: it is the woman, not the man, who threatens violence, for the lightning "flashes" in her eyes and she carries the thunder "deep" in her heart. The threat of female violence against men is made explicit in the video, which depicts a battered woman killing her husband. While the video reinterprets the song so that the woman's violence is a justified response to her husband's violence against her, not just a reaction to his unfaithfulness, it was still judged as having stepped too far over the line and was banned from the Country Music Television (CMT) channel because of negative viewer response. In an article entitled "Garth Brooks's Black Eye" (which interestingly links Brooks's relationship with his fans to the domestic abuse depicted in his video), *People* magazine quoted a spokesperson from The Nashville Network (TNN) as saying that the depiction of domestic violence in the video was excessive and lacked an acceptable resolution.[25] The backlash against the video appears to represent a crucial policing of the gothic bluegrass plot: excessive violence becomes unacceptable only when it is (visibly) directed against patriarchal control instead of being perpetrated in the service of it. Reversing the plot of "boy kills girl" appears to be a violation of law and order. However, it is when the plot is reversed that its excesses become most apparent—and most threatening. All efforts to contain the video's violence, even the attachment of a disclaimer in which both wife abuse and vigilantism are condemned, were judged insufficient. When Brooks was quoted as saying, "I'm kind of disappointed . . . they want to see the good side of real life . . . but they want to turn their backs to the bad side," he seemed to be missing the point.[26] Country music's "dark side" can be shown, at least in its "cleaned-up" form, but only within the traditional parameters of patriarchal control.

The policing of the gothic bluegrass plot in the gendering of country music was perhaps most strikingly articulated in a 1992 article on Mary Chapin Carpenter in *Pulse!* that was curiously titled "American Gothic."[27] Best known for upbeat songs like "Passionate Kisses" and "Down at the Twist and Shout," it is difficult to imagine what could be labeled "gothic" in Carpenter's music. Indeed, the article does little to illuminate its title, referring only to Carpenter's creation of an "American Gothic for the 90s" in her song "He Thinks He'll Keep Her," which depicts a woman finally revolting against a picture-perfect but restrictive domestic situation. Not even hinting at the violence of "The Thunder Rolls," the wife in this song merely tells her husband that she does not love him anymore and is then rewarded with a minimum-wage job in a typing pool. Gothic? Not unless leaving one's husband is a felony, which the article implies it might be when Carpenter is asked if there are "any *Thelma and Louise* motivations here." *Pulse!* readers apparently expect even a hint of female empowerment to be demonized as "gothic." What is striking is how such a minor threat to patriarchal control gets configured in these extreme terms: this woman, who is now policed by her culture instead of being killed by her man as she drowns in the typing pool instead of the river, is associated with the wild lawlessness of *Thelma and Louise*. Gothic? Only if the gothic now represents every minor transgression of the social order. But, as we have seen, any threat to the patriarchal order, no matter how slight, provokes an extreme response. Carpenter quickly disassociated herself from any threateningly feminist, not to mention Southern lawless, connection to *Thelma and Louise* by labeling herself as merely different. Indeed, Carpenter's notion of her difference entails being just slightly outside mainstream country, for she identifies with other artists who write "incredibly dark but uplifting songs." Even though Carpenter imagines the "darker" side of life only within safely defined bounds, she still gets portrayed as "gothic."

If merely pointing toward the "dark side" is enough to label an artist "gothic," then the resonance of the gothic in country music has itself become quite muted and contained. Instead of representing the transgressive and the subversive, the gothic in new country music has become a traditional device in service of the status quo. Domestic abuse and its repression in Brooks's and Carpenter's songs look tame in comparison to the violent, unmotivated murders of women in such classic bluegrass songs as "The Knoxville Girl" and "Banks of the Ohio." Far from stretching the parameters of country music, Carpenter has acceded to their constriction. The difference between bluegrass and new country music, then, is a matter of degree, not of kind. By reconstructing its bluegrass roots in more palatable ways, these new-country backlash songs domesticate the gothic even as they expose the dangers of domestic space. The new country music, like bluegrass, remains constituted by violence against women.

Instead of exorcising its gothic roots, new country continues to be haunted by the themes of bluegrass, whose bloody ground, in fact, becomes the necessary, if marginalized, background to the new country songs: mainstream country music is finally intelligible only through bluegrass. Without hearing the traces of bluegrass gothic within the new country songs, a listener might miss the return of its repressed violence against women and, hence, the significance of that return. Indeed, the very popularity of the new country music may depend upon its audience's failure to hear these gothic echoes. By refusing to acknowledge what haunts it, country can continue to reproduce the narrative of what men must do to women in order to "feel good," but without alienating its nominally more socially conscious audience. Country music, then, depends on both the presence and the absence of bluegrass. Bluegrass is the necessary foundation upon which new country is based, yet it is also the tradition that must be repudiated. As its "dark side," bluegrass is the haunting force in country music that must remain unacknowledged.

Garth Brooks's video of "The Red Strokes," a cut from his 1993 album *In Pieces,* reflects new country's repackaging of the gothic. Having decided that his "music shouldn't be something that causes trouble," Brooks is currently recasting his excesses in a more acceptable form.[28] The "Red Strokes" video, which one *Rolling Stone* reviewer termed "somewhat overlush," shows a white-clad Brooks sitting at a white piano in an all-white room singing sinisterly into the camera.[29] As the song progresses, blood begins to well up from the piano keys and then to pour out of the piano and splash down his face. By the end of the video, Brooks and the entire room are covered in blood. Brooks would seem to be once again stepping over the line; however, despite its bloodiness, this video's violence is sanitized since it does not reflect perversely gendered social relationships but stage effects. Indeed, the song itself transforms excessive passion into a "work of art." Instead of seeing the lovers, we glimpse only their "shadows," which converge to paint a picture. The "erasing" of borders here no longer entails the transgressive act of murder, but, like the video in which it is visualized, a transgression that occurs only in the realm of art. By abstracting passion, Brooks can indulge his excesses without suffering any of the consequences. Indeed, the AIDS subtext that haunts this gratuitously blood-stained video can easily go unrecognized. Brooks further protects himself by displacing the excesses of his video: he informs his American television audience, who have just seen it, that this video will only play in Europe. By insisting on the "foreignness" of the image he is presenting, Brooks frees his American fans to indulge their passion for transgression without having to admit any deeper connection to it. Brooks's clever repackaging of the gothic notwithstanding, we should not forget its indigenous—or its gendered—roots: the bloody baby grand reflects a long, ongoing gothic tradition in American country music. As we are invited by the new country music to (as the old Carter Family song puts it) "Keep on the Sunny Side," we would do well to listen for its dark and troubled side as well.

NOTES

I wish to thank Mark Schoenfield and Valerie Traub, who read drafts of the essay and discussed many aspects of the argument with me. I am also grateful to Tracy Todd and Jeremy Wells for suggesting songs and to Yoshikuni Igarashi for discussing *Deliverance* with me. I would especially like to thank Cecelia Tichi, who first introduced me to country music and made her enthusiasm for the music contagious.

1   Cecelia Tichi, *High Lonesome: The American Culture of Country Music* (Chapel Hill, 1994), 266–67.

2   John Egerton, *The Americanization of Dixie: The Southernization of America* (New York, 1974).

3   Richard Peterson and Paul DiMaggio, "From Region to Class, the Changing Locus of Country Music: A Test of the Massification Hypothesis," *Social Forces* 53 (1975): 497–506.

4   See Don McLeese, "Did Nashville's Cross-Over Dreams Come True at the Expense of Its Soul?" *Rolling Stone* (December 1992): 75.

5   Anthony DeCurtis, "Opinion," *Rolling Stone* (November 1992): 23.

6   Jack Temple Kirby, *Media-Made Dixie: The South in the American Imagination* (Athens, 1986).

7   Quoted in Kirby, *Media-Made Dixie*, 155.

8   See James C. Cobb, "From Muskogee to Luckenbach: Country Music and the 'Southernization' of America," *Journal of Popular Culture* 16 (1982): 81–91.

9   Kirby, *Media-Made Dixie*, 159.

10  Bill C. Malone, *Country Music U.S.A.*, rev. ed. (Austin, 1985 [1968]), 1.

11  See Jan Harold Brunvand, *The Study of American Folklore: An Introduction* (New York, 1968), 156.

12  Robert Cantwell, *Bluegrass Breakdown* (Urbana, 1984), 212.

13  Ibid., 214.

14  Kenneth D. Tunnell, "Blood Marks the Spot Where Poor Ellen Was Found: Violent Crime in Bluegrass Music," *Popular Music and Society* 153 (Fall 1991): 101.

15  Lee Smith, *The Devil's Dream* (New York, 1992), 97.

16  Unless otherwise noted in the Selected Discography, songs are taken from Peter Wernick, *The Bluegrass Songbook* (New York, 1976).

17  Alan Lomax, *Folk Songs of North America* (New York, 1975), 183–84.

18  Roger Abrahams and George Foss, *Anglo-American Folksong Style* (Englewood Cliffs, NJ, 1968), 114.

19  Cantwell, *Bluegrass Breakdown*, 29.

20  Catherine Marshall, *Christy* (New York, 1967), 414.

21  Cantwell, *Bluegrass Breakdown*, 13.

22  See Ruth Banes, "The Dark Side: Southern Gothic in Country Music," in *Developing Dixie: Modernization in a Traditional Society*, ed. Winfred B. Moore, Jr., Joseph F. Tripp, and Lyon G. Tyler, Jr. (New York, 1985), 279–93.

23  Tony Scherman, "Wild Kentucky Skies by Marty Brown," *People,* 26 April 1993, 22–23.

24  Jackson Griffith, "Johnny Cash," *Pulse!* (June 1994): 46.

25  "Garth Brooks's Black Eye," *People,* 20 May 1991, 93.

26  Ibid.

27  Tom Lanham, "American Gothic," *Pulse!* (July 1992).

28  "Garth Brooks's Black Eye," 93.

29  Paul Evans, "Review of Garth Brooks: *In Pieces*," *Rolling Stone,* 14 Oct. 1993, 114.

# A Musical Legacy, A Way of Life

*A Photo Essay*

❧ ———————————————————— **Charmaine Lanham**

I remember the stacks of dusty sheet music and the abandoned piano lessons of my youth, spending hours at the keyboard, feet not quite touching the floor. The practice rooms always seemed subdued, windows covered by heavy curtains, and the air smelled like old pianos. We played songs exactly the way they were written. Creative exploration or improvisation, the infamous "playing by ear," was strictly forbidden.

For a child, this was solitary practice, and I quickly lost interest in learning to play music. As a young adult I rediscovered music, this time Appalachian string music. Instead of a passing interest, traditional music became my way of life. The music community has become like family.

Overlapping styles of American stringed music are called by many names including Old Time; Gospel (with heavy emphasis in "by ear" piano rhythm); String Bands; Jug Bands; Blues; and most widely known, Bluegrass. Musicianship involves years of devotion and a lifestyle involving expense, travel, and long hours of practice. Following the trail of tunes involves whole families traveling in Gypsy-like excursions across the United States during the festival season.

For more than twenty-five years my world has been music, playing it and recording images of those around me in the music community. Because I am one of those people who see the world more clearly through a camera lens, I am able to share these scenes with you.

Baby and Dad pack instruments at the Mark O'Connor Fiddle Camp, Montgomery Bell Park, Tennessee, 1993.

The Lesson: Catherine Woodward learns technique on her half-size cello with master cellist Michael Cobb. Fiddle Camp, 1993.

Fiddlers Hans and Natalie Holzen gather around Carroll Best and his banjo to learn a tune at the Tennessee Banjo Institute, 1990.

Jazz fiddler Claude Williams, age eighty-six, jams with one of several "kids."

One of the young fiddlers. Fiddle Camp, 1993.

Bill Monroe, "Father of Blue-grass Music." Ryman Auditorium, Nashville, 1995.

Jam Session: Bill Monroe shares his musical style in a break from filming the award-winning film, *High Lonesome Sound*. Goodlettsville, Tennessee, 1988.

Singer Emmylou Harris and fiddler Deanie Richardson, age twelve, prepare to perform together. Nashville Bluegrass Music Association Festival, Mother Maybelle Carter's Farm, Madison, Tennessee, 1984.

Earl Scruggs's is the most imitated five-string banjo style in the world. This was one of the rare and wonderful moments when the master musician appears with his admirers, Vince Gill and Ricky Skaggs. Grand Ole Opry, Nashville, 1995.

Buckdancing is a style that developed along with string music. Nashville Summer Lights, 1995.

Jacky Christian, old time buckdance instructor, shares her dancer with the old banjo player. Grass Roots Days, Nashville, 1985.

Buck and Pat White with daughters Sharon and Cheryl perform one of their first Nashville gigs at Earl Sneed's Bluegrass Inn, 1972. In 1984 the Whites became members of the Grand Ole Opry.

From the old to the young: Granpa Jones, star of the Grand Ole Opry, joins a group of students and faculty at the Tennessee Banjo Institute, 1990.

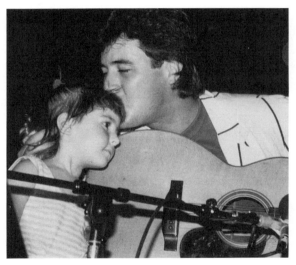

Roland White and Marty Stuart at the Ryman, 1995. Roland and his brother, guitarist Clarence White, had a great influence on country music star Marty Stuart.

Vince Gill invited daughter Jessica onstage at Nashville's Summer Lights Festival, 1986. Gill, a veteran of two decades in music, was about to be discovered by Music City—one of the success stories.

Cordell Kemp, banjo player from Defeated, Tennessee, was a faculty member for the Tennessee Banjo Institute, Cedars of Lebanon Park, 1988.

# Commercial (and/or?) Folk

*The Bluegrass Industry*

*and Bluegrass Traditions*

 _____ **Mark Fenster**

Like nearly every nonmainstream, "niche" music in the contemporary American popular music marketplace, bluegrass survives through a network of relatively small, independent businesses, including record companies and distributors, mail order and specialty retailers, periodicals publishers, festival promoters, and booking agents specializing in folk and bluegrass artists. While these businesses compete with each other for both musicians and consumers, they also attempt to coordinate their activities informally, through social networks, and formally, through organizations like the International Bluegrass Music Association (IBMA), the trade organization founded in 1985, so that bluegrass can be most effectively and efficiently produced, distributed, and marketed. The bluegrass "industry" is a relatively small but widely dispersed community made up of friends and fellow enthusiasts. The importance of such a community lies in its position as a focal point around which efforts are made to coordinate and streamline business activity, to represent bluegrass to a wider audience and thereby gain wider recognition for the music, and to change the way people outside bluegrass perceive the music.

However, like many other contemporary cultural forms and practices with strong historical ties to American traditional culture and to the musical styles of American ethnic and racial groups (e.g., polka, Cajun, blues, etc.), bluegrass represents for many of its devotees far more than simply a musical style, with recordings and performances available at the local record store and concert hall, respectively. Instead, bluegrass is for many a point of identification, a music that would seem to express something "authentic" about emotional attachments to family, home, and traditional Appalachian culture, as well as a source of "affective alliances" among fans, jam session partners, and professional musicians.[1] This is true both for the devoted listeners and amateur pickers who constitute much of the primary audience of bluegrass and for the professional and semiprofessional musicians, many of whom could be making far larger incomes playing other forms of music or taking up nonmusical careers (a commonly cited joke claims that the only person to make a million dollars playing bluegrass began with two million).

Like musicians and fans, bluegrass business people are themselves concerned with the music as a cultural entity rather than as a mere commodity, and most of them work for low wages or on narrow (if any) profit margins, treating the business as a hobby that they enjoy and care about rather than as a primary source of income. Since the development of bluegrass as a style of commercial country music in the 1940s, its survival, even on the margins of the music industry today, has depended on this enthusiasm to keep the music "alive" for successive generations; bluegrass has always been a commercial music, yet it has always been closely associated with Anglo-Irish rural and folk traditions, inflected with blues rhythms and sounds.[2] If the music is to be securely established, for the health and well-being of the bluegrass industry, and if the compensation for professional bluegrass musicians, who make far less money than their counterparts in mainstream country music, is to improve, the market base of bluegrass must not only remain stable, but grow. Such growth, however, cannot be attained at the expense of what is seen as the "integrity" of bluegrass music. Ultimately, bluegrass is understood by fans, musicians, and the industry itself as an *artistic*—and specifically *traditional*—musical genre that must be protected by an industry that will not "sell it out"; bluegrass is thus often contrasted to more commercial genres like country and rock, which, as part of the mainstream music industry, are seen as mass-cultural types of music. The goal for most bluegrass musicians, fans, and business people, then, is the formation of a nonintrusive commercial structure by which bluegrass can be successfully produced and distributed without despoiling the music of its integrity and traditions.

This goal entails a series of apparent contradictions: the bluegrass industry attempts to function as a relatively noncommercial business, marketing a *traditional* yet *commercial* music, while protecting it from the influence of *commerce*. The ongoing attempt to resolve these contradictions is one of the most pressing problems facing the bluegrass business community, and it infuses such decisions as how bands choose material, how record labels sign artists, how promoters conceive of and arrange festivals, and how fans describe and debate the music. The economic and institutional problems faced by bluegrass, which are discussed in IBMA meetings as well as in the pages of many bluegrass fan publications, must be resolved within the context of these contradictions. And because the music means so much both to bluegrass business people and to its knowledgeable, active fans, the problems of the bluegrass industry, notably, the contradictions within which it works, are perceived as crucial issues for the music. At stake in the attempt to work through and resolve these contradictions, then, is the survival of bluegrass as a distinct cultural and commercial musical genre.

The dualisms of traditional/commercial production, mass/folk culture, and authentic/manufactured art that have been so much a part of debate over the general cultural shift to modernity are thus still very prominent in the discourse of bluegrass participants.[3] Such dualisms are themselves complicated by the numerous definitions of "authenticity" in popular discourse, including the forms and practices that emanate from a shared culture and community, the "true" expression of an individual artist's inspiration, and the freedom from commercial contamination or determination in cultural production. For many fans, bluegrass would seem to fit all three definitions: it was developed within traditional Appalachian culture; many great, innovative musicians, beginning with Bill Monroe and, later, Earl Scruggs and others, have contributed to the music's development and popularization; and bluegrass continues to flourish outside the tainted structures of the mainstream music industry.

From its inception, however, bluegrass has been commercial music. Developed by musicians who made their living as touring and recording artists and disseminated by radio broadcasts, bluegrass has always been produced and distributed within an industrial context, whether that context was the country music industry of the 1940s or the contemporary bluegrass industry. Bluegrass was initially most popular in the rural upland South, particularly the Appalachian regions of Tennessee, Virginia, Kentucky, and North Carolina, as well as among migrants of rural origin in the Midwest and the Middle Atlantic states (particularly Maryland and Pennsylvania). Even though it was not itself a "folk music" (in the sense of being produced and experienced within an orally based, relatively closed folk community), then, bluegrass was immediately associated, especially by virtue of its stylistic similarities to the music of old-time string bands and the commercial country music of the 1930s, with social groups who would be increasingly perceived in the postwar period as representatives of an "authentic" culture that was threatened by the industrial and mass-cultural forces of modernity. And, moreover, this association was itself partly constructed through the work of such bluegrass "pioneers" as

Bill Monroe, who consciously tried to produce a commercial form of country music that could reach these audiences.

Thus, claims of the "authenticity" of bluegrass are "false," and the dualisms on which they are based are specious: bluegrass was a new, commercial articulation of musical elements that were already in circulation, some with strong ties to traditional music, some without; "commerce" was neither imposed on Bill Monroe and his successors nor foreign to them, but was integral to their artistic goals and ambitions; and finally, the entire notion of "the folk" rests on a simplified, nostalgic vision of the culture and economic conditions of early twentieth-century Appalachia.[4] Yet the "falsity" of such claims to authenticity in no way diminishes their significance relative to bluegrass; the traditions of bluegrass may be more the result of modern (as opposed to premodern) forces, but they are substantive traditions nonetheless, with bluegrass festivals, recordings, and amateur jam sessions representing meaningful practices in people's lives.[5]

Bluegrass "traditions," then, could be dismissed as mere nostalgia for a time that never was, but such a dismissal fails to recognize the complex process by which modern, commercial forms of culture reconstruct and rearticulate the past. As Susan Stewart argues about narratives of nostalgia: "By the narrative process of nostalgic reconstruction the present is denied and the past takes on an authenticity of being, an authenticity which, ironically, it can achieve only through narrative."[6] In other words, the reenactment of tradition in contemporary bluegrass music attempts to deny the present (and specifically the Other[s] of such mainstream popular forms as commercial country music) by constituting its traditions as an authentic past and by basing this authenticity on the practice of bluegrass itself. If the past described in bluegrass is available only through playing or listening to bluegrass music, then the work of the bluegrass industry is utterly crucial and completely contradictory: it must enable tradition and the experience of the past, but can do so only by selling it in the present, in a degrading marketplace that has itself imposed commerce upon tradition, the "mass" upon the "folk." The important issues raised by the bluegrass industry, in other words, do not concern the simplistic notion that the process of marketing bluegrass does or does not effect the "traditionalness" of bluegrass, but instead concern tradition's meaning and identification, as these are understood and struggled over within the industry and in discussions about the industry.[7]

BLUEGRASS IS USUALLY DESCRIBED as a hybrid form of country music that combines elements from old-time string band music, the "hillbilly" sounds of

1930s and 1940s country music, and African-American blues. There are a number of specific musical conventions associated with bluegrass, including the use of particular acoustic instruments (guitar, five-string banjo, fiddle, mandolin, acoustic upright bass, and the Dobro, which was not introduced into bluegrass until 1955); fast, "driving" tempos played in duple meter (usually 2/4 or 4/4);[8] a high-pitched singing style elaborated in duet and trio harmonies; and songs whose lyrics tend to focus on "down-home" topics, such as the "old homeplace," the family, the difficulties of urban life, and religious faith, and whose musical structure is based on relatively simple harmonic progressions using major keys and I, IV, and V chords.

Instrumental virtuosity is prized in bluegrass; the most famous performers in the genre have typically been musicians rather than singers, and those perceived as having "founded" a particular sound (e.g., Bill Monroe's mandolin playing or Earl Scruggs's three-finger banjo technique) are legendary figures in bluegrass history. In instrumental arrangements, the bass and guitar generally provide the backing rhythm, while the fiddle, banjo, mandolin, lead guitar, and, in some bands, Dobro alternate between playing leads and providing rhythmic and melodic backup. The interplay of these instruments, and the ways in which they tend to alternate leads in songs, is more reminiscent of jazz than country and old-time string band music, and such instrumentation highlights the individual musician far more than string bands, which concentrated on cohesive rhythm and interplay.

IF THE MOST IMPORTANT COMMODITY in popular music is the recording, and if the mainstream music industry is dominated by transnational music companies that are owned by large, multinational conglomerates, then the "bluegrass music industry" would seem to exist almost entirely in another commercial universe. The only bluegrass performer currently on a major record label is Bill Monroe, who has been on MCA (and, earlier, Decca) for over forty years. By contrast, during the early years of bluegrass many "first-generation" musicians (e.g., Monroe, the Stanley Brothers, and Flatt & Scruggs) recorded for the country music divisions of major record labels. Other than Monroe's records and the occasional reissue of "classic" material by major labels, all bluegrass records released in the United States are currently produced and distributed by independent record labels and distributors with some commitment to the survival of bluegrass as a musical form. Major labels pay little attention to bluegrass, except to recruit individual performers who are willing to cross over to mainstream country music. For such performers as Marty Stuart, Ricky Skaggs, Vince Gill, and Rhonda Vincent, as well as musicians like Jerry Douglas and Mark O'Connor, the bluegrass industry has served as a "minor league" from which stars could emerge.[9] An exception who proves the rule is singer/fiddler/bandleader Alison Krauss, one of the most prominent young bluegrass performers, whose success has led to ongoing attempts by major record labels to sign her. Krauss's desire to remain strongly identified with the bluegrass genre has gained her an exalted position within the bluegrass industry and community, while her induction into the *Grand Ole Opry,* her national exposure via mainstream media outlets (such as *Rolling Stone,* the *New York Times,* and TNN, the major country music cable-television network), her stints as the opening act for a number of Garth Brooks's stadium concerts, and her important role as a woman in a historically male-dominated genre have widened the exposure of bluegrass music among new audiences. Krauss's success within, and commitment to, the bluegrass genre, community, and industry has been somewhat anomalous in the past two decades of bluegrass and has cost her the far greater financial rewards and institutional support (i.e., promotion, distribution, radio airplay, etc.) to be gained from major record labels and mainstream country music.[10]

For the most part, however, the bluegrass industry survives and, to a limited extent, thrives at a stable level on the margins of the mainstream music industry. And rather than being identified with a central location in Nashville, New York, or Los Angeles, the bluegrass industry comprises a number of geographically dispersed business venues, as three of the largest record companies that release bluegrass are located in Durham, North Carolina, Roanoke, Virginia, and Cambridge, Massachusetts. Bluegrass record companies range in size from what could be called the "major" independents, which release a steady flow of albums and are distributed nationally by larger independent distributors and often by their own distribution companies, to the mid-sized independents, which release a few records per year and are distributed through networks specializing in bluegrass, down to the very small companies that are often owned by a musician who releases and distributes cassettes of his or her recordings exclusively. Bluegrass recordings are sold through a number of different venues, including independent specialty shops, "superstore" record store chains with large inventories (e.g., Tower Records and HMV), and mail order, as well as by the artists themselves at performances. With the exception of superstore chains (which are relatively few and concentrated in large cities), all of these markets operate outside the domain of the major music companies, distributors, and retail chains, which produce, distribute, and sell the vast majority of recordings in the United States.[11]

As bluegrass began to be distinguished from country music and as independent record labels became the only recourse for even the most popular blue-grass artists, the music's institutional position within broadcasting began to shift as well. Throughout the late 1950s and early 1960s, the exposure of blue-grass on country radio steadily declined as radio stations, following the lead of major record companies and the Country Music Association (CMA), perceived bluegrass as "too country" and thus as representative of the wrong kinds of demographics (i.e., less "attractive" types of audiences to sell to advertisers).[12] In addition, as country radio programmers began to be more influenced by trends in the national country music scene and industry, they tended to ignore musicians and subgenres of country, such as bluegrass, which survived at the local and regional levels. With increasingly tight playlists on the largest coun-try radio stations, which have enormous power to influence chart position and record sales, bluegrass was virtually shut out of commercial country radio by the mid-to-late 1960s.[13]

Currently, bluegrass is relegated to a form of radio exile, being mainly broad-cast from ghettos at the left side of the FM dial (i.e., the part of the band reserved for college and public radio stations) or, to a lesser degree, in brief, specialized time slots on country radio stations in the South and Southeast. There are as many as 800 radio stations, many of them nonprofit, that include some blue-grass on a regular basis.[14] Some of the most important bluegrass programs on commercial radio are syndicated, and a number of syndicated shows on pub-lic radio stations include bluegrass within a broader, folk music format. Most bluegrass radio shows, however, are locally produced by disc jockeys who rely on bluegrass recordings (either culled from personal collections or provided gratis by record companies) and occasional live performances. Most of these disc jockeys are bluegrass enthusiasts working at small or noncommercial sta-tions for little or no pay. Bluegrass is thus presented in a much different way from mainstream, commercial, country music radio formats: on most locally produced radio shows, it effectively becomes a fan's or enthusiast's genre, with the music presented as a rarity unavailable through mainstream broadcasting or retail channels.

Periodicals devoted to bluegrass serve important roles in educating fans and consumers about the music, as well as in fostering communication within the regionally dispersed bluegrass community. The oldest and most prominent national periodical devoted to bluegrass is *Bluegrass Unlimited,* published in Broad Run, Virginia (Figure 1). Launched in 1966 and clearly produced by and for bluegrass fans, the magazine provides a central forum for arguments over the aesthetic and institutional directions that bluegrass is or should be taking; such discussions are usually conducted in occasional guest editorials by musi-

Figure 1. A selection of *Bluegrass Unlimited* covers. Courtesy of *Bluegrass Unlimited,* Inc. Photograph by Jamie Adams.

cians, fans, and bluegrass business people, in interviews with performers, and in fans' responses printed in the magazine's letters section. A number of other, smaller and less well-circulated bluegrass periodicals are also currently published, including a myriad of local and regional association newsletters produced throughout the United States, some of which are quite substantial and professional, as well as magazines published in Canada, Europe, and Japan.

Local and regional bluegrass associations constitute an important part of the bluegrass industry in terms of their ability to coordinate activities among fans. These associations are located in large cities (e.g., Boston, Toronto, and New York) as well as in the rural and suburban areas of such states as Florida, Georgia, and Texas, and they are often launched by an individual or a small group of people who perform most of the organizational duties. The associations' primary activities include arranging jam sessions, where members bring their instruments and play in small groups; printing newsletters, which list upcoming local and regional concerts and jam sessions as well as news and gossip about members and bluegrass musicians; and attempting to increase community awareness of bluegrass by sponsoring public events like concerts and festivals. Many associations, such as the Society for the Preservation of Blue Grass [sic] Music of America (SPBGMA), emphasize the preservation of the musical traditions of bluegrass and thus limit the use of nontraditional instruments in the festivals that they sponsor. For example, the Southeastern Bluegrass Association of Atlanta, Georgia, describes itself as "a non-profit organization of fans, musicians, vendors, and friends of BLUEGRASS [sic] music, joined together to preserve, promote, and publicize the music," while the Spring Creek Bluegrass Club of Spring, Texas, "is an organization for Bluegrass music fans and musicians who are dedicated to preserving good clean family entertainment." [15]

The focus of many associations on the preservation of tradition places them in a somewhat conflicted relationship with those institutions of the bluegrass industry that would like to expand the music's base of support. On the one hand, associations serve as grassroots survival mechanisms that strengthen support for the music on a local level, which is seen as crucial by the rest of the bluegrass industry; the IBMA, for example, expended a good deal of effort in its early years trying to convince these associations that the new trade organization would not take over their functions and could instead coordinate their activities and facilitate communication among them, while promoters of bluegrass shows often solicit the support of bluegrass associations for their festivals and concerts. But, on the other hand, the conservative constraints of "preservation," in terms of the associations' notion of "tradition," their regulation of the instruments that can be played on stage or in jam sessions, and their commitment to preserving the body of material that comprises the bluegrass "canon," are perceived by some institutions and performers as potentially limiting the commercial opportunities for bluegrass to reach new audiences. "Tradition" and "preservation" often work within bluegrass discourse as crucial notions on which distinctions between "aesthetic" and "commercial" are drawn, and while tradition denotes an essential difference between authentic bluegrass and non-bluegrass for "preservationists," others in the bluegrass industry view "traditional" as one style among many (including "contemporary," "progressive," and various hybrids and shades) that are popular with record and ticket buyers and radio audiences.

The most important sites for bluegrass are festivals, weekend-long concerts in private or public parks that feature a number of professional acts. The festival season, which generally runs from Memorial Day through the Labor Day weekend, is the most important period for fans, who consult the festival guides published in *BU* and other publications, and who drive their recreational vehicles or cars packed with camping equipment (and, for those who play, musical instruments) to one or more festivals around the country each year. For professional musicians, this is the most lucrative period of the year, as the top bands play at least one and as many as three festivals per weekend at the height of the season, making money from their fees and sales of their records and merchandise. For musicians and fans alike, these festivals are events that redeem and renew their faith in bluegrass as a highly personal and personable music through the coming together of fans in campgrounds and in the jam sessions that erupt across the festival grounds; the proximity of a large number of bluegrass artists, who mix and mingle with each other and the crowd; and the general atmosphere of enthusiasm that pervades most successful festivals.[16] While a number of professional individuals and organizations run the largest annual bluegrass festivals, many of those who put on one-day or weekend-long events are amateurs or nonprofit groups; in either case, the profit margin is generally slim, and many of the nonprofit sponsors of festivals use surplus earnings to finance subsequent bluegrass-oriented events. In addition to festivals, two other sites for live, paid performances by bluegrass musicians are nightclubs and cultural centers, but both usually book only the most widely known national acts and then only infrequently throughout the year.

The distance between the most successful bluegrass performer and his or her fans is relatively slight, whether measured in income or in the interaction between artist and audience at festivals and concerts. The notion of the performer as a "normal" person, "one of us" but with perhaps a bit more talent—which is an important notion in many types of folk music as well as in the discourse of country music—is central to the relationship between bluegrass artists and audiences. In fact, not all musicians want to become national, touring performers; some are quite content with their amateur or local status. At the same time, however, the rungs on the ladder of success for professional bluegrass performers are relatively fixed. Climbing to the top of the ladder, from the local and regional levels to the heights of national success, can take as long as ten years for bands or individual artists; once there, performers can establish a loyal following large enough to support them on the bluegrass circuit and in record sales for an extended duration. Bluegrass fans, who are known for their appreciation and sophisticated knowledge of bluegrass bands and their lineups, never abandon their favorites and will support acts—particularly first-generation and popular second-generation performers—for decades. In addition, bluegrass fans and musicians celebrate the music's history and traditions to a stronger degree than even those of country music, thus lending considerable stability to bluegrass, in contrast to the continual turnover of musical performers and styles that has marked country and other commercial forms of popular music over the last thirty years.

Because bluegrass is distinguished by both the faithfulness of its fans and its slow growth, its market has likewise remained relatively stable, especially over the past five years; at all levels of the professional bluegrass hierarchy, this has meant a somewhat static market in which, with some notable exceptions (such as the breakup of a nationally recognized band like Hot Rize), a small, finite number of bands can hold the top positions in the field (i.e., can charge the most money for festival appearances and sell the most records) for a decade or more. Moving up in this hierarchy therefore continues to be a long process that requires, as a *BU* article giving advice to new bands puts it, "a combination of good management, dedication, consistent practice and hard work, talent, and a bit of luck."[17] A band can attain a high level of local support, but without a willingness to suffer through the inevitable hard work and an ability to market and sell itself—both of which are required to attain wider regional support— the band will do little more than release self-produced cassettes and appear at local functions and festivals. Most areas of the country have well-established festivals and other venues where a band with a certain degree of regional popularity can play, often on the same bill as national bluegrass performers, thereby reaching new and larger audiences. Sometimes, regionally established bands are able to record for nationally distributed labels, thereby opening up the possibility of a national audience for themselves and, should their recordings receive good word of mouth and positive reviews in publications like *BU,* a chance to perform outside their home regions at festivals or on tour.

While regional distinctions within bluegrass do not usually prevent a band from recording for a nationally distributed label, a band that attains a high level of regional acclaim can often find it difficult to move up and on to national success. For example, the West Coast band The Good Ol' Persons is perceived by some, particularly in regions with stronger ties to traditional bluegrass like the South and Southeast, as something other than a bluegrass band because of its contemporary folk sound and the absence of banjo from most of its recordings. For this band, scheduling a tour outside the West, which is necessary to build up national support, is economically difficult because of the lack of available shows in large areas of the country.[18] Similarly, a more traditional band like The Warrior River Boys, from Alabama, has a difficult time building support on the West Coast and in the Northeast because it is perceived as too traditional and Southern. Such regional distinctions are not as important as they once were, largely because bluegrass musicians are better versed in different bluegrass styles and those styles are no longer so tightly tied to specific regions, but it remains fairly difficult for bands to move from regional to national status if they are identified too closely with a particular sound and/or a specific region.

An established bluegrass band that regularly releases albums on a national bluegrass label and annually conducts national tours of bluegrass festivals and other venues can attain a secure, but still not very large, income. In addition, unless the band has performed at that level for a long period and also features one or more important first- or second-generation bluegrass figures (e.g., Bill Monroe, Ralph Stanley, etc.), it must continue to work hard—including traveling thousands of miles around the festival circuit each summer—in order to remain on that level. For many performers, the status of being a nationally recognized artist within the field of bluegrass is often not matched by their incomes, and a number of artists are forced to keep some type of "day job" or find a position that can provide financial security during the winter months.

The other option for such artists is to cross over and out of the bluegrass field and into country music. The country stardom of Ricky Skaggs, Marty Stuart, and the late Keith Whitley, among others, as well as the success of a number of bluegrass musicians who have become session "pickers" in Nashville (e.g., Mark O'Connor and Jerry Douglas), demonstrates both the power and the problem of bluegrass for artists schooled within its ranks: bluegrass provides a solid background and excellent training for developing musicians, but it also limits them in terms of how much acclaim can be achieved and how much money can be earned. The shift of mainstream, commercial country music to a more "traditional" sound over the past decade has been both an effect of and a reason for the shift by younger artists like Skaggs and Stuart to major labels and success with "roots"-sounding country music. The pressing issue within the bluegrass community has thus become retaining its most promising stars while not "selling out" the traditions and conventions of bluegrass for commercial gain.

The bluegrass industry, then, is made up of small, independent businesses of varying size and importance that are motivated more by their owners' and employees' devotion to the music than by the hope of financial gain. In this sense, the divisions among fans, business people, and professional musicians—so evident in the international star system and transnational media conglomerates of mainstream popular music and the major companies of the music industry— are virtually nonexistent in bluegrass, where a record company owner and a festival producer remain "fans," a musician or a member of a musician's family often runs a festival or books tours, and a "fan" is often a practicing, if amateur, musician who will at times play for other enthusiasts on stage or in festival parking lots.

This situation both corresponds to the notion of bluegrass as an "authentic," "folk" form and conflicts with the nature of bluegrass as a commercial enterprise: How can bluegrass survive and maintain its identity as the former within a market economy for music that demands the latter? One attempt made by members of the bluegrass industry to resolve this issue was the establishment of the International Bluegrass Music Association, which is the subject of a more in-depth analysis in the next section.

IN A PAMPHLET soliciting new members, the International Bluegrass Music Association (IBMA) defined its purpose and objectives as follows:

> The IBMA exists 1) to promote the bluegrass music industry and create unity within it and 2) to coordinate the bluegrass music community's public image and recognition. We work as a "chamber of commerce" for our music community, not as a dictatorial or regulatory agency. The IBMA does not define bluegrass music nor does it tell anyone how to run their business or play their music.[19]

The discourse of this pamphlet is marked by both the organization's pride of accomplishment and its defensiveness: the IBMA is simultaneously touted as something that "couldn't be done," that "had to be done," and that "was done"; it promotes bluegrass, yet adamantly eschews any "definition" of it; and it coordinates activities that it neither dictates nor regulates. The problem of unifying the bluegrass industry is seen by the IBMA as one of its most difficult yet important tasks; as Art Menius, former executive director of IBMA, said in a 1987 interview,

> We've suffered from splitting off into so many sub-genres: people interested only in traditional bluegrass and people who like the contemporary sound; those who are into newgrass, or into new acoustic music; and people interested only in old-time string band music. We need to put all this together in an organization. . . . There's a tremendous strength in unity.[20]

As the history and current operations of the IBMA demonstrate, the act of organizing the diverse, nonmainstream, and often locally situated musical practices comprised by bluegrass within a unified, national (and international) institutional framework is extraordinarily difficult. In the decade following its formation, the IBMA has become the single most important trade institution representing bluegrass, and through its various activities and projects it continues to coordinate the enterprises of the bluegrass businesses and to promote the music among the broader sectors of the mainstream music industry and the national media. Yet the IBMA's difficulties in establishing itself, particularly during its early years, and its ongoing need to explain itself to fans, who are still wary of what they perceive as a creeping commercialization of bluegrass, illustrate the persistent polarization of "tradition" and "commerce," "authenticity" and the seeming diminishment or lack thereof.

Fear of such resistance was manifested by the IBMA and its proponents from the organization's beginnings. The IBMA's first meeting in 1985 was covered by *Bluegrass Unlimited,* an early supporter of the association, which both celebrated the IBMA's formation and attempted to calm its critics: "During the question and answer period, . . . it was emphasized that the association will neither be a preservationist organization nor will it seek to change the music to make it more popular. . . . The IBMA is a trade organization intended to promote and publicize bluegrass music and increase unity within the field."[21] In other words, the IBMA would have little to do with "the music"—rather, it would concern itself only with the commercial aspects of the music, and specifically with publicizing and promoting bluegrass. The article also discussed the IBMA's intention not to interfere with the local structures of fan involvement, quoting from remarks made by Menius: "We want to contact every [local and regional fan] association. . . . Most importantly, we want to know what they want the IBMA to do."[22] The work of the IBMA, in other words, would be conducted outside the realms of aesthetics and participation, perhaps the two most important aspects of bluegrass cited by those who define it as a traditional or folk form of music rather than a commercial one.

By 1990, the organization's membership had grown from 150 in its first year to approximately 1,500 members throughout the United States and abroad. The IBMA's major annual event, held at the organization's headquarters in Owensboro, Kentucky, is the World of Bluegrass Music trade show, a weeklong conference and showcase for the bluegrass industry. A pamphlet advertising the trade show urges the reader to attend because "the people you need to meet will be there." Bluegrass business people and organizations are assured of opportunities to book acts, meet the talent, discuss common problems, examine the latest in bluegrass-related products and services in the trade show exhibit hall and hospitality suites, and enjoy the informal jam sessions that take place throughout the week. The panels, seminars, and workshops focus on particular concerns and issues facing the various professional groups, such as "Developing a Press Kit and Band Marketing," "Making Bluegrass Green: Expanding the Retail Market," and "Playlists and Audience Development" (for bluegrass radio show and station programmers). The week ends with the IBMA Awards Show, in which respected professional awards are presented in a setting similar to

*International Bluegrass Music Association*

The Fourth Annual
## International Bluegrass Music
### Awards Show

Figure 2. Poster, IBMA Awards Show. Courtesy of International Bluegrass Music Association. Photograph by Jamie Adams.

awards ceremonies for other kinds of music, and with Fan Fest, beginning on the concluding Friday afternoon of the trade show, which has become one of the largest and most important bluegrass festivals of the year (Figure 2).

The World of Bluegrass Music trade show has had a major impact on the bluegrass industry by providing an annual opportunity for a large number of individuals and business groups scattered across the country to meet, make deals, and discuss common problems. In this sense, the trade show would seem to fulfill an important IBMA objective by facilitating a stronger alliance among people working in the bluegrass industry and by fostering their identification of common goals in the process of solving their common problems.

In addition, the IBMA has initiated, and designed a building for, an official bluegrass museum, which will be part of a cultural and performing arts complex in Owensboro. Intended to help establish bluegrass as a vital and historical musical genre, the project will also reinforce the IBMA's image as a central bluegrass institution. With a museum, bluegrass—or, more precisely, those musicians, historians, business people, and organizations involved in its planning and creation—will be able to articulate and represent the music's history in a setting that institutionally legitimates bluegrass as a cultural, historical, and commercial art form.[23] IBMA's role in coordinating the efforts behind such an endeavor is an integral part of its mission to establish an institutional identity for bluegrass both within and beyond the bluegrass community.

IN SPITE OF SUCH SUCCESSES (and perhaps, for some "preservationists," because of them), the IBMA has been forced, even recently, to confront various suspicions concerning its nature and intentions. Would a "trade" association inevitably make bluegrass, an avowedly "traditional," "folk" form of music, a more commercial "package" or "product" and force irrevocable changes on the music? Indeed, could the notion of "trade"—with its connotations of commerce and profit—be applied to bluegrass at all? Various articles and editorials in *Bluegrass Unlimited,* the most important forum for fans, and in *International Bluegrass,* the IBMA's trade publication, have raised and debated these questions.

Around the time of the IBMA's formation, *BU* published a guest editorial by Dick Spottswood, a founder of the magazine and a disc jockey at one of the most important stations with bluegrass programming, who voiced a number of these concerns in a powerful way. Spottswood began by saying, "The time has come for banjos and fiddles to join forces with lawyers and advertising agents—to the certain benefit of the latter and the hoped-for benefit of the former." Commerce—in the guise of legal and mass-media professionals— was thus placed at the outset in opposition to bluegrass, which was represented, interestingly, not by musicians, but by "banjos and fiddles," two of the trademark instruments of bluegrass. Going further, Spottswood explicitly questioned whether the IBMA would become for bluegrass what the Country Music Association has been for country music (as well as, indirectly, for bluegrass): a commercially oriented organization that has attempted to dictate what form country music should take in order to be most profitable, and, many bluegrass supporters believe, one that has helped to force bluegrass and other forms of traditional country music out of the mainstream. Would the IBMA, Spottswood asked, want to encourage the defection of more bluegrass performers like Ricky Skaggs and Keith Whitley to mainstream country music? Would the IBMA ignore or disregard local organizations and performers to focus exclusively on established national stars? He concluded: "What I want to emphasize is the dependence of bluegrass on its traditions—and the older country music traditions—for its long-term health and survival, and that a trade group can be in danger of emphasizing the quantity of trade over the quality of product."[24] Spottswood also noted the IBMA's potential to positively affect bluegrass through its efforts to procure better insurance rates as well as through its trade shows, its attempts to increase radio airplay, and its other promotional efforts. Furthermore, he announced that he would join and that he hoped others would as well, so that all those concerned with bluegrass could pool their efforts on its behalf. Despite this support for the IBMA, however, Spottswood's editorial articulated a number of conflicts at the heart of bluegrass that the organization would face in establishing itself: commerce versus culture, modernization versus tradition, (inter)national versus local, and "crossing over," or worse, "selling out" versus integrity or authenticity.

Over the course of the organization's existence, letters to *BU* and internal IBMA communications have raised similar concerns. Two letters published in the *BU* issue that immediately followed the one in which Spottswood's editorial appeared described bluegrass and similar music as somewhat frail folk genres threatened by the potential destructiveness of an overtly commercial IBMA. Letter writer Joe Ross warned that the organization could "prostitute or misrepresent" the music in order to get more airplay and create a wider appeal. It was essential, he went on, that the IBMA not change the music "if the identity of bluegrass is to survive."[25] A letter from Linda Higginbotham in direct response to Spottswood's editorial noted that bluegrass was itself a commercial form of country music and warned the IBMA not to ignore the more traditional music that she played—old-time string band music. A similar argument and conception of the conflicts within which bluegrass operates was thus transposed to another folk music, which was, Higginbotham claimed, "the traditional form from which [bluegrass] sprang."[26]

Two recent disagreements that arose within the IBMA and were aired in the pages of its bimonthly publication, *International Bluegrass,* demonstrate the persistence of these conflicts, although at a relatively minor level, even within the organization. A panel of musicians at the 1988 trade show issued a statement opposing the taping of live performances by fans (a common practice, particularly at festivals) and also proposing that fans be barred from the backstage areas of outdoor festivals and concert halls. Four letters published in *International Bluegrass* expressed strong reactions to the statement. One argued that "the day a bluegrass artist is escorted to and from the stage . . . will be a sad day for bluegrass. The charm of bluegrass is the accessibility to the stars."[27] Another fan asked, "What effect do you think [searching people for tape recorders and video recorders] will have on the intimate, comfortable relationship that now prevails between bluegrass fans and bluegrass artists? . . . The last thing this music needs is barriers."[28] Bluegrass, so this line of argument goes, is a music without *social barriers,* allowing fans and musicians to interact in local settings like the festival, and a music without *commercial barriers,* where performances are in the public domain and can be taped for posterity. Changes like those suggested by the IBMA artists' panel, warned these fans, threatened to erect such barriers. Similarly, in remarks made at the 1989 general membership meeting of the IBMA and printed in *International Bluegrass,* a self-described "small" bluegrass business owner criticized "large" bluegrass businesses and the IBMA for ignoring the interests, concerns, and needs of "grass roots" institutions.[29] Again, the notion of large commercial entities eroding the participatory, grassroots tradition of bluegrass was at the core of this argument. Thus much of the resistance to the IBMA was and—to a much lesser extent, given that these resistances are now being articulated within the established, accepted communications structures of the IBMA—still is based on fear of the organization's potential to undermine the identity of bluegrass as a traditional, relatively "pure" and somewhat fragile, local and participatory cultural practice.

Many of the activities and communications of the IBMA have been either direct responses to or attempts to circumvent such criticism and skepticism (Figure 3). Perhaps most importantly, the organization has been careful to work closely with the strong network of grassroots associations that has developed across the continent in the past twenty years. A *BU* editorial by an active member of the IBMA explicitly dismissed suspicions that the organization wanted to issue guidelines for local clubs and organizations; instead, the author asserted, the IBMA wanted to improve communication among local associations in order to "make it easier for the clubs to share positive, workable ideas with one another."[30] In addition to publishing occasional reports from local and regional groups and a regular "Association Business Briefs" column in *International Bluegrass,* the IBMA has reserved a seat on its board of directors for an association representative. Chuck Stearman, president of SPBGMA, one of the largest and most important bluegrass associations, is a longtime member of the IBMA and regularly rents a booth at its trade show. He explains the relationship between his organization and the IBMA as a partnership in which the two can work together—the IBMA to "grab the ear of the younger folks," and SPBGMA to preserve the music in its "traditional" form—for the benefit of bluegrass.[31]

More explicitly, such *BU* pieces as Ray Hicks's January 1987 editorial, "What IBMA Isn't," and Jack Bernhardt's November 1987 profile of Art Menius have attempted to allay what the organization sees as "misconceptions" about the IBMA and its purpose, particularly the fear that it will work to somehow trans-

Figure 3. A selection of IBMA promotional materials. Courtesy of International Bluegrass Music Association. Photograph by Jamie Adams.

form and "commercialize" the music. Hicks, a disc jockey and former member of the IBMA board of directors, responded in his *BU* editorial to the suspicion that the IBMA wanted to change bluegrass, arguing that such changes are ultimately made by musicians and fans; as a trade association, the IBMA had no desire to change the music. Similar assertions were made by Menius, who argued that bluegrass had been changing ever since its inception because it was a "living, vital music."[32] The IBMA's refusal to articulate a definition of bluegrass has made it difficult to judge the acts that apply for a slot in the showcase performances held during the trade show; the IBMA's call for applications describes the talent committee's judgments as "subjective evaluation[s] based on [an act's] entertainment value, level of professionalism, potential appeal, and quality of work," going on to explain that "since the IBMA does not promulgate a definition of bluegrass music, the showcases include musical acts which desire to play bluegrass events and venues."[33]

In response to the suspicion that the IBMA would be most directly concerned with helping "bluegrass professionals," both Hicks and Menius have maintained that the organization's structure is democratic, with every member casting an equal vote. In addition, argued Hicks, any success achieved by "professionals" would "filter down" to local amateur bands, smaller festivals, and the fans themselves. He stated in conclusion that the IBMA intended "to promote and enhance that which is already out there—and known as bluegrass. . . . It is our aim to promote and provide help and support to [groups, clubs, artists, and festival promoters] in any way we can, not [to] regulate them."[34]

The trade association, then, is not interested in involving itself in the music or institutions of bluegrass, except to unify and provide aid to those structures and practices that are already in place. As Menius wrote in a 1987 *International Bluegrass* editorial:

> We [are] going to need to change not how we pick, but how we market. We need to upgrade our media relations with modern press releases and press kits in order to stimulate outside interest in our music and to let the rest of the world know about our events. . . . We have systematically cut ourselves off from reaching out to people who like the music, but don't know when or where it's happening. As long as bluegrass remains hard to find on the radio, on stage, and in record stores, we'll only be reaching the hardcore, dedicated fan who is willing to seek it out.[35]

Countering the assertion made by Spottswood (and echoed by other critics of the IBMA) that the commerce of "lawyers and advertising agents" conflicts with the tradition of "banjos and fiddles," Menius and other IBMA proponents have offered a competing account in which the agents of commerce become the means for promoting and distributing bluegrass music. Rather than attempt to harmoniously articulate two opposed and mutually exclusive terms—"commerce" and "tradition"—the IBMA's efforts to foster alliances within bluegrass in order to further the music's marketing represent an attempt to balance commerce and tradition, to promote bluegrass as a traditional *and* commercially viable form of music, as well as one that embodies a unified and powerful set of institutions.

In his speech at a reception held during the first IBMA trade show in 1986, association president Pete Wernick presented a powerful image of the past, present, and future of bluegrass, in which its pioneers, including Bill Monroe, the Stanley Brothers, and Flatt & Scruggs, represented the foundation; the launching of *BU* and the establishment of annual bluegrass festivals represented critical developments in the "mushrooming" of the bluegrass industry; and the formation of the IBMA, twenty years after *BU* and the initial festivals and forty years after bluegrass had first been heard, would "be the catalyst for another level of growth of the world of bluegrass so that people in the future [would] look back to the mid-80s and say, 'What they did then is the key to all the good that's happening now.'"[36] If the IBMA continues to prove successful, the seemingly conflictual relationship between commerce and tradition/authenticity should be resolved within the context of a better distributed, more unified, and more profitable bluegrass, yet one that remains faithful to its distinct musical and institutional practices.

A COMMON JOKE among bluegrass folks answers the question "How many bluegrass fans does it take to screw in a lightbulb?" with "Three: one to screw it in, and two to complain about how it was better the old way." Clearly, this joke can be transposed to other cultural forms that champion or fetishize some sense of "tradition," but there is an undeniable measure of truth to it in relation to bluegrass, as the arguments over the IBMA demonstrate. Bluegrass musicians and business people alike work under conditions in which "tradition" and "commerce" can coexist or, at times, clash, and part of the struggle to legitimate their music and their goods and services is the ongoing attempt to resolve issues of "authenticity" in meaningful yet popular ways. Ironically, many of these same issues recur on a daily basis via one of the newest means by which bluegrass fans, musicians, and business people can communicate with each other: an electronic mailing list (BGRASS-L) based at the University of Kentucky. Here, more than 400 U.S. and European subscribers can discuss the legitimacy of bluegrass traditions via their personal computers at home or in the workplace.[37] The E-mail list thus further reconfigures and recontextualizes an avowed "folk" art in the most modern of contexts—successfully, but not without the occasional conflict over precisely what "real" bluegrass really is.

NOTES

Many thanks to all those whom I interviewed, especially Ken Irwin, Pete Wernick, Dave Freeman, Barry Poss, Bruce Kaplan, Cash Edwards, Dan Hays, Alison Krauss, Dudley Connell, and Keith Case. Thanks also to Larry Grossberg, Neil Rosenberg, and Tom Turino for comments on earlier drafts of this paper.

1   The phrase is borrowed from Lawrence Grossberg's discussion of rock and contemporary culture in *We Gotta Get Out of This Place* (New York, 1992), 397. He describes an "affective alliance" as "a particular segment or articulation of a cultural formation; a configuration of texts, practices and people."

2   Neil Rosenberg's *Bluegrass: A History* (Urbana, 1985) is the most significant resource for bluegrass history and represents one of the best histories of twentieth-century popular music. Many of my assumptions and assertions here concerning the aesthetic, social, and economic development of bluegrass are based on his work.

3  See Hanno Hardt, "Authenticity, Communication, and Critical Theory," *Critical Studies in Mass Communication* 10 (1993): 49–69.

4  The latter is David Whisnant's argument in *All That Is Native and Fine* (Chapel Hill, 1983), a historical study of various attempts to "understand" and "display" the culture of the mountain areas of the Southeast in the pre–World War II era; see specifically his discussion of the White Top Folk Festival in the 1930s for an interesting analysis of the ways in which "traditional" music was perceived and represented by various outside forces and individuals.

5  See Joli Jensen, "Honky-Tonking: Mass-Mediated Culture Made Personal," in *All That Glitters,* ed. George H. Lewis (Bowling Green, 1993), 119–31, for a similar argument concerning honky tonk music.

6  Susan Stewart, *On Longing* (Baltimore, 1984), 23.

7  On issues of authenticity and rock music, see Simon Frith, " 'The Magic That Can Set You Free': The Ideology of Folk and the Myth of the Rock Community," *Popular Music* 1 (1981): 159–68; and *Music for Pleasure* (London, 1988), esp. 1–8.

8  As Rosenberg has described it, this "drive" or "punch" is accentuated by the tension between the instruments that lay down basic rhythms, which stress the first and third beats, and the instruments that take the lead or play melody, which stress the second and fourth beats. In addition, the drive often "surges" in leads as the single instrument being played at times pushes ahead of the basic rhythm, a surge that is generally resolved by the end of the solo or the beginning of the next verse; see *Bluegrass,* 7–8.

9  See Rosenberg, *Bluegrass* (especially 348–61), for a discussion of this transition from major to independent record labels.

10  See my article "Alison Krauss and the Contemporary-Traditional Conflict in Modern Bluegrass," in Lewis, ed., *All That Glitters,* 317–28.

11  One exception that proves the rule is the Disc Jockey/Wax Works chain of predominantly mall stores, which carries a good selection of bluegrass recordings mainly because the chain's chairman is an important personal supporter of bluegrass and a member of the IBMA board of directors.

12  For discussions of these developments within country music history, see Bill C. Malone, *Country Music U.S.A.,* rev. ed. (Austin, 1985 [1968]); and William Ivey, "Commercialization and Tradition in the Nashville Sound," in *Folk Music and Modern Sound,* ed. William Ferris and Mary L. Hart (Jackson, 1982), 129–38.

13  See Malone, *Country Music U.S.A.,* 265; and Richard Peterson, "The Production of Social Change: The Case of Contemporary Country Music," *Social Research* 45 (1978): 292–314. The latter does an adequate job of covering this period in terms of the institutions and economics of country radio, but ultimately makes a somewhat simplistic argument concerning the power of program directors.

14  "IBMA Promotes Bluegrass with CD Samplers," *International Bluegrass* (November/December 1990): 5.

15  *The SEBA Breakdown* (publication of the Southeastern Bluegrass Association) 8

(February 1991): 8; *Spring Creek Bluegrass Club Newsletter* (January 1991): inside back cover.

16   See Michele Kisliuk, "'A Special Kind of Courtesy': Action at a Bluegrass Festival Jam Session," *The Drama Review* 32 (Fall 1988): 321–42.

17   F. Paul Haney, "Successful Bands: Myth, Magic, or Miracles," *Bluegrass Unlimited* (May 1988): 70–73.

18   See J. D. Keinke, "Omnigrass Anyone? The Good Ol' Persons and the Can't-Label-Us-Blues," *Bluegrass Unlimited* (March 1991): 18–24.

19   IBMA, "Proud of our past . . . building our future," membership solicitation pamphlet, n.d.. The pamphlet is circulated at bluegrass festivals, concerts, and other events attended by bluegrass fans and musicians.

20   Jack Bernhardt, "Art Menius: Working to Make Bluegrass Grow," *Bluegrass Unlimited* (November 1987): 54–58; quotation from 57.

21   Ray Hicks, "Bluegrass Trade Association Created," *Bluegrass Unlimited* (December 1985): 66–67.

22   Ibid.

23   "Building on a Legacy Campaign: Questions & Answers," International Bluegrass Music Museum pamphlet, n.d. (c. 1993).

24   Dick Spottswood, "IBMA: A Chamber of Commerce for Bluegrass?" *Bluegrass Unlimited* (February 1986): 5.

25   Joe Ross, "Nashville Recognizes Bluegrass" (letter), *Bluegrass Unlimited* (March 1986): 11.

26   Linda Higginbotham, "IBMA Editorial" (letter), *Bluegrass Unlimited* (March 1986): 10.

27   Solange ("Sally") LaPorte (Peebles, OH), Letter, *International Bluegrass* (March/April 1989): 11.

28   John Wright (Evanston, IL), Letter, *International Bluegrass* (March/April 1989): 11.

29   Stephanie P. Ledgin, "At the Microphone," *International Bluegrass* (September/October 1990): 14.

30   Ray Hicks, "What IBMA Isn't," *Bluegrass Unlimited* (January 1987): 20–21.

31   Interview with Chuck Stearman, 27 November 1990.

32   Bernhardt, "Art Menius."

33   "How You Can Showcase in Owensboro in 1991!" *International Bluegrass* (November/December 1990): 2.

34   Hicks, "What IBMA Isn't," 21.

35   Art Menius, "Executive Directions," *International Bluegrass* (May/June 1987): 14.

36   Pete Wernick, Speech to IBMA (August 1986), *International Bluegrass* (November 1986): 9–10.

37   BGRASS-L, started in 1991 by Frank Godbey, a longtime bluegrass musician (mostly amateur) and bluegrass journalist/record reviewer, includes a few professional musicians, a number of bluegrass disc jockeys, a couple of prominent mem-

bers of the bluegrass industry, some bluegrass historians, and many amateur musicians among its subscribers. Because BGRASS-L sends and receives messages via Internet and Bitnet, both of which primarily serve academics and government employees, most of its subscribers are affiliated with universities or government agencies, although the list has become more diverse as access to Internet has expanded.

# Mountains of Contradictions

*Gender, Class, and Region in the*

*Star Image of Dolly Parton*

**Pamela Wilson**

Dolly Parton has achieved broad popularity over the past twenty years as an exceptional country musician who successfully "crossed over" into pop music and is now perceived as one of the industry's most respected and prolific singer/songwriters. Her distinctive voice is noted for its lilting clarity and "shimmering mountain tremolo," and her repertoire ranges from Appalachian ballads to African-American gospel tunes to hard-driving rockabilly numbers. Parton was one of the first female country musicians whose career developed in front of the television cameras: first as Porter Wagoner's partner on *The Porter Wagoner Show* (1967–74), then as the first woman to host her own country and western variety show, *Dolly* (1976–77). Securing her position as a multimedia star, Parton has played major roles in a number of notable Hollywood films, including *9 to 5, The Best Little Whorehouse in Texas,* and *Steel Magnolias.* In addition to her musical fame and her starring roles on television and in films, Dolly Parton has become well-known through the popular media as an icon of hyperfemininity and as a hero to or role model for women of varying class and cultural backgrounds.[1] As Mary A. Bufwack and Robert K. Oermann explain, "Dolly Parton is the most famous, most universally beloved, and most widely respected woman who has ever emerged from country music," making her "a role model not only for other singers and songwriters, but for working women everywhere."[2]

Dolly Parton has fashioned her star image visually to accentuate her ample, voluptuously overflowing body, particularly her large breasts, a body image that she has embellished with showy, garish costumes and an exaggeratedly sculptured blond wig. This persona is a caricature that juxtaposes the outlandish style of the country singer (in a predominantly male tradition of gaudy costuming) with the stereotypical self-display of the "painted woman," or prostitute, whose sexuality is her style. In ironic contrast to the parodic nature of her visual style, the articulate Parton has perpetuated an image that has gained her respect as a smart, wholesome, sincere person with traditional rural values (Christianity, family, rootedness, and "old-fashioned" integrity) who has managed, through perseverance and resourcefulness, to transcend the disadvantaged economic and social circumstances into which she was born and to use her talents to realize many of her dreams. These "dreams," when materialized and activated, entail another set of contradictions since they represent a lifestyle which, on the surface, is decidedly nontraditional for someone with any combination of her social identities: female, Southern, rural, Appalachian, working-class. Yet, through the construction of her persona, Parton manages and actively exploits the contradictory meanings associated with the social categories of gender, class, ethnic, and regional identity.[3]

Parton is often compared to Mae West, Marilyn Monroe, Bette Midler, and Madonna for her manipulation and burlesquing of femininity. In fact, she has incorporated an acknowledgment of her place in this tradition of subversive white femininity into her 1990s persona through mimetic references in her costumes, makeup, and performances.[4] Yet there is something about Parton that distinctively resonates with a rural and/or working-class audience and that seems to strengthen her appeal as a popular role model rather than a mere visual icon. As a fluent and savvy promoter of "Dolly," Parton provides a fascinating case study in the construction of a star image, specifically one that mediates the often contradictory ideals of gender, region, and class.[5]

AN EXAMINATION of national magazine stories about Dolly Parton reveals that different popular periodicals, the discourses of which strategically target different demographic constituencies, have appropriated Parton for their own discursive realms or purposes and have contributed to the construction of her persona in a number of different ways.[6] Music and musical technology magazines (e.g., *High Fidelity, Stereo Review, Crawdaddy*) have depicted her as a musician and songwriter, tending to focus on her extraordinary talent and her status in the music industry. Men's magazines (e.g., *Esquire, Playboy*) have claimed her as an icon for the desiring male gaze, focusing on her body and sexual image. Supermarket tabloids (e.g., *The Star, National Examiner, National Enquirer,* and *The Globe*) have variously portrayed her as a sexual icon, as a transgressor of patriarchal conventions, and as the occasional victim of personal crisis. They have also focused on her body and the unconventionality of her long-distance marriage and have offered projections of various scandals that lurk on the horizon of her life, so to speak. Middlebrow women's magazines (e.g., *Good Housekeeping, Ladies' Home Journal, Redbook*) have promoted Parton's womanliness, speaking of her as if she were a potential friend and focusing on Parton's "private side": her personal history, her family and her home, her nurturing motherliness, her problems with her weight, her emotions, and her ability to balance an "ordinary" marriage and home life with an extraordinary career. The feminist magazine *Ms.* has promoted what it reads as Parton's feminism, praising her as an empowering agent for women and the working class: "a country artist, a strong businesswoman, and a mountain woman with loyalty and love for her roots."[7] Finally, mainstream news magazines (e.g., *Newsweek, Time*) have billed Parton as a phenomenon of popular culture, focusing on her astute financial management in the entertainment industry and business world.

Dolly Parton's appearance, notably, the images of her body and especially her breasts, has become the terrain for a discursive struggle in the popular press over the social meaning of the female body and the associated ideologies that compete for control over the meaning of "woman" in our society.[8] Parton has consciously and strategically created a star persona that incorporates and even exploits many of the gender contradictions that currently circulate in society. Her complex encoding of these contested meanings via multiply accentuated signifiers defies any easy or uniform interpretation and categorization—in fact, her image encourages a plurality of conflicting readings, which she seems to relish playfully.

The Dolly persona *embodies* (there being no other word for it) excessive womanliness, in any interpretation. Parton displays this excess through her construction of a surface identity (her body and appearance) and through her representation of interiority, or a deeper identity (her emotions, desires, and "dreams"). As one interviewer noted, "Dolly built overstatement into what she calls her 'gimmick,' that is, looking trashily sexy on the surface while being sweet, warm and down-to-earth on the inside."[9] Parton openly discusses the strategies she employs for the construction of her image in almost every interview, and she makes no secret of the fact that the Dolly image is a façade she has created to market herself. This "masquerade" might be interpreted in the psychoanalytic terms theorized by Mary Ann Doane (based on the work of Lacan and Joan Rivière). Yet it might also be seen, following Claire Johnston, as a social parody, a hyperbolic stereotype, a tongue-in-cheek charade that playfully and affectionately subverts the patriarchal iconography of female sexuality.[10] As Parton has explained,

When I started out in my career, I was plainer looking. I soon realized I had to play by men's rules to win. My way of fighting back was to wear the frilly clothes and put on the big, blonde wigs. It helped that I had a small voice that enabled me to sing songs of pain and loneliness and love and gentle things like butterflies and children. I found that both men and women liked me.[11]

Parton's construction of the "inner" Dolly, though just as carefully controlled, is not as readily evident since she attempts to elide the constructedness of the Dolly persona by conflating it with public perceptions of the "real" Dolly Parton, thus diverting attention from the aim of such strategies (i.e., as marketing ploys) as well:[12]

I'm careful never to get caught up in the Dolly image, other than to develop and protect it, because if you start believing the public persona is you, you get frustrated and mixed up. . . . I see Dolly as a cartoon: she's fat, wears a wig, and so on. . . . Dolly's as big a joke to me as she is to others.[13]

In many ways, it is difficult to deconstruct the issues of gender, class, regionalism, and ethnicity as distinct facets of Dolly, since many of the signifiers Parton uses connote and connect two or more. Parton never decontextualizes herself from her rural, working-class, Southern Appalachian identity; from her interviews it is clear that she does not distinguish the abstract condition of being female from her personal experience as a Southern Appalachian, working-class woman. Parton "plays herself," constructing an image from the very contradictions of her own culturally grounded experience and social identity. However, many popular discourses (particularly those addressed to a gendered audience, either masculine or feminine) foreground gender issues. They focus on Dolly as a (more abstract) "woman," buying into her image without necessarily considering the relationship between her "woman-ness" and her class and regional/ethnic origins.

In a 1977 issue of *High Fidelity,* a country music columnist addressed Parton's corporeal contradictions:

Inevitably, the recent national notice accorded Dolly Parton has focused more on the improbability of her image than on her art. A voluptuous woman with a childish giggle, she finger-picks the guitar, the banjo and the mountain dulcimer with inch-long, painted nails. She composes delicate lyrics of Tennessee mountain innocence and performs them in finery a stripper would happily peel. And through layers of lipstick, she pushes a voice fervent with fundamentalist religion. . . . Today she would like to be a little more listened to and a little less ogled. But the reams of copy about her fashion and physiognomy can hardly be blamed on anyone but herself; she donned the gaudy garb and high-piled hair specifically to make us stare.[14]

Critic Ken Tucker has also addressed the tactical strategy of Parton's self-marketing:

> Now, there is no doubt that the major reason non-country fans initially took an interest in Parton was the outer package—"People will always talk and make jokes about my bosom," was the way she put it with typical forthrightness. This, combined with her Frederick's of Hollywood high heels . . . and cartoonish hairpieces ("You'd be amazed at how expensive it is to make a wig look this cheap"), transformed Parton into the country version of Mae West, and made her a highly telegenic figure.[15]

The traditional masculine perspective that fetishizes the female body (particularly large breasts and an hourglass figure) for the male gaze has long been a visual staple of men's magazines. However, the fact that Parton's appearance is such an exaggeration of that aesthetic (plus, I suspect, the fact that she has maintained such a mystique about her sexuality) seems to make her male admirers too uncomfortable to directly address this fetish, relying instead on nervous puns, laughter, jokes, and euphemisms to communicate their desire. For example, humorist and *Esquire* columnist Roy Blount, Jr., once wrote:

> Folks, I am not going to dwell on Dolly's bosom. I am just going to pass along a vulgar story: "They say old Dolly's gone women's lib and burned her bra. Course it took her three days." Dolly's bosom, horizontally monolithic in its packaging, is every bit as imposing as her hair. And then abruptly her waist goes way in. . . . And she wears very tight clothes over it. . . . I imagine you would have to know Dolly a good while before you could say hello to her without suddenly crying, "Your body!"[16]

Prefacing his extended 1978 interview with Parton in *Playboy,* Lawrence Grobel remarked:

> Although she appears larger than life, she is actually a compact woman—dazzling in appearance; but if you took away the wig and the Frederick's of Hollywood five-inch heels, she'd stand just five feet tall. Of course, her height isn't the first thing one notices upon meeting her. As she herself

kids onstage, "I know that you-all brought your binoculars to see me; but what you didn't realize is you don't need binoculars."[17]

Grobel continued with another anecdote about a little girl whose parents brought her backstage to greet Dolly; it too articulates the discourse of male desire:

> The picture I'll always remember was of the father telling his wife to take a shot of him behind Dolly. He had this crazy gleam in his eyes, his tongue popped out of his mouth, and I was sure he was going to cop a feel. But he restrained himself, as most people do around her. Because she is so open and unparanoid, she manages to tame the wildest instincts of men.[18]

What the *Playboy* interview reveals is Parton's complicity in (and ultimate control of) this discourse of male desire. Several factors enter into the carefully constructed mystique that Parton maintains. First, her long-distance, part-time marriage to the mysterious, never-interviewed Carl Dean of Tennessee has generated questions about outlets for her sexual energy. There is an implicit assumption that since she appears to be hyperfeminine, she must be hypersexual. One of the most prevalent topics in "Dolly" discourse is speculation about her relationship with her husband, about how much time she spends with him, and, often implicitly, about the terms of their marriage vis-à-vis fidelity (about which questions are posed but evaded in several interviews). The tabloids have linked her sexually to a number of singing partners and leading men; there have also been suggestions of a lesbian relationship with her best friend and companion. This obsessive concern with the intimate details of Parton's sex life is found primarily in men's magazines and the tabloids. In contrast, when women's magazines have addressed the issue of her marriage, the focus has primarily been on her interpersonal/emotional relationships in general.

Throughout the *Playboy* interview, Grobel repeatedly raised questions about Parton's sexuality, to which she responded teasingly and unabashedly, but always stopping short of any personal disclosures. She admitted that she frequently flirts; however, the reader can observe her flirtations with the interviewer as her way of tactically taking control of the situation; her witty and manipulative comebacks frequently seemed to take Grobel by surprise and usually served to keep the ball in her court. The late Pete Axthelm once wrote about this aspect of Parton's persona:

> What Dolly is, it seems to me, is more than the sum of her attractive parts. Aside from her talent, she represents a vanishing natural resource—the mountain woman who understood independence and manipulation of

men long before the first city girl got her consciousness raised. Dolly has a seldom-seen husband . . . she also employs a number of men to help build her career. But there is no doubt about who's boss. "I need my husband for love," she says, "and other men for my work. But I don't depend on any man for my strength." [19]

Although some feminists have spoken out against the objectification of women's bodies as fetishes of male desire, on the grounds that such objectification reduces women to a passive state that victimizes them, one counterargument attributes power to the woman who controls—and controls the use of— her own image. Dolly Parton, by managing and manipulating her sexual image in such a way as to attain the maximum response from the male gaze while maintaining her own dignity and self-esteem, is making patriarchal discourse work to her own advantage. She is keeping the upper hand and stage-managing her own "exploitation."

If Dolly's appearance seems to signify excessive femaleness in the discourse of male desire and the magazines that articulate it, in such women's magazines as *Good Housekeeping* and *Ladies' Home Journal* it is identified with a different kind of excess: exaggerated womanliness. There, Parton's literal embodiment of excessive womanliness is represented in two domains: that of her attitudes about her weight and body image, and that of her reproductive capabilities and speculations about whether her future holds motherhood. Both domains function as grounds for identification with Dolly by many female readers. While the evocation of male desire constructs Dolly as an object of voyeurism and aggressive sexual fantasy, the emphasis on female identification constructs Dolly as an ordinary woman who has the same types of physical and emotional problems as other women. In contrast to the physiological oddity constructed by men's magazines, in women's magazines Dolly becomes "Everywoman," and efforts are made to minimize her exceptionalness. [20]

The first discursive domain of women's magazines deals respectfully with the *imperfections* of Dolly's body, as noted by Parton herself, and the associated psychological aspects (a very different reading of the same physical "text" on which the masculine reading of sexuality is based):

> I look better fat, though, don't you think? Skinny, my face looks too long. I'm just very hefty. People are always telling me to lose weight, but being overweight has certainly never made me less money or hurt my career. . . . Besides, everybody loves a fat girl. . . . See, I know I'm not a natural beauty. I got short legs, short hands, and a tiny frame, but I like the way I am. I am me. I am real. [21]

After an extended illness and gynecological surgery in the early 1980s, Parton lost a good deal of weight. This generated a surge of interest in—and a number of women's magazine articles about—her body and her relationship to it:

> Dolly admits she was overeating. Although she confesses, "I'm a natural-born hog. . . . I also eat when I'm happy," the protracted illness added more pounds to an already overloaded five-foot frame. "See, I'd always had this eating problem. I'd gain twenty pounds, lose it, gain it back the next week. In ten days I'd put on ten pounds. . . . I'd binge, diet, gain, start all over again. . . . Overeating is as much a sickness as drugs or alcoholism."

> To the suggestion she's too thin, that she looks anorexic, Dolly guffaws, "Honey, hogs don't get anorexia."

> Boy, it burns me up to see people look at a fat person and say, "Can you believe anybody would let herself get into that kind of shape?" That's easy for someone who looks like Jane Fonda to say. When I see a really over-weight person, I feel sorry for her, because I've been there. . . . I know I could gain the weight back any minute, and it scares me to death."[22]

Through this admission, Parton brings herself down from any pedestal on which her star status might have placed her and aligns herself with the every-day concerns of ordinary women. Yet she also specifically identifies with working-class women, sarcastically criticizing the class-based aesthetic of thin-ness among the upwardly mobile:

> "My doctors would tell me, 'Okay, you have about twenty pounds to lose, but you can do that easily. Just eat right.' Well, that's easy to say. I just love those beautiful people who tell you, 'I *cahn't* see how anybody could let themselves get in that awful shape. Oh, my dear. That's gross,'" says Dolly, aping a fancy society voice.[23]

The other discursive domain of women's magazine articles about Dolly, the intense interest in her childbearing potential, has included speculation about her desire and possible plans for motherhood:

> Dolly doubts whether they'll have children because of the demands of her career. "I'm not saying women can't do both, but I'm on the road so much that it wouldn't be fair to the child. I love children so much that I'd want to be a mother all day long if I was going to be one. . . . But remember, I was one of the oldest in my family. I've been raising babies all my life. . . . There's no shortage of kids around our home."[24]

This interest in the nurturing, maternal side of Dolly continued after her hysterectomy, shading into curiosity about her emotional reactions to the loss of her childbearing potential:

> Dolly had a partial hysterectomy and can no longer become pregnant. "Carl and I wanted children for years," she says. "I used to grieve after the hysterectomy, but since I turned forty, it doesn't bother me as much. I think God meant for me not to have children. My songs are my children, and I've given life to three thousand of them." Had she had kids, Dolly admits, most of those songs would never have been written.[25]

This metaphoric link between childbearing and the cultural production of songs recalls the Appalachian folk tradition (as described by Bufwack and Oermann) of women's collecting and amassing huge repertoires of ballads and other songs that were then shared and exchanged among themselves.[26] Songs, like stories, have been a vital part of the cultural economy of Appalachian women; producing songs, like producing children, has been important to their social identities.

In contrast to women's magazines, recent tabloid articles have created masculinist scenarios, such as this one:

> Dolly Parton wants a baby. The country music star, who's pushing 43, always insisted motherhood wasn't for her. But now she's pining for the patter of little feet. Though she knows she can't become pregnant—surgery has eliminated that possibility—she wants to tear a page out of 44-year-old Loni Anderson's book and adopt a child.[27]

Tabloid discourse thus works hard at trying to "push" Parton back into a normative patriarchal structure, to contain and/or deny the creative potential of other forms of cultural production for women.

One of the contradictions between Parton's Dolly persona and her "real-life" image is that while the former has attained wealth and fame, the latter is projected as a humble Tennessee housewife who merely puts up with the demands of fame and fortune until she can get home and relax, slip into something more comfortable—her private life—which is just like everyone else's, well, almost. These conflicting images are paralleled by the dualistic roles that Parton models for women. On the one hand, she represents the modern, nonrepressed woman who can "have it all"—marriage, strong family ties and friendships, and a successful, self-managed business/career that has brought her financial independence and a commensurate degree of social power; on the other hand, she represents the traditional values of rural American womanhood. The women's magazine articles reflect both a strong interest in how she manages to balance all of these aspects of her life and an intense curiosity about what that life entails/who that woman is—hence their focus on the private, emotional side of the star. By contrast, articles in mainstream, business-oriented news and music magazines (as well as in *Ms.*) have charted the (nontraditional) economic accomplishments of Dolly Parton. Particular interest has been paid to her business acumen and to her success as a crossover, both of which are associated with overcoming institutional and social obstacles. Parton has been successful as a country music singer and songwriter, a Hollywood actress, and a television performer in both specials and series. She has also proved to be an extremely successful entrepreneur as the owner of several production companies, publishing companies, toy companies, and music studios, and as the developer of Dollywood—the theme park she created to strengthen the economy of her native Tennessee county, which celebrates both her own career and the culture of the Appalachian region where she began.[28]

DOLLY PARTON'S STAR IMAGE is the terrain for a struggle over not only the contested meanings of gender—the social construction of "woman"—but also the nature of and relations among class, regional culture, and ethnicity.[29] The Dolly persona, as an intersection of multiple social categories, raises the question of what it means to be Southern, Appalachian, rural, working-class, and female—or any one of these social identity categories.

In today's cosmopolitan, rapidly globalizing society, the construction of cultural identities is increasingly becoming a symbolic process rather than a result of geographic positioning. Although the role of the media in this symbolic construction needs further exploration, I want to suggest that the country music industry contributes to it by constructing notions of "Southernness" or "country-ness" to which consumers can subscribe. Today, many cultures are geographically situated in or otherwise associated with the American South, such as the cultures of black, rural, working-class Southerners; white, rural, working-class Southerners; the "old South's" white aristocracy; urban black Southerners; urban Southern Jews; Southern Appalachian whites; urban/suburban white Southerners; Louisiana Cajuns; Southern Mennonites; and Cherokee, Choctaw, and Seminole Indians. All are distinct, but their cultural boundaries are permeable, and social agents may be associated with more than one of these subcultures. Class, race, ethnicity, and place are the most significant markers of cultural group identity. As a result, "Southern" is clearly a generic construct rather than a label for a distinct culture. It is used as a classifying and stereotyping term by outsiders; the signifiers of Dolly Parton's distinctive white Southern Appalachian culture are collapsed into a nonspecific "Southernness" and "country-ness" by the popular culture discourses relating to country music.

"Southernness," as a symbolic and discursive construction, has acquired distinct connotations and cultural referents that are usually associated with white Southern cultures.[30] The political history of the Southern states, beginning with their secession from the United States during the Civil War period, through the stark, Depression-era WPA images of impoverished sharecroppers, to the civil rights movement of the 1960s, has generated a host of internal and external discourses and stereotypes about the "South," which are reproduced and further fueled by conflicting images and representations of the region in literature, the media, and popular culture.

The specific subculture represented by Dolly Parton (Southern Appalachian mountain culture) has also been subject to stereotyping in popular culture, from the socially inept and "primitive" hillbillies of the "L'il Abner" comic strip and television's *Beverly Hillbillies* to the violent, sexually deviant villains of James Dickey's novel *Deliverance* and its 1972 film adaptation. Parton parodies these popular images in her persona, even as she promotes the more "authentic" cultural elements that reflect her heritage, particularly the culture of Appalachian women. Historically and culturally, kinship has been the central organizing principle of Southern Appalachian society, and a matrilineal orientation has resulted in strong affective ties among women.[31] Each rural community tended to form an independent, kinship-oriented, egalitarian social group, without clear social-class differences (most group antagonism stemmed from tensions between a social group and the outside world—meaning, since the mid-nineteenth century, the Northern industrial society—as well as from minor tensions between communities or between families). Relationships between women have been primarily kin- and neighbor-oriented, and a strong women's culture has been maintained. Members of a traditional mountain community have tended to share a common history and ideology, with their code of morality primarily informed by localized inflections of fundamentalist Christianity.

In the traditional, preindustrial economy, there was a gendered division of labor: the woman's domain was her household, where she was responsible for raising food and children and for serving as a repository of cultural knowledge (history, genealogy, and the moral code). As industrialization overtook the agrarian mode of life in this century, mountaineers have been gradually assimilated into this economy as working-class laborers, and both men and women now participate in the wage-labor force.[32] Although this culture is generally perceived as strongly patriarchal (a perception largely due to the work of early male "ethnographers," such as John C. Campbell), studies by women who have examined the culture challenge that assumption; they see instead a gender-based system of coexisting models for cultural practice, whereby Appalachian women maintain a great deal of power within and through a facade of patriarchal control.

On the matter of the oppositional relationship between Southern Appalachian culture and the dominant American social order, some readings of Gramsci's work on early twentieth-century rural and urban societies in Italy are especially useful.[33] Gramsci describes rural intellectuals as "for the most part 'traditional,' . . . linked to the social mass of country people and the town (particularly small town) petite bourgeoisie, not as yet elaborated and set in motion by the capitalist system."[34] Anne Sassoon's explanation is significant:

> These intellectuals are considered traditional from . . . the point of view of the dominant, capitalistic mode of production. They are still linked to a world which is pre-capitalist. In this terrain they weld together a sub-bloc which has its own particular coherence. Although they are traditional vis-à-vis the dominant bloc, they can at the same time have *organic* links to surviving pre-capitalist modes and classes. They live, as it were, in two different historical times.[35]

The dualistic historical inscription of Southern Appalachian culture—one inscribing mountaineers as residual remnants of the past and the other transposing them to contemporary lower- or working-class status—is an important key to understanding the multiple sources of oppositional sentiment represented in Southern Appalachian cultural expression: the traditional agrarian mode versus postindustrial capitalism, and rural working-class culture versus mainstream/middle-class American culture (especially as constructed by film and television).

A great deal of the "Dolly" discourse in popular magazines has been devoted to authenticating her "country" life history and cultural roots, particularly the conditions of poverty, rural isolation, and familial heritage in which she developed.[36] In interviews, Parton herself has emphasized her working-class background:

> I can think like a workingman because I know what a workingman goes through. . . . Where I came from, people *never* dreamed of venturing out. They just lived and died there. Grew up with families and a few of them

went to Detroit and Ohio to work in the graveyards and car factories. But I'm talking about venturing out into areas that we didn't understand.[37]

Parton has also discussed the farming/working-class mentality of her husband, an asphalt contractor:

He's really bright. He's not backward at all. I just really wish that people would let him be. He's a home-lovin' person. He works outside, he's got his tractor and his grader, he keeps our farm in order. He wouldn't have to work no more, because I'm making good money now, but he gets up every morning at daylight. If he ain't workin' on our place, he'll take a few jobs, like grading somebody's driveway or cleaning off somebody's property, to pick up a couple of hundred bucks. . . . He'll say, "Well, I ain't in show business, I got to work."[38]

Many magazine articles underscore Parton's refusal to be assimilated into a Hollywood celebrity lifestyle and her preference for maintaining a home near Nashville. However, this brings up the complex issue of the subcultural hegemony represented by the Nashville-based country music industry.

In relation to the mainstream music and entertainment industries centered in Los Angeles and New York, the Nashville industry represents a successful regional-cultural force that has gained a national audience, yet remains independent and appears somewhat radical in its advocacy of Southern, white, working-class culture. In the course of being disseminated nationally through radio and, most recently, cable television, the "country" culture has been appropriated by a generalized working-class audience, both urban and rural, that represents various racial and ethnic backgrounds.[39] As a result of its folk music origins, country music has long been a genre of self-defined "ordinary folks," whose sense of humor has frequently generated both oppositional satire and a somewhat self-mocking tone (often read as straight by outsiders, but recognized as ironic and self-parodying by insiders).[40] Since the 1950s, country music has increasingly become a genre for female artists, who have aligned themselves with rural and working-class women.

However, the country music industry has recently changed, shifting away from its folk roots (though still incorporating them in the construction of "country-ness") and moving into the postmodern popular-music mainstream market. In an insightful essay, Patrick Carr discusses the changing social image of and audience for country music in the 1980s:

Historically in America, the rural working class has been the object of prejudice, of stereotyping amounting to contempt, on the part of the urban population. . . . Not long ago, to "be country" meant that you had been cast by a geo-socio-economic accident of birth with an almost automatically adversarial relationship with the dominant urban/suburban culture; in effect, you belonged in a cultural ghetto. Now it's a matter of free consumer choice.[41]

Carr argues that the country music industry has structured its current place in the entertainment industry in such a way as to commercialize those adversarial voices, thereby economically insinuating them into a capitalist order to which they have been traditionally opposed.[42] This is indeed a major paradox of country music in general and of stars like Parton in particular. The bristling tension between the proudly rebellious, rough-hewn rural style of "authentic" country music culture and the glossy, slickly packaged commercialized style of the mainstream entertainment industry has become the defining mark of the country music industry today.[43]

I find Raymond Williams's insights on "residual" cultural elements helpful in analyzing how Southern Appalachian and rural Southern subcultural elements are incorporated into the dominant economy and culture: "The residual, by definition, has been effectively formed in the past, but is still active in the cultural process, not only and often not at all as an element of the past, but as an effective element of the present."[44] This notion of "the residual" illuminates the active role that the past plays, not just in subcultures, but in their incorporation into the dominant culture:

> A residual cultural element is usually at some distance from the effective dominant culture, but some part of it, some version of it . . . will in most cases have had to be incorporated if the effective dominant culture is to make sense in these areas. . . . It is in the incorporation of the actively residual—by reinterpretation, dilution, projection, discriminating inclusion and exclusion—that the work of the selective tradition is especially evident.[45]

In constructing her star persona, Dolly Parton has played with and exploited cultural stereotypes of style and taste—not only in terms of femininity, but also with respect to Southern Appalachian, rural and/or working-class culture—often exaggerating them in her persona or emphasizing them in interviews:

> I always liked the looks of our hookers back home. Their big hairdos and makeup made them look *more*. When people say that less is more, I say *more* is more. Less is *less;* I go for more.

Dolly, who commands $350,000 a week in Las Vegas—making her the highest paid entertainer there—says she prefers shopping at K-Mart or Zayre's, where she can get several articles of clothing for the price she'd pay for one at a more upscale establishment.

I'd much rather shop in a mall and buy some cheap clothes than go into some fine store and buy something that costs a fortune. . . . I want to design something for the average woman, something that could be sold at Sears or Penney's.[46]

By foregrounding such stereotypes, Parton not only celebrates working-class tastes and values, but also parodies her male predecessors in the country music world of the 1950s and 1960s, particularly her former partner, Porter Wagoner, and others who perpetuated country music's most distinctive visual symbol—the extravagantly expensive, gaudy, spangled-and-rhinestoned stage costume, which became the haute couture of male country music performers of that era.[47] The "down-home" side of Dolly thus advocates "authenticity" by making fun of the superficial stylistic elements that have encrusted the dominant society's image of (and that have been internalized as identificatory values by) women on display, country music performers, Southerners, and the rural working class. As Gloria Steinem points out, "Her flamboyant style has turned all the devalued symbols of womanliness to her own ends. If feminism means each of us finding our unique power, and helping other women to do the same, Dolly Parton certainly has done both."[48] If we extend Steinem's statement to include the other categories of social identity and oppression that the "Dolly" image enunciates, Parton can be understood as a self-empowered woman whose image, challenging social stereotypes through parody, becomes empowering and counter-hegemonic.

MY MAIN INTEREST HERE is in the type of feminism Dolly Parton represents, which seems to be "organically" rooted in and intertwined with the multiply oppressive conditions of class, regional ethnicity, and gender. Through her practices and her discourse, Parton has made public what had previously been tacit or private strategies used by rural, working-class, Southern Appalachian women to negotiate power for themselves within patriarchy and the capitalist class structure. Nevertheless, Parton is not an anomaly, but is instead drawing upon a model of feminine action in which women subvert, and gain strength from within, the dominant patriarchal system.[49] The apparent purpose of this subversion is not to overthrow patriarchy altogether, but to create opportunities for women to control their lives within it.

Michel de Certeau's theories of the resistance practiced by working classes within a capitalist class structure, or by subcultures resisting assimilation into dominant culture, provide insights that can be extended to gender negotiations of power within patriarchy:

> [She] creates for [herself] a space in which [she] can find *ways of using* the constraining order of the place. . . . Without leaving the place where [she] has no choice but to live and which lays down its law for [her], [she] establishes within it a degree of *plurality* and creativity. By an art of being in between, [she] draws unexpected results from [her] situation.[50]

De Certeau's model is one of subversion from within an order of power: not overthrowing or necessarily transforming it, but exploiting its resources (time and materials) for one's own purposes, constructing one's own space and strategies for action within the boundaries, and tactically identifying and exploiting the loopholes in the structure of dominance to acquire power for oneself. Both de Certeau's model and the case of Southern Appalachian women illustrate the dual operations of orders of power—a top-down presumption that the legitimately powerful are in control, complemented by a bottom-up pretense of endorsing that presumption: although "they" think they are in control of "us" (and "we" pretend to be controlled by "them"), "we" are in fact manipulating the structure for our own purposes, taking advantage of every opportunity to informally (and quietly) exploit the system. In the coalescence of multiple oppressions (gender, social class, economic group, etc.), these mechanisms operate on multiple levels, against a variety of "systems" of power.

Feminism, class, and regional/ethnic consciousness become personal rather than political, rhetorical, or structural issues for women like Dolly Parton. She represents a type of popular feminism that has little knowledge of or use for the political rhetoric of the women's movement, although Parton herself has never publicly opposed its goals and has always aligned herself with other strong, self-sufficient women. In citing the qualities that Parton hails in her 1991 song "Eagle When She Flies," Bufwack and Oermann describe this type of feminism among female country artists of the 1960s and 1970s, who "sang proudly of the enduring strength of womanhood": "They portrayed the country woman as the powerful life force, the resilient mother, the source of love, and the rock of support."[51] In a May 1991 (week of Mother's Day) appearance on *The Tonight Show,* Parton introduced "Eagle When She Flies" with these comments:

> I wanted to do a song for all the mamas out there. This is a song I actually wrote about my own mother, and about myself—about people like

Mother Teresa, Amelia Earhart, Harriet Tubman, Eleanor Roosevelt, Ann Richards, and all the great women who've helped make this world more wonderful. I hope maybe you guys will appreciate this, too.

In spite of this tribute to female humanitarians, politicians, and adventurers, Parton dissociates herself from the rhetoric of mainstream feminism, insistently personalizing and individualizing feminist ideology in terms of lived experience, as in this segment of the 1978 *Playboy* interview:

Grobel:  Do you support the Equal Rights Amendment?
Parton:  Equal rights? I love everybody. . . .
Grobel:  We mean equal rights for women.
Parton:  I can't keep up with it.
Grobel:  Do you read any books on the women's movement?
Parton:  Never have. I know so little about it they'd probably be ashamed
         that I was a woman. Everybody should be free: if you don't want
         to stay home, get out and do somethin'; if you want to stay home,
         stay home and be happy.[52]

And, in another interview:

I think if women, or people in general, would just listen and not think they're still listening to their father or to their mother or their husband, or to this or to that, but listen to what *they* think they can do. . . . I always said, with my accountants, with my managers, or my bankers or agents: "Look, I don't need advice, I need information. I will make my own decisions."[53]

Parton applies her belief system to the management of her own life and career. She openly discusses her determination to control the construction of her image, even as she also chooses to express herself in language that marks her by class and region:

People have thought I'd be a lot farther along in this business if I dressed more stylish and didn't wear all this gaudy get-up. Record companies have tried to change me. I just refused. If I am going to look like this, I must have had a reason. It's this: if I can't make it on my talent, then I don't want to do it. I *have* to look the way I choose to look, and this is what I've chose.[54]

She has also exhibited a strong-willed determination to master and manipulate the social codes and conventions of the patriarchal and capitalist systems, deploying these codes to her own advantage without transgressing them.[55] This is a key to her acceptance as a nonthreatening but powerful influence. Parton, in forging new traditions from old ones, is serving as a model for others to do the same. As one music magazine describes her, she is "a woman taking possession of her destiny."[56] Or, as Parton's occasional collaborator Linda Ronstadt puts it:

> I think Dolly is a girl who was born with an amazing amount of insight into people. It's like an intelligence of compassion. Shakespeare really understood human behavior. Tolstoy could write the greatest novel ever because he really understood what makes people tick. And I think Dolly Parton is one of those kinds of people. She has that kind of intelligence; she is amazingly perceptive.[57]

Basing her feminism and class consciousness on cultural knowledge and emotion rather than intellectual rhetoric, Parton's impassioned, popular feminism speaks to segments of the working class who are probably beyond the reach of liberal feminist rhetoric. It is also significant, I believe, that she reaches this population through the vehicle of musical expression (and its attendant discourses) rather than through political or intellectual rhetoric. As Gramsci articulated the dichotomy:

> The popular element "feels" but does not always know or understand; the intellectual element "knows" but does not always understand and in particular does not always feel. . . . The intellectual's error consists in believing that one can know without understanding and even more without feeling and being impassioned. . . . One cannot make politics-history without this passion, without this sentimental connection between intellectuals and people-nation.[58]

As a popular feminist and an advocate of the rural working class, Parton employs a counter-hegemonic rhetoric that seems sentimental, emotional, and nonthreatening to those in the power bloc, who often perceive it as comical and ineffectual. Yet her subversive strategies are powerful. Far from serving as a vehicle for the dominant ideology, Parton's star image provides a rich, multidimensional configuration of signifiers that exploit the contradictory meanings inherent to that image. "Dolly" may well make Parton's fans aware of their own social positioning and thereby encourage alternative readings and practices.

NOTES
Many thanks to Lynn Spigel, Julie D'Acci, John Fiske, David Morley, Greg Smith, and Cecelia Tichi for their insights and suggestions at various stages in this paper's development.

1  Mary Bufwack and Robert K. Oermann's *Finding Her Voice: The Saga of Women in Country Music* (New York, 1993) provides a thorough and fascinating account of the central, though often overlooked, role of women in the growth of country music throughout this century. See also Joan Dew's *Singers and Sweethearts: The Women of Country Music* (Garden City, NY, 1977); and scattered references in Bill C. Malone's *Southern Music, American Music* (Lexington, 1979); and in John Lomax III, *Nashville: Music City USA* (New York, 1985). Patrick Carr also provides an insightful look at the industry; see "The Changing Image of Country Music," in *Country: The Music and the Musicians,* ed. Paul Kingsbury, Country Music Foundation (New York, 1988), 482–517.

2  Bufwack and Oermann, *Finding Her Voice,* 360.

3  See Richard Dyer, *Stars* (London, 1979).

4  During the U.S. military engagement in the Persian Gulf ("Operation Desert Storm"), a story on Parton in *Vanity Fair* featured photos of Dolly attired in the style of various 1940s pin-up queens and posing atop the shoulders of American fighter pilots. Another stylized image mimetically invoked Dolly "doing" Madonna "doing" Marilyn Monroe: A photo in *People,* taken during a concert performance, shows Parton with a brassiere-like contraption of two huge cones—a mocking parody of Madonna's contemporaneous act. The caption reads "Dolly Parton finally found a way to contain herself and still delight fans at the Brady Theater in Tulsa, where she sang 'Like a Virgin' with a pointed reference to the originator." See Kevin Sessums, "Good Golly, Miss Dolly!" *Vanity Fair* (June 1991): 106–11, 160–66; and *People,* 29 June 1992, 7.

5  To clarify my terminology here, since it has potential political implications, I use the name "Dolly" to refer to the constructed persona or image and "Parton" to refer to the social agent responsible for the act of constructing. I realize, however, that even this distinction is problematic since Parton's construction and representation of her "authentic" self amounts to creating a media persona as well. Admittedly, it is difficult to refer to her as "Parton" because in almost all of the literature (with the exception of three articles, two in music magazines and one in *Ms.*) she is referred to as "Dolly" with a familiarity that I suspect would be less acceptable in journalistic writing about a man.

6  These magazine articles represent only a small portion of the available media coverage of this star, which also addresses her recordings, films, two television series and numerous specials, as well as other promotional coverage.

7  Gloria Steinem, "Dolly Parton," *Ms.* (January 1987): 95.

8  Consider the dual cultural meaning of women's breasts in our society: as charac-

teristics of sexual attractiveness, and as sites of maternal life-giving, nourishment, nurturance, and mother-child bonding.

9   Cliff Jahr, "Golly, Dolly!" *Ladies' Home Journal* (July 1982): 85.

10  See Mary Ann Doane, "Film and the Masquerade: Theorizing the Female Spectator," *Screen* (September-October 1982): 74–87; Joan Riviere, "Womanliness as a Masquerade," *Formations of Fantasy,* ed. Victor Burgin et al. (London, 1986 [1929]), 35–44; and Claire Johnston, "Feminist Politics and Film History," *Screen* 16 (Autumn 1975): 115–24.

11  "Love Secrets That Keep the Magic in Dolly's Marriage," *The Star,* 27 November 1990, 12.

12  For example, regarding the emphasis on family and traditional rural values in much of the popular discourse about Parton, Ken Tucker notes that "the invocation of family is an emotional button that country stars like to push—it seems to produce instant sympathy among tradition-minded fans." See his "9 to 5: How Willie Nelson and Dolly Parton Qualified for 'Lifestyles of the Rich and Famous,'" in Kingsbury, ed., *Country,* 386.

13  Jahr, "Golly, Dolly!" 85, 139.

14  Jack Hurst, "You've Come a Long Way, Dolly," *High Fidelity* (December 1977): 122.

15  Tucker, "9 to 5," 383.

16  Roy Blount, Jr., "Country's Angels," *Esquire* (March 1977): 131.

17  Lawrence Grobel, "Dolly Parton: A Candid Conversation with the Curvaceous Queen of Country Music," *Playboy* (October 1978): 82.

18  Ibid.

19  Pete Axthelm, "Hello Dolly," *Newsweek,* 13 June 1977, 71.

20  See Dyer, *Stars,* on "ordinariness" as an important aspect of star-image construction, especially among women (49–50).

21  Jahr, "Golly, Dolly!" 142.

22  Cindy Adams, "Dolly's Dazzling Comeback," *Ladies' Home Journal* (March 1984): 153; Nancy Anderson, "Dolly Parton: A Home Town Report," *Good Housekeeping* (February 1988): 186; and Mary-Ann Bendel, "A Different Dolly," *Ladies' Home Journal* (November 1987): 120.

23  Adams, "Dolly's Dazzling Comeback," 153.

24  Joyce Maynard, "Dolly," *Good Housekeeping* (September 1977): 60.

25  Bendel, "Different Dolly," 182.

26  Bufwack and Oermann, *Finding Her Voice,* 7.

27  Gary Graham, "Dolly Parton to Adopt Baby," *The Star,* 14 April 1989, 6.

28  See Charles Leehrsen, "Here She Comes, Again," *Newsweek,* 23 November 1987, 73–74; see also Hurst, "You've Come a Long Way," 122; Grobel, "Candid Conversation," 108; and Alanna Nash, "Dollywood: A Serious Business," *Ms.* (July 1986): 12–14.

29  I use the term "ethnicity" in the anthropological sense established by Barth and

by de Vos and Romanucci-Ross, that is, as referring to cultural groups within a pluralistic and hegemonic society who define themselves (through a perception of common origins or common beliefs and values) as culturally distinct from the dominant group and who use a variety of mechanisms to maintain symbolic boundaries and delineations from other groups. In this sense, I perceive Southern Appalachian culture to be one of regional ethnicity, but I do not perceive "Southernness," as an external construction of regionality, to be a kind of ethnicity in itself, although it incorporates many. See Fredrik Barth, *Ethnic Groups and Boundaries* (Boston, 1969); and *Ethnic Identity: Cultural Continuities and Change,* ed. George De Vos and Lola Romanucci-Ross (Palo Alto, 1975).

30　In the working-class South, the races (white, black, and American Indian) have lived in relative isolation from each other, maintaining fairly separate but parallel cultures. The black population in the Appalachian region has always been much smaller than that of the lowland South, according to Phillip J. Obermiller and William W. Philliber, *Too Few Tomorrows: Urban Appalachians in the 1980's* (Boone, NC, 1987), 11. For useful overviews of Southern cultural issues, see Carole Hill, "Anthropological Studies in the American South: Review and Directions," *Current Anthropology* 18 (1987): 309–26; Marion Pearsall, "Cultures of the American South," *Anthropological Quarterly* 39 (1966): 476–87; and John S. Reed, *The Enduring South: Subcultural Persistence in Mass Society* (Chapel Hill, 1974).

31　Relevant works on the Southern Appalachian culture of Parton's region include John C. Campbell's 1921 classic, *The Southern Highlander and His Homeland* (Lexington, 1969 [1921]); *Appalachian Ways: A Guide to the Historic Mountain Heart of the East,* ed. Jill Durrance and William Shamblin (Washington, DC, 1976); Elmora Messer Matthews, *Neighbor and Kin: Life in a Tennessee Ridge Community* (Nashville, 1965); and Jack Weller, *Yesterday's People: Life in Contemporary Appalachia* (Lexington, 1965). For insights into the culture of Southern and Appalachian women, see Margaret Jarman Hagood, *Mothers of the South: Portraiture of the White Tenant Farm Woman* (New York, 1977 [1939]); and Pamela Wilson, "Keeping the Record Straight: Conversational Storytelling and Gender Roles in a Southern Appalachian Community" (Master's thesis, University of Texas at Austin, 1984). Obermiller and Philliber, *Too Few Tomorrows,* also provide insights into Appalachian ethnicity.

32　With this century's increasing economic dependence upon industry and the corresponding breakdown of the agricultural economy, many farmworkers have been integrated into the dominant capitalist system as part of the working class and now tend to fill that slot in the social and economic structure (although it is important to point out that this rural working-class society exhibits characteristics that are quite different from those of an urban/industrial working-class society). In addition, as Obermiller and Philliber report in *Too Few Tomorrows,* from 1940 through 1970, over three million people migrated from the Southern Appalachian region to industrial urban centers in the Midwest (primarily Cincinnati, Detroit, and Chicago) to find work as unskilled laborers; some returned after a few years, but many stayed and created cultural ghettos of Appalachian people in these cities.

33 My understanding of Gramsci is based on the interpretations of Anne Showstack Sassoon, as well as on the neo-Gramscian interpretations of Raymond Williams, John Fiske, and Dick Hebdige. See Sassoon, *Gramsci's Politics* (Minneapolis, 1987); Williams, *Marxism and Literature* (Oxford, 1977); Fiske, *Television Culture* (London, 1987); and Hebdige, *Subculture: The Meaning of Style* (London, 1979).

34 Antonio Gramsci, *Selections from the Prison Notebooks,* ed. and trans. Quintin Hoare and Geoffrey Nowell Smith (London, 1971), 14.

35 Sassoon, *Gramsci's Politics,* 144.

36 Parton's family history and the photographs that visually document her rags-to-riches story feature prominently in women's magazine articles (see, e.g., Anderson, "Home Town Report"; and Jahr, "Golly, Dolly!"). Grobel's 1978 *Playboy* interview also extensively investigates the details of Parton's life growing up, and the two articles in *Ms.* (by Nash and by Steinem) focus on the rootedness of Parton's life and image in her region and hometown community. See also Willadeene Parton, "My Sister, Dolly Parton," *McCall's* (July 1985): 74–125; and Connie Berman, "Dolly Parton Scrapbook," *Good Housekeeping* (February 1979): 140–43, 203–9.

37 Grobel, "Candid Conversation," 88, 102.

38 Ibid., 88.

39 On the predominance of working-class and female consumers in the composition of country music audiences, as well as the prevalence of working-class backgrounds among country music performers, see Mary A. Bufwack and Robert K. Oermann, "Women in Country Music," in *Popular Culture in America,* ed. Paul Buhle (Minneapolis, 1987), 91–101.

40 On the folk origins of country music, see Hurst, "You've Come a Long Way," 123. He traces Parton's musical style to the convergence of three components: (1) Elizabethan ballads preserved for centuries by isolated Appalachian mountaineers; (2) the wildly emotional religious music of Protestant fundamentalist churches; and (3) the country music on early 1950s radio.

41 Carr, "Changing Image," 484.

42 Ibid.; see also George Lipsitz, *Time Passages* (Minneapolis, 1990), esp. 99–160; and Bufwack and Oermann's "Women in Country Music."

43 This is particularly true of country music videos; see Mark Fenster, "Country Music Video," *Popular Music* 7 (1988): 285–302.

44 Williams, *Marxism and Literature,* 122.

45 Ibid., 123.

46 Jahr, "Golly, Dolly!" 85; Kingsbury, ed., *Country,* 258; and Bendel, "Different Dolly," 182.

47 Carr, "Changing Image," 494.

48 Steinem, "Dolly Parton," 66.

49   Willadeene Parton, in "My Sister," 125, tells of vacations that all the women of the Parton family take together each year ("It's so secret that not even our husbands and children know what we do"), and she articulates the patriarchal myth: "For the first years of their life together, we were sorry for Mother because Papa's word was law; and the last years, we were sorry for Papa because Mother keeps breaking the law."

50   Michel de Certeau, *The Practice of Everyday Life,* trans. Steven Rendell (Berkeley, 1984), 30.

51   Bufwack and Oermann, *Finding Her Voice,* 320–21. The lines from "Eagle When She Flies" that seem particularly relevant in this context are as follows:

> She's been there. God knows, she's been there.
> She has seen and done it all.
> She's a woman. She knows how to dish it out or take it all.
>
> . . . . .
>
> She's a lover, she's a mother, she's a friend and she's a wife.
>
> . . . . .
>
> Gentle as the sweet magnolia, strong as steel, her faith and pride.
> She's an everlasting shoulder, she's the leaning post of life.
>
> . . . . .
>
> And she's a sparrow when she's broken,
> But she's an eagle when she flies.

(For recording information, see Selected Discography.)

52   Grobel, "Candid Conversation," 110.

53   Susan McHenry, "Positively Parton," *Ms.* (July 1986): 14.

54   Grobel, "Candid Conversation," 82.

55   On Parton's tenacious control over her own business affairs, see Noel Coppage, "Dolly," *Stereo Review* (September 1979): 82–84; Scott Isler, "Where Town Meets Country," *Crawdaddy* (February 1978): 74; Karen Jaehne, "CEO and Cinderella: An Interview with Dolly Parton," *Cineaste* 17 (1990): 16–19; and Leehrsen, "Here She Comes," 73–74.

56   Hurst, "You've Come a Long Way," 124.

57   Quoted in Bufwack and Oermann, *Finding Her Voice,* 429.

58   Gramsci, *Prison Notebooks,* 418.

# Keeping Faith

*Evangelical Performance in Country Music*

♦🎼 ————————————————————————— **Curtis W. Ellison**

It's Saturday night at the *Grand Ole Opry* in Nashville, Tennessee. The date is 22 January 1994, and country music fans, artists, family, friends, and well-wishers are gathered to honor Hal Ketchum. *Opry* star Bill Anderson tells his cable television audience there are so many floral arrangements backstage that it smells like a flower shop. Ketchum has said that he's "scared to death," but is having fun visiting with friends and family who have flown in from around the country. Hal's father, who introduced him to country music, has left his hospital bed to be present. Frank Ketchum will die of cancer on 18 February, but tonight he's here to see his 41-year-old son inducted as the 71st living act of the *Grand Ole Opry*.

At 7:30 P.M. (CST), the *Opry* goes live on The Nashville Network (TNN). Hillbilly rocker Marty Stuart—decked out in a glittering black and white jacket and blue jeans with riding chaps—is tonight's host. He begins the induction with a comment meant to illustrate the special character of the moment:

> When you grow up singing country music, the ultimate milestone is to become a member of the *Grand Ole Opry*. And if you're just gonna have to get inducted, there's one man that can do it probably better'n anybody in this world. And it's kinda like gettin' married by the right preacher— you know it took. And you know it took when this guy does it.[1]

The performer who now comes forward wears his signature fire-engine-red rhinestone suit and large cowboy hat. Only two acts performing in 1994 have been here longer than Little Jimmy Dickens, a member of the *Opry* for forty-six years. Dickens politely thanks the assembled fans and artists, then introduces

Ketchum by reading from Hal's autobiographical poem, written for tonight, about the influence of country entertainers on him:

> My father brought these people home,
> One by one,
> And they all stayed.
> They told me even then
> That I was welcome,
> They knew I understood.
> A thousand souls and singers
> Have beckoned me to this
> Hallowed place,
> And tho' some would say
> I've come a long way,
> I would say simply
> That tonight, I arrive.[2]

Dickens reads with considerable gravity, then solemnly announces: "Ladies and gentlemen, the newest member of the *Grand Ole Opry* family is Mr. Hal Ketchum!"

As Ketchum strides vigorously on stage with his acoustic guitar, shaking his thick mane of steel-gray hair and dressed in black jeans, black shirt, and a sparkling black, fitted jacket, the packed house rises to a standing ovation and Ketchum's younger fans, particularly the women, scream. He walks straight to center stage and formally shakes hands, first with Jimmy Dickens, then with Marty Stuart. Moving onto the stage extension that juts out into the audience, he bows formally from the waist, then turns to the microphone. Ketchum's first words are "God bless you, one and all. Thank you." Then he tilts his head far back, yells a sharp "Owoo!," leans into the microphone, and begins Ferlin Husky's 1960 hit, "On the Wings of a Dove."

Written in 1959 by Bob Ferguson, this was a song that Husky had difficulty recording for the secular market because of its overtly religious content. Yet, by 1994, Husky claimed there were over 400 cover recordings of the original. Ferguson based "On the Wings of a Dove" on the scriptural account of the aftermath of Jesus' baptism, when a dove was sent to earth as a sign of God's love. In the song, the image of a dove is a reminder that God does not forget ordinary people during hard times, "when troubles surround us" and "the spirit grows numb." After this opening rendition, Ketchum gestures toward stage right and gently says, "Mr. Ferlin Husky." Husky himself then strides eagerly to Ketchum's side, and together the 68-year-old star and the *Opry's*

Figure 1. Hal Ketchum (l) and Ferlin Husky (r) on the *Grand Ole Opry,* 22 January 1994. Photograph by Gary Layda. Courtesy of Gaylord Entertainment.

newest member sing the refrain: "He sends His pure, sweet love / A sign from above on the wings of a dove."[3] For the second verse, Ketchum stands back respectfully while Husky performs alone, but continues to play a guitar accompaniment and, near the end, adds vocal harmony. When Ketchum again takes the lead, Husky raises his hands toward the fans in a gesture of tribute, and the television camera cuts to a young woman in the audience, singing ardently along with the second chorus. By the third verse the camera is panning the audience, where female fans are crying as Ketchum solos and Husky waves to the crowd, urging them to sing along. During the final chorus, fans gaze in awe at the stage, swaying back and forth, and singing in unison with Hal Ketchum as Ferlin Husky signals the crowd-rousing finale by taking the song's last line up an octave. Then the two country singers embrace warmly, Marty Stuart reclaims center stage, and a long ovation rolls (Figure 1).

Later in this same *Grand Ole Opry* segment, reigning Country Music Association Entertainer of the Year Vince Gill praises Hal Ketchum's behavior at the moment of his induction: "What meant more to me than anything is he had enough respect for where he learned how to do what he does, and that showed me an awful lot about Hal Ketchum." Fans immediately greet this compliment with loud applause. When Ketchum returns to sing his own hit, "Small Town Saturday Night," Marty Stuart comments that he has become a member of one of the most exclusive fraternities in the world. An unidentified fan immediately calls out, "He's worth it," and Stuart, turning to the fan, replies, "He *is* worth it."

Hal Ketchum is the twelfth singing star to become a member of the *Grand Ole Opry* since Garth Brooks was inducted in 1990. Ketchum's induction ceremony vividly exemplifies the confirmation ritual reserved for popular stars who have also demonstrated sincerity, worthiness, and fidelity to conventions of country music culture. Foremost among those conventions is paying active homage to a living past. Ketchum's confirmation has featured the touching of hands, the embracing of younger performers by older stars, and the presentation of the inductee to fans, who shower him with applause, compliments, and flowers. Another feature, the symbolic performance, here enacted in the Ketchum-Husky duet, is a literal representation of the presence of the past. Ketchum's chosen song exemplifies a basic theme of country music performance by invoking the transcendent power of heavenly love over earthly hard times to elicit an ecstatic response from fans. And this authentic moment of country music culture was witnessed by fans across the nation in prime time as it was broadcast from a multimillion-dollar entertainment and telecommunications complex that has become a leading example of American popular-music marketing in the 1990s.

COMMERCIAL COUNTRY MUSIC was launched during an intense period of modernization in the American South. It rapidly evolved from rustic radio programs of the mid-1920s through the marketing of regional recording artists to a national community of performers and fans unparalleled in other forms of popular music—a self-conscious entertainment community that shares a set of accumulated attitudes, values, traditions, gestures, and ritual/ceremonial events. The culture of country music is a complex phenomenon promoted aggressively by its business interests through print and electronic media, record companies, radio, film, network and cable television, and via festivals, theme parks, and other tourist attractions, yet for nearly seventy years this culture has maintained a distinctly personal tone and a strong focus on domestic social life. In the persistence of these values lies a striking irony: while the marketing of country music and its trappings has fully embraced the commercialism of modernity, the resulting popular-culture community functions as a means for imaginatively transcending modernity's negative effects.

In the everyday life of the country music community, its members behave something like a vast extended family at a never-ending church supper in a rural American small town. This suggests a sustained affection for tradition, perhaps as an antidote to the dislocations so pervasive among twentieth-century white Southerners and working-class Americans. While country music is probably best known to the uninitiated as an expression of heartbreak, hard times, and failed hopes, the music has in fact been a significant agent of social change through its lucrative entertainment, media, and tourist marketing. Because it has brought impressive fame and wealth to many informally trained performers, who were fans themselves before becoming inspirations to others dreaming of success, the country music business has itself become an object of romance. That romance feeds (and feeds on) an awareness of the past that links stars, musicians, business people, fans, and the music's interpreters in a still-evolving sense of community. True fans of country music tend either to ignore or, sometimes, to revel in the implicit irony of an entrepreneurial and increasingly complex entertainment business that is focused mainly on evocations of hard times, painful relationships, romantic love, religious salvation, or the music's own traditions. By virtue of their adulation of stars, their affection for country music events, sites, and shrines, and their identification with one another in organized groups, these fans essentially serve as agents of the culture, forgiving its sinners, adoring its saints, and keeping its traditions alive.

While these traditions look to the past, country music is also actively innovative, incorporating elements of other musical genres into both its vocal and its instrumental stylings. It blends these imported elements in musical formulas that are emotional narratives of romantic love, spiritual love, and loving relationships in family life. Country songs are dominated by stories of broken hearts and hard times, but this emphasis masks the culture's assumption that such traumas can be overcome. The public and private lives of major stars are regularly made into object lessons on that theme. Country stars provide fans with exemplary images of personal tragedy endured or spiritual salvation found, demonstrations of individual grit, lessons in handling the financial rewards of popular success, or living commentaries on gender relationships.

Fans show their deepest devotion to country music during live performances, especially when their stars actively evoke a sense of living in hard times and of transcending them. Hard times are usually expressed as financial strain or distress, marital discord, family problems, personal loneliness, or the undesirable conduct resulting from these, such as domestic violence. Whatever their cause, hard times in country music are typically presented as an individual's *personal* condition, which can best be relieved romantically or spiritually, rather than as an economic or social-class experience that might be addressed by collective political action. This emphasis on personal experience in country music parallels the emphasis on individual salvation in Protestant, especially evangelical, traditions. And just as salvation can follow sin, hard times in secular country music are accompanied by the implicit hope of escaping them.

Country music's dynamic shifts our attention from hard times to heaven, and singing stars are its central agents. Through countless elaborations upon traditional vocal and instrumental formulas, they affirm the possibility of finding better times in the rewards of romantic, familial, or spiritual love. The prospect of love is a given—always offered as an ultimate personal goal and frequently in contrast to deluded desires for wealth or social status. (In that respect, country music is a distant cousin to some genres of popular fiction, such as gothic novels, where intense lovers regularly triumph over the vividly depicted hardships of broken hearts and social maladies.)

The *Grand Ole Opry* is definitely an entertainment business, yet as country music's "Mother Church," it is also much more. The informality of its stage production combined with the professionalism of its stars, the sense of an extended family rooted in a historic enterprise, the vital bonding of fans and artists, and the honorific status of membership have been leading models for this music culture since the 1920s. The *Opry*'s warm sense of the past, like its cultivated rusticity, projects a congenial invention of tradition, an image of common values in a familiar time and place. To its fans the *Opry* is about fame and fortune, and it is about supporting people, feeling at home, being part of a family, and embracing spiritual values.

In 1992, Iris DeMent recorded a song that draws on these dimensions of country music. In "Mama's Opry," DeMent tells the story of her mother, who grew up in a farm community. As a child, her mother had listened to the Carter Family, to Jimmie Rodgers, and to the *Grand Ole Opry* on radio—and she had dreamed of singing on the *Opry* stage. As a child in turn, Iris sang along with gospel records played on her mother's phonograph. In 1992, she remembered those songs: "Sweet Rose of Sharon," "Abide with Me," "The Gospel Ship to Heaven's Jubilee," "I Don't Want to Get Adjusted to This World," and others. From the perspective of adulthood, DeMent saw that in singing gospel music she "was singin' in the grandest opry." "Mama's Opry" links DeMent's memory of her own and her family's past to the *Opry*'s spiritual tradition. *Infamous Angel*, the album carrying "Mama's Opry," concludes with the gospel number "Higher Ground." It features Flora Mae DeMent, Iris's mother, as lead vocalist. By moving from an artist's remembered image of family to the realization of her actual family through a shared gospel heritage, *Infamous Angel* literally enacts the spirit of the "Mother Church."

IN A DISCUSSION of Victorian-era American evangelism, historian Peter W. Williams describes an important reformulation of piety that occurred in the mid-nineteenth century. Although still characterized by the fear of a masculine, wrathful God that American popular religion owed to its Puritan antecedents, nineteenth-century Protestantism also reflected a new strategy for redeeming sinners that featured in such literary works of the period as *Uncle Tom's Cabin*. Here, says Williams, "redemption came about not through the active mastery of the external environment and the aggressive conquest of sin, but through a passive, exemplary role exerted by the saintly." The preaching of popular evangelist Dwight L. Moody exemplified this shift. Moody's theology, according to Williams, "could be reduced to the proposition that salvation was available for the asking. All that the sinner had to do was make a simple decision, symbolized in 'hitting the sawdust trail,'" to publicly demonstrate the desire for salvation. The theatrical form of an evangelical revival, to which Williams is alluding here, emphasized the direct, personal response of an individual to charismatic preaching, culminating in the act of walking forward into an area near the evangelist, where an emotional demonstration of the acceptance of redemptive love would occur. Moody was particularly effective because he spoke with sincerity to the everyday experiences of converts:

> Instead of theological reflections, Moody's sermons were anecdotal— usually pathetic stories invoking premature death, longing for mother, and a gentle Jesus whose message of redemption was open to all. Judgment was largely gone, and mercy was everything. Sentimentality—the appeal to the heart, even in contradiction to the dictates of the head— had been raised to an ultimate principle.

To emphasize the shift in gender orientation that accompanied this change, Williams adds: "And sentimentality was the province of woman."[4]

The exemplary piety at the heart of evangelical traditions is prominent in gospel music. Demonstrating piety is an important function of gospel singers, as they move the congregation toward an emotional display of faith in their personal salvation. In this way gospel singing invokes the tradition of Victorian-era evangelism by showcasing the role of the saintly person, here one whose songs often tell stories about life in a future heaven that will be a victory over current hard times in this world. Such direct references to the power of salvation are prolific in all forms of country music. The *Grand Ole Opry* has featured gospel singing prominently since its earliest days, and bluegrass music is replete with evangelical allusions. One of Hank Williams's signature songs was a work of personal testimony, "I Saw the Light," and Williams wrote twenty other gospel songs, for a total of 15 percent of his entire output as a songwriter.

In June 1993, TNN showcased 37-year-old country singer Mark Collie on its autobiographical series *Path to Stardom.* A native of Waynesboro, Tennessee, who has named Hank Williams, Jimmie Rodgers, John Lennon, Paul McCartney, Jerry Lee Lewis, Ray Charles, and Elvis Presley as figures he admires, Collie chose to focus his life story for the TNN audience on his spiritual values. The songwriter responsible for such phrases as "My baby did but now she don't, and if I don't say 'I do,' it's a safe bet that she won't," Collie said on TNN, "I had a difficult time as a young man trying to understand, to resolve what I was doing, because my relationship to God is important to me. It's the most important thing, I think, in the lives of all of us." *Path to Stardom* showed Mark Collie as a small-town boy who made good in an entertainment field requiring a lifestyle that is difficult for a diabetic, as Collie is. A vivid stage performer who can bring an audience to its feet with rockabilly renditions where he wriggles energetically in tight gold pants, Collie spoke softly on TNN of his inner faith: "I believe in a higher power. I believe we all need to be connected spiritually. . . . Music is a very supernatural thing." At the end of *Path to Stardom,* Collie is shown listening respectfully to 88-year-old Parker White playing "We Shall See the King Someday" on his dulcimer. They are seated in Russell's Chapel Church of Waynesboro, where Collie once played piano and where White has worked since 1932.

Established country stars often have a spiritual side that is well-known to their fans. One of seven children of a sharecropper family from Dyess, Arkansas, Johnny Cash, born in 1932, worked as a young man in a Detroit automobile plant before enlisting in the Air Force. While stationed in Germany, he learned to play the guitar and began to sing the country and gospel songs he had heard as a child. In 1955, Cash was working as an appliance salesman in Memphis, where he formed a gospel group and pitched the act to Sam Phillips at Sun Records. Phillips signed Cash, and, aided by the rise of such singers as Elvis Presley, Carl Perkins, Jerry Lee Lewis, and Charlie Rich, Cash hit the charts as a rockabilly artist. Then, in a pattern reminiscent of Hank Williams's career, Cash spent ten years on pills and in pursuit of personal destruction. Of this time in his life he would later say, "There is something important in worshipping together with other believers. And missing it left me vulnerable and easy prey for all the temptations and destructive vices that the backstage of the entertainment world has to offer." Cash was saved by June Carter, daughter of Mother

Maybelle and E. J. Carter, who took him on as a rehabilitation project. Cash said of her efforts, "June was never afraid of me, and she was serious about the battle she was waging against the pills. 'I'm just trying to help,' she'd say. 'God has His hand on you, and I'm going to try to help you become what you are whether you want me to or not.'" In 1968, Cash and Carter were married, and by the following year he was able to perform without drugs. A network television show followed, then Grammy awards, five CMA awards in 1969 alone, and a public commitment of his life to Christ. Cash went on to write his autobiography, *Man in Black,* and a novel about Jesus' disciple Paul, *Man in White.* His albums have included recordings made in prisons, social commentaries on the plight of Native Americans, and observations on war.[5]

Barbara Mandrell, a major country music star who has hosted a television series and is well-known for her recovery from an automobile accident (graphically depicted at her personal museum in Nashville), has also spoken frankly about her religious faith. She told Don Cusic that she was "saved" at the age of ten and grew up a Pentecostal Christian of no particular denominational affiliation. Mandrell believes that her success as a secular singer is related to her spiritual commitment:

> I really feel like if He meant for me to be totally in gospel music, that is where I would be. Because He doesn't pull any punches with me. Besides, I reach so many, many people, and I don't say this in any ugly way—I am just stating fact—that I would never reach if I were not a secular singer. Introducing a gospel song into a secular show has a larger strategy. . . . When I sing the gospel songs, they see something in my eyes that lets them know I mean what I'm singing about. I think that is why they turn to me.[6]

The gospel tradition likewise lends emotional force to one of Dolly Parton's most powerful songs, "Appalachian Memories," an autobiographical account of her family's attempt to migrate out of Appalachian poverty to a more economically secure life in the North. When she played the Fraze Pavilion in Kettering, Ohio, on 1 August 1993, Parton used "Appalachian Memories" as the penultimate production number within a quartet of autobiographical ballads. Comprising almost 20 percent of her twenty-song concert and performed about a third of the way through, this quartet, especially "Appalachian Memories," was a major production piece that established a dramatic context for the rest of her concert. Parton introduced the song by telling a story about her father. He was a hard-working farmer who never went to school and couldn't read or write. Told that he could "do better" in Detroit, he went there to look for work, but came home two weeks later, telling his family: "Whatever happens, I'm gonna live and die in these mountains." Parton wrote "Appalachian Memories" from her memory of her own loneliness after first leaving home. A ballad sung from the perspective of an Appalachian family living in the North, the song is framed by an opening and closing melancholy flute line supported by long violin strokes that create a wistful, nostalgic tone. The tempo of the song builds gradually from very slow to moderately slow through two verses, a chorus, then another verse and chorus, to a climactic finale. At the beginning, Parton's voice is accompanied solely by piano, played in a style distinctive to piano accompaniments in evangelical church services. As the song builds intensity, violins are added to provide fills, then to increase tension. The singer recounts how the family was told to go north because there, "fortune falls like snowflakes in your hands." We "hitched our station wagon to a star," she says, but instead of finding a promised land, the family found that life in the North meant "a struggle keepin' sight of who you are." The refrain evokes images of old folks back home and promises to "keep leaning on sweet Jesus" because "He'll love and guide and lead us." Evangelical faith and keeping faith with the past become one, as the last line of the refrain pointedly affirms: "Appalachian memories keep us strong."

By imaginatively confronting migrant loneliness with spiritual salvation, "Appalachian Memories" links the secular and sacred traditions in country music and builds on the culture's sense of the past. This might be regarded as a response to traumas of modernization, a response that has a parallel in regional religious expression more generally. In his study of Baptist traditions, *Giving Glory to God in Appalachia,* Howard Dorgan concludes that the worship practices of Appalachian evangelicals serve in part to create a usable sense of the past. "The past is terribly important to these fellowships. Their particular understanding of it has fostered their sense of certainty, of place, of belonging, of heritage, of an ongoing covenant. And the value of this past to them does not diminish with the encroachments of modernity—just the opposite, in fact."[7]

IF BEING SAVED by the evangelist's Jesus is an enduring subject of sacred country music, there is a parallel tradition in secular country music that also relies upon a salvation motif, but that replaces the love of Jesus with the love of women. This salvation theme—good women working tirelessly to save their men from the debilitations of domestic turmoil and a tragic troubadour's life—is central to many depictions of country music culture by novelists and Hollywood filmmakers. It's also likely that the romantic salvation motif has fueled the growth of a distinctive fan culture associated with country music.

No country singer has earned more fans than Elvis Presley. He came to high visibility in American popular culture via television, with a stage-performance style that bore some resemblance to the ecstatic displays of evangelical worship. Before television, that style had never been so widely and systematically disseminated to white middle-class youth, and it proved to be surprisingly attractive. Elvis Presley's debt to evangelical traditions also included the distinctive music that his performances showcased. At a famous jam session on Tuesday, 4 December 1956, at the Sun Records studio in Memphis, Presley was joined by Sam Phillips's three other most prominent rockabilly artists, Jerry Lee Lewis, Carl Perkins, and Johnny Cash. Performances recorded during that session were recently released as *Elvis Presley: The Million Dollar Quartet* (see Selected Discography). This impromptu encounter in the early days of rock & roll suggests that white gospel music, country music, and blues all contributed to its genesis. Yet the unequal representation of these three traditions on the album is striking: of the thirty-eight cuts, thirteen are clearly white gospel songs and ten are country (four of those bluegrass), thus amounting to more than half of all the songs performed during this session. At least nine cuts on *The Million Dollar Quartet* may be described as rock & roll, including four blues numbers and two covers of pop songs. Thomas Poole has pointed out that the "gospel set" takes up twenty-two of the album's fifty minutes.[8] In his liner notes for the album, Colin Escott describes the significance of this imbalance:

> The country roots ran deep but the true common ground for *The Million Dollar Quartet* was gospel music. Between songs there is inside chatter about white gospel groups such as the Statesmen Quartet, and one of Presley's first moves after he got a little recognition was to bring the Jordanaires into his entourage. He would warm up for every session with gospel music just as he does here. However, Presley's gospel recordings never captured the atmosphere of pure church as vividly as these performances. There was no need for rehearsal because the songs were so deeply embedded in all the participants; after one singer took the lead, the others instinctively knew where to follow.

When Sam Phillips felt a need to defend rock & roll from charges that it was inspired by Satan, he was able to point to the religious beliefs of his singers. "I dare say that there were never any 'infidels'—or agnostics even—that came in my studio," he said. "There was a deep-seated feeling for God, very much so, in probably every artist I ever worked with. Whether they knew how to express it in any way, they showed it to me in the way they did what they did."[9] Phillips probably did not have Elvis Presley's stage demeanor in mind here, but if one compares his body motions in early performances with those depicted in Randall Balmer's television documentary on evangelical religion, there are intriguing parallels. As shown in the Balmer film, Pentecostal services are characterized by ecstatic singing and by jerky or spasmodic bodily movements. These occur when participants experience what they describe as the Holy Spirit entering their bodies. Like rock & roll, this spirit crosses racial boundaries to attract both urban-black and rural-white working-class adherents.[10]

The documentary film *Elvis '56,* a close look at one year in Presley's career, examines the strong impact of Presley's body movements as displayed on national television.[11] Here we can see the "Hillbilly Cat" exhibiting a variety of bumps, grinds, pelvic vibrations, leg and body shakes, and spasmodic jerks of his head, punctuated by a sneering lip roll that is immediately followed by a smile and a widening of the eyes—all performed in time with the crisp, driving rhythm of his guitar accompaniment. It's clear that Presley is acting. While his body movements seem effortless and involuntary, like the uncontrollable movements of an ecstatic religious seizure, Presley clearly controls his performance and always brings each song to its finale with a winning smile and a bow to the audience. We might think of Elvis-on-stage as the novel persona that Presley created from elements of his religious heritage, a performance persona that a detractor might call a secular holy-roller.

In 1956, Presley was all the rage on television, playing the *Dorsey Brothers, Milton Berle, Steve Allen,* and *Ed Sullivan* (three times). Videos of these performances can be viewed at the Country Music Hall of Fame and Museum in Nashville, testifying to their revolutionary impact on American popular culture. For example, when Presley covered Big Mama Thornton's recording of "Hound Dog" on *The Milton Berle Show,* broadcast from Los Angeles on 5 June, 40 million viewers watched him deliver a series of powerfully suggestive sexual gestures, including what many regarded as phallic ones with the microphone stand. Dubbed by critics "Elvis the Pelvis" for this performance, Presley responded: "It's one of the most childish expressions I've ever heard." He described his stage act as a natural reaction to the music: "Rock and roll music, if you like it, if you feel it, you can't help but move to it. That's what happens to me. I mean I have to move around. I can't stand still. I've tried it, and I can't do it." Asked if he believed that his stage behavior contributed to juvenile delinquency, the non-smoking, non-drinking 21-year-old Elvis replied, "If someone saw me singing and dancing, I don't see how they could think that it would contribute to juvenile delinquency. If there's anything I've tried to do, I've tried to live a straight, clean life and not set any kind of bad example." Presley was filmed backstage during a rehearsal break for *The Steve Allen Show* on 28 June; as a national controversy over his television performance raged, Elvis sat himself down at a piano in a corner of a New York City television studio and began singing one of his favorite gospel songs.

Presley died unexpectedly in 1977, and fan devotion to his memory has become the object of considerable attention because it has continued to grow for almost two decades. The tenth anniversary of his death brought 15,000 people to the candlelight vigil at Presley's Graceland burial site, and 25,000 attended ceremonies marking the fifteenth anniversary in 1992. One critic has described the phenomenon of this fascination with the memory of Elvis as "a chronicle of cultural obsession." [12] Yet the most persuasive account of what Presley's fans may be feeling as they remember him is a small book published in 1992 by two younger fans, Cindy Hazen and Mike Freeman. *The Best of Elvis: Recollections of a Great Humanitarian* tells the story of a private Elvis—one who loved people and, without calculation, gave profusely of his personal wealth for their individual benefit (Figure 2). Beneath all the gaudy marketing that would later surround him, in his fans' view, Elvis maintained an inner life that was true to the spirit of the young performer seen both in *Elvis '56* and on his fan-initiated postage stamp. To his fans, he was a man of religious conviction and of deep feelings openly expressed, a sincere and sensitive man.[13]

IN THE LATE 1980s and early 1990s, female country singers increasingly recorded songs that challenged the "domestic turmoil" tradition of country music by raising expectations for male behavior. In Lorrie Morgan's recording of Beth Nielsen Chapman's "Five Minutes," for example, a woman tells her mate that he looks "disbelievin'" as she packs her bag and calls a taxi. "Lately you've forgotten what lovin' me's about," she sings, and "now you've got five minutes to figure it out." The couple's problems in "Five Minutes" seem to be boredom and a lack of communication. The singer implores her partner to talk to her, to tell her what she needs to hear, to ask her to stay, to be passionate, to kiss her. What she's asking for is personal commitment, "to show me that you're really sincere." Lorrie Morgan's song demanding commitment is part of a current trend among younger female singers who are giving voice to higher expectations for male behavior than country music has conventionally expressed. Michelle Wright's song "Take It Like A Man," showcased on the 1993 CBS television special "The Women of Country," delivers an unequivocal challenge to 1990s men. She introduced "Take It Like A Man" not as a "man-bashing song," but rather as "a guideline" (she said with an assertive smile) "for all you fellows out there." This song tells the story of a woman who wants both a lover *and* a friend in a romantic relationship. But the men she has encountered have all failed to meet her criteria, wanting a maid or a mother, too much or too little space. Yet the

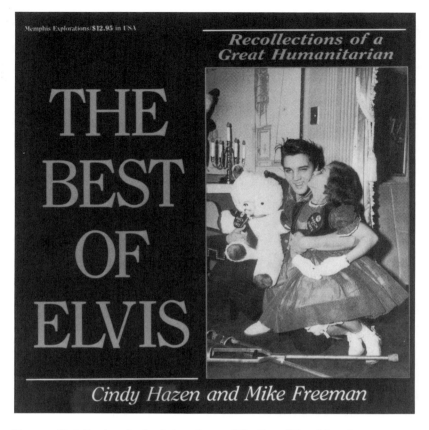

Memphis Explorations/$12.95 in USA

**Recollections of a
Great Humanitarian**

THE
BEST
OF
ELVIS

*Cindy Hazen and Mike Freeman*

Figure 2. Elvis Presley: the fans' view. Cover of *The Best of Elvis* (Memphis Explorations, 1992). Courtesy of Cindy Hazen and Mike Freeman.

song is not a lament. In an upbeat tone Wright issues a challenge and an invitation to someone who will "take it like a man, steady and strong," someone who will be true to his promises, someone who will be sincerely committed.

Some rising male stars of the nineties have taken up the challenge in song. John Michael Montgomery went to #1 on the *Billboard* Top Country and *Billboard* 200 charts in 1994 with an album featuring a song that earnestly pledges devotion, "I Swear." "You can be sure I know my part," he sings. "I'll make mistakes," but "I'll never break your heart." Montgomery's "I Swear" represents a trend in country music, where sensitive males devoted to women constitutes a leading masculine image in the 1990s. That trend was precipitated by the success of Garth Brooks and Vince Gill, but it had an earlier voice than theirs.

Early in the authorized biography of the late Conway Twitty, he describes his motivation for abandoning a successful career as a rock music performer in 1965. Twitty's managers, producers, and agents couldn't understand why a singer with a series of hits, including a #1 single on the pop music charts in 1958, would want to give up rock & roll in order to sing country music. "They kept bringing up the subject of money," Twitty said, "and I kept trying to tell them singing country meant a lot more to me than making money." [14] When he made the switch, Conway Twitty deliberately fashioned his new country image in order to appeal to women:

> I've understood that the way to develop an appeal was to aim at women as the primary audience. I knew it way back then, and almost every song I've ever written was created first of all with women in mind and anticipating how they were going to react. Second, and very close to that, most men want to say these things to women, but they just don't know how. They may end up expressing themselves all wrong, and not even knowing why or how they've hurt a woman's feelings. A lot of us men have made this mistake. [15]

One of Twitty's compositions, "Hello Darlin'," became the signature song of his effort to attract female fans by addressing them in songs that reflected the romantic experience of a sensitive man. Twitty used "Hello Darlin'" as a show opener, beginning the song offstage with house lights down, then slowly walking out on stage to a crescendo of applause. And he stayed with his successful formula of sensitive-man love songs as a way to build fan trust.

> Women understand why and how I select the songs I do. They reach a point where they trust me to deal with their feelings and emotions. That confidence takes a long time to develop, for one reason because women need time to reach the point where they can trust you to be able to deal with the emotions they go through. It may take years. [16]

For more than twenty years in "a world of tight-lipped macho American males," Conway Twitty stood apart, presenting himself as "powerful, communicative, and daring to reveal his vulnerable side to a woman." He did this almost entirely in his concerts and hit records; Twitty avoided both television and awards shows, fearing that they would blunt the live stage effect of his cultivated persona. When Twitty appeared at Cincinnati Gardens on 21 March 1992, his show, which was opened by George Jones and Lorrie Morgan, attracted 16,000 fans. The audience was heavily female; in the two sections nearest my own seat, 122 of the 181 seats were taken by female fans whose average age I estimated to be over forty-five. In my own section, 127 of the 173 fans were female. The youngest fans visible appeared to be of high school age, but there were far more who seemed to be retired couples or grandmotherly women. Unlike the dress typically worn for concerts by younger country stars, this audience sported very little cowboy clothing, although many were dressed casually in T-shirts and bluejeans. The men in this audience had "haircuts," not "stylecuts," and many women seemed to have had "home perms." The crowd was quiet and orderly, indulged in modest drinking and smoking, and observed the sign for no alcohol inside the arena. There was little "dating" behavior.

The billing order for this concert was Jones, then Morgan, and Twitty as headliner, with an intermission between each act. At the end of the second intermission, the house went dark and a spotlight hit a sparkling ball that began to revolve just above and in front of the stage. Offstage, Conway Twitty began to sing the opening words of "It's Only Make Believe," then paused for an announcer's dramatic introduction: "One of the best friends a song ever had, please make welcome Conway Twitty!" As the announcer drew out the syllables of Twitty's name, a long drum roll began, the sparkling ball threw confetti-like light over the crowd, smoke spread across the stage, and Twitty walked from stage left into a blue light that shifted to a white spotlight as he began the opening words of "Hello Darlin'." The crowd rose to its feet in unison, cheering ecstatically. Twitty was dressed in a dark blue suit, black patent leather shoes, and a pink, high-necked satin shirt decorated with a single jewel at the throat. Spotlighted against a dark background, Conway Twitty impressively fulfilled his image as "the high priest of country music." Twitty stood alone on stage, holding a hand mike during "Hello Darlin'," while a mob of camera-clicking fans streamed forward in an orderly line to capture the moment on film, as others remained standing or sat on the edges of their seats.

At the end of his first song, Twitty nodded politely, with a soft "thank you," and the band promptly hit a fast beat as Twitty picked up a small electric guitar to open a medley of hits with "Boogie Grass Band." Twitty's next five numbers were "sensitive man" love songs, including "I'd Love to Lay You Down," in which a man propositions his wife; "Tight Fittin' Jeans," a commentary on the dalliance of an upper-class woman in a workingman's world; and "Desperado Love," a pledge of romantic commitment. The songs in this set were performed in a rapid, back-to-back arrangement, highlighting key lines from hits, with Twitty accompanying himself on guitar and introducing some understated body language. Then, at the set's end, the stage went black. When the lights came up again, Twitty was standing center stage, his guitar replaced by a hand mike, his right knee slightly bent in a partial genuflection. His pose suggested intense concentration, as he prepared for the eighth, and centerpiece, song of his concert. A slow production number in which the emotional intensity builds, "Good-bye Time" sets a tone of resignation at the dissolution of a long marriage. The song begins with gentle questions: "How can you walk away?" "Don't I matter anymore?" And then, an emotional shrug: "Well, it's been fun. What else can I say?" The refrain plaintively alludes to the marketplace of emotions: "If being free's worth what you leave behind," Twitty says, "then it's good-bye time." This song proceeds through a range of moods, from quiet questioning to painful wailing, drawing the listener in. Twitty's delivery was intense, and, at the song's conclusion, he made a finger-pointing gesture, with his right hand moving rhythmically up and down in a manner resembling a blessing of the multitudes, before uttering a polite "thank you."

The next six songs continued to elaborate "Good-bye Time"'s slow-tempo mood of sincerity in romantic relationships. "Crazy in Love" reminisces about a time when the romance was more alive in a couple's relationship. "Who Did They Think He Was?" is a song with a gospel tint that jointly memorializes Elvis Presley, John F. Kennedy, and Jesus Christ. Twitty's latest single at the time of the concert, this song questions the enigma of hero worship, but doesn't dismiss its significance. At the end, Twitty addressed his fans briefly, the only time during this concert when he did so. "Isn't that a pretty song?" he asked. "If you like it, when you get back to wherever it is that you came from, call your local radio station and tell 'em you like it, and sock it to 'em one time for ol' Conway." This set ended with one verse and the chorus of "Slow Hand." A slightly up-tempo number, "Slow Hand" is a good example of the double meanings that can often be found in Twitty's songs. The refrain, "when it comes to love, you want a slow hand," is both sexually suggestive and connotes attentiveness. At the end of "Slow Hand," Twitty again made his blessing gesture, then the auditorium was blacked out entirely.

When the light returned, it was a soft red spotlight shining directly down on Twitty, who was seated on a stool at center stage in preparation for the theological statement of the show, his cover of "The Rose." "The Rose" was originally a pop hit, recorded by Bette Midler for the sound track of the film that was based on the career of Janis Joplin. For Conway Twitty, "The Rose" offered an extended commentary on the power of love, depicted here as a gentle force of nature that will overcome loneliness and counter those moments when "the road has been too long." It was also an opportunity for theatrical display by Twitty. With the entire Cincinnati Gardens audience in a state of eerie silence as he began the song, Twitty spoke the first two verses in a slowly building, rumbling growl, with several hesitations and long pauses. As he gained intensity and his voice became louder, members of the audience responded to the intensifying mood with spontaneous yells and screams. When Twitty reverted abruptly to a softer delivery for the second verse, the audience responded by becoming totally silent. Then, as he built up vocal power again, his louder growls provoked more screams. By the end of the song, couples in the audience were hugging and crying, many hands were raised in a gesture reminiscent of praise responses during evangelical services, and the clapping, shouting, and screaming of other fans urged Twitty on to a more emotional vocal intensity. Although lighters were prohibited at the Cincinnati Gardens, when Twitty reached this same point during concerts at Hara Arena in Dayton thousands of butane lighters flared and were held aloft in a quasi-religious candle-lighting act of emotional communion.

By the end of "The Rose," his fans were fully engaged, and Twitty gave them three more songs. "That's My Job" focuses on warmth and nurturing in a father-son relationship, while "You've Never Been This Far Before" is another song with double meanings that alludes either to adultery or, as Twitty explained elsewhere, to unrequited love:

> The lyrics are really about a woman who's married, and you in the song have admired her for years. It's an off-limits situation. She doesn't love her husband and she's outside the boundaries of her marriage for the first time. And that's what the line means, 'You've never been this far before.' Now she's with you, this woman you've admired, and simply holding her hand has been a forbidden thing. And that's what the words really mean— not something dirty or risqué. The implication is just like putting your arm around her. Women are sensitive like that and they understood that line.[17]

For his final number, Twitty returned to his opening song and completed his rendition of "It's Only Make Believe." Here, he was bringing the image of Conway Twitty to full visibility, framing his entire concert with a comment on its character as an entertaining artifice and revealing himself to fans as a conscious showman within the show itself. Fans loved it. While spotlights scanned the crowd, Twitty again made his finger-pointing gesture, waved to the floor, to the bleachers on each side and in the back, gave a nod of appreciation, and slowly walked off stage. The show had been carefully constructed theater, performed through a sequence of songs serving as statements, and no encore was planned or expected. As the announcer asked for one more round of applause for Conway's band, the Twittybirds, the lights came up and the crowd—now that the experience was over, amazingly subdued by comparison with their prior ecstatic demonstration—filed out of the hall in an orderly way.

VINCE GILL HAS ACKNOWLEDGED the importance of Conway Twitty to male singers of the 1990s who subscribe to the notion of sensitive masculinity, and Gill himself has elaborated that image by fashioning a public persona of the road musician as caring husband, friend, and benefactor of the music business. Born in Norman, Oklahoma, in 1957, Gill played bluegrass music with a variety of groups before signing a recording contract as a solo artist with MCA Records in 1984. By 1985, two of his singles had made the Top 10, and in 1990 "When I Call Your Name" hit #1. The following year Gill joined the *Grand Ole Opry*. His national visibility has grown substantially as a result of his appearances on televised music awards programs, where his self-effacing manner, boyish good looks, and aura of personal sincerity have proved highly appealing.

At the June 1993 fan-voted TNN/*Music City News* Country Awards ceremonies, targeted to country music fans and broadcast on the TNN cable network, Gill received his third Instrumentalist of the Year award. In an unrehearsed moment of generosity and gratitude, Gill called John Hughey, now a steel guitarist with Gill's band, to the stage and gave him the award in honor of Hughey's years of performance with Conway Twitty. During that same program Gill received the Minnie Pearl Award in recognition of his humanitarian efforts on behalf of various charitable causes supported by the country music community. Upon receiving that award Gill cried openly, and as the camera panned the assembled stars and music business figures in the audience, many appeared to weep with him. Gill's most important awards-show moment, in terms of his image as a caring husband, occurred in March 1993 at the *Music City News* Country Songwriters Awards. Readers of *Music City News* chose "I Still Believe In You" by Vince Gill and John Barlow Jarvis as Song of the Year. In the course of the evening Gill, dressed in a conservative dark suit, white shirt, and tie, appeared on stage several times, and each time he did so, he commented on his marriage. "Sometimes what I'm doing takes me away from Janis and our daughter, Jenny. It's really tough," Gill said. At another point, he described how "I Still Believe In You" came to be written—he went directly to a songwriting session after "probably the worst fight of our thirteen-year marriage." During his acceptance speech for the Song of the Year honors, Gill again cried. This time he invited his wife, Janis Gill (of Sweethearts of the Rodeo), who was also crying—to join him on stage, where, before the entire viewing audience, Gill presented her with the award. Noting that she was an entertainer, too, and that female performers were, in his opinion, notably absent from music awards shows, he said: "There is no better inspiration than my wife. She's done this for a long time. She's a good songwriter, too. So, Honey, I'm giving this to you." [18] By this gesture Gill effectively endorsed the stance of assertive female country singers who expect men to pay serious attention to the needs of women. And by commenting publicly on the music industry's resistance to recognizing the achievements of female artists, he positioned himself as the colleague of a long line of successful women.

On 20 March 1993, Mary Chapin Carpenter and Vince Gill appeared in concert at Hara Arena in Dayton, Ohio. Carpenter was the opening act. She played a one-hour set that, in this traditional, working-class venue, did not emphasize her political views. For her encore of "Party Doll," she leaped from the stage to mug with fans on the floor, and, picking out a large young guard, sang to him, then, to the delight of fans, kissed him forcefully on the mouth. Gill's set picked up the "party" mood set by Mary Chapin Carpenter, with mostly fast numbers emphasizing instrumental virtuosity and frequently showcasing John Hughey on steel guitar. Gill stood front-and-center stage, with seven players in a crescent arc behind him. His stage manner was animated, yet he did not rely on such theatrical effects as dramatic movements across the stage, smoke machines, or elaborate lighting. During his uninterrupted two-hour set, Gill played twenty songs in a snappy, back-to-back style reminiscent of Conway Twitty. His concluding number was the signature song "I Still Believe In You."

For this moment, the house, which had been highly raucous during previous numbers that featured Gill's guitar playing, fell silent, and a sea of lighters flared. Gill chose a single white rose from the array of flowers brought to the stage and inserted it in his guitar strings. On the second chorus, Gill said gently to his fans, "Y'all sing it for us now; come on, one more time, everybody, come on." The song itself is a confession by a musician who recognizes his failure to give proper attention to his spouse and who asks for a chance to make amends. He's been thinking only of himself, but now says, "For all the times I've hurt you, I apologize." As fans at Hara Arena sang along softly with Gill on the refrain, he spoke again, verbally paralleling Conway Twitty's gesture of blessing: "This is for Margaret and Vesy," he said. "May it heal all your pain. God bless you." After four repetitions of the chorus of "I Still Believe In You," with the sold-out crowd singing along, Gill received a standing ovation. Then, waving gently, he said, "Good night, thank you," and left the stage.

AT THE END of the first third of his 1993 show at Hara Arena, Vince Gill told his fans, "I got something real special now." He then brought his father on stage, with the introduction, "It's always special for me to come to Ohio because that's where my Dad lives. I've not forgotten where I learned these three chords. I want him to come out and do the one he first taught me." Then Gill's father, dressed in a black sport coat, gray slacks, a white shirt, and a tie, walked to center stage and sang the pop hit "When My Blue Moon Turns to Gold Again," while Gill stood slightly back to accompany him on guitar. At the end of this display of family feeling, Gill gave his father flowers in the midst of an ovation from his fans.

At the very moment when Gill was performing with his father to warm applause at Hara Arena, across town at the Ervin J. Nutter Center the "pop metal" band Def Leppard was rocking their audience of 9,123 fans with "a menacing rendition of 'Gods of War'" from their album *Hysteria*. During a heavy metal concert at Nutter Center three months later, the lead singer of Megadeath, Dave Mustaine, left the stage in fury after forty minutes of confrontation with fans that included "challenging one fan to a fight for flipping him the finger," trying to goad "a girl down front into exposing her breasts to the crowd, belittling her when she refused," and berating fans "for shouting out requests." This four-hour event, which also featured the bands Pantera and White Zombie, included such Megadeath numbers as "Angry Again," "My Darkest Hour," and "Symphony of Destruction." [19]

As the American pop music scene of the early nineties fragmented into diverse tones, Garth Brooks took up the challenge issued by country music women to demonstrate a more sensitive masculinity, projecting himself as a devoted family man who deeply identified with white, middle-class social concerns. In his commitment to a music of "message," Brooks did not shrink from cultural politics. In six albums released between 1989 and early 1994 and in numerous appearances on cable and network television as well as in interviews in the print media, Brooks embraced the causes of hungry children, exploited fans, homosexuality, war, the environment, domestic violence, foreclosures, civil rights, and date rape. In early September 1992, when Brooks had sold 21 million albums and was releasing two new ones, he told a reporter for the *New York Times* that "We Shall Be Free," the lead single from one of those albums, was a song about "family values." Then he explained:

> I think the Republicans' big problem is that they believe family values are June and Walt and 2.3 children. To me it means laughing, being able to dream. It means that if a set of parents are black and white, or two people of the same sex, or if one man or one woman acts as the parent, that the children grow up happy and healthy: that's what family values are.

Brooks also pointed out that one dollar from the sale of each CD of his Christmas album would be donated to Feed the Children, a group that "specializes in helping to fight poverty and starvation in the United States." The *Times* reported that "at some of Mr. Brooks' shows he has the charity collect canned goods to distribute locally" because, to Brooks, "it's an effective way to have people think of what's going on: to get involved."[20]

A massive wave of publicity launched Brooks as a popular-culture icon. It penetrated all segments of American electronic and print media and was particularly pervasive in sources targeted to white, working- and middle-class families. One of the ways in which Brooks was promoted was as a sensitive man. A 1993 biography written for fans by Rick Mitchell established this image in its opening pages by quoting Brooks on his father:

> If I could wrap my Dad up in two words, it would be thundering tenderness. He's a man with the shortest temper I ever saw, and at the same time he's got the biggest heart. Some of the greatest conflicts are not between two people but between one person and himself. He knows what's right and he doesn't have any tolerance for what isn't right but at the same time he is so forgiving. I learned from him that you gotta be thankful for what you got and treat people like you want to be treated.[21]

"Thundering tenderness" might also aptly describe the impression Garth Brooks hoped to make on American popular culture. Edward Morris's 1993 biography presents a chronology of Brooks's achievements that centers on family experiences. Among the major events of his thirty-three years are his birth on 7 February 1962 in Tulsa, Oklahoma; getting a banjo for his sixteenth birthday; graduating from high school; listening to George Strait in 1981 and deciding to become a country singer; winning a talent show in college at Oklahoma State University; making a one-day trip to Nashville in 1985; and marrying Sandy Mahl on 24 May 1986. At this point in the chronology, the significant events selected by Morris shift to music industry activities: Brooks's second attempt to get a recording contract in Nashville; the agreement (on a handshake) to record for Capitol Records after a performance at Nashville's Bluebird Cafe in 1988; making the video of "The Dance" in 1990, when he also won the CMA Horizon Award and released the breakthrough hit, "Friends in Low Places"; publicity surrounding the TNN ban on the video of "The Thunder Rolls"; 1991 and 1992 CMA awards; a 1992 Grammy for *Ropin' the Wind;* and being selected by *Entertainment Weekly* as America's favorite male singer.[22]

Morris's account of Brooks's career includes a story about Brooks's handling of domestic turmoil. In 1989, while Brooks was touring, Sandy Brooks learned "that Garth was cheating on her." On 4 November she telephoned her husband and issued an ultimatum demanding faithfulness. Her bags were packed, she allegedly told him, and his choice was "my way or the highway." The next day, while performing in Cape Girardeau, Missouri, Brooks allegedly broke down on stage as he was singing "If Tomorrow Never Comes"—a song he wrote to express his love for Sandy. Brooks has said that, at the end of the concert, an unidentified fan called out, "Go home to her, Garth." He did.[23]

Soon, stories that Sandy was pregnant began to appear in the press. Garth's baby-boomer fans who had delayed their own childbearing were able to follow every detail of the pregnancy's impact on the Brooks family, including Brooks's failure to appear at the 1992 American Music Awards ceremonies (when he won the awards for Best Country Male Performer, Best Country Album, and Best Country Single) because Sandy Brooks had been hospitalized to prevent a miscarriage. Vince Gill's public affirmation of male sensitivity and commitment to his marriage happened on cable television during an awards show, but Garth Brooks got more attention. His declarations of sensitive masculinity were so enhanced by media attention that his entire nuclear-family life developed under the watchful gaze of national television, radio, and print media.

In 1992, Garth Brooks appeared in fan publications, financial magazines, music business magazines, tabloids, and on the covers of *Time, Life,* and the *Saturday Evening Post.* The latter three were particularly aimed at the middle-class "family" market, and here Brooks stressed his sensitivity. He told Marjie McGraw of the *Saturday Evening Post* that meaning in his music was more important to him than showmanship. "It has to mean something to me," he said. "I would rather have one song that was from the heart than 80 songs that were clever and went to No. 1 on the charts. If I get a song that I feel is on a parallel from my heart to yours, instead of coming from my mouth to your ears . . . then I think I've got something." Brooks also emphasized the richness of his family life. He stayed off the road during the latter months of Sandy's pregnancy to "be a husband" to her. "I introduced myself to her and she introduced me to one of the neatest people I've ever met—I've been living with her for six years and didn't know her." All of his awards were hidden under the stairs in the basement, he said, because he didn't want the music business to intrude on his family life. "Our house is a house for loving, for fighting and making up, for learning, for screaming at each other, for laughing—it's not a house for music. Music has given us the house, music has given us the food to eat, but that house is for Sandy and me as a family."[24]

So pervasive was the Garth Brooks media image of male sincerity in 1992 that readers of *Country America* magazine, polled that year along with a panel of music business figures to name "the Top 100 country songs of all time," ranked "The Dance," written by Tony Arata and performed by Brooks, #3. The following year a coffee-table book of photographs illustrating the lyrics of "The Dance" was published. True to the connotations of Brooks's image, every photograph depicted an intense moment of family experience or a major life event—birthday celebrations of the elderly, the birth of a child, a high school football game, a christening, a college graduation, a Little Leaguer at bat, children hearing Halloween stories from elders, teenagers victorious in small-town sporting events, a young couple introducing their infant to an elderly gentleman, groups of children eating watermelon at a local festival, veterans at a reunion, a young girl on a swing, a happy bride preparing for marriage, a young boy's early haircut, and a couple at a country dance. Only four of the twenty-two images omit family situations, and these show pastoral scenes, one of them a peaceful graveyard.[25]

Brooks himself was nearing a major life event: the birth of his first child in the summer of 1992. She would be named Taylor Mayne Pearl Brooks, after James Taylor, Minnie Pearl, and the vacation spot where Brooks said the child was conceived.[26] At Nashville's Fan Fair in June, Garth and Sandy were treated to an impromptu, public baby shower. Brooks had made an advertised commitment to spend at least five minutes with each of his fans, and they lined up across the entire Tennessee State Fairgrounds parking lot in the early morning hours, willing to wait all day, if necessary, to meet him. The media reported that Brooks signed autographs for more than nine hours each day (Figure 3). At the Liberty Records show on the third morning, Brooks performed his cover of Billy Joel's "Shameless," dropping to his knees near the edge of the stage, then lying down to bestow a symbolic kiss on an adoring fan. Throughout his showcase performance, which included renditions of "Rodeo," "The Thunder Rolls," "Friends in Low Places," and "The Dance," fans streamed forward in an assertive but orderly fashion to offer flowers, notes, and gifts for the eagerly awaited baby. This scene would be repeated at the "Grand Ole Opry Superstar Spectacular" that same evening, with Brooks accepting each gift personally and thanking every fan individually. Before his final number at Fan Fair, Brooks brought his visibly pregnant wife on stage, to the excited applause of fans, and introduced her, saying, "I know a lot of you might be wondering how Sandy's doing. Well, I brought her here with me today." At the end of his show, Brooks gave what Edward Morris described as "a long, benign wave, strongly reminiscent of a papal benediction." Then, after carefully loading up every gift, the Brooks family left the stage.[27]

Taylor Mayne Pearl Brooks was born on 8 July 1992. Two months later,

Figure 3. Fans meet Garth Brooks at Fan Fair, Nashville, 11 June 1992. Photograph by Curtis W. Ellison.

Garth Brooks was talking about retiring from country music, which provoked another burst of media publicity. On 17 November, Brooks expressed deep concern about his personal future in an NBC interview with Jane Pauley, wiping away tears as he talked. In September, *Billboard* had reported Brooks's concern as front-page news: "I feel God put me down here to play music," he was quoted as saying, "but it's very evident to see because of the baby, God put me down here to be a father also." The problem seemed to be achieving the proper balance between money and time, ambition and family life:

> Sandy and I have 50,000 times more money than we could spend in the rest of our lives. . . . The parents, the whole crew is set up on pension plans, so I can walk away from it. I must decide what I want to do. I think parents work to provide for their children because they have to, and if I don't have to, is it my duty to stay home? And that's a war that's going on right now.

The authenticity of Brooks's dilemma was surely rooted in his actual family situation. Yet at the end of the *Billboard* story, passing reference was made to a more commercial factor: Brooks was at that moment renegotiating his contract with Liberty Records. "I've been amazed at all the other labels who have given me numbers and said, 'Look, if you're ever unhappy, give me a call.' I'm not in this thing to be the highest-paid ball player on the field," Brooks said. "I did, however, want to negotiate a deal that stated if I did sell [a] product, I got rewarded and that's what we've worked out."[28]

GARTH BROOKS'S PROJECTION of male sincerity and his cultivation of an image as a devoted family man have been essential ingredients in his unprecedented appeal. But there is more to him. Brooks established a performing style that gave country music culture its perhaps most flamboyant live concert experiences in almost seventy years. The Liberty Home Video *This Is Garth Brooks* provides a good sample of his stage maneuvers and strategies for engaging his fans as he performs fifteen songs. Compiled from films of two sold-out concerts in Dallas on 20 and 21 September 1991 and aired by NBC on 17 January 1992, the video documents the performance style that has become the preoccupation of Brooks's critics. Influenced by his fondness for such rock & roll groups as Boston, Journey, REO Speedwagon, and Fleetwood Mac, Brooks's style blends frenetic, extravagant on-stage activity (swinging over his fans on lighting cables, bashing guitars, and commandeering a spotlight to connect with small groups throughout the concert hall) with tenderly sung ballads evoking sensitive masculinity and ritualized moments of emotion that project an image of Brooks as a popular theologian.

Daniel Cooper has described Brooks's appeal as part of "a musical überculture that's very middle American, very 1970s, and unfortunately very white." According to Cooper, 1970s rock & roll was an emotional expression by white teenagers living in safe suburbs where white flight had placed them, and Brooks's merging of country music with this tradition is consequently undesirable. Says Cooper, "Garth serves one master: the spectacle."[29] While Cooper's critique may be pertinent to the social origins of 1970s rock & roll culture, the "spectacle" of fan behavior at a Garth Brooks concert has roots in earlier, secular country music performance and in evangelical worship practices going back to at least the nineteenth century. There is no doubt that Brooks loves spectacle. Perhaps the largest audience he ever had heard him sing the national anthem at the Superbowl on 30 January 1993. And the following September he filled a Texas stadium for three consecutive days of concert performances—drawing audiences of unprecedented size for a single country music performer. Such massive audiences are reminiscent of revival meetings from the days of Billy Sunday and Captain Ryman's Nashville auditorium or, in contemporary experience, the crowds drawn by Billy Graham. It's hardly surprising, then, that the Garth Brooks Fan Club magazine is titled *The Believer*.

Trends in American religious practice may suggest one context for the phenomenon of Garth Brooks concerts. Church membership has increased by approximately 30 percent since 1960, although the percentage of church members in the U.S. population has declined by 4 percent. These changes mask internal shifts in the nature of American churchgoing. Since 1965, membership in Methodist, Presbyterian, Congregationalist, and Episcopal churches has declined by 20 to 33 percent, while evangelical and culturally conservative denominations and movements have grown rapidly—especially in metropolitan areas.[30] Robert K. Oermann has reported the results of a study suggesting that the retail market for "Christian music" may grow "by an estimated 50.5 million" people in the 1990s.[31] The cumulative significance of these discrete indicators—revival-style concerts in Texas, dramatic growth in evangelical church membership, expectations of a sharply increasing sales volume of "Christian" religious music—remains to be seen. Yet when you attend Fan Fair and watch Garth Brooks greeting his fans beneath a large banner spelling out *The Believer,* and you see those fans wearing shirts that define the "true lesson" of life not as the outcome, but as the struggle "between the dream and reality," some link between "Garthmania" and a secularized expression of religious feeling seems plausible.

ON 10 DECEMBER 1992, Garth Brooks appeared at the Ervin J. Nutter Center in Dayton, Ohio. This concert featuring Brooks and his opening act, Martina McBride, sold out in unprecedented time for this venue. Early in his career Brooks had opened for Reba McEntire and the Judds; now, as a headliner, he promotes female artists by choosing them as his own opening acts. The crowd had clearly come to see Garth Brooks, however. The audience included more teenagers than is usual for a country music event, and many were dressed in highly stylized "Garth shirts" with bold stripes or striking color patterns, worn with crisply clean blue jeans, and black, Garth-style cowboy hats. This was also a well-manicured audience, with many women costumed in country garb and appearing to be in their mid-to-late twenties. The black Garth-style hat, with its silver band and rhinestones, could be seen on six-year-old girls, teenage boys, or grandfathers. The age range of this crowd included babies, toddlers, preteens, teenagers, young and middle-aged adults, and couples who appeared to be in their sixties. In contrast to a Conway Twitty crowd, this audience was not dominated by late-middle-aged, working-class couples. The crowd was extremely orderly and polite; virtually no drinking, smoking, or rowdy behavior was visible.

At 9:10 P.M., the announcer told the sell-out crowd that while no video or audio recording was allowed, flash photography was encouraged. At this announcement, the crowd began to anticipate the show by clapping intensely. At

9:17, the house lights went down and the crowd rose to its feet—not to sit again for the entire evening. Smoke puffed across the stage, a loud explosion was heard, then a countdown of rim shots and a drum roll filled the hall. A mechanical platform rose from the rear of the stage, lifting Brooks into view, posed in his characteristic bowlegged cowboy stance, with guitar in hand and head bowed. Ecstatic cheers erupted in the packed arena as bright lights came on, Garth's band of six musicians (displaying red and blue guitars) fanned out on the stage, and Brooks came forward, carrying his guitar and wearing his black hat, a red, white, and black shirt, and blue jeans.

Without any introduction Brooks launched into "Rodeo." As an opening statement, "Rodeo" both comments on entertainment culture in general and summarizes, in a catalog of specific images, "the joy and the pain" of rodeo entertainment specifically. From the moment Brooks appeared, couples in the audience began to hug in excited pleasure and women formed a line, moving in an orderly but urgent procession toward the stage, where they held up their babies for him to touch. As Brooks sang each song, individuals in the crowd watched him closely, as intent upon his words as if they were following an important text, many of them singing along with him. Yet at the end of every song, they erupted in ecstatic applause. After his first number, Brooks spoke directly to his fans, inquiring, "Is everybody okay?" Through the next few numbers, fans responded by taking up armloads of flowers and more children to be touched. "Two of a Kind, Workin' on a Full House" began a trio of numbers focused on domestic commitment. Brooks introduced the first of these by earnestly confiding to his fans: "Something very sweet has happened to me." In honor of that, tonight he would dedicate "Two of a Kind, Workin' on a Full House" to himself. If this song represented a testimony about Brooks's conversion to devoted family man, the crowd liked the idea. They sang along ardently. Brooks's next song, "Somewhere Other Than the Night," from his then-current album *The Chase,* tells the story of a mature married woman's need for passion and her husband's discovery of that need. "Papa Loved Mama" concluded the trio of songs about marriage with a humorous account of misplaced passion and revenge for infidelity.

So far, Brooks had opened with a framing song about entertainment in a manner reminiscent of Conway Twitty, then offered a sequence of instructive story songs about passion in romantic relationships, including one of personal testimony. Now the concert shifted to a new tone. The next two songs spoke to the role of God's will in everyday affairs, asserting that life is not directed by an individual's desire, but instead flows "like a river." Brooks's performance of "Unanswered Prayers" proved to be one of the concert's two emotional high points for fans and the most unequivocally theological statement of the evening. A ballad about meeting an "old flame," this song recounts a man's realization that an unanswered adolescent prayer had in fact been answered. As a mature man looking at his wife, he realizes that divine will and momentary human desire don't always coincide. This song is evocative of Conway Twitty's ambition to say what men would like to say, but often cannot. Garth Brooks's fans listened to "Unanswered Prayers" in respectful silence — until Brooks, accompanied only by his guitar, invited the audience to sing along. They knew all the words. Brooks's next number, "The River," generated more armloads of flowers and a vast expanse of lighters held aloft. Many couples embraced as Brooks sang that we should dare to "chance the rapids" and to "dance the tide," even though rough waters are doubtless in store.

The next three songs were all statements about justice. Brooks introduced "We Shall Be Free" as a "righteous song," a "gospel song" that takes up matters of public justice. "The Thunder Rolls," a story of domestic violence and retribution, describes a type of private justice. "Much Too Young (To Feel This Damn Old)," Brooks's first hit, is about a rodeo rider who admits that he got his just reward when his partner left him.

Brooks then shifted gears again, reverting to the theme of domestic commitment in order to give a sermon and to illustrate its lesson. "If Tomorrow Never Comes" advises listeners to tell their lovers how much they care now in case their "time on earth" ends before they have another opportunity to do so. And in his cover of Billy Joel's "Shameless," Brooks went on to demonstrate *how* one should express that love — passionately, directly, and with open emotion. During these two songs, which served as testimony to Brooks's credo of passion and commitment in romantic relationships, the audience took action. They filed up to the stage during "If Tomorrow Never Comes" as Brooks paced back and forth, shaking hands with fans in a ritual reminiscent of communion. They hugged and kissed each other as Garth stood alone on stage to deliver his rendition of "Shameless" while holding a single flower. At the song's conclusion, he gently presented the flower to a woman in the front row, provoking a tremendous ovation from the audience.

This moment of intense feeling was followed by one of comic relief — from Brooks's sermonizing — a bawdy rendition of "Friends in Low Places." A witty commentary on romantic relationships gone awry, this ballad recounts the story of a rejected man who brashly tells off his former lover on the day she is about to marry into high society. (Just before beginning the song, Brooks threw a towel into the audience, provoking another burst of ecstatic applause from the audience, who then clapped and sang along with him on "Friends.")

After this moment of humor, Brooks turned serious again. In a farewell speech to his fans, Brooks returned to family matters. This tour would end in two days because, he said, "I'm gettin' ready to take a few months off and go home and be a dad." Brooks had resolved the issue of his retirement: "After that I'm gonna pack up Sandy and Taylor and come back out" on the road, to be with the fans again. Brooks then launched into the finale with his signature song "The Dance." A hymn to the role of chance in ordinary lives, it stresses the importance of taking chances and making passionate commitments. Lighters flared throughout the hall and fans sang in solidarity with Brooks, who stood alone under a single spotlight. At 10:35 P.M., Brooks waved good-bye and humbly requested of his fans, "In our eight months off, please don't forget us."

As Brooks left the stage, the hall erupted in a deafening roar. It was the most intense gesture of appreciation that I had witnessed in more than two years and five thousand miles of travel, during which I had seen over seventy-five artists with their fans in live-performance situations. This response to Brooks was even more impressive because it came from a mixed audience of both traditional and new country music fans. Their genuine desire for an encore could be neither doubted nor denied. When Brooks returned to the stage with a long drum roll, the fifteenth song of the evening provided an occasion for his only significant display of rock & roll stage effects. Up to this point, with the exception of moments when he was kissing babies, taking flowers, or shaking hands, Brooks had remained in center stage with his band spread out on risers behind him in a semicircle—a stage setting not much different from other country music concerts. But during his encore, a fervent rendition of the rock & roll number "Keep Your Hands to Yourself," Brooks engaged in the theatrics that have so preoccupied his critics. He threw a water bottle into the crowd, climbed a rope ladder, swung on a dangling cable out over the heads of the audience, picked up a spotlight and focused it on small groups of fans, took off his hat, and let his shirttail hang out, building up enthusiastic fan involvement with every trick. This performance was intense but brief; after seven minutes, and without further comment, Brooks and his band left the stage, the house lights came up, and the crowd filed out of the hall in its typical orderly way. Although the sidewalks outside the arena were crowded, there was no rude jostling, or even any loud talk. Many fans had to take crowded shuttle buses to distant parking lots, and even here their demeanor remained polite and considerate, with no pushing. At that moment, it seemed that Garth Brooks's fans were inspired to be good to one another.

NOTES

1   As I heard him to say on *The Grand Ole Opry Live,* The Nashville Network, 22 January 1994.

2   "Hal's Induction Poem," *The Opry Observer* (Winter 1994): 1.

3   Dorothy Horstman, *Sing Your Heart Out, Country Boy* (New York, 1986 [1975]), 69.

4   Peter W. Williams, *America's Religions: Traditions and Cultures* (New York, 1990), 233.

5   Don Cusic, *The Sound of Light: A History of Gospel Music* (Bowling Green, 1990), 179.

6   Ibid., 181–82.

7   Howard Dorgan, *Giving Glory to God in Appalachia: Worship Practices of Six Baptist Subdenominations* (Knoxville, 1987), 216.

8   Thomas Poole, "Rock and Roll: A Country and Gospel Connection?" (paper presented at the International Country Music Conference, Meridian, Mississippi, 1992).

9   See Charles K. Wolfe, "Presley and the Gospel Tradition," in *The Elvis Reader: Texts and Sources on the King of Rock 'n' Roll,* ed. Kevin Quain (New York, 1992), 17.

10   Randall Balmer, *Mine Eyes Have Seen the Glory: Exploring the Amazing Vitality and Diversity of Evangelicalism and Its Role in American Life* (PBS documentary, Chicago, 1992).

11   *Elvis '56* (Cinemax television documentary, 1987).

12   Greil Marcus, *Dead Elvis: A Chronicle of a Cultural Obsession* (New York, 1991).

13   Cindy Hazen and Mike Freeman, *The Best of Elvis: Recollections of a Great Humanitarian* (New York, 1993 [1992]).

14   Wilber Cross and Michael Kosser, *The Conway Twitty Story: An Authorized Biography* (Toronto and New York, 1987), x.

15   Ibid., 135.

16   Ibid., 134.

17   Ibid.

18   *Music City News* (April 1993): 38–40.

19   Dave Larsen, "Tantrum Highlights Megadeath Debacle," *Dayton Daily News,* 5 July 1993, 6B.

20   Peter Watrous, "Brooks Seizes a Chance to Make Changes," *New York Times,* 2 September 1992, B5.

21   Rick Mitchell, *Garth Brooks, One of a Kind, Workin' On a Full House* (New York, 1993), 17.

22   Edward Morris, *Garth Brooks: Platinum Cowboy* (New York, 1993).

23   Ibid., 77, 188.

24   Marjie McGraw, "Garth Brooks: Hitting 'em in the Heart," *Saturday Evening Post* (July-August 1992): 102–3.

25   *The Dance.* Lyrics by Tony Arata (New York, 1993).

26   Mitchell, *Garth Brooks, One of a Kind,* 110.

27   Morris, *Platinum Cowboy,* 135–38.

28   Malinda Newman and Edward Morris, "Garth Bows Latest (Last?) Set," *Billboard,* 5 September 1992, 1, 85.

29   Daniel Cooper, "No Fences," *Journal of Country Music* 16 (1993): 55–57.

30   William J. Bennett, *The Index of Leading Cultural Indicators: Facts and Figures on the State of American Society* (New York, 1994), 115–16.

31   Robert K. Oermann, "Christian Music May Be Booming," *The Tennessean,* 27 May 1993, 1E.

# Girls with Guitars

*—and Fringe and Sequins and Rhinestones,*

*Silk, Lace, and Leather*

**Mary A. Bufwack**

There is a story that circulates around Nashville about a letter that was mailed from California with only a picture of a woman's straw hat, a price tag dangling from the brim, on the envelope. The letter found its way to its recipient—Minnie Pearl (Figure 1).

It is no surprise that country music, with its distinctive sounds and lyrics, and its distinct social identification with working-class America, should also have a strong visual identity. Women have always had a role, albeit a changing one, in country music. An overview of country music women's changing styles can therefore illustrate how working-class women have developed their own visual identity. Women's changing styles are a particularly rich area for analysis because of the consistent attention historically given to establishing norms for women's self-presentation. We are fortunate that photography has preserved many images of female performers, images that can still speak to us even though we may never again hear these women's voices (or, in many cases, even know their names).

How the individual country music artist makes "choices" and handles the dilemma of what to wear in her musical performance is greatly influenced by issues of group and class identity as well as by the forces of commercial entertainment. These choices cannot be reduced to a simplistic explanation whereby they are attributed to individual expression, mass culture, or women's dressing for the male gaze. Such choices are as complex as working-class women's lives. With the media and critics ever ready to pass judgment on their "good" or "bad" taste, female country performers have had an additional problem when trying to decide what to wear. They not only want to be visually accepted by

Figure 1. Minnie Pearl and Rod Brasfield in a 1945 *Grand Ole Opry* performance. Robert K. Oermann collection. Reproduced with permission.

the audience as country performers and to provide entertainment value, but also to express their individuality, to have pride in their performance, and to avoid the condemnation and ridicule of groups outside country music. Dolly Parton has met such criticism and disdain with humor and wit. In 1993, when she was promoting her new cosmetic products line, Parton was asked if she was wearing her own makeup. "Yes," she said, "and plenty of it."

Country music's first successful recording group—the Carter Family—included its first female stars as well. It is the voices of the two women cousins that we hear on the recordings. In the pictures that remain from their successful career (1927–43), Sara and Maybelle Carter, together with Sara's husband,

A.P., stare directly and solemnly into the camera. When the Carter Family traveled to Bristol, Virginia, on that hot August day in 1927 to let Ralph Peer record their music, it was for income to supplement their meager living from the soil. Although they outfitted themselves in dresses and hairdos current to the period of their career, their beautiful and soulful harmonies of folk songs, sentimental ballads, and mournful hymns spoke of older musical traditions. There was no adornment to their music, their performance, or their dress, poignantly reflecting the plain, hard mountain life in which music was passed down from generation to generation. Theirs was not the clothing of the dance hall or nightclub. Nor did they wear the work clothes typical of the poor rural farmers they were, though in an interview Ralph Peer would later claim that they showed up in denim and calico. Theirs was the practical, sturdy, Sunday-go-to-meeting "best" clothing (Figure 2). Many Southern rural families recorded and performed music throughout the 1920s and 1930s. Their photographs are like family portraits, showing women and men dressed in their Sunday best, holding their instruments and staring straight ahead. It is their demeanor rather than their clothing that hints of an awkwardness and unease.

Recording for Ralph Peer during that same trip he made to Bristol, Jimmie Rodgers presented a very different image. Considered the first modern country star and a top record seller, Rodgers had a casual, urbane style. His background included extensive work on the vaudeville stage, and, because he had worked on the railroad and sang blues-type songs, he put on the costume of a railroad man and cultivated the image of a "singing brakeman" in the late 1920s. But in most of his photos he looks very dapper and stylish. Billed as "America's Blue Yodeler," his costume was nevertheless what you would find on a college quartet performer of the era. The brakeman costume gave him a definite identity as a workingman, but Rodgers's own preference was for the sporty clothing that was his usual attire. Even as a railroader he had liked perfume and ignored the fact that some people found it odd for a man. His success allowed him to indulge his taste for new cars and high living, but this was not the image cultivated by his successors and imitators after his death in 1933, at the age of thirty-five, had cut short his growing national popularity.

There were also women who combined this rural-sounding acoustic music with the style of veteran entertainers. In a 1924 photograph, fifteen-year-old Roba Stanley looks like a young flapper (Figure 3). She had begun performing with her father before recording a number of songs, such as "Devilish Mary," "Single Life," and "Old Maid Blues." Her career ended soon after making these recordings when she married. Veteran vaudeville performers Adelyne Hood and Ada Jones also wore relatively glamorous dresses.

Figure 2. Carter Family songbook (1940). Photograph courtesy of the Country Music Foundation, Inc.

Despite the incredible commercial success of both the Carter Family and Jimmie Rodgers, the style that came to dominate country music in the late 1920s and early 1930s was neither the Carter's Sunday-go-to-meeting look nor the fashionable style of Jimmie Rodgers. The newly defined market for "hillbilly" music encouraged the search for a corresponding identity, and the already well-established commercial convention of the vaudeville "rube" was an obvious vehicle, reinforcing the music's rural and working-class identity. The rural poverty stereotype that was part of the image of so many groups with such names as the "Hill Billies," "Fruit Jar Drinkers," and "Skillet Lickers" included overalls, work shirts, and bandannas. The musical talents and the hu-

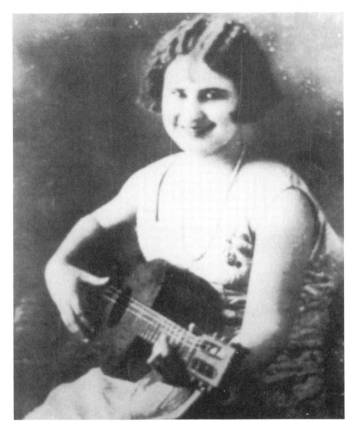

Figure 3. Roba Stanley in a 1924 publicity photo. Robert K. Oermann collection. Reproduced with permission.

mor of these groups made them extremely popular with the growing radio and record audiences in the South and Midwest.

This hayseed image was not new, but at this time, when the South was less industrialized than the North, it came to represent rural Southerners and their folk music. The rube, or country bumpkin, image had gained popularity in traveling shows of the late 1800s. Characters like Minnie Pearl made the rube a complex "liminal" type of the sort that has parallels throughout the history of entertainment. The bumpkin is an individual whose rustic and ignorant qualities allow him/her to comment on the world in insightful and comedic ways, saying and doing things that are proscribed for the properly socialized

Figure 4. Rose Melville as stage character Sis Hopkins in 1915. Robert K. Oermann collection. Reproduced with permission.

person. The bumpkin is both ridiculed in society and capable of inadvertently exposing sophisticated and cosmopolitan society to ridicule. The bumpkin is the common person or little guy who exposes people with "airs" and their big institutions, hence the character's great appeal to audiences of the poor as an expression of both their hostility toward the wealthy and powerful and their belief in their own worth.

The dress of the female rube has remained startlingly frozen in time for over 100 years. Pigtails were tied with large bows, while a loose-fitting gingham dress was worn over mismatched pantaloons, with the costume completed by high-button shoes (Figure 4). The female rube had greater freedom than the male in that her break with acceptable female behavior was more transgressive. Her behavior was "unladylike," she was indifferent to her appearance, and she often joked about chasing men. But these freedoms made her neither a "loose" woman nor a man.

The "hillbilly gal" became a very popular image for female country music performers during the Depression, the era of the new radio barn dances. Barn dances developed from the vaudeville tradition, but were radio shows performed for live audiences by an ensemble of musicians and other entertainers. None of these shows was more popular than the *National Barn Dance,* broadcast from Chicago on WLS. It had a rural audience, and, when not performing on the radio, the troupe would travel to nearby small towns for live performances. Many young women seeking employment (often to help their families through the horrors of the Depression) found work on the *Barn Dance.*

Among the most popular cast members was Myrtle Eleanor Cooper, who came to be known as Lulu Belle, the name given her by John Lair, producer of the *Barn Dance.* At age sixteen she auditioned for the *National Barn Dance,* singing the songs she had learned during her North Carolina childhood. Lair encouraged Myrtle to pattern herself after the female rube vaudevillian "Elviry." As Lulu Belle acknowledged in later years, her comedy was not as good as Elviry's, but her costume certainly was. Her mother sewed her a calico "Mother Hubbard," to which she added old high-top shoes and a braid pinned to her hair. She sang her songs loudly and boisterously, chased the male stars, and was generally mischievous. By 1936, Lulu Belle was the most popular woman on radio (Figure 5).

While commercially exploiting the backward/bumpkin stage character, WLS also promoted the performers as "normal." The show's "Family Album" booklets, which were sold to members of the live audience, pictured the performers, often with their families, in everyday clothes and engaged in family activities. Rural audiences could appreciate the bumpkin humor and costumes of the performers, knowing that behind the persona was a person who looked like themselves.

The sweetheart image typified by Linda Parker was an alternative, respectable gingham character available to women. A singer of parlor songs and old ballads, the sweetheart embodied a more dignified role than the rube, but also exacted greater conformity with propriety and social conventions. As the Depression wore on, the dominance of the "hillbilly" image did not go unchallenged. However, it was superseded not by a conservative character like the sweetheart, but by the heroic cowboy/cowgirl. This romantic and dignified image seemed to capture the qualities and spirit of resistance necessary to withstand the hardships of the times. The cowboy/cowgirl provided an em-

Figure 5. Lulu Belle in a 1935 WLS *National Barn Dance* advertisement. Robert K. Oermann collection. Reproduced with permission.

battled people with a simple, stripped-down hero/heroine. Completely American, this physical laborer, plainspoken and plainly dressed, was a man/woman with heart and style. As disseminated in movies and country music, the image became a national preoccupation.

There had been women in vaudeville who pioneered this style, and some were real cowgirls. Female country performers who adopted the image escaped the confines of the sunbonnet girl, and the cowgirl was a better fit with the lifestyle and work demands on these early, independent female artists. Cowgirl dress and music were unconventional and innovative. Like cowboys, they wore hats, pants, and boots; like men, and like women in mainstream popular music, these female performers became the "leads" in their musical groups. The repertoire of the cowboy/cowgirl singer could range from old ballads to contemporary swing.

Patsy Montana (originally Rubye Blevins, from Hope, Arkansas) went to Hollywood at the age of nineteen to seek her fortune in show business. In 1931, she joined one of the first singing-cowgirl groups and later took the image with her to WLS in Chicago. By 1935, Patsy had written the western swing/string number "I Want to Be a Cowboy's Sweetheart," the first million-selling country recording by a woman. Patsy began her career as a Jimmie Rodgers imitator who dressed like her other role model, popular singer Kate Smith:

> I won a theater contest in 1931 wearing a black, lace dress and played my guitar without a strap. I had to pull out a chair to put my foot on. After I won the contest a lady back stage suggested I wear a western costume. I thought a dress would be more professional.[1]

Her father wanted her to be billed as "Ruby, the Jewel of Arkansas," but she preferred "Rubye Blevins, The Yodelling Cowgirl from San Antone." When "Patsy" was given to her by fellow performer Monty Montana, it stuck. Patsy's first cowgirl costumes were like functional western dress, with all the basic elements—boots, hat, bandanna, and fringe (Figure 6). And Patsy's songs were likewise about being able to rope cattle and ride the range with her cowboy by her side. The cowgirl's relationship with men was companionable.

Meanwhile, the continuing entertainment value of the traditional rube character was exploited in movies by the multitalented Judy Canova. While she began her career as part of a family group known as the "Three Georgia Crackers," it was as a musical-comedy star in movies that she gained wide popularity. From 1940 to 1955 she starred in seventeen films for Republic Pictures. Her vocal abilities were astonishing: she yodeled, called hogs, and even sang opera in movies with titles like *Scatterbrain, Puddin' Head, Lazybones, The WAC from Walla Walla,* and *Singin' in the Corn.* As Joan of Ozark, she saved her town from the Nazis. Her hair remained in pigtails whether she wore gingham, a maid's uniform, or a tailored suit (Figure 7).

Throughout the Depression and into the World War II era, women emerged as independent performers and developed their own stage acts. In many cases, they objected to the images created for them by powerful men in the entertainment industry. Far from compelling women to adopt more sexual or alluring images, these men forced a conservative image on them, and audience preference, rather than the men's ideology, was used as the rationale. In 1936, John Lair hired nineteen-year-old Lily May Ledford to perform on WLS. The seventh of fourteen children in a family of sharecroppers, Lily May picked up banjo and fiddle playing from her father at a very young age. By the age of sixteen, she was walking eight miles to a local tourist attraction where she would play

Figure 6. Patsy Montana sheet music (1935). Photograph courtesy of
the Country Music Foundation, Inc.

for travelers on the excursion train, making as much as two dollars a day (in
contrast to the fifty cents a day she earned for hoeing in the cornfields of
surrounding farms). In Chicago, Lair had his secretary make Ledford a red
calico dress trimmed with white rickrack, then put her together with other
performers in a group called the "Pine Mountain Merry Makers." In 1980, remembering those early days, she wrote:

> In the long old-fashioned dress and high-top lace-up shoes that Mr. Lair
> had me wear, I felt like an old lady and not at all pretty. Mr. Lair dis-
> couraged my buying clothes, curling my hair, going in for make-up or

Figure 7. Judy Canova song folio (1944). Robert K. Oermann
collection. Reproduced with permission.

improving my English. . . . I . . . would not wear my hair pulled back in a
bun except on stage.[2]

When John Lair left WLS and moved to Renfro Valley, Kentucky, to establish
a "Barn Dance" of his own, Lily May went with him and was joined by her sister
Rosie, a talented guitarist. John Lair teamed them up with Esther Koehler (mandolin) and Evelyn Lange (fiddle) to form the Coon Creek Girls — the first all-
female string band. (The women hit it off when they met, and Evelyn and Esther
adopted flower names — Daisy and Violet, respectively. They wanted to call
themselves the "Wildwood Flowers," but John Lair preferred the "Coon Creek

Figure 8. The Coon Creek Girls in a 1940 publicity photo. Robert K. Oermann collection. Reproduced with permission.

Girls" [Figure 8].) During the band's career, Lily May was uncomfortably aware that their music and image were objects of ridicule, especially to the men on some of their shows who played more "polished" music. The Coon Creek Girls often played four or five shows a day at theaters, in between movie screenings:

> Sometimes, if it was a short movie we wouldn't have time to change so we would wear our gingham or calico costumes to eat in. If I could see a group of college kids coming down the street, I'd cross to the other side to keep from coming into direct contact with them, because invariably one would say something and the rest would laugh.[3]

The cultural conservatism of radio directors was reflected in the "WLS Creed": "Radio is far more than a mere medium of entertainment. It is a God-given instrument which makes possible vital economic, educational and inspirational service to the homeloving men, women and children of America."[4] George Hay, who had helped to create the WLS *Barn Dance,* was hired by WSM in Nashville in 1925. He believed that rural people should be able to hear their own music on the radio. Many years later, he wrote about the *Grand Ole Opry* show:

> Above all we try to keep it "homey." Home folks do the work of the world, they win the wars and raise the families. Many of our geniuses come from simple folk who adhere to the fundamental principles of honesty included in the Ten Commandments. [The show] expresses those qualities which come from these good people.[5]

Entertainers and audiences were not as conservative as the image developed within the radio format. Performers were often asked to do something differently because it was too modern, and their comedy was always censored to avoid off-color jokes. In the case of wsm, the station's conservative philosophy actually kept women in minor roles for years. When Minnie Pearl joined the *Opry* in 1940 she was a single woman and had developed her rural character on theater tours through the South during the Depression. She had always played the character in her regular clothes, relying on dialect and mannerisms, until one day, when

> I spotted a pale yellow dress made of sleazy organdy. It had a round collar and a cheap-looking grosgrain bow at the neckline that had been attached with a safety pin. I was as thin as a rail, and the dress made me look like Olive Oyle. . . . I found some white cotton stockings (you never saw country girls wearing silk stockings because they couldn't afford them) and a tacky straw hat, with a brim, . . . I bought some flowers to plop on the hat. . . . I never intended her to be a caricature. I dressed her as I thought a young country girl would dress to go to meeting on Sunday or to come to town on Saturday afternoon to do a little trading and a little flirting.[6]

Following World War II, the rube image did not fare well, while the cowboy/cowgirl continued to prosper. The cowgirl moved from the moviehouse and radio show to the dancehall with admirable adaptability. And the dancehall and honky tonk were the main entertainment venues in the country music centers of Texas and California.

It was Rose Maddox and her brothers who developed the cowboy/cowgirl image, adding a spangled costume, adapting it to both their folk music past and the honky tonk music of the booming factories and dancehalls of California, and billing themselves as the "Most Colorful Hillbilly Band in the Land." In 1933, Rose's parents took their five children on a cross-country exodus from their Alabama farm, by way of the railroad yards, to migrant worker camps in

Figure 9. The Maddox Brothers and Rose in a 1954 publicity photo. Robert K. Oermann collection. Reproduced with permission.

California. In 1937, when Rose was ten, she and her brothers began to make money by performing at rodeos, bars, radio stations, and other country music venues. After the war, their mother took them to a tailor who outfitted movie cowboys and they emerged in satin costumes with fringe, embroidery, and spangles, complete with boots and neckerchiefs (Figure 9). The flamboyant costumes matched their energetic, flamboyant stage act, and their innovative blend of rockabilly and honky tonk music was equally groundbreaking.

This image of the cowgirl—in its many varieties—dominated the female country style during the postwar years. Some performers preferred shorter skirts and tighter blouses, while others wore pants, but the costume could be adapted to all types and shapes. The cowgirl image had a versatility that allowed female performers to adopt new roles, play innovative music, and experiment. The image could also be continually updated, and few country music women avoided the cowgirl look altogether. Patsy Cline's first incarnation in the 1950s was as a cowgirl, as was Loretta Lynn's in the 1960s. In the 1970s, Lynn Anderson developed a reputation as a real equestrian, and Dottie West was a glamorous cowgirl all in white. Emmylou Harris cultivated the long-skirt-and-boots look in the 1980s, and Reba McEntire became known for her jeans and big rodeo buckle. By the 1990s, Tanya Tucker had developed her own line of western wear, Suzy Bogguss was designing leather-fringed jackets, and Carlene Carter had made boots with short skirts popular again.

In the 1950s, however, the standard costume for female country performers became the gingham dress. The style of the women, whether old or young, bore a striking resemblance to the internationally fashionable "New Look" introduced by Christian Dior in 1947. The New Look was a great contrast to the utilitarian style of women's clothing during the war years: the broad-shouldered/straight-skirt look gave way to soft shoulders and a full skirt with a nipped-in waist. High heels were impractical, but, like the full skirt and exaggerated bust line, they emphasized the difference between men and women. The impracticality of this clothing seemed to reinforce the view that women belonged in the home just at the time when women were being encouraged to leave the workforce. Country music's women gave their own twist to the New Look. Their dresses had nipped-in waists and full skirts, but they were generally made of gingham check or plaid, trimmed with rickrack or lace, and had puffed sleeves. Their dresses looked more like the feedsack housedresses of the 1930s and 1940s than Dior's Paris creations.

Kitty Wells was a 33-year-old mother when she recorded the groundbreaking song "It Wasn't God Who Made Honky Tonk Angels" in 1952. While her image resembled the country sweetheart of the 1930s, her song not only expressed the tensions between men and women in a postwar world where divorce was becoming common, but it had the new hard, barroom, honky tonk sound (Figure 10). Wells made a significant breakthrough for women at a time when country record companies had decided that "girl" singers weren't popular. In a restrained, mountain voice she indicted men for loving and leaving women — and was banned from singing the song on the *Grand Ole Opry* stage — but the song was reminiscent of old broadsides and Carter Family songs like "She is More to Be Pitied than Censored."

Other women, pursuing musical styles that were on the fringes of country music, adopted images considered unladylike or rebellious. Lorrie Collins had the sweetheart look of a homecoming queen, but Janis Martin wore dungarees and a peasant blouse (Figure 11). Jo-Ann Campbell wore tight dresses with side splits, while the great rockabilly singer Wanda Jackson performed at the age of nineteen in tight dresses with silk fringe that would swing:

> My mother and I designed a tight-fitting sheath with rhinestone spaghetti straps and a little short silk fringe. . . . I dreamed it up because I said

Figure 10. Kitty Wells in a 1954 publicity photo. Robert K. Oermann collection. Reproduced with permission.

that way I don't have to wiggle. I can just pat my foot, and the fringe will shake. I didn't want to look vulgar, I wanted to look sexy. I wanted to look like a lady, but I wanted to cause a little stir, too.[7]

Many country music performers were seeking a larger audience in the 1960s, and the sound that most appealed to mainstream audiences then was the "Nashville Sound," crafted by Chet Atkins, Don Law, Owen Bradley, and Anita Kerr. Smoother than honky tonk music, it combined acoustic guitars with echoes, a string section, rippling pianos, and vocal backup. The more sophisticated Nashville Sound suited country's heartfelt songs, and, as performed by singers like Patsy Cline, it helped to make female country artists more com-

Figure 11. Janis Martin in a 1957 publicity photo. Courtesy of Bear Family Records.

mercially successful. But Cline also embodied the identity crisis of country music in the 1960s. She was a hard-talking, hard-drinking woman, but a dyed-in-the-wool traditional country artist as well (Figure 12). Nevertheless, she had wide appeal, becoming a popular music star—not just a country star—and her dress style reflected this versatility. A photo spread in a fan magazine from 1958 depicts Cline variously attired in a gingham sundress, slacks, formal evening dress, and an evening gown plus a fur. As the accompanying text explains, "She has something in her wardrobe to answer every requirement—fringed costumes, full-skirted dresses with tight bodice, formal-type wear, and skirts and blouses. Slacks and blouses answer most of her at-home requirements, and one of her major concerns always is that everything must have that

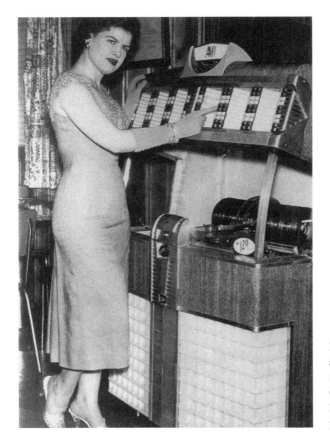

Figure 12. Patsy Cline
at the jukebox in
1962. Robert K.
Oermann collection.
Reproduced with
permission.

'just pressed' look." The article stresses Cline's good taste, noting that she likes jewelry, particularly the sparkly type, "but again, in excellent taste because she doesn't 'overdress' with it."[8]

Throughout the 1960s many country performers were eager to adopt popular cultural styles. The bouffant hairdo is an example of a high-fashion look that country music women made their own. Originally created by French hair stylists (the "bubble") in the late 1950s, big hair was intended to lend interest and balance to such fashions as Givenchy's sack dress. After Jackie Kennedy adopted the bouffant in 1961, mounds of hair began to appear on Hollywood stars like Audrey Hepburn (in her 1961 portrayal of Truman Capote's kooky Holly Golightly in *Breakfast at Tiffany's*). The beehive followed, and in 1963, Priscilla Presley's big hair caused a stir when she couldn't fit into her Corvair coupe. But by 1969, Kenneth had declared the look outdated, perhaps because regular people were sporting the hairdo, but country music performers clearly weren't letting their styles be dictated by Kenneth. They added ribbons to their high and flowing tresses, wore short skirts and granny dresses made of gingham, and traded in their cowboy boots for go-go boots. But just as country music's women were breaking through the gingham curtain and experimenting with contemporary fashions in a way that might bring them further into the cultural mainstream, popular music artists, with audiences of college-educated young adults, were developing a more casual, unadorned mode of dress that resembled earlier country styles. This trend toward folk simplicity was part of a critique of materialism and consumer culture that eventually developed into a feminist critique of Western culture's manipulation of women as sex objects. The attendant folk music trend appealed to many country performers. Stars of prior decades, such as Maybelle Carter, rebuilt their careers, while Johnny Cash and Glen Campbell, among others, found new audiences.

The social distances and stylistic differences between performers of folk and popular music and those of country music blinded many to the content of country women's music. In 1968, when activists in the women's movement were protesting the Miss America Pageant in Atlantic City with a "liberation trash can" into which they threw bras and makeup, female country music performers were writing and singing songs from a woman's point of view that were very popular. Dolly Parton's "Dumb Blonde" (1967) was an angry song about how she was treated by men, and her 1968 hit, "Just Because I'm a Woman," argued against the double standard for men and women. That same year, however, Tammy Wynette released her own hit, "Stand By Your Man." Wynette's high hair, thick Southern accent, and song, which counseled women to be patient because "after all he's just a man," became a symbol of female opposition to women's liberation. Only stylistic prejudice against country music can explain why this honor was not given to Janis Joplin, who was singing "Piece of My Heart" in 1968, telling her man to break her heart if it made him feel good.

The 1970s were exceptional years for country music's women, who dominated the charts as never before or since. Lynn, Wynette, and Parton not only had distinct (and very country) styles, but also brought women's songwriting and the woman's point of view to prominence. However different their songs, their sounds, and their dress styles were from each other's, together they revolutionized country music. Loretta Lynn's background as a coal miner's daughter had allowed her little exposure to fashionable styles, and her essential modesty has always been evident in her dress (Figure 13). It wasn't until after she had begun performing professionally that she started wearing makeup, high heels, and dresses that she hadn't made for herself. Her preference has always

Figure 13. Loretta Lynn in a 1966 publicity photo. Robert K. Oermann
collection. Reproduced with permission.

been for either pants or long dresses. But, again, as with Kitty Wells, her modest image did not prevent her from recording a song about "The Pill" that was
banned from much of country radio.

Lynn's poor-but-proud persona and music showed an awareness of the fact
that women of different classes have different lifestyles. In "One's On the Way"
(1971), she contrasts overworked mothers with women marching for women's
lib, living modern lives and dancing in discotheques. This class consciousness
pervaded women's material. In 1970, for example, Melba Montgomery sang
"Something to Brag About" with Charlie Louvin: while she might not be able
to brag about the "swingin' minnie skirt" she makes from "Mama's kitchen curtains and a bed sheet," she can and does brag about her man.

Figure 14. Dolly Parton in a 1987 Marlboro advertisement.
Photograph courtesy of Robert K. Oermann.

Dolly Parton uses clothing and physical descriptions in her songs in ways that emphasize how such things are symbols that are often misunderstood. In her autobiographical "Coat of Many Colors," for instance, a child loves a coat of rags at which her schoolmates laugh. Parton is also extremely aware of how negatively her current style is viewed by some, but staunchly defends her different standard of beauty. She has acknowledged that she looks like a hooker, but emphasizes that her heart is bigger than her "boobs" (Figure 14). She has also spoken of how she sees fashion through the innocent eyes of a child:

> I was impressed with what they called "the trash" in my hometown. I don't know how trashy these women were, but they were said to be trashy because they had blond hair and wore nail polish and tight clothes. I

thought they were beautiful. . . . They were like "strollops," as my mother called them—strumpets and trollops.[9]

The appearance of her hair has been of special concern to Parton, who owns several hundred wigs. (Asked by a journalist how long it took to do her hair, she said that she didn't know. She was never there.) Her cultivation of the "big hair" look dates back to adolescence:

> When I was a freshman in high school hair teasing came out. I'd already bleached my hair and got in big trouble. I have blonde hair, but it just wasn't radiant, it's sandy blonde. When teasing came out I just thought I had died and gone to heaven. Being creative with my hands, I started teasing. I fixed everybody's hair. I had the biggest hair in school.[10]

Often saying that "Cinderella" and other fairy tales had a great influence on her, Parton wants people to appreciate the creative and fun aspects of her self-presentation as well as the positive feelings that come from looking good: "I want my looks to match what I feel like inside, and I want it to be overwhelming, whether it looks appealing or not. Because how it looks isn't the point. I want it to fit my personality and I want to feel good livin' inside what I created." [11]

Tammy Wynette cultivated a more refined image and, contrary to her characterization in the popular press as extremely country, has always avoided the gingham look: "I think I just dressed classy, but conservatively classy. . . . I make two clothes changes in my show because I think the women really appreciate fashion and like to see different clothes. I never want to go out there and be a threat to any of those women" (Figure 15).[12]

The adoption of contemporary styles was not an easy or unproblematic choice for female country music performers. On the one hand, a short skirt could mean liberation from a stifling "family entertainment" image, but, on the other hand, it could mean bondage to commercial forces. Jeannie Seeley was forbidden to wear a short skirt on the *Grand Ole Opry* stage in the late 1960s. Her response was to tell the *Opry* management that if they agreed to stop every customer with a short skirt from coming in the front entrance, she would not wear a short skirt when coming in the back. Leona Williams recorded "Country Girl with Hot Pants" and dressed the part as well. Jeannie C. Riley's experience, however, was very different. She made her reputation with a short skirt and go-go boots (Figure 16). As the sassy girl of "Harper Valley P.T.A." (1968), she sang of small-town bigotry, but later confessed in her 1981 autobiography to some ambivalence about her image:

Figure 15. Tammy Wynette in a 1967 publicity photo. Robert K.
Oermann collection. Reproduced with permission.

The photographers were always saying "hike your skirt," "lift your eye-brow," "pout a little bit." They were building a Harper Valley PTA image. But deep inside I felt that the real person was buried behind my miniskirt and boots. In the long run I felt the sex symbol would destroy me.[13]

When Riley's big moment came to receive the Country Music Association's 1968 award for Single of the Year, she was humiliated:

I had asked Elsie Of Nashville, a leading dress designer, to make my dress for the awards ceremony. It was to be a blue velvet top with old-fashioned, puff-type sleeves that continued down the arm with long rows of old-fashioned covered buttons. It was to have a little scoop neckline with an

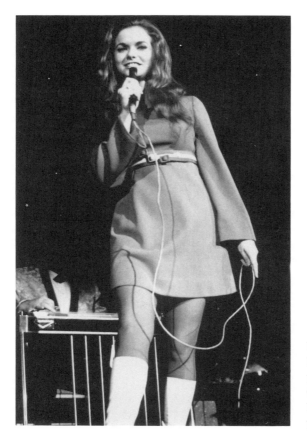

Figure 16. Jeannie C. Riley in a 1968 performance. Robert K. Oermann collection. Reproduced with permission.

empire waist. Then, under the bust and continuing all the way to the floor, was to be layer after layer of organza. The craze for old-fashioned clothes was just coming in and I wanted to be a model for the way a country girl should look.[14]

When she went to pick up the dress, it had been cut off just below the panty line—her manager had warned the dressmaker that if Riley appeared in anything but a mini skirt, her job was on the line.

With their expanding commercial opportunities, country music women's styles became even more like those of mainstream entertainers, with few distinguishing "country" characteristics. In 1980, records by women on *Billboard's* country music chart held all of the Top 5 slots plus #8, #10, and #11. Barbara Mandrell, Lynn Anderson, Dolly Parton, Tammy Wynette, Dottie West, and Crystal Gayle dominated the airwaves. Starring in glittering shows, they wore stylish gowns. Crystal Gayle's style included long hair and glamorous clothes, which complemented her smooth singing style. Barbara Mandrell also cultivated a more glamorous image when she brought country music to national television audiences. Mandrell has named Patsy Cline as one of her greatest influences and has said that as a child star she was impressed with Cline's glamorous clothes. What had once been a means of challenging a culture that stifled women had become a sign of conformity to a broader popular culture.

There was opposition to this trend within country music. The Outlaws of the early 1970s cultivated a scruffy, hippie kind of look, and the "urban cowboy" craze brought many of these Texas-based singers and songwriters to national attention. Songwriter and "Blue Jean Country Queen" Linda Hargrove released a song entitled "Nashville, You Ain't Hollywood," lamenting the watering down of country music. With a Janis Joplin-style delivery and denim attire, Lacy J. Dalton promoted a casual country image in the late 1970s.

As country music's identity crisis was deepening in the mid-1980s, Emmylou Harris moved to Nashville. Already successful, she brought a cultural outlook that fused the roots of country music with the casualness of the California rock culture. Harris was uncompromising in her love and respect for all forms of traditional country music, but she also had impeccable hip/rock credentials, having sung with California country-rock star Gram Parsons, who died of the effects of alcohol and drug abuse in 1973. Harris's success as a traditional country music performer without Las Vegas glitz and glamour gave a boost to country's most traditional artists. Her long, center-parted hair, her jeans, cowboy boots, and long, prairie-style dresses set a new style (Figure 17). She has also allied herself with other women in country music, recording the *Trio* album in 1987 with Dolly Parton and Linda Ronstadt (see Selected Discography). Harris's image is distinctly feminine, according with her strong belief in women's difference from men, including their different communication styles, and in the importance of women's voices for human communication and understanding. Her approach to country music thus converges with the music's working-class tradition, which has always expressed the differences between men and women in their experiences, their concerns, their attitudes, and their understanding of the world.

An androgynous image is one that has never really been cultivated by country music performers. Even k. d. lang, an acknowledged lesbian who experienced popularity and success in 1989 as a country artist before attaining mainstream stardom, built on a distinctly female identity. She claimed to be a reincarnation of Patsy Cline and wore full skirts as part of her country costume. Although her shoes were clunky, her hair was short, and her face was

Figure 17. Emmylou Harris in a 1976 performance. Robert K. Oermann collection. Reproduced with permission.

not covered with makeup, her passionate vocals said *woman,* and her recording project with classic country stars Kitty Wells, Loretta Lynn, and Brenda Lee was a statement of a sisterhood.

For female country artists of the 1990s, visual style is more important than ever. Music videos have become as important as recordings for promoting the music, marketing a release, and reaching a broad audience. Following the successful launching of MTV in 1981, two country music networks, The Nashville Network (TNN) and Country Music Television (CMT), were established in 1983, adding to the available venues for videos. By 1986, most country hits spawned a video. While videos focus on the visual performance and thereby increase the likelihood that women's looks will become even more important, this medium has also offered women a greater opportunity to showcase their talents and personalities than ever before. Performers can now project a multiplicity of images with each recording. It is standard, in fact, for video performers to appear in many different settings and costumes, showing many sides of themselves. Videos add dimensions to performances that would otherwise be impossible to convey.

The opportunities for stardom represented by the advent of videos in country music notwithstanding, the 1990s have not been good years for many female country artists so far, with the notable exception of Reba McEntire. Her stylistic development over a fifteen-year career has been very conscious. At a time when record companies are again questioning if they should invest in female stars, McEntire is the only current country female star who can compete with men in album and concert sales. Her early recordings in 1976, at the age of twenty-one, were not successful, however. At this point in her career, she wanted to sound like Patsy Cline and was recording many of her songs. Her image, which was initially that of a lace-and-high-collar sweetheart, went through several transformations. She got more sophisticated: her hair became redder, her eye makeup became heavier, and she wore tops with more sequins: "I got to playing around with it, and the more I wore sequined tops, spandex britches and knee boots, the sassier I felt and the better I performed. I felt kind of cocky." [15] After consulting a Los Angeles choreographer, she developed a new stage show in 1980.

Then in 1984, with her album *My Kind of Country,* she went back to the basics with her material and style. Her signature rodeo belt with jeans or a prairie-style skirt or dress matched her fresh face and her outgoing personality. That same year she was honored by the Country Music Association's Female Vocalist of the Year award. Her songs became more adventurous, with a specific orientation to women's concerns: "I'm trying to sing songs for women, to say for them what they can't say for themselves." [16] Her clothes changed, too: "I quit wearing spandex pants. Because, although they're the most comfortable britches I've ever had on, since they stretch, I thought women might be offended by me walking out there in a pair of tight pants. So I went to western skirts and boots." [17]

With a driving ambition and a commitment to being the best and the biggest, McEntire has invested herself in developing innovative road shows, acting in videos and films, and writing an autobiography, *Reba: My Story* (a 1994 bestseller). Her material translated well to video when she played a hurt wife in "Whoever's in New England" (1986), and she has continued to make videos in addition to performing in films. By the 1990s, McEntire had developed a stage show that included multiple costume changes (nine changes in one hour and twenty minutes), elaborate sets, video screens, and lighting effects: "A woman's gotta do more. She's gotta dazzle more, do more steps and—most of all—she's got to win the women over!"[18]

Whether it was in a song about women finding themselves in new roles and skills ("Is There Life Out There?" [1992]) or about women angrily confronting their men ("Take It Back" [1992]), like many of the other great female country singers and songwriters, McEntire has embraced her female audience and given special attention to selecting material that she believes speaks to their needs, emotions, and dreams. Who would have predicted even a decade ago that a female country performer could plausibly don a sexy business suit and play the character of a lawyer, as she did in "Take It Back"?

With her increasing popularity and her drive to be as successful as the biggest popular music performers, McEntire has cast off her boots, jeans, and rodeo buckle and costumed herself in more glamorous styles (Figure 18). Like Wynonna Judd, Lorrie Morgan, Kathy Mattea, and other female and male country performers, she has hired designers and stylists to work with her on her clothing, hair style, and overall image. In 1994, the low-cut gown she wore on the Academy of Country Music awards show stimulated a debate among country fans over the appropriateness of such cleavage. Sandi Spika, who has been designing McEntire's hair styles and wardrobe for seven years, felt that the dress was "revealing in a classy way."[19] But it caused such a stir that McEntire joked during the show, "I wish Sandi would have told me I had that on backwards."

While most current male country performers have a standard uniform of jeans, some sort of casual shirt, boots, and a hat (as well as a sound) similar to Merle Haggard's, female country performers are exploring diverse images and innovative types of songs. Perhaps this creativity comes from being on the margins of the industry. Although record companies know that they have signed some highly talented women, and many company executives believe that women can be successful, they do not know *which* women will be successful. There is no mold into which female country artists easily fit. This uncertainty has actually benefited the women by allowing them greater diversity and the freedom to craft their own styles. As a result, Emmylou Harris and other female artists with fresh sounds were able to pave the way for today's country music women. Rosanne Cash's 1981 success with "Seven Year Ache" ushered in the "new country." Her confessional writing style and deep voice were enhanced by contemporary keyboard and guitar arrangements. One observer quipped that she was "the queen of the hip parade" in rock-style clothes and hair color that changed from black to eggplant to orange. In performances, she might wear a

Figure 18. Reba
McEntire in a 1991
performance.
Photograph by Beth
Gwinn. Reproduced
with permission.

rhinestone bandanna with an evening gown and spiked hair. Her introspective
1990s songs (e.g., "Interiors") were critically acclaimed but less successful with
country radio, and, following her divorce from Rodney Crowell in 1991, she
moved to New York City, where she felt more comfortable pursuing her music.

The Judds, on the other hand, like Harris, were taking country back to its
roots. Naomi Judd's romanticized folk music style and Wynonna's strong vocals
landed the mother-daughter team a recording contract soon after their arrival
in Nashville. In 1983, when Wynonna was just nineteen, the Judds launched an
eight-year career that would make them country's top-selling and most award-
winning women. Their songs ranged from the sentimental to the fun-loving
and the plain-spoken, while their videos showcased them with a style that was
neither artificial nor glamorous, but rather the casual elegance of California
with the country twist. The Judds combined the ultra-feminine with the hip

and made it work, although not without provoking some comment. As Naomi Judd recalls, "Much attention was paid not only to our flamboyant clothes but also to these startling contrasts between our individual styles. I was called a 'barbie doll.' They'd compare Wy with Elvis because of her black pants, rhinestoned rock and roll jackets and matching boots."[20]

The stylistic elements of most contemporary female country performers' music and image have been more influenced by the country/folk/rock sounds of such artists as Linda Ronstadt and Emmylou Harris. These women along with folk troubadours like Joan Baez, Judy Collins, and Joni Mitchell constitute the musical roots of Mary Chapin Carpenter, Kathy Mattea, Trisha Yearwood, Suzy Bogguss, and Wynonna. Carpenter is a distinguished songwriter as well as a performer. Her moving and insightful lyrics are considerably enhanced by the grace and naturalness of her performance style, but she can also write and perform more up-tempo songs as well as poignant ballads of love and loss. Mattea, Bogguss and Wynonna have not established themselves as songwriters, but they emphasize the values of the songs they perform, and, like their folk music predecessors, they demonstrate their musical knowledge by accompanying themselves on guitar. Their voices have the quality and conviction that distinguish artistic interpreters of songs from mere singers.

Although in the same folk tradition, K. T. Oslin has cultivated a more sophisticated, torch-singer image in a transformation reminiscent of Patsy Cline's. Oslin's " '80's Ladies" was the first song by a female songwriter ever to be selected Song of the Year (1988) by the Country Music Association. Her songs had been recorded by other Nashville performers in the 1980s, but when she successfully recorded her own material for the first time at the age of forty-six, it marked a milestone for women in Nashville. With her witty, interesting songs and commanding personality, her gloves, suits, high heels, and fans (not to mention her keyboard playing), Oslin defied the music marketers and showed that commercial success does not come only to the young.

Even such female country artists as Lorrie Morgan and Patty Loveless, who were raised within a strong, traditional, country music environment, have not been musically or imagistically bound by tradition. Lorrie Morgan was the fifth child of *Grand Ole Opry* star George Morgan, and she made her own *Opry* debut (at age thirteen) in 1972. Morgan cites Tammy Wynette, with her ladylike composure and beautiful way of dressing, as her early ideal. Like Wynette, Morgan is a blond beauty, and she has likewise made the heartfelt ballad her signature style. In a more 1990s vein, however, she has also performed such sexual material as the song (and video) "My Night to Howl." Patty Loveless began her country music career at the age of twelve in 1969. Daughter of a coal miner and cousin to Loretta Lynn, Loveless broke with tradition and was doing hard country with a rock edge by 1986. With her growing success, she (like Reba McEntire) dropped her original country-sweetheart image and made her hair redder, her clothes more provocative.

Carlene Carter and Pam Tillis are two other artists with ties to Nashville's country music industry, both of whom pursued rock music careers before coming home to country. The daughter of Mel Tillis, Pam Tillis sang everything from rock to new wave. While commercial success eluded her for years, she became a favorite of Nashville club audiences, for whom her 1986 "twang nights" brought out the soul and the fun of country music. Tillis finally attained commercial success in the 1990s with a country format that showcased her incredible range of styles. Passionate and kooky, her hits have included the torrid "Maybe It Was Memphis" as well as the witty "Cleopatra, Queen of Denial," the videos for which exhibited the same sense of freedom. Carlene Carter, granddaughter of Mother Maybelle Carter and daughter of June Carter and honky tonk singer Carl Smith, returned to Nashville in 1987 at the age of thirty-two. She had married at fifteen, divorced, married again at nineteen, divorced again, and headed for Los Angeles to sing rock when she was twenty-two. She married British rocker Nick Lowe in 1979 and moved to London, plunging into the rock scene there. Her 1980 recordings were on the frontier between country and rock that is often referred to as "cow-punk." Her rock covers of such classics as "Ring of Fire" were interesting, but the music had no home. When Carter returned to Nashville, frustrated and confused, she began performing with Helen, June, and Anita Carter. Then, in 1990, she came into her own with hit recordings that brought out her lighthearted country-rock style. Between them, Tillis and Carter revived the short-skirt-and-cowboy-boots costume, and when they take up their guitars they also show how a woman can rock (Figure 19).

In terms of both style and content, female country artists are making exciting music that builds on the strengths of the genre's traditionalist women. A survey of their songs reveals a strong and enduring preference for those that speak meaningfully of the lives of women. They have released songs that address the experience of and feelings about domestic violence (Martina McBride's "Independence Day" [1994]), their feelings about being female artists (Wynonna's "Girls with Guitars" [1994]), the experience of marriage gone stale (Lorrie Morgan's "Something in Red" [1993]), and their anger with men (Patty Loveless's "Blame It on Your Heart" [1993]). These performers are singing for women, as their predecessors did, and while there are still record company executives who are looking only for the female artists whose recordings men will buy, country music's new women are comfortable writing, singing, and performing

Figure 19. Carlene
Carter in a 1991
performance.
Photograph by
Alan L. Mayor.
Reproduced with
permission.

for other women. Newer performers also seem confident that today's audiences like country music with attitude and style. When Trisha Yearwood's "She's in Love with the Boy" went to #1 on the charts in 1991, it was the first time a woman's debut single had topped the charts in country music since 1964. And when the CD sold a million, it was country's first female platinum debut in twenty years. Speaking of her song about a modern-day dream partner, "That's What I Like About You," Yearwood said, "I don't like wimpy lyrics. I like to find things women don't normally say or are afraid to say."[21]

It is this desire to be different, to break out and yet to be true to women's lives, that seems to drive so much of these artists' creativity today. And unlike past eras, when men told women performers that other women wouldn't like them if they were too sexy and that they had to dress demurely as a result, country music's women are now following their own impulses and listening to all segments of their female audience. Tanya Tucker, for example, is nothing if not herself. The "bad (country) girl" of the tabloids has been very successful as a rebel, and her success raises questions about the validity of characterizing the country music audience, and female country fans in particular, as conservative or prudish. Sexuality has been a part of Tucker's image since she recorded "Would You Lay with Me" at the age of twelve. And her cover photo on a later rock album showed her posed in a red jumpsuit with the microphone cord drawn between her legs. She made two versions of a recent video, "Soon," which featured her wrapped in wet bed sheets. One version was toned down to accommodate TV programs and networks that found the video too suggestive. Her performance style can be captured in one word—*strut:*

> I was singing "Woman of the World" when I was nine. I've got some movies of me when I'm singing "Harper Valley P.T.A." with my hair out to here. I was struttin'. I love to strut. My mom always told me, "Now, honey, don't move so much on stage. Be a little lady: friendly without familiarity." But I just moved to the feel of the music.[22]

Tucker describes herself as a fun-loving good ole gal and a devoted mother to her two children, both born out of wedlock. She draws on these roles and many others for her creative energy: "There is no certain look, I mean I go on stage one night and I might look like a cowgirl and [the] next night I might want to wear my Tina Turner outfit, my minidress, and one night I might want to go out in jeans, so it really depends on how I feel and what I feel like doing that night."[23]

Despite the many images that female country music performers adopt and the great variety of costumes they wear in videos and concerts, there are some standard country styles that most adopt at one point or another: the short skirt or jeans with boots, the suit coat with jeans or with leggings and boots, the prairie dress or skirt, or the jeans with just a T-shirt.

All-female "cowgirl bands" are one of the latest developments in country music, and they bring together many of the stylistic trends of the last twenty years. The Dixie Chicks, Ranch Romance, and Evangeline are all-female instrumental bands. Much of what they wear is vintage western clothing that suits a musical style ranging from honky tonk to swing and bluegrass. Kathleen Stieffel, of Evangeline, says that everyone in the band "loves a good pair of boots and jeans. Our look is feminine, but not too cute—jeans, short skirts, long dresses, black dresses and lace. We have a kind of retro look, partly as a result of our photo shoots."[24] The popularity of jeans among rock performers and middle-class audiences as well puts country music performers at the center of fashion today. An unpredictable social process has made the denim clothing of rural farmers and urban laborers the fashionable style for affluent people at leisure.

The image of women in country music, their styles and their music, will continue to be an arena where individual, gender, and class identities are confronted and debated, for the same identity problems that fuel working-class women's search for an image with reality and dignity also emerge in this arena. While a working-class identity may bring a male some (at least grudging) respect—namely, the respect for physical/productive labor versus the paper-pushing work of middle-class male occupations—a working-class identity, whether as a laborer or a country music performer, does not bring women respect. Women traditionally gain respect as mothers, as wives of respected men, or, more recently, as professionals in occupations that bring wealth or power. In fact, in the larger society, women with working-class occupations continue to be portrayed as dumb or naive, as having loose morals and bad taste, despite the fact that most working women are employed as secretaries, waitresses, nurses, and service sector and industrial workers. Such derogatory terms as "secretary hair" or "trailer trash" are an indication of this persistent prejudice. The prejudice extends to country music as a whole, manifesting itself every time a journalist writes about a popular female star and feels obligated to tell us how different she is from other "country" women—her hair is flatter, her makeup less thick, her politics more liberal, her clothing less glamorous, her reading list longer, her wit sharper, and so on.

As female performers search for and find those styles that will simultaneously bring them respect, appeal to their audiences, and convey some degree of personal expression, they provide the women in their audiences with style alternatives, images they can experiment with in their own lives, as well. As Dolly Parton puts it:

> People don't come to the show to see you be you, they come to see you be them, and what they want to be. . . . I spend time trying to look good but that comes from my insecure place. We all try to look as good as we can and make positives out of negatives, but makeup and hair and image is born from a serious place.[25]

NOTES

1   Personal correspondence, 27 March 1980.
2   Lily May Ledford, *Coon Creek Girl* (Berea, KY, 1980), 16.

3   Ibid., 23.

4   *WLS Family Album* (Chicago, 1938), 1.

5   Quoted in Jack Hurst, *Nashville's Grand Ole Opry* (New York, 1975), 75.

6   Minnie Pearl, with Joan Dew, *Minnie Pearl: An Autobiography* (New York, 1980), 129–30.

7   Interview with Wanda Jackson, April 1986, Nashville.

8   "Patsy Cline," *Trail* (March–April 1958): 34.

9   Unpublished interview with Robert K. Oermann, July 1990, Nashville.

10  Maura Moynihan and Andy Warhol, "Dolly Parton," *Interview* (July 1994): 36.

11  Leo Janos, "Dolly Parton: No Frets, No Regrets!" *Cosmopolitan* (September 1980): 259.

12  Unpublished interview with Robert K. Oermann, 9 February 1992, Nashville.

13  Jeannie C. Riley, with Jamie Buckingham, *Jeannie C. Riley: From Harper Valley to the Mountain Top* (Lincoln, VA, 1981), 99.

14  Ibid., 100.

15  Quoted in Don Cusic, *Reba McEntire: Country Music's Queen* (New York, 1991), 93.

16  Quoted in Jack Hurst, "McEntire Uses Songs to Speak for Women," *Palm Beach Sun Sentinel,* 17 October 1986.

17  Cusic, *Reba McEntire,* 154.

18  Ibid., 213.

19  Debra Evans Price, "Sandy Spika: Design from A-Z," *That's Country* (February 1994): 54.

20  Naomi Judd, with Bud Schaetzle, *Naomi Judd: Love Can Build a Bridge* (New York, 1993), 376.

21  Unpublished interview with Robert K. Oermann, April 1992, Nashville.

22  Quoted in Victoria Balfour, "I'm Still a Party Girl," *Us Magazine,* 2 June 1986, 24.

23  Unpublished interview with Robert K. Oermann, 26 January 1992, Nashville.

24  Quoted in Michelle Broussard, "Cowgirl Bands," *That's Country* (February 1994): 75.

25  Unpublished interview with Robert K. Oermann, 2 March 1992, Nashville.

# Event Songs

Charles K. Wolfe

In January 1925, the long and fruitful relationship that was to develop between the commercial phonograph industry and country music was just beginning. In 1922, puzzled engineers of the Victor Talking Machine Company had completed the first, landmark recording session by a traditional Southern fiddler, Eck Robertson.[1] In July 1923, an A&R man for the General Phonograph Company (Okeh Records) had reluctantly authorized the manufacture of a record by Atlanta entertainer Fiddlin' John Carson, whose singing he judged to be "pluperfect awful." Today, these discs by Robertson and Carson are considered the first two "country" records ever made. Throughout 1924, most of the major record companies—Vocalion, Victor, Columbia, Okeh, Brunswick—brought a number of Southern artists to their New York studios. By June 1924, the General Phonograph Company had run an advertisement in the trade publication *Talking Machine World* that featured John Carson and asserted: "The craze for this 'Hill Country Music' has spread to thousands of communities north, east and west as well as in the south."[2] Yet the companies were not really sure what this "new" music was: their 1924 catalogues listed numerous recordings of fiddle tunes, sentimental numbers from the 1890s, gospel songs, banjo tunes, white blues, and ballads. The music had no clearly defined identity, and the record companies were not even agreed on what to call it. (The terms "country" and "country and western" would not be commonly used until the 1940s.)

There are a number of possible reasons why, at this particular time, the record companies suddenly got interested in country music. I have suggested elsewhere (e.g., in *The Illustrated History of Country Music*) that one factor was the popularity of the new medium of radio, with the attendant drop in record sales (some major record companies were seeing sales decline by almost 50 percent). Another factor was the decision by such companies as Sears and Montgomery Ward to add records to their increasingly popular mail-order catalogues, which had an especially strong appeal in rural areas and in the South. A third factor may have been the campaign by Henry Ford to revive old-time music and dance as an antidote to the "Communist" plots represented by jazz and dances like the Charleston; not only did Ford propagandize in such magazines as *The Dearborn Independent,* but he sponsored a national series of fiddling contests that, among other things, helped to establish radio programs like the *Grand Ole Opry.* Probably related to Ford's program was a general interest in and curiosity about the whole idea of folk music on the part of the American public: major song collections, such as those of John Harrington Cox and Henry M. Belden, had recently been published, and companies like Victor were even producing records specifically marketed for folk dancing.[3] Another factor, though, and one which may have had the most direct influence on the record companies' decision to get into country music in a big way, was a powerful new fad that reached its height during 1925: the fad of what were then called "event songs." While such songs have long been recognized as an important subgenre of hill country music, recently discovered sales figures reveal that their popularity was far greater and more widespread than had been thought. During 1925, at the dawn of the country music record industry, event songs dominated the scene as did no other genre. Their success not only encouraged the companies to more actively pursue the country music market, but also helped to define an aspect of country music that would survive into the present. Exactly how the genre of event songs came into being, and how dramatic an impact it had on the early country music scene, is my topic here.

EVENT SONGS, as they emerged on records of the 1920s, were first cousins to the much older topical ballad broadsides that were sold on the streets of London and Dublin and later circulated throughout the American colonies before the Revolution. Mainly ballads, event songs took as their subject recent disasters or controversial items from the news, recounting the events and capping them off with a moral. Unlike many of their older British or nineteenth-century counterparts, event songs did not serve to actually spread the news of an event, but rather to recapitulate what people already knew, to comment on an event and put it in perspective. They were the creatures of the growing trend toward sensational journalism of the time; by 1900, the Associated Press service was well established among even the midsize newspapers, and by the 1920s wire-photos and "photogravure" sections were featured in many papers. Such technology lent itself to the sensationalizing of news and to the luridly headlined "human interest" stories about those who were caught up in disasters. A prime example of such journalism was the 1925 coverage of the death of spelunker Floyd Collins in a Kentucky sand cave.[4]

Even before then, however, the fledgling country recording industry had released two major event ballads. In 1924, Ernest "Pop" Stoneman, a carpenter from Galax, Virginia, recorded for the Okeh label a version of "The Sinking of the *Titanic,*" one of the numerous folk ballads that had been inspired by the sinking of the luxury liner twelve years earlier. Although some would later claim that the Stoneman disc sold in huge numbers, there is little hard evidence to suggest this—but Stoneman's version of the song would later be covered by many other country stars.[5] The other event song, which garnered bigger sales, was a ballad originally called "The Wreck on the Southern Old 97" but later shortened to "The Wreck of the Old 97." It was based on the train wreck that occurred on 27 September 1903, when an express mail train running between Washington and Atlanta flew off a trestle and crashed into a gorge near Danville, Virginia.[6] Unlike the case of the *Titanic* song, over two decades had passed before this event was recorded, literally, in song. On 12 December 1923, barely five months after Fiddlin' John Carson's country music "first," a Virginia millhand named Henry Whitter recorded the first version of this ballad, also on the Okeh label. It was released in January 1924 and sold moderately well.[7] "Cover" versions on the Columbia and Edison labels soon followed, and on 13 August 1924, a journeyman singer named Vernon Dalhart recorded the ballad for Victor, then as now one of the largest labels. This turned out to be the most popular version of the song, and following its release on 3 October 1924, it began to sell with amazing speed. Dalhart's recording racked up verified sales of over a million copies within the next three years—making it country music's first Gold Record.[8] In the years since then, the song has become a country standard, recorded by everyone from Johnny Cash to the Statler Brothers to Hank Snow.

Thus, as 1925 dawned, the record company executives were getting clear signals that at least one variant of this new "hill country" music was fully commercial: the type of song represented by "The Wreck of the Old 97." They watched with envy as Victor's recording racked up sales through November and December. Then, in January, the newspapers began filling up with stories about a young man trapped in a Kentucky cave, Floyd Collins. After Collins died in February, it occurred to one of the record company men that the event could mark an opportunity for the music business. Polk Brockman, an Atlanta furniture store owner and the man who had earlier brokered the 1923 recording by John Carson, contacted an Atlanta songwriter and singer, Andrew Jenkins. An evangelist, Jenkins was also a radio performer with an incredible ear for vernacular music. Could he, Brockman asked, compose an old-time-sounding ballad about Floyd Collins? He did so, and, on 15 April, Brockman's hill country music star, Fiddlin' John Carson, recorded it on the Okeh label. Carson performed "The Death of Floyd Collins" in an archaic manner, with just his fiddle-playing and his singing, and no guitar or other back-up. Carson's recording was scheduled for release on 15 June, but in the meantime, executives at Okeh's rival, Columbia, heard about the song, got a copy, and signed up Vernon Dalhart to record it. Using the pseudonym "Al Craver," possibly to conceal his Columbia contract from Victor, Dalhart recorded the song on 27 May. Columbia had no great hopes for the record and initially pressed slightly more than 4,000 copies, about average for the typical hill country record of the time. On the flip side of the record was Dalhart's version of another topical song, "Little Mary Phagan," about a 1913 Atlanta murder case that had gotten considerable coverage in the newspapers.

Columbia 15031, the Dalhart recording of "The Death of Floyd Collins," was released two weeks after Carson's, on 30 June 1925—four and a half months after Collins's death and about two and a half months after Jenkins had composed the song. Its opening was in the classic form of the old British ballad broadside:

> Oh, come all you young people and listen while I tell,
> The fate of Floyd Collins, a lad we all know well.

After the narrative came the moral, modeled closely on the final stanza of the "Old 97" song:

> Young people, oh, take warning from Floyd Collins' fate
> And get right with your maker before it is too late.

The tune was singable, Dalhart's stiff singing made the lyrics comprehensible, and the record took off, selling not only in the South, but all over the country. As an account of the Floyd Collins incident in a 1937 issue of *American Mercury* magazine noted, "Phonograph records that recited *The Death of Floyd Collins* in doleful lament to the accompaniment of hillbilly music outsold all others of the American series."[9] In fact, CBS files reveal that Columbia 15031 eventually sold some 306,000 copies—more than any other recording in Columbia's hill country catalogues of the 1920s—making it Columbia's biggest hit for many years to come.

Even before the release of "Floyd Collins" on 30 June, Columbia executives felt they were on top of a trend. Rather than bringing genuine traditional musicians such as Carson up to New York and trying to teach them freshly minted "old-time" songs, why not sign up a studio-savvy, music-reading professional tenor like Dalhart to record topical songs commissioned from composers like Jenkins? Thus on 22 June, eight days before "Floyd Collins" was even issued, Columbia had Dalhart in the studio recording another event song, "The Wreck of the 1256." Recounting a January 1925 train wreck on the James River in Virginia, this song was one of the first compositions by a young writer who would become a master of the genre, Carson J. Robison.[10] Like Jenkins, Robison was not a denizen of New York's Tin Pan Alley or a composer in its Broadway-show-tune tradition; unlike Jenkins, who grew up in Atlanta, Robison was from Kansas. In a 1929 interview in *Collier's*, Robison described his event-song writing practices in detail:

> First I read all the newspaper stories of, say, a disaster. Then I get to work on the old typewriter. There's a formula, of course. You start by painting everything in gay colors. . . . Then you ring in the tragedy—make it as morbid and gruesome as you can. Then you wind up with a moral.[11]

"The Wreck of the 1256," Robison's first disaster-song hit, was released by Columbia on 10 July. Columbia 15034, just three issue numbers after "Floyd Collins," sold over 178,000 copies, making it Columbia's second-biggest hit of the decade, with sales figures exceeded only by those of "Floyd Collins."

At this time, the head of Columbia's country music division, then called "Old Familiar Tunes," was Frank Walker, a competent yet somewhat romantic executive who saw the songwriters and singers in his series as "poets."[12] He quickly sensed in Carson J. Robison a songwriting parallel to singer Vernon Dalhart: someone who could imitate rural Southern styles yet was sophisticated enough to work within the rapidly developing recording industry. Walker hastened to encourage Robison, who soon provided him with several, even more current event songs. Less than three weeks after recording "The Wreck of the 1256," Dalhart recorded two more Robison songs on 10 July—the very day that "1256" was released—"The Scopes Trial" and "The Santa Barbara Earthquake." The earthquake of the latter song had occurred on 29 June, only eleven days before the recording session, while the Scopes trial (the landmark case about teaching evolution in the public schools) was even more current. It had not, in fact, even started yet and would not begin until 10 July, when Dalhart's recording session for "The Scopes Trial" also occurred. Released on 10 August, the record sold almost 80,000 copies. Walker recalled "thousands" of copies being sold on the steps of the Dayton, Tennessee, courthouse during the last days of the trial.[13]

By 1925, then, things were moving as fast as one of the shrieking mountain trains that Dalhart sang about. Columbia and Victor had their respective
recording, manufacturing, and distribution systems in high gear, and their
ability to respond to (and capitalize on) topical events was impressive even by
modern standards. When William Jennings Bryan died on 26 July, soon after
the Scopes trial had opened, it took Columbia only two weeks to get "Bryan's
Last Fight" recorded by Dalhart and into the stores one month later. When
the U.S. Army dirigible *Shenandoah* crashed near Ava, Ohio, during a storm on
3 September, Victor was able to get Dalhart into the studio in less than a week
to record "The Wreck of the Shenandoah"; two days later, on 11 September, he
recorded the same song for Columbia under a pseudonym. The Columbia version was in the stores by 20 October, and the Victor version soon followed. (On
15 November, however, Victor announced that it was withdrawing its record
in deference to the family of the airship's captain.) Other event songs that were
released in the fall of 1925 included one about the sinking of a submarine S–5;
one that commemorated the dedication of Georgia's Stone Mountain Memorial
(a tribute to Confederate soldiers); and the first of a series of modern outlaw
ballads, this one about Frank Dupree, who had been executed for committing
a 1922 murder in Atlanta.

The extent to which these event songs dominated the record sales of 1925
can be measured by the sales figures of Columbia's best-selling releases. During that year, Columbia issued 53 records in its 15000, "Old Familiar Tunes"
series, and their combined sales reached almost two million. Most of these releases sold in the neighborhood of 20,000 copies, but the spectacular sellers—
the top seven—achieved much higher averages and, by themselves, accounted
for some 980,000 records sold—almost 50 percent of Columbia's total sales
for 1925. Based on figures drawn from the CBS-Sony archives, the top sellers of
this first real year of country music as a specific genre were as follows:

| | | | |
|---|---|---|---|
| 1. | 306,044 | Co 15031 | Vernon Dalhart, "The Death of Floyd Collins" / "Little Mary Phagan" |
| 2. | 178,029 | Co 15034 | Vernon Dalhart [Al Craver], "The Wreck of the 1256" / "The Roving Gambler" |
| 3. | 112,993 | Co 15032 | Vernon Dalhart, "New River Train" / "The Sinking of the *Titanic*" |
| 4. | 108,938 | Co 15049 | Vernon Dalhart [Al Craver], "Zeb Turney's Gal" / "The Letter Edged in Black" |
| 5. | 102,431 | Co 15038 | C. Poole, "Can I Sleep in Your Barn Tonight?" / "Don't Let Your Deal Go Down" |

6.   92,048   Co 15042   Vernon Dalhart, "Sydney Allen" / "Frank Dupree"

7.   79,814   Co 15037   Vernon Dalhart, "The Scopes Trial" / "The Santa Barbara Earthquake"

Of the top seven records, only two (Co 15049, Co 15038) did not have an event song on at least one side. And only one was not sung by Vernon Dalhart. Such sales figures stunned the record companies, and convinced them that (a) there was a future in country recordings, and (b) that country music was inextricably bound up with topical event songs. They were to be proved right about (a), but not so right about (b).

IN NOVEMBER 1925, a Victor catalogue supplement listed a Vernon Dalhart disc featuring "The Death of Floyd Collins" on one side and "The Wreck of the Shenandoah" on the other. In its advertising copy, Victor set a tone about event songs that would be echoed for years.

> Popular songs of recent American tragedies. They belong with the old-fashioned penny-ballad, hobo-song, or "come-all-ye." The curious will note that they are even in the traditional ballad meter, the "common meter" of the hymnodists. They are not productions of, or for, the cabaret or the vaudeville stage, but for the roundhouse, the watertank, the caboose, or the village fire station. Both have splendid simple tunes, in which the guitar accompanies the voice, the violin occasionally adding pathos. These songs are more than things for passing amusement; they are chronicles of the time, by unlettered and never self-conscious chroniclers.

As we have seen, neither of the "chroniclers" of these ballads, Carson J. Robison and Andrew Jenkins, was "unlettered" or unself-conscious. Both knew exactly what they were doing, as did such later composers as Bob Miller and Dan Hornsby. In its ad, Victor was blatantly presenting these new songs as something they were not, and as something akin to what folklorist-historian Richard Dorson would later call "fakelore." What is intriguing, however, is that many of these pseudo-folk ballads did in fact make it into folk tradition. Given the huge numbers of Victrola records of these ballads in circulation, it is not surprising that many of them were learned and put into oral circulation. Virtually every one of the ballads on Columbia's best-selling records listed above, with the exception of "Wreck of the 1256," appears in Malcolm Laws's definitive *Native American Balladry*.[14] Although Laws himself noted that some ballads were "of dubious currency in tradition," the point is that at some time some folk-song collector gathered each text "in the field" from some informant. In Edwin C. Kirkland's "Check List of the Titles of Tennessee Folksongs," an index to various collections made prior to 1946, there are no fewer than five versions each of "Floyd Collins" and "Little Mary Phagan," three of "The Santa Barbara Earthquake," and one each of "Frank Dupree" and "Sydney Allen." [15] In the 1930s and 1940s, Library of Congress fieldworkers collected folk variants of "The Santa Barbara Earthquake" and "The Scopes Trial." [16] Most folk-song collectors of this period, with the exception of Vance Randolph, were largely unaware of the early recordings of hill country music, and when they encountered versions of Robison's or Jenkins's event ballads, they simply assumed that these were part of the older tradition that such songs were in fact imitating.

By the end of 1925, many record company executives and much of the public associated the new hill country music with event songs. An editorial in a December issue of *Talking Machine World,* the recording industry's trade journal, speculated about "what the popularity of Hill-Billy Songs Means in Retail Profit Possibilities." The editorial began by noting that "the 'Death of Floyd Collins,' 'Wreck of the Shenandoah,' 'At My Mother's Grave,' and other such songs which have had fairly widespread popularity may mark the initial move in the passing of jazz." Music buyers, it was argued, might be turning away from the "over-arranged" fox trots and toward the "weird funeral musical offerings" that represented "the most simplified song form." [17] Although the editors of *Talking Machine World* were wrong about jazz (its greatest years were just beginning), what is significant is the way in which they exemplified "hill-billy" music with two event ballads.

This association was still strong many years later when Frank Walker, who had been in charge of Columbia's 15000 series, gave an interview to folklorist/singer Mike Seeger during which he classified old-time country music into four categories: gospel songs, fiddle tunes, sentimental songs—and event songs. The event song, according to Walker, was a genre that had "passed out to a degree today and was terrific in those days." Interestingly, he defined the subject matter of an event song as "something that had happened, not today, maybe years ago, but hadn't permeated through the South because of a lack of newspapers and no radio and no television in those days, but they had heard of it." Walker singled out Carson Robison as his premier writer of event songs.

> Carson was a natural writer, and if I were down South and found some tale of a local nature down there, I'd sit down and write Carson to tell him

the story of it. Then twenty-four hours later, in New York, Carson would be in, and say here is the story of whatever it happened to be. It would be done. We might make a few changes to make it a little more authentic.[18]

Walker and his counterparts in other record companies were by now convinced that "hill-billy" music was a viable commodity for the recording industry, and most of the major labels followed Columbia's and Okeh's lead by starting their own special "hill country" record series. These had titles similar to Okeh's "Old-Time Tunes" and Columbia's "Old Familiar Tunes": "Native American Melodies" (Victor), "Songs from Dixie" (Brunswick), and "Old Southern Tunes" (Vocalion). By the start of 1926, primarily as a result of the sales of 1925 event songs, the companies were charging full tilt into this new market. All of them eagerly sought new event songs, hoping to find the next "Floyd Collins" or "Wreck of the 1256."

A complete list of these post-1925 recordings is far beyond the scope of this study. Suffice it to say that all the companies entered the sweepstakes, some with more gusto than others, and that between 1926 and 1930 (when the Depression seriously curtailed the recording industry's production and sales) well over 100 event songs were recorded. Columbia, thanks to Walker's cultivation of Carson Robison, and Okeh, with its comparably prolific songwriter, Andrew Jenkins, issued the majority of these recordings. Among the most influential and enduring post-1925 event songs were "Billy Richardson's Last Ride" (1926; issued on the Brunswick, Columbia, and Vocalion labels), a train wreck ballad coauthored by Robison and a railroad worker named Cleburne C. Meeks; "The Wreck of the No. 9" (1927; issued on all five major labels), another one of Robison's train wreck songs; and a series of ballads, such as "Little Marian Parker" and "The Hanging of the Fox (Edward Hickman, Slayer of Little Marian Parker)," released in 1928 after the kidnapping and murder of the daughter of a wealthy Los Angeles banker in December 1927.

One popular series of ballads that Walker remembered with special fondness was inspired by an outlaw named Kinnie Wagner:

> Kenny [sic] was a bandit, but he was a clever bandit. . . . He seemed to be able to master every jail that he was ever in. Well, it was all very good for us from a record standpoint. We would have a record telling of the capture of Kinnie Wagner and then a record of the escape of Kinnie Wagner.[19]

Columbia released "Kinnie Wagner" in March 1926 (Co 15065), followed by "Kinnie Wagner's Surrender" in October 1926 (Co 15098) and "The Fate of Kinnie Wagner" in February 1927 (Co 15109). Curiously, the first two songs were written by Andrew Jenkins, the third by Carson J. Robison—testimony to how well each had mastered the style.

Another series of ballads centered on the sinking of the steamship *Vestris:* "The Heroes of the *Vestris*" (1927; Brunswick); "The *Vestris* Disaster" (1928; Gennett); "Storm at Sea [Sinking of the Steamship *Vestris*]" (1929; Columbia); and "The Sinking of the *Vestris*" (1928; Victor, Vocalion, and Okeh). Natural disasters were chronicled in such songs as Robison's "Miami Storm" (1926; Columbia and Vocalion) and Jenkins's "Alabama Flood" (1928; Okeh), while manmade ones were described in Bob Miller's "Ohio Prison Fire" (1930; Columbia), Dan Hornsby's "Shelby Disaster" (1928; Columbia), Robison's "West Plains Explosion" (1927; Okeh), and Jenkins's "Tragedy at Daytona Beach" (1929; Okeh). In between were dozens of other event songs, often featuring disasters or murders or clever con men, such as "The Story of C. S. Carnes" (1929; Columbia), about the alleged larceny of a church official. Up until his career ended in 1938, Vernon Dalhart recorded many of these songs, although he often used his pseudonym, "Al Craver," on the Columbia sides.

In spite of this rich variety of event songs, the new country record series soon began to include other types of hill country music: the driving fiddle tunes of string bands like the Skillet Lickers, the comic vaudeville tunes of Uncle Dave Macon, the "blue yodels" of Jimmie Rodgers, and the clear, mountain harmonies of the Carter Family. It did not take long for the stiff, formal singing of Vernon Dalhart to be replaced by the more authentic Southern styles of such singers as Charlie Poole, Dock Boggs, and Frank Hutchison, among others. And these more traditional singers seldom showed any interest in event songs—especially the ones that were generated in New York. After 1925, the percentage of event songs released by the major record companies steadily declined. They constituted 11 percent of all releases in 1925, but only one percent in 1931. While most of the seven top-selling country records released by Columbia in 1925 were event songs, only one event song made it into the top seven after that year. Overall, of the approximately 1,400 songs recorded by Columbia in its 15000 series, only thirty-seven were really event songs, and other labels had similar percentages. The event songs, like colorful butterflies, died out almost as quickly as they had emerged, after a single season.

For years afterward, Walker, Dalhart, Robison, and others kept trying to rekindle the spark, and, as country music developed in the 1930s and 1940s, sporadic attempts to revive the genre were made with songs about Will Rogers and Wiley Post, Amelia Earhart, the 1937 Ohio flood, and such outlaws as John Dillinger and Pretty Boy Floyd. Folksingers Woody Guthrie and Huddie Ledbetter (Leadbelly) won early popularity with the genre. None of these songs or singers, though, replicated the kind of commercial success that had occurred with the 1925 releases, and the event, or topical, song survived only as a minor subgenre of modern country music.

Carson Robison, perhaps sensing that his original speciality was living on borrowed time, honed his skills as a studio musician in New York and began to develop a repertoire of sentimental and novelty songs—including such hits as "Left My Gal in the Mountains," "Little Green Valley," and "Open Up Dem Pearly Gates." When he began to publish his own song folios in 1930 and 1931, his event songs were conspicuously absent. In fact, by the time he was interviewed by *Collier's* in 1929, he was already virtually finished with the genre. He soon went into radio and adopted a cowboy image, but he located his office in New York, not Nashville. Vernon Dalhart, on the other hand, dropped into total obscurity after making his last recordings in 1938, although in his final years he was still corresponding with old fans who had bought and cherished his fragile 78 rpm records.

This brief explosion of event song popularity did more than just launch a minor but curious subgenre of country music. The dramatic sales figures for 1925, as well as the data on recording and release dates, reveal just how much these songs contributed to the early commercial success of country music. At the start of 1925, few record company executives had any clear sense of what hill country music was, or any real faith in a market for it. By the end of that year, however, they had discovered, to their amazement, how well country music records could sell—and not only to fans in the South. The event song fad was very short-lived, but its advent was propitious for country music in general. Probably more than any other single factor, the success of event songs encouraged the big record companies to seriously pursue the country music market and thus to help define and promote a major new commercial art form.

NOTES

1   Details of Robertson's first recordings can be found in Charles K. Wolfe, "What Ever Happened to Country's First Recording Artist? The Career of Eck Robertson," *Journal of Country Music* 16 (1993): 33–41.

2   See *Talking Machine World,* 15 June 1924, 17.

3   John Harrington Cox, *Folk-Songs of the South* (Hatsboro, PA, 1963 [1925]); Henry M. Belden, "Balladry in America," *Journal of American Folklore* 25 (1912): 1–23.

4   Much of this journalism was dramatized in Robert Penn Warren's novel *The Cave* (New York, 1959).

5    For more on Stoneman's early career, see Ivan M. Tribe, *The Stonemans: An Appalachian Family and the Music That Shaped Their Lives* (Urbana and Chicago, 1993).

6    For a full history, see Norm Cohen, *Long Steel Rail: The Railroad in American Folksong* (Urbana and Chicago, 1981), 197–226.

7    The classic study of Carson's early career is Archie Green, "Hillbilly Music: Source and Symbol," *Journal of American Folklore* 78 (1965): 204–28.

8    Cohen, *Long Steel Rail,* 203.

9    Oland D. Russell, "Floyd Collins in the Sand Cave," *American Mercury* (November 1937).

10    The best overview of Robison's career is Robert Coltman, "Carson Robison: First of the Rural Professionals," *Old Time Music* 29 (Summer 1978): 5–14.

11    Hugh Leamy, "Now Come All You Good People," *Collier's,* 2 November 1929, 58.

12    See Mike Seeger, "Who Chose These Records? A Look into the Life, Tastes, and Procedures of Frank Walker," in *Anthology of American Folk Music,* ed. Moses Asch, Josh Dunson, and Ethel Raim (New York, 1973), 12.

13    Ibid.

14    Malcolm G. Laws, *Native American Balladry,* AFS Bibliographical and Special Series, Vol. 1 (Philadelphia, 1950).

15    Edwin C. Kirkland, "A Check List of the Titles of Tennessee Folksongs," *Journal of American Folklore* 59 (1946): 423–76.

16    See *American Folk Poetry: An Anthology,* ed. Duncan Emrich (Boston, 1974).

17    *Talking Machine World,* 15 December 1925, 177.

18    Seeger, "Who Chose These Records?" 11–12.

19    Ibid., 12.

# Country Green

*The Money in Country Music*

❧ ———————————————————————— **Don Cusic**

In 1979 Wal-Mart sold one billion dollars' worth of merchandise in its 230 stores; by 1989 there were 1,402 stores, with sales totaling $8.1 billion. These simple facts also pertain to the growth in sales of country music during the same decade. The history of U.S. retailing in the 1980s and 1990s is dominated by the phenomenal growth of Wal-Mart and other mass merchandisers. K-Mart overtook Sears as the nation's largest retailer during the 1980s, while Wal-Mart moved up to third place. During the 1990s Wal-Mart overtook both Sears and K-Mart to become the number one retailer in the United States.

The reason this is important for country music is that around 75 percent of country music is sold by mass merchandisers. And nobody sells more country music than Wal-Mart. Indeed, if the truth be known, the explosion in country music sales during the 1980s and 1990s owes more to Sam Walton than to Garth Brooks, Randy Travis, George Strait, or any other country singer. Ironically, the spread of Wal-Mart stores and other mass-merchandising outlets has helped country music, on the one hand, by exposing more consumers to the product, while, on the other hand, it has undermined the very values and traditions expressed in the music. The arrival of a Wal-Mart in a suburban community or small town has usually meant the death of the town square as its marketplace, especially the independently owned drugstore, among other "Mom and Pops." The small-town drugstore has been replaced by the large chain store located far from downtown.

The mass merchandisers, as well as other retailers, have electronic scanners at their checkout counters that scan bar codes and automatically record the items purchased, subtract them from store inventory, tally up their prices, and show the customer how much to pay. In addition to their impact on consumers, these scanners have also had a tremendous impact on country music. Sales figures on recordings are collected each week by *Billboard*, a trade magazine that compiles national charts of the top singles and albums in all music genres, ranking them on the basis of sales and airplay. The SoundScan technology used by *Billboard* has been in place since 1991; it gives a quick, accurate reading of what sells and what doesn't, unlike the way charts used to be compiled.

Before SoundScan, *Billboard* and other trade papers regularly called a prese-lected group of record stores and distributors (known as "reporters") around the country and asked a manager or assistant manager (or whoever was in charge of making the report) what the top sellers were in the various categories (country, rock, rhythm & blues, etc.). The actual sales figures were *not* col-lected; the stores merely provided a relative ranking. Since country music con-sumers generally do not shop in traditional record stores—either freestanding shops or those in malls—these stores didn't sell many country albums. Further-more, such stores generally employed young people who loved rock & roll or some other popular music of the day and who often had an antipathy toward country music, so they usually didn't report country sales along with pop sales.

Then there was the psychological factor of display. Country music had its own section, generally at the back of the store, while pop records were dis-played up front. So country music was not even considered in calculating pop sales unless an album sold so well that it was moved to the front of the store. This move was made by the albums of some artists, such as Charlie Rich in the early 1970s and Kenny Rogers in the late 1970s; thus the key to big sales for country music became "crossovers," or records that "crossed over" from the country to the pop music charts. Not only did this mean that such albums ap-peared on both charts, but also that they were moved up front in the stores and were ranked by the reporters along with pop music releases. Although much has been made of the heights attained by country music on the pop charts in the 1990s, the sales of records by such country artists as Waylon Jennings and Willie Nelson during the Outlaw movement of the mid-1970s; Kenny Rogers, Alabama, and Willie Nelson in the early 1980s; and Randy Travis in the mid-1980s compared favorably with country music sales in the 1990s. But since SoundScan wasn't available before 1991, the popularity of country music couldn't be accurately assessed. Simply put, it was generally assumed that rock ruled and that country could not really compete in terms of sales.

With the advent of SoundScan, all those assumptions had to be revised. Once the raw data of unbiased sales figures began to be collected, it was dis-covered that country music was competitive with pop music and sometimes even outsold it. While this had been no secret within the music industry for a number of years, at least among the accounting departments of the major record companies, the pop music world had generally refused to believe that country releases could sell in such huge numbers. In fact, while Fleetwood Mac's albums were setting the pop music world on fire in the mid-1970s, ole Slim Whitman was outselling them with his *Greatest Hits*. But that was different, some would argue: Fleetwood Mac sold in retail stores, whereas Whitman sold over TV. Still, it was a harbinger of things to come.

THE DEMOGRAPHIC AGE GROUP of country music buyers has generally been in the 25- to 50-year-old range. But in the 1990s that age range has widened to include teenage consumers—and this is important because it is young people who set the trends. Record companies depend on the youth market not only because American culture is obsessed with youth, but also because consumers aged ten to twenty-four purchase the most records. Actually, the age groups of the record-buying public fall roughly into three categories: 10- to 19-year-olds, 20- to 24-year-olds, and 25- to 50-year-olds. Although each group buys about one-third of the total recordings sold, the oldest group (25–50) tends either to mirror what the younger groups are buying or to purchase catalog "oldies." So, with older people wanting to remain young, or at least connected to "youth," younger people are setting the trends.

For country music to reach the youth—who tend to be more prone to fads—it had to become "hip." This happened in two ways. First, the rise of Country Music Television (CMT), with its emphasis on videos, broke down many of the old stereotypes of country music. Second, record companies began to sign attractive young artists who appealed to younger audiences. Meanwhile, the term "country" was being redefined as a result of rural/urban shifts in the American population.

Before World War II, almost two-thirds of the U.S. population lived in rural areas. In 1940, about 23 percent of the population lived on farms, a figure that had been declining throughout the twentieth century (in 1900, it was 39 percent). But during the Second World War, as manufacturing plants opened in cities, there was a tremendous exodus into urban areas. By then the cities had nearly all modern comforts, which added to their appeal. Urban life and work was no longer limited to the daylight hours, as farming still was. (Rural areas did not begin to receive electricity until after the Rural Electrification Act had been passed in 1936, and it was not until after World War II that rural America was fully wired.) By 1950, only 15 percent of the population lived on farms, and a decade later that figure dropped to 8 percent (it now hovers at around

2 percent). Within cities, the image of the rural person was that of a country "bumpkin," a "hayseed," "hick," or "rube." The image of the city dweller was that of someone cultured and sophisticated, or at least "streetwise." So the term "country" had negative connotations for people who were or wanted to be "citified," and these connotations likewise applied to "country music."

The 1990 census showed the United States to be an urban nation, although more people actually live in the suburbs that surround a city than anywhere else. Nevertheless, about 80 percent of the U.S. population is now to be found in metropolitan areas, with the other 20 percent of the nation living in rural areas but only 4.6 million (or less than 2 percent) on farms. By 1990, however, the cities had acquired a negative image and were viewed as areas of widespread violence, rampant crime, crowded living conditions, and—for many inner-city dwellers—hopelessness. Country living, on the other hand, had gained a lot of appeal. To live in the "country" meant having fresh air and freedom from inner-city conditions. A home in the country became a status symbol, and "country" clothing, furniture, and music became increasingly popular. Establishing this change of image has largely been the work of the media, especially television: The Nashville Network (TNN) went on the air in 1983, and Country Music Television (CMT) debuted at about the same time. Originally, these were two separate companies, but in 1991 the Gaylord Broadcasting Company, which owned TNN, purchased CMT.

THERE'S AN OLD ADAGE that says if you want to find the answer to any question, follow the money. Well, the answer to the question of why country music became so popular during the decade from 1984 to 1994 lies, to a large extent, in the money. Country music has always been profitable, but the money was made in different ways. Since World War II, the big money in country music has come from publishing; a strong publishing industry was essentially what made Nashville the country music capital of the nation. Sales of country music recordings were always limited by a variety of factors: (1) lack of marketing, such as the major labels undertook (Nashville record companies generally didn't have marketing departments until the 1970s); (2) lack of retail outlets where country music customers could feel comfortable; (3) lack of accurate reporting of sales figures, which distorted the picture of country record sales and tended to perpetuate the stereotype of the music's weak sales; and (4) "country's" negative image among a significant segment of the U.S. population.

During the 1980s and 1990s all that changed—now it is the record labels that reap huge profits on country music. Furthermore, the internal restructuring of record companies brought about by the restructuring of major corporations in response to the changing American economy, and the fact that the music industry is now dominated by six multinational corporations (five of which are headquartered outside the United States), has meant that the money from country music record sales for most labels now flows directly into Nashville bank accounts. Prior to the recently gained autonomy of Nashville labels, this money had been deposited in a label's New York or Los Angeles accounts before being allocated to the Nashville operation. But because country music generated so much money (often enough to "carry" the pop music divisions of several major labels during the 1980s) and because New York and Los Angeles executives did not want to deal with country music (preferring to stick with their pop music superstars), country music executives, whose divisions earned big profits for the labels, wielded an increasing amount of power. Nashville thus emerged as a major power center in the corporate music world.

To get some idea of the growth in income from country music, let's look at the growth of its radio airplay. In 1961, the first year for which the Country Music Association compiled data on radio stations, and the year that probably marked the low point for country music programming (numerous stations had switched from country to rock & roll between 1956 and 1961), there were only 81 stations playing country music full-time. By 1969, however, there were 606, and during the 1970s that figure grew to 1,434. In 1980, there were 1,534 country stations, but by the end of that decade there were 2,108. And those numbers have continued to rise in the 1990s; as of 1994, according to the latest figures from the Country Music Association, 2,427 radio stations now program country music full-time. With more people able to listen to country music on the radio, which constitutes advertising for each recording given airplay, country music reaches a lot of potential buyers.

Within the country music business community, the primary beneficiaries are the publishers because income from radio station airplay goes to publishers and songwriters—not to record companies or artists. Record company income derives only from the sales of recordings, while the artists' primary source of income is their personal-appearance fees, although they also earn some income from the sales of their recordings. Since the Nashville music industry's main enterprise is publishing, this expanded radio programming has strengthened Nashville's position as the country music capital.

There are three revenue streams in the music industry, all of which converge in the successful artist. First, there are fees for personal appearances. Such appearances occur in a variety of performance venues, ranging from small clubs to large concert halls or even stadiums. Booking agents and concert promoters work together to get an artist into each venue, with the promoters generally assuming the financial risk when the agent makes a commitment for the artist. The income is generated by ticket sales: the artist earns either a set fee or a percentage of the gate, less the booking agent's percentage—usually 15 percent of whatever the artist makes. Lucrative sales of merchandise (T-shirts, caps, pictures of the artist, etc.) also generate income from these personal appearances. In fact, artists can often make as much as or more than their fees or gate percentages from such merchandising. As a rule, the money an artist earns for a personal appearance usually covers only his or her expenses, while the profits are generated by merchandise sales. (Obviously, this ratio between fees and merchandising varies from artist to artist. Major acts command high personal-appearance fees or percentages, while lesser-known acts must settle for less and must depend more on merchandising to generate income.)

The second revenue stream is the income earned from the airplay—on radio and TV—of recordings. Each radio and TV station pays a certain amount of money (based on a formula by which the station's advertising revenues, market share, and audience size are calculated) to the performing-rights organizations—BMI, ASCAP, and SESAC—which then pay the respective songwriters and publishers of the songs that get airplay. Consumers indirectly pay for performing rights when they buy the products that a station has advertised. The retail price of each advertised product is high enough to cover or absorb the cost of its advertising on radio and TV, which constitutes income for the stations.

The third revenue stream is the income earned from sales of recordings to consumers. When someone walks into a store and buys a recording, the money paid for it is split among the retailer, the wholesaler, the artist, and the record company. This is the only revenue stream from which the record company makes money.

All of the music industry's income is generated by these three revenue sources. For example, the musicians who play on a label's releases are paid through their union by the record company, which advances the money (much as a venture capitalist would do) for production. Studios and engineers earn income this way as well. Publishers also record songs (as "demos") and pay the singers, musicians, studios, and engineers, usually less than the "master" rate paid to them for commercial recordings. Managers, on the other hand, earn a percentage of artists' incomes; this is generally 10 to 20 percent, although for some ventures, such as merchandising T-shirts or setting up a publishing company, an artist and a manager will often go into business together and split the income.

NASHVILLE BECAME the country music center for a variety of reasons, including the success of the *Grand Ole Opry,* which was created by an insurance company (the National Life and Accident Insurance Company) in order to help sell policies, as well as the establishment of publishing companies, record companies, and booking centers for country music by individuals, most of whom were connected to the *Opry*. But there were several reasons for the major labels' choosing to let recording be done in Nashville. First, there was obviously a talent pool at the *Opry,* and some studios developed around it, notably, Castle, which was founded by three WSM engineers. But there was also the fact that the major label executives in New York right after World War II simply did not want to handle country music or blues. These executives liked popular music, which they knew and understood, so there was no power grab for country music, since neither big money nor prestige was attached to it, and Nashville thus became the center for country music almost by default.

Still, the major labels retained control in New York or Los Angeles, although they had offices in Nashville and staffs to oversee their country music divisions. But as country music flourished and prospered, its success made Nashville less and less of an outpost until the point was reached where it became a financial center for the U.S. music industry. And when a place generates too much revenue to be ignored, first with publishing and booking and then through sales of recordings, a power shift in the corporate world is inevitable.

Because the *Opry* made so much money, and attracted so much attention to Nashville, the National Life and Accident board decided to create the Opryland theme park. And when this proved successful in turn, plans were made for a cable TV network centered on country music. Since Nashville had established itself as a stronghold of music publishing, first with the formation of Acuff-Rose in 1942 and later with Cedarwood and Tree, more songwriters were attracted to the city and more publishing companies were formed there. This led the performance-rights organizations (ASCAP, BMI, and SESAC) to establish offices in Nashville. The Country Music Association was formed in 1958 to serve as a sort of Chamber of Commerce for country music, promoting the music to advertisers in order to secure radio airplay, which would widen the music's exposure. The CMA also established the Country Music Hall of Fame, which further enhanced Nashville as a major tourist attraction for country music fans and generated a new revenue stream that complemented those of the music industry. Finally, an awards show and a network TV show gave Nashville (and country music) more exposure, prestige, and income.

The major labels produced country music because it made money, especially when it was recorded in Nashville studios that employed local musicians.

The famous Nashville Sound was simply the product of a handful of musicians who worked together quickly and efficiently to turn out albums economically. Since it didn't cost much to record a country album, it was easy to make a profit. Major label executives didn't have to bother too much with the music or the people; they just sat back and let the money roll in. There was always somebody in charge of the Nashville office to oversee all this, but at first these managers were usually musicians who would hire other musicians and organize a recording session for some talent they'd found. Gradually, support staffs were hired and then expanded to include promotion and publicity people as well as sales and marketing staffs. With greater profits being made by the Nashville offices, the country music executives who ran them wielded more power within the record companies, which then had to give the Nashville offices more autonomy. (After all, as the old saying goes, "if it ain't broke, don't fix it.")

COUNTRY MUSIC SUPERSTARS have had an impact on the pop music world since Jimmie Rodgers, the Blue Yodeler, began his career in 1927. During the 1950s there were such stars as Eddy Arnold, Hank Williams, Tennessee Ernie Ford, Kitty Wells, and Elvis Presley; in the 1960s, Roger Miller, Merle Haggard, Johnny Cash, Charley Pride, Jim Reeves, Patsy Cline, and Loretta Lynn; in the 1970s, Dolly Parton, Charlie Rich, Waylon Jennings, and Willie Nelson; in the 1980s, Alabama, Randy Travis, George Strait, and Reba McEntire; and now, in the 1990s, there is superstar Garth Brooks. But since the late 1980s, there has been a big difference in how such superstars have emerged. Prior to this time the success of country music depended on its "crossover" capability, or appeal to the pop music market. This meant that country artists had to have an appeal *outside* the field of country music. Since the mid-to-late 1980s, however, country artists have been able to become superstars *within* the country music field, and this has subtly changed the music itself. Country artists could now attain superstardom *as* country artists because enough money was being generated by the country music industry to make crossovers and appeal to the pop music market unnecessary.

The development of new technologies for the information-based economy, specifically cable TV, bar codes and scanners, and computer networks within and among companies, changed the country music industry more than its own new technologies of CDs and digital sound did. These information-based technologies demonstrated the popularity and success of country music in hard numbers.

In the 1990s, information and money are power. And that's why country music has emerged as such a powerful force in the mainstream music industry. Country music no longer has to be held hostage to the whims, tastes, and prejudices of record company executives in New York or Los Angeles, but can now market itself in its own way. Ironically, since it has become so successful, country music has attracted a number of highly talented musicians, singers, songwriters, and executives to Nashville, as they flee the dirty, crime-plagued cities of New York and Los Angeles for the environs of country green.

NOTE

This article draws on the knowledge of and experience in the music industry that I have gained over the last two decades, including my stints as the country and gospel music editor of two trade publications, *Record World* (1974–76) and *Cashbox* (1979–80), and as an executive of Monument Records (1976–77). I have also relied here on the following sources: *Statistical Abstract of the United States: 1993* (Washington, DC, 1994); *World Almanac: 1994,* ed. Robert Famighetti (Mahwah, NJ, 1994); Sam Walton, with John Huey, *Made in America* (New York, 1992); and Joel Whitburn, *Top Country Singles: 1944–1988* (New York, 1989).

# Country Music and the

# Contemporary Composer

*The Case of Paul Martin Zonn*

 **Michael Kurek and Cecelia Tichi**

In 1981, Joel Krosnick, cellist of the Juilliard String Quartet, commissioned a work from composer Paul Martin Zonn, winner of two Ford Foundation fellowships and a Rockefeller Foundation fellowship and chair of the Composition-Theory Division of the School of Music, University of Illinois, UrbanaChampaign. Zonn, a clarinetist and conductor of the UI Contemporary Chamber Players and New Music Ensemble, responded with a composition entitled *Prairie Songs* (1983), scored for violin, cello, acoustic guitar, oboe, mandolin, and bass (Figure 1). The work was performed at Lincoln Center and the Library of Congress, and musically knowledgeable listeners were immediately able to identify its indebtedness to bluegrass (a genre whose position on the country music spectrum is discussed by Mark Fenster and Teresa Goddu elsewhere in this volume).[1]

The story of an avant-garde composer's foray into country music seems like a family tale worthy of a made-for-TV movie. It begins with Paul Zonn's parental anxiety when his ten-year-old daughter, Andrea, balked at continuing her violin lessons. Musically speaking, Zonn's *Prairie Songs* came directly out of a father's determination to find some kind of music that would keep his talented daughter interested in the violin when the frustrated Andrea threatened to quit because of her inability, after five years of lessons, to play the violin classics of Mendelssohn and Tchaikovsky. Her composer-father was thankful when Wayne Logue, a violin repairman, suggested a book of "old-time" fiddle tunes as the sort of music that might interest the child sufficiently to bridge the next few developmental years.

Unknown to bluegrass newcomer Andrea Zonn or her parents, the notation

Figure 1. *Prairie Songs* by Paul Martin Zonn. Reproduced with permission. .

in this "old-time" fiddle book was at best skeletal, since bluegrass microtonal inflections are too complex to be fully notated. The crucial improvisational dimension of bluegrass was nowhere indicated on the printed music. Unaware of this, Andrea began learning the tunes in the most literal, note-by-note way. When her father suggested that she enter a county fair fiddling contest, Andrea at first resisted performing such "backwoods" music, but then reluctantly agreed. While pleased enough to win the seventy-five-dollar second prize, Andrea was thrilled by the attention of the veteran fiddlers she met, who offered to teach her their tricks of the trade. (Says Andrea Zonn: They'd "sit down and show you their tunes and play them over and over again and get their left hand right in your face so you could see exactly what they were doing. . . . [They'd] play them until you learned the tune. And that's how the tradition is carried on. You learn it and work on it at home . . . and change it up a little . . . until it becomes your own.")[2]

If his daughter's threat to abandon her classical violin led the composer serendipitously into country music, her fiddle book proved to be the entire family's introduction to bluegrass, which became so compelling an interest that the Zonns were soon traveling the interstates to attend summer bluegrass festivals in Illinois and neighboring states (Ohio, Kentucky, and Kansas), as well as Indiana's Bean Blossom Festival, instituted by the "father of bluegrass music," Bill Monroe.

The profound extent to which these festival vacations proved to be educational is revealed in the sequel to the family story. At college age, Andrea moved to Nashville and completed her education in classical music at Vanderbilt University's Blair School of Music (winning a concerto contest and playing the Mozart A-major violin concerto with the university orchestra), while studying voice and also working as a fiddler and harmony vocalist for such country music stars as Vince Gill, Ronnie Milsap, Pam Tillis and, most recently, Lyle Lovett. In fact, when the teenage Andrea had complained that female country vocalists sounded insipid, Paul Zonn once again came to the rescue, persuading his daughter otherwise with a gift of three albums by Emmylou Harris: *Elite Hotel* (1975), *Luxury Liner* (1977), and *Quarter Moon in a Ten Cent Town* (1978). (Zonn names Vince Gill and John Anderson as country vocalists he especially admires.)

But country music, especially bluegrass, had meanwhile become a Zonn family affair. Andrea's younger brother, Brian, learned guitar and now sings and plays with the country-rock band Six Shooter, while their mother, Wilma Zonn, a professional oboist, regularly performs in concert and teaches music in the Nashville Public Schools, including a stint at Hunter's Lane High School, which may be the only secondary school in the United States to have a program in bluegrass. As for their father, Paul Zonn added mandolin to his instrumental repertoire of piano and clarinet so that he could form his own bluegrass band, which won the Indiana Bluegrass Band Championship in 1983, with Paul himself singing and playing mandolin. In terms of classical or concert music, this family story might be encapsulated by a photograph of the performers of Zonn's *Prairie Songs* on the Lincoln Center stage: among the musicians pictured are Wilma Zonn, playing oboe, Andrea Zonn on violin, and composer Paul Zonn playing mandolin.

The Zonn family chronicle, from county fair fiddling contest to Lincoln Center concert, may seem entirely unremarkable, a sweet story of parental guidance, musical discovery, and career development. The compositional indebtedness of *Prairie Songs* to bluegrass music seems both anomalous and inevitable, yet essentially serendipitous—an accident of geography and personal circumstance. But the temptation to read it this way obscures the cultural barriers that a classical composer must ignore or transcend in order to participate in certain musical styles and traditions, especially country, for which he or she may be criticized (e.g., for commercialism, wasting talent and education, letting his or her musical standards plunge, and even for pandering to debased taste). On the other hand, Aaron Copland effectively quoted Shaker hymns in *Appalachian Spring* (1944), commending what he understood to be the Appalachian ideals of quiet strength, simplicity, and fundamentalist faith. (And Copland was himself quoted, in a musical turnabout, in the arrangement of Dolly

Parton's 1984 ballad "Appalachian Memories.") In recent years, contemporary composers affiliated with the academy and/or the conservatory have shown their commitment to certain popular musical traditions, especially jazz (e.g., the virtually single-handed revival of ragtime and promotion of its performer-exponent Eubie Blake by the New England Conservatory's Gunther Schuller).

Country music, however, has not enjoyed this attention, largely because of the stigma of its "hillbilly" origins. "Hillbilly," "redneck," "hick," "bumpkin"—these are the pejoratives haunting country music, many of whose performers do not read standard transcribed music. (In fact, Nashville musicians have developed what is called "the Nashville number system," which is structured on the diatonic scale, but this system is used locally and has no place in academic music.)[3] Country music, in addition, is scorned for its typical three-chord structure, one considered musically simplistic. Institutionally, moreover, the academy has not accessed the venues of country and bluegrass music (with the notable exception of East Tennessee State University, whose faculty includes mandolinist Jack Tottle). Country/bluegrass vocalist Kathy Chiavola recalls that during her doctoral work in voice and vocal pedagogy at the renowned Indiana University School of Music, none of her cohorts or teachers knew of the Bean Blossom Festival, held annually just a short drive from Bloomington. If jazz and black blues have found a warm reception among those segments of the music intelligentsia eager to embrace an American music whose origins—African-American and Caribbean—are perceived as exotic and distinctly "other," the same welcome has not been extended to a music identified with lower-class, uneducated whites.

Country music practitioners, what's more, have cultivated, perhaps inadvertently, the notion that theirs is a music requiring little knowledge or skill. The songwriters, in particular, downplay any rigor, difficulty, or problems of composition (word choice, rhythm, rhyme). Instead, they have presented their work as music that is innocent of technique. We hear this over and over again from the songwriters quoted in *Sing Your Heart Out, Country Boy* by Dorothy Horstman. One important feature of this useful collection of twentieth-century country songs is the commentary provided by the writer or a close companion, explaining something about the origin of each song. Hank Williams's second wife, for instance, recounts driving with him from Nashville to Louisiana in a top-down convertible as Hank described marital problems with his first wife, whom he characterized during that conversation in the car as a "cheatin' heart." Billie Jean Williams Horton recalls Hank's exclaiming, "Hey, that'd make a good song! Get out my tablet, Baby; me and you are gonna write us a song." According to Horton, Williams dictated "Your Cheatin' Heart" in a matter of minutes.[4]

The speedy song is virtually a staple of country music composition—that is, as the songwriters report it. It is said to be the serendipitous product of an off-hand phrase or an overheard remark. Harlan Howard, the legendary Nashville songwriter and member of the Country Music Hall of Fame, recounts over-hearing a couple arguing and the woman flinging the line "Well, you can just pick me up on your way down." A year later, Howard recalls, "All of a sud-den, I sat down and just wrote the song ["Pick Me Up on Your Way Down"] from beginning to end, and I've never changed a word. It just kind of fell into place." Anecdotes such as these make country music songs seem like the result of virtually natural processes. No struggle is required. The writer does not sweat or agonize over the lyrics or the melody line, does not shift phrases around in search of coherence or the most satisfying form. The songwriter, in these accounts, meets no resistance: a key phrase is simply overheard or spon-taneously spoken, and the song immediately takes shape. Thus Merle Haggard recalls that "Okie from Muskogee" "probably took twenty minutes to write," while Jay Miller reports pulling his car over and taking a pad of paper from his glove compartment in order to immediately write down the lyrics to "It Wasn't God Who Made Honky Tonk Angels." Holly Dunn says that her signature song, "Daddy's Hands," occurred to her one morning and was "a reality" by night-fall.[5] Numerous songs are similarly described, including Ted Daffan's "Headin' Down the Wrong Highway," Mel Tillis's "Ruby, Don't Take Your Love to Town," and John Volinkaty's "Satin Sheets." The writers all tell the same story: "It took about ten minutes, including the melody. . . . I wrote the story in about an hour. . . . It took thirty minutes to write."[6] And so on.

But speed of composition is not really the issue: the important thing is the notion that the song is created whole, virtually intact, existing before it is written down. The act of writing only formalizes what already *is*—or what is already gestating. The songwriter becomes something between a stenographer, a spiritual channeler, and an incubator or midwife. "I give birth every time I write a song," says Dolly Parton. And, as the late Roy Acuff said, in elaborat-ing this theme, "Nobody really writes our music, you know. If we write a song, we're only writing what we've felt and heard."[7] Country music composers who reminisce about the short time it took to get the song down on paper are really voicing the Romantic tenet of the organic song or poem. Their conception of the song is part of the same tradition that led Thoreau to describe poetry as "a natural fruit," or to say that "man bears a poem . . . as naturally as the oak bears an acorn and the vine a gourd."[8] The country music song, like Thoreau's poem, is a "natural." Rodney Crowell, who is acknowledged to be a major country songwriter, describes himself more modestly: "I'm just here with a butterfly net, catching . . . the music." Country songwriters who gauge their work in stopwatch terms or describe it in the language of fruition share Thoreau's viewpoint. Their songs are organic entities that come into being at the moment of ripeness, ready to be "picked" (as it were), or harvested. "I caught a song and set it free," goes a line in the Rodney Crowell/Will Jennings song "Many a Long and Lonesome Highway"—the country song as a creature, captured and then set loose in the world.[9] Marty Brown, the Kentucky Kid, used the same maternity image we heard from Dolly Parton when he explained, during a TV appearance: "Writing a song's just like . . . having a baby. If it's going to come, it's going to come. And when it does, you'd better have a pen and pad around just like you'd better have a doctor around delivering that baby."

Country music's organic self-representation is, of course, contrary to the very idea of *composition,* which brings us back to Paul Zonn. The composer who wants to compositionally exploit bluegrass or any other country music can do so only if he (or she) ignores the barriers of cultural stereotypes, of musically generic self-representation, and of musical self-identification with diverse—and often mutually exclusive—genres and traditions. In order to understand the genesis of Paul Zonn's *Prairie Songs,* we need to address the issue of what is loosely called "crossover."

The term "crossover" is commonly applied to a performer of one popular music style who veers toward, or shifts completely into, a different style (for example, a "rock" singer who records a "country" album). As remarkable as these musical crosscurrents may seem, they are nothing new. They have been going on in classical music (which we tend to call "concert" music) throughout its history. Specifically, concert music composers have a long tradition of borrowing elements of style from the popular music of their day. (To cite only a few examples, Bach's suites are modeled on courtly dance music, Mahler used Jewish klezmer-style music in his symphonies, and Stravinsky employed various jazz and tango references in several of his pieces.) However, what is important to our focus here is the current concert music scene and, more specifically, three distinct types of interaction between concert music and popular music. Using examples of country and bluegrass styles, we aim to distinguish musical "crossover" from "postmodern simulation" and from "eclecticism."

By "crossover," we mean a situation in which a composer or performer departs (perhaps temporarily) from his or her normal venue/medium/genre in order to pursue a different one, although the new work that results may retain elements of the old. Certain general assumptions or problems inherent to the crossover, however, need to be clarified before we take up our example, Mark

O'Connor's fiddle concerto. The term "crossover," itself at risk of a pejorative connotation, clearly raises an intriguing question of value judgment: How skillfully *can* an expert in one musical style "cross over" to make music in a different style? For example, the "white bands" of the big-band era, such as the Paul Whiteman Orchestra, whose roots were in European ballroom music, are generally considered by jazz aficionados to have produced a relatively poor product because they often failed to "swing." That is, the music represented only a watered-down or superficial approximation of the rhythms and harmonies found in genuine jazz. Likewise, if George Gershwin's *Rhapsody in Blue* (1924) is a popular composer's crossover into concert music, it is generally consigned by classical musicians to the lower ranks of their literature. This is not because the piece alludes to jazz—many respected contemporary concert works do that—but because Gershwin, like Whiteman, was not particularly skilled in the stylistic conventions of the music into which he was crossing. Not only did Gershwin lack the formal training at that time to orchestrate *Rhapsody in Blue,* which Ferde Grofé orchestrated (unlike his later work *Porgy and Bess,* which he orchestrated himself), but his composition is considered by some to be formally flawed—several tunes strung together with little development or formal coherence of the sort one expects from, say, Brahms.

So, judging only by such examples as these, one might be tempted to propose a hierarchy of aesthetic standards for crossover music. The best crossovers would exhibit as much mastery in the composer's adopted style as in his native style (or as if the composer were equally skilled in both styles from the start); the next best would be music whose combination of two distinct styles demonstrates greater skill in the composer's native style than in the style with which he is less adept (whether through some technical deficiency or a fundamental misunderstanding of that style or aesthetic). Last or lowest would be music that is weak in both styles or that guts the effectiveness of both by awkwardly combining them. (Pavarotti's operatic rendition of "I Left My Heart in San Francisco" comes to mind.)

As described above, *Rhapsody in Blue* would seem to fit into the second category, being strong in Gershwin's native style (popular music) but flawed by the standards of his adopted style (concert music). This might lead us to predict the work's ultimate demise. So far, however, it has lived on, probably because listeners simply find it charming enough to put aside style labels; likewise, they may generally overlook its formal "flaws," which seem to be based more on apple-and-orange stylistic comparisons than on audibly objectionable faults (the piece does not aim for Brahmsian formal structure). We may conclude that the charm of the music itself (the melodies, the harmonies, etc.) is what makes it work, not how effective it may be in "crossing over," or how well it may conform to concert style.

Perhaps this conclusion is confirmed, from the creative point of view, by the early work of Gunther Schuller (the 1994 Pulitzer Prize winner in music composition), who endeavored in the 1950s to integrate jazz with contemporary atonal concert music in what he called a "third stream" style (e.g., *Seven Studies on Themes of Paul Klee* [1959]). Most of these works are seldom, if ever, performed anymore, being equally unsatisfactory as *music* to both jazz and classical listeners, in spite of a well-articulated theoretical justification. Had the particular works created in this crossover vein been more compelling, they would have survived as performance pieces.

Crossover works, then, cannot be adequately judged by their conformity to either the standards of the style being crossed "away from" or the standards of the style being crossed "over to." Rather, these works must be allowed to create their own categories and stylistic norms. It can thus be acknowledged that Paul Whiteman was indeed hugely successful (musically, as well as financially), even if his epithet, "The King of Jazz," was a misnomer. Nevertheless, most of us can't seem to avoid placing music into a few basic categories, lest a practical chaos ensue in keeping track of them—like assigning a different name to each individual tree in the world instead of grouping some as maples, say, and others as elms. The dilemma is illustrated well by the early minimalist music of Philip Glass. Glass was not accepted in the professional circles of either concert or popular music, but in this case it was members of the *audience* (for both popular and concert music) who "crossed over" to provide Glass with his own category, idiosyncratic as he seemed to be.

In the case of Mark O'Connor's *Fiddle Concerto for Violin and Orchestra* (1993), we encounter a situation not unlike that of Gershwin's *Rhapsody in Blue:* a concert composition created by a popular musician (but one whose music-reading skills were extremely limited and who needed help to write out the composition in full orchestration). Like Gershwin, O'Connor's knowledge of the music literature of the classical tradition was more limited than that of the typical concert composer, and he lacked formal training in the harmony, counterpoint, and form used in that literature. His approximation of classical style, as he understood it, was ahistorical; that is, it did not conceptually fit within a chronology of works that would constitute an aesthetic frame of reference. (Indeed, it is doubtful that O'Connor was aware of much of the concert music composed since 1900.) As such an approximation, the resulting concerto may be likened to American primitive or folk art, painted naively by rural artists whose freshness has appealed to "high art" circles since the 1920s. O'Connor's concerto has been well-received in much the same way by a segment of the concert audience, and time will tell whether its own musical merits will gain it a place in the standard repertoire of works like *Rhapsody in Blue* that have atypically "crossed over" to the concert hall.

In contrast to such crossovers, many concert compositions employ what we call "postmodern simulation." This technique bears a strong resemblance to "eclecticism," in that various types of music may appear in the same composition and the composer may be motivated by the same desire to acknowledge the musical pluralism of our culture (or of his own musically polyglot background). But rather than striving for an eclectic blend or synthesis of contrasting musical elements, this composer tends to simulate several different styles sequentially in a single piece. William Bolcom and John Corigliano are perhaps the two most prominent composers who exemplify postmodern simulation. Bolcom's *Songs of Innocence and of Experience* (1984) is a mammoth work that sets Blake's poetry to music not only for large orchestra, but for many vocal soloists and choirs as well as rock and country western bands. One song, "The Shepherd," is an unabashedly Hank Williams-style number, stylistically pure from the moment it begins until it is interrupted by atonal bombast, signaling the next section. (Bolcom's piece also incorporates bluegrass fiddle, rock, and reggae in discrete sections, among its several styles.) According to the composer's program note, an eclectic integration is supposed to emerge: "The apparent disharmony of each clash and juxtaposition eventually produces a deeper and more universal harmony, once the whole cycle is absorbed." However, many listeners report that they have difficulty perceiving this larger context and find the music unsettling. Just as they begin to enjoy one "program," Bolcom seems to go "channel-surfing" with a remote control and jerks them into a completely different program. Then, just as they begin to "believe in" this new music, he jerks them around again. For many listeners, this experience seems typically "postmodern," that is, "art about other art," with the music becoming too self-referential and too stylistically self-conscious. The listener is impressed by its cleverness, but is so distracted by the changes of style that it is difficult to become emotionally involved with the work, which in the end seems more like a collage than a hybrid.

An essentially different type of musical crosscurrent is represented by the recent trend in concert music called "eclecticism." The eclectic composer does not cross over from one particular style into some other one. Rather, he remains in the concert tradition, retaining its media (e.g., the string quartet) and its venues, but he embraces and wishes to integrate other styles in his work.

The eclectic composition is generally intended to be a truly organic hybrid, not just a collocation of musical allusions or quotations—which brings us back to Zonn's *Prairie Songs,* a chamber work reconciling bluegrass and fully chromatic, atonal, concert music traditions. At some points in the piece, the two traditions are allowed to speak separately, while other sections either gradually integrate them into or let them evolve away from a hybrid union. This convincing union is accomplished in various ways. First, fragments of what will become a tonal melody are woven into a complex, (mostly atonal) polyphonic fabric so that when the tonal context emerges, it has been prepared and is unified. Second, the atonal music sometimes employs performance practices associated with bluegrass: the violin will at times be played with the rhythms and gestures of a fiddle, but with atonal pitches, while bluegrass mandolin tremolos periodically articulate atonal melodic motifs and the double bass is sometimes used to pluck out atonal lines in the manner of a bluegrass bass fiddle. Finally, each style is always kept in check by the other. Even when bluegrass elements seem to dominate the texture, an oboe (a distinctly concert instrument) keeps the listener's ear attuned to the concert style. When the two traditions seem co-equal in presence, each is fragmented rather than monolithic, sounding not so much superimposed on each other as woven together into a variegated fabric. The coherence of Zonn's eclecticism (or "fusion," as he prefers to call it) may owe something to his mastery of the distinct skills mandated by each style. Both a country songwriter (e.g, "Water, Earth, and Air" [1991] and "Hotel Shelby Park" [1992]) and a purely classical composer (e.g., *String Quartet No. 5* [1985]), Zonn has produced convincing, noneclectic works in each style.

AT THIS POINT, the "Paul Zonn Story" can be taken up again, in relation to his eclecticism. As Zonn himself says, "My music has always been concerned with the very new and the very old, and the integration of diverse elements." He continues, "I frequently use the many languages of the world's music, binding them together with common syntax. All of my musical interests and performance skills reveal themselves very naturally in my own compositions." *Very naturally?* Is Zonn acceding to the Romantics' organicist ontology? No. He speaks as a composer identifying his relation to many musics (Figure 2).

In accounting for Zonn's eclecticism, we must also consider his unconventional career trajectory. His was not the typical B.F.A.–M.F.A.–Ph.D. route to university faculty status. Growing up in Miami, Florida, Zonn learned to play the clarinet (the cheapest instrument in the pawnshop and the only one his father could afford), and he earned spending money in high school by "playing the Beach"—performing in the bands playing nightly at Miami Beach hotels

Figure 2. Classical Zonn. Courtesy of Paul Zonn.

like the Eden Roc (and doing orchestral arrangements for them as well). While a music student at the University of Miami, Zonn was trained in the European concert tradition and studied theory and composition. Upon graduation, Paul and Wilma Zonn, newly married, headed for New York City, where the couple played gigs in a range of musical styles, from Mozart to Broadway show tunes, over the next few years.

A pivotal point in their life together occurred with Wilma's decision to enter graduate school at the University of Iowa, where Paul also began graduate work, played in the university orchestra, and listened to the New Music. His performance of Milton Babbitt's avant-garde *Composition for Four Instruments* so pleased the composer that he recommended Zonn to Lucas Foss, director of the Center for Performing and Creative Arts at the State University of New York,

Figure 3. Country Paul. Courtesy of Paul Zonn.

Buffalo, where Zonn joined the faculty as a clarinetist and composer. When the Lenox String Quartet visited the Center, they persuaded the Zonns to return to Iowa, but this time to Grinnell College, the quartet's musical home base, where Wilma continued her graduate work. From there came Tanglewood and Berkshire Music Center fellowships. The opportunity to join the University of Illinois faculty in composition came about through the Zonns' widening circle of musical acquaintances.

Paul Zonn's curriculum vitae now lists performances with the Lenox String Quartet, the Miami Philharmonic, and the New Orleans Jazz Band—as well as shots with the Nashville Jug Band and Vince Gill. Avant-garde and traditional jazz and music of the sixteenth through the twentieth centuries are among his interests and his resources. So are country music and bluegrass (Figure 3). Zonn's career can be viewed as the basis for an interrogation of the ways in which musical hierarchies are culturally established and naturalized—and rejected. When Zonn says that his diverse musical interests are expressed "very naturally" in his compositions, he is claiming a barrier-free musical outlook for himself. He is saying that he takes (and makes) his music where he finds it, and one place where he finds it is in country.

NOTES

1    This essay is based on an interview with Paul Zonn in Nashville, January 1994. It also draws on a discussion of country music songwriting and a profile of Andrea Zonn in Cecelia Tichi, *High Lonesome: The American Culture of Country Music* (Chapel Hill, 1994), 198–200 and 233–39. Conceptually, our discussion here is indebted to Leonard Meyer's distinction between "borrowing" and "simulation," with the latter term referring to music written in a certain style as opposed to a virtually verbatim transcription of existing music. See Leonard Meyer, "The Aesthetics of Stability," in *Music, the Arts, and Ideas* (Chicago, 1967), 199–205.

2    Tichi, *High Lonesome,* 236.

3    See Chas. Williams, *The Nashville Number System* (Nashville, 1988).

4    Dorothy Horstman, *Sing Your Heart Out, Country Boy: Classic Country Songs and Their Inside Story, by the Writers Who Wrote Them,* rev. ed. (Nashville, 1986 [1975]), 209.

5    Ibid., 180–81.

6    Ibid., 240, 224.

7    Ibid., 220.

8    Henry David Thoreau, "Homer, Ossian, Chaucer," *The Dial* 4 (April 1844): 290–305; quotations on 290–91.

9    Horstman, *Sing Your Heart Out,* 207, 184.

# "My name is Sue! How do you do?"

*Johnny Cash as Lesbian Icon*

 ——————————————————— **Teresa Ortega**

> I used to hang out in this bar in Baltimore that was *really* heavy
> duty, I mean, where many of the women looked like Johnny Cash.
> And I met Johnny Cash this year and I . . . almost told him that.
> —John Waters
>
> I know I had it comin',
> I know I can't be free.
> —Johnny Cash, "Folsom Prison Blues"

The special affection that many gay men have for certain female stars has been firmly established for years in mainstream American folklore about gays. A less well-told tale by far is that of the equally intense way in which many lesbians relate to various popular icons of masculinity, including male movie stars, singers, and athletes. In fact, lesbians idolize certain male celebrities in significant enough numbers to create a recognizable canon of male lesbian icons. Such a list would doubtless include Elvis, James Dean, and Marlon Brando at the top (though a non-celeb, dear old Dad, ranks with them), followed by a range of lesser gods roughly equivalent to, say, Karen Black or Maria Montez in the gay males' pantheon of celebrities. It is among these quirkier, yet still widely admired objects of lesbian idolatry—who include the likes of Sal Mineo and Bruce Lee—that Johnny Cash may be justifiably placed as a lesbian icon.

If there is an organizing principle to this temple of lesbian worship, a deep, beating heart within this conundrum of non-manhating behavior, it is lesbian identification with troubled and suffering masculinity. In his songs chronicling men's painful dealings with railroads, prisons, God, drugs and alcohol, lousy automobiles, bad dogs, and women, Johnny Cash relates plenty of tales of masculinity gone strange with grief, remorse, and loneliness. I have found the legendary path toward butchness that Johnny Cash embodies to be a perfect correlative to many lesbians' experiences of becoming gendered as "mannish." Taking place on the terrain between lesbian childhood and adulthood, this process of identification with Cash covers the peculiar ground between stardom and fandom that is home to intense curiosity, lip-synching, and occasional minor fame.

I REMEMBER WELL, as a child in grade school, the first time I heard the Folsom Prison album. Of course, when I mention listening to Johnny Cash as a child, I really mean to say, *as a lesbian child*. It is lesbian children who do the pioneering work of seeking out heroes and role models to help them through the calamity of gay childhood, and it is therefore on their reception of Cash that I will focus. After hearing *Folsom,* I became intensely interested in Johnny Cash, imitating him—swearing and repeating, "Hello, I'm Johnny Cash," in the lowest voice I could muster—singing along with him, trying to play harmonica as well as guitar like him, and eventually dressing like him, in all-black men's clothes and heavy, black boots. If that description doesn't immediately make you see what a big dyke Johnny would have been if he'd been born a woman, you are probably convinced that Wynonna is a sweet flower of femininity, too. But best leave that one alone, for now.

What did I like about Johnny? Well, what's not to like? Johnny Cash is, after all, a mysterious, sexy, perverse man, and no album shows off his dangerous appeal more than his 1968 release, *At Folsom Prison*. Yet despite its being a one-man thriller showcase, *Folsom* is at the same time quintessential family entertainment, offering much to please both adults and kids. Although it was certainly never intended for children, *Folsom,* recorded live with an audience of prisoners, manages nonetheless to pack in more perverse fun and child-oriented yucks than an episode of *Pee-Wee's Playhouse*. For starters, nearly every song demonstrates one of the age-old first principles of child's play: engage in some prohibited activity and have lots of fun doing it ("Hey kids, everybody SCREAM REAL LOUD!"). The famous line in "Orange Blossom Special"—"I don't care if I do-dah-do-dah-do-dah-do-dah-do"—serves as a slogan for this type of jubilantly contrary behavior. Plus, there's plenty of rowdy ambience to enjoy, what with Johnny yelling "Suuuueey!" at the audience and cracking up in the middle of songs. No self-respecting fifth grader could fail to enjoy the joke lyrics to "Dirty Old Egg-Sucking Dog" or "Flushed from the Bathroom of Your

Heart." Add W. S. Holland's railroad percussion to all that and you've got a child-pleaser to rival anything put out by *Sesame Street*.

However, the lesbian child who listens and identifies with the perverse antics on *Folsom* also finds herself imaginatively placed in some very adult situations. In the first song ("Folsom Prison Blues"), for instance, Cash describes how he lands in prison when, despite his mother's warnings not to mess with guns, he shoots and kills a man "just to watch him die." The catcalls of approval from the audience following this revelation encourage the child listener's identification with this shit-eating bravado, despite its unhappy results. While the murderer in "The Long Black Veil" shows remorse for his crime, Johnny interrupts his delivery of the climactic lines expressing the criminal's regret with his own laughter and the question "Did I hear somebody applaud?" thereby undermining the lyric's anguish. The gallows humor of "25 Minutes to Go" invites the listener to empathize with the doomed man and to identify with the prisoner's defiance, pleasures only slightly tempered by the fact that the prisoner is hung at the end of the song. In fact, *Folsom* is characterized by its relentless depiction of the attractiveness of the wrongdoer, as in Cash's charismatic rendition of "Cocaine Blues," which creates empathy for a prisoner facing a life sentence by describing the fateful day he "shot his woman down."

*Folsom*'s invitation to identify with criminality is reinforced by Cash's showmanship. During his remarks between songs, he makes several jokes at the expense of authority figures, including the prison warden and Columbia Records (who, he claims, will censor his frequent cussing), creating a cozy us-against-them relationship with his audience. I can attest to the curiosity and excitement, as well as the frustration, of the listening child who wants to know what words those repeated bleeps are replacing, so she can share in the prisoners' experience of the live stage. Cash's skill at creating a rapport with his audience seems so natural that it places the listener in the odd position of a sort of aural voyeur, as she attempts to insert herself into this intimate though confining space, within the imagined walls of prison. In "The Long Black Veil," the listener is let in on the tantalizingly secret crime that "nobody knows / nobody sees / nobody knows but me," namely, that the doomed speaker had "been in the arms" of his "best friend's wife" on the night of a murder for which he cannot reveal his alibi. The power of Cash's songs to invoke prison, even the ones that do not deal directly with the prison experience, stems from the loneliness and isolation of those he sings about and from the queer cage of desire in which his music's cast of characters often find themselves trapped. For example, the poor miners lauded in "Dark as the Dungeon" are depicted as incapable of leaving a profession where the "danger is double," lusting for the "dark, dreary mines" like "a pig with his dope / and a drunkard with his wine." Like these miners, the lesbian child also desires forbidden yet compelling company, despite the fact that the danger already inherent to the sexual longings of girls and women is at least doubled for lesbians by virtue of their unlawful bent. The song's metaphor of wallowing like a pig in forbidden pleasures likewise strikes a familiar chord in lesbian children, who associate their early gender nonconformity or "masculinity" with both being dirty and its resulting punishments. To be dirty is a condition consistently allowed only to boy children, who routinely dig, stage adventures, and otherwise play in dirt and mud. Different standards of conduct and appearance apply to girl children, just as today's grown-up women are encouraged to maintain strict regimens of cleanliness through shaving, douching, and other prescribed hygienics. When, in the movie *Fried Green Tomatoes,* kid lesbian Idgie Threadgoode walks down the stairs dressed for her sister's wedding, smudged with dirt from head to toe, the audience's laughter is not simply or merely situational, since a male child in the same sequence would most likely register an attitude of light censure or a "boys will be boys" dismissal. Rather, audience laughter at Idgie's appearance is an indicator of how transgressive the image of a dirty girl child is. As funny to a modern audience as Jack Lemmon in a dress, perhaps dirt is the female comedic form of male drag (cross-dressing being the tragic form). For the lesbian child, punishment for being dirty or "acting like a boy" is oftentimes the state of cleanliness itself, with its humiliating "revelation" of feminity—though a femininity that cleanliness and physical purity themselves define and construct.

At the time of the Folsom·Prison recording in 1968, Cash had only recently (and temporarily) recovered from a drug addiction that landed him in jail on seven different occasions over a period of seven years. These well-publicized troubles, as well as the success of the Folsom and San Quentin albums, helped to create a legendary connection between Johnny Cash and prisons in the mind of the public. Prisons also played an important role in Cash's private life: it was a sheriff's words after a night spent in a Georgia jail that initiated his turning away from drugs and toward God. Prisons, like convents and military barracks, are fantasy locations with a particularly strong hold on the lesbian child's imagination. All three of these same-sex institutions proffer a lifelong career option to single women, and women who do not conform to conventional gender expectations are visibly at work in each one, often performing manual tasks traditionally thought of as belonging to men. As popularly depicted in movies, television, and other media, nuns, servicewomen, and female convicts provide lesbian children with powerful, sustaining images of a plausible working future, even when the media's portrayal of these nonconformist women is negative or explicitly homophobic. The discipline and enclosure that are the hallmarks of these institutions offer the young lesbian a means to defend herself against societal disapproval, while at the same time protecting and indulging her sexuality by way of the accidental inevitability of *faute de mieux* sexuality. "Faute de mieux," meaning "for lack of something better," as in the disclaimer "I'm sorry, Warden/Sergeant/Reverend Mother, but what choice did I have?" Faute de mieux, meaning not congenital homosexuality, not the rooted, irresistible, unyielding force of lesbian desire, not *that* prison. Finally, these cloistered, same-sex institutions afford lesbians the not insignificant opportunity to wear a gender-concealing or gender-neutral uniform without recrimination. Of the three, the slammer clearly wins out in the fashion department, for a complete fantasy ensemble includes not only the de rigueur gray and white stripes, but also the chic black of the criminal.

ALL IDOLS HAVE THEIR NICHES, their singular groups of devotees who wear the right clothes, make the appropriate sacrifices, and worship in the designated areas, revering the distinctive qualities of their special gods. As a lesbian icon, Johnny Cash enjoys the attention of a particular dyke crowd who stand by their man for his notable contributions to the world of lesbian fashion. With his homely face, starkly cut hair, and unfashionable black clothes, Cash's star image is determinedly antiaesthetic, a style that owes more to folksiness than to artiness. Cash's unapologetic self-presentation symbolizes many lesbians' view of their own relationship to ideals of physical beauty, both masculine and feminine. In addition, lesbians admire the particulars of Cash's wardrobe and the weathered but durable masculine persona his clothes define and project. To understand the origins of the lesbian fan's appreciation of Cash, and of male stars generally, we must look once again to the lesbian child and the disquieting path to adulthood she must travel.

Homophobic U.S. culture rejects the very idea of gay children, challenged and reviled by the paradox of innocence and guilt that they represent. Most parents, however, are well acquainted with the child types of the tomboy and the sissy, whose prefiguring of the lesbian and gay adult makes them the focus of parental concern. Although our society is no longer as virulently anti-tomboy or anti-sissy as it used to be, what with Alan Alda and all that, when I was growing up in the pre-Stonewall 1960s the situation was still rather . . . tense. I remember my parents nervously taking in my requests to play with neighborhood boys and to have boys' clothes and toys as if each new query held some mysterious power to set our house on fire. Yet the stigma of tomboyism comes not from a girl's actual desire or ability to throw a ball harder than the boy next door, but from adults' palpable fears of what not-so-innocent pastimes such ball-playing might lead to and from the policing, monitoring, and disciplining that thus attends tomboyish behavior. Perhaps, we might speculate, it is this initial watchfulness that first evokes the trinity of prison, convent, and military in the mind of the lesbian child. In any case, and despite my earlier caveat, over the past twenty years things probably haven't changed so much for tomboys. Although feminism has helped to loosen some of the strictures placed on tomboys, homophobia and the acceptable limits of child-watching have increased by way of the Reagan/Bush years, strengthening rationales for punitive observation. So, while my comments here draw on the experience of a pre-feminist, pre-gay lib era, they should be broadly descriptive of a segment of today's tomboy children.

It is important first to acknowledge that distinctions must be made among tomboys, with gradations of experience often determining what a girl's tomboyism will mean, both to herself and others, over the course of her development. There are tomboys who become heterosexual, for example, just as there are tomboys who become lesbians. Most pertinent to this discussion, there are tomboys who know they are lesbians—or if that word is beyond their conceptual reach—who may simply feel that, as the cinematic Idgie Threadgoode puts it, "God's made a mistake."

There are some girls so strongly imprinted with a butch sensibility that you can almost see the young dykes they will become. The girls' own mothers, like as not, are afraid of them, the backwards outcome of being too afraid for them. Sometimes the girl is involved in an incident or has specific talents or inclinations, none of which may be sexual in nature, that link her to lesbian sexuality in the mind of her community. In my case, early and persistent cross-dressing made a strong impression on friends, family, and others. Boyishness is not what attracts attention to these tomboys; rather, it is the "mannishness" that their future holds, their potential growth into adult butch lesbians, that leads parents and peers to stare as if into a monstrous looking glass. Such intense scrutiny will likely lead the young butch in turn to seek out, in one form or another, the trouble so clearly expected of her, perhaps leading her to repeated detention, juvenile hall, or worse (again, the specter of prison hovers). Given the predictability of this course of events, one can readily see how role models for the junior butch set might be in order.

But for all lesbian children (tomboys or not) born pre-Stonewall, and, I suspect, for those lesbian children born in the 1970s as well, there were no lesbian role models. Nor were any images, stories, or other useful information about being a lesbian available within popular culture. As is typical for most dykes

of my generation or older, I cannot remember ever once before I turned sixteen seeing or hearing about another real-life lesbian—not on television, not
on the street, not in print—so complete was the media blackout on the everyday existence of lesbians, so complete was our pre-Stonewall invisibility. In my
day, then, and in the many other days before Martina and k. d. lang, lesbian
children had to look elsewhere than in the conventional consumer resources
for details on how to live as lesbians. Many went to the library to find such
information and later made themselves professional homes there, hence the
popularity of this profession among grown-up lesbians. Meanwhile, the young
butches, like myself, were already negotiating lesbian existence in the most
visible and harrowing way, always looking for something that could help us
understand what it meant to be masculine-gendered females. We found it in
the most secret, most safe, least-likely-to-be-found-out place you could look.
Enter male-celebrity fandom.

Madonna has been quoted as calling lesbian singer k. d. lang "the female
Elvis." Lang self-consciously borrows from the styles, repertoires, and mannerisms of several male stars, including Elvis, Frank Sinatra, Roy Orbison, and
Dean Martin. In her live act, lang will break into an Elvis-style hip gyration one
minute, then grasp the microphone in a Sinatra-style pose the next. Similarly,
acclaimed lesbian performer Peggy Shaw pays homage to such outlaw stars as
James Cagney and Willie Nelson in her one-woman performance piece "You
Look Just Like My Father," which she also wrote. On stage, Shaw talks about
how, as a baby butch, she would practice curling her lip like Elvis. In fact, if
we were to count as Elvis impersonators all of the lesbians who have copied
one significant element of manner or dress from him, there would probably
be more female than male Elvis impersonators in this world. Far from being a
"fringe" practice, male-celebrity fandom is a shaping force in lesbian culture.

In contrast to the remote stardom of Elvis, Johnny Cash's populism lends
depth to lesbian imitation and adulation. Unlike many black-clad singing stars,
Cash's enduring image has little to do with trendy fashion stances, but rather
can be traced to his first humble performances in his hometown church in
Dyess, Arkansas. "Black [was] better for church," Cash is fond of saying; it
was also the only color in which he and his backup musicians had matching
clothes. A homely fellow with a voice that his own publicity releases describe as
"rangy, big, [and] hollow," Cash testifies to hard-earned success against tough
odds, an image that has won him fans from many backgrounds. That same
triumph-in-the-face-of-adversity persona is transposed into a model of masculinity in the well-known Cash hit "A Boy Named Sue." Tormented by "a lotta
laughs / from a lotta folks," the boy named Sue grows up fighting his "whole

life through," but learns to survive in the rough world, just as his father hoped he would. Cash's Sue is a natural point of identification for the butch lesbian child, in whom the line "life ain't easy for a boy named Sue" particularly strikes a sympathetic chord.

The toughness of Cash, expressed in the single-mindedness of his black wardrobe, answers the iconic needs of the butch lesbian child, whose masculinity serves a totemic, armoring function against the constant threat of harm engendered by her difference. Cash's Everyman look also appeals to lesbians because of how easily his style can be adapted, transformed into the fashionable habit of Everydyke. Black jeans or other black pants, black boots, and a black belt are staples of the adult butch's wardrobe (Figure 1). All-black is the lesbian cross-dresser's dream outfit: hiding hips, adding height, creating a line to conceal feminine curves. And, in Cash's awkward voice, which wanders and cracks on many of his songs like some transgendered butch on hormone therapy, the adolescent butch can hear the sound of her own willed efforts to pitch her voice low, fighting the inevitable and undesired changes of puberty. According to Cash, the long hum in the middle of "I Walk the Line" occurred as a result of his efforts to stay on key throughout the course of the song. At all ages, the butch lesbian hums to herself her own song of gender, in order to stay true to her vision of her sex.

Male celebrities have served as important role models for the butch lesbian child in the absence of visible older butches who might serve the same purpose. Toughness and the ability to face the sometimes difficult consequences of American manhood are lessons that lesbians have taken to heart in great numbers. Cash provides a model of the homely but hardworking man that corresponds to the butch child's experience of growing up as a masculine (therefore "ugly") female. Cash's classic example of masculinity thereby encourages the hard labor of survival entailed by growing up differently gendered, or gay. Such models are priceless, for without them and without lesbians' resourceful and imaginative appropriations of images never intended for their use, the already astronomical gay-teen suicide rate might be much higher. I would contend, in fact, that the relationship between the lack of role models for lesbian youth in our culture and the high suicide rates among lesbian teenagers is precisely causal, for to deny a foreseeable future to the lesbian child is at one and the same time to invest in the nonexistence, the extinction even, of the lesbian adult.

DESPITE THE FACTIONALISM and quarrelsomeness of the U.S. lesbian community—with butch and femme lesbians facing off against separatists, poor and

Figure 1. Johnny Cash, sporting perfect dyke hair, wears one of his signature all-black outfits. Photograph courtesy of Photofest.

working-class lesbians struggling with so-called lipstick lesbians and entrepreneurs, lesbians of color protesting the homogeneous whiteness that dominates middle-class lesbian culture, and old lesbians rallying against the ageism of the young, among other ongoing battles—the outlaw character of lesbianism is still a unifying principle of this diverse community. I once heard the "mother of lesbian folk music," Alix Dobkin, encourage an audience largely made up of p.c., New Age-type, white feminist lesbians to commit more acts of political resistance. She told the crowd that if they were smart and worked in twos and threes, no one would notice that they were doing anything illegal because nobody pays attention to women. Of the truth of this statement I have absolutely no doubt, even though one of my own early acts of resistance, cross-dressing (which, as a political act, marks the other, non-p.c. end of the lesbian spectrum from that of Alix's listeners), reveals the opposite truth: being a lesbian can make you visible as a target for harassment by the police and others. For example, an incident that convinced me I was going to be hauled off to jail occurred when I was an earnestly cross-dressing seventeen-year-old. I was tracked by armed police with two enormous dogs after using a women's restroom. (A woman who had seen me in there reported me as a potential male rapist.) When I showed the police my driver's license, with its "F" under "sex," they looked at me uncomprehendingly. Although I shouted, "I'm a woman!" over and over again, they did not believe me and demanded that some friends living nearby vouch for my sex. In many ways, this episode was unsurprising, bearing out the painful conspicuousness, delinquency, and threat of punishment so familiar from my butch lesbian childhood. What was new and frightening was my *adult* lesbian visibility, brought home to me for the first time when the police failed to recognize me as a woman. I stopped cross-dressing several years later, finally self-conscious and scared enough to hide myself in women's clothing, before resuming the practice a few years afterward. By then, I knew how precious and integral this self-constructed gender identity that I had briefly lost was to my sense of self. My childish attempts to fashion an identity out of clothes copped from my father and male cousins were efforts to make me more recognizable to myself by adapting my sense of my gender to my sex. Ironically, I made myself more recognizable to others as well, though not in a way I intended, by unwittingly turning myself into someone who "looked like a lesbian." In those years before my first sexual encounter with another woman, I was both a lesbian and not a lesbian, inhabiting the liminal and little-understood state of child sexuality to which Johnny Cash complexly spoke. Yet it is within the seemingly inherent ambiguity of childhood sexuality that the defining experience of becoming-as-lesbian for me created the most long-lasting and sharply focused tendencies. "Corrupting children" indeed.

As a lesbian born in 1964, I am also part of Generation X, and I find it fascinating that Cash has become an icon to my twentysomething peers. I can only speculate that Xers—media outlaws in the generational wars between the "Blowin' in the Wind" children, who grew up with the Kennedys, and those MTV kids who grew up with Reagan—identify with and are attracted to Cash's outsider status. Besides being a legendary outlaw himself, Cash has aligned himself with many disenfranchised groups, from coal miners to Native Americans. It is fitting, then, that butch lesbians look to Cash, as well as to other male icons, not to lead us deeper into the prevailing capitalist culture, but to teach us how to master cultural isolation. Like Shane riding out of the picture screen, some gay women choose to turn away from society's gaze altogether, either by passing as men or through transsexual passage—quite the opposite of the male transvestite's traditional courting of an audience. Gay men have long looked to the glamour girls of the past as a way to mediate the desire to be "fabulous." Lesbians, by contrast, have always been more reluctant to invest in dreams of no-holds-barred fame and outright attractiveness. Given our less powerful socioeconomic situation and our greater degree of estrangement from consumer culture, it is not surprising that lesbians interpret and appropriate pop culture in dramatically different ways from gay men.

The culture of late capitalism makes desire itself a commodity, selling identities and lifestyles through advertising. Lesbians of all types, many of whom were inspired by Adrienne Rich's "Compulsory Heterosexuality and Lesbian Existence," have especially decried the selling of heterosexuality to women; all lesbians are engaged, to various degrees, in protecting our sexualities and sexual identities from the voyeurism and hype to which all women's sexuality is subject. Lesbians who idolize male stars frustrate market appropriations of lesbian imagery by creating secret networks of identification and desire incomprehensible to a culture that equates lesbianism with man-hating and refuses, as a general principle, to meet lesbian sexuality on its own terms. In this era of increasing social visibility, lesbians must keep in mind the fact that visibility does not equal intelligibility: the preservation of our secret meanings is both our greatest weapon and our smallest hope.

My hope is that the pluralism of U.S. lesbianism, as well as its resistant character, will become known in the coming years, regardless of whether such information comes to the public through well-distributed gay and lesbian venues like *Out* magazine, mainstream TV shows like *Roseanne,* or the anti-gay, watchdog publications of the religious right. For, despite the appearance of such new phenomena as lesbian chic and lesbian-targeted market research on the horizon of our national identity, as long as gay women still grow up valuing and, more importantly, eroticizing solitude, inwardness, and endurance, large segments of the lesbian nation will continue to resist mainstream U.S. culture and will throw in their lots with the other outsiders populating Cash's country.

NOTE
This essay is dedicated to my butch buddy, Ronda Cohen.

# The Dialectic of Hard-Core and Soft-Shell Country Music

        **Richard A. Peterson**

Conventional histories of twentieth-century country music trace a virtually linear development from folk-like to commercial and pop-like music. Resonating with both the American ideal of progress and the equally American nostalgia for a time of imagined simplicity, this view of change in country music is shared by academic and popular chroniclers alike.[1] The conventional story of the music's development is illustrated by a chapter from the conventional history of the *Grand Ole Opry*. Starting in 1926 with an old-time fiddler, Uncle Jimmie Thompson, so the story goes, the *Opry* became the province of a number of ever-more proficient string bands that did not feature many vocals. Roy Acuff himself contributed to the popularization of this version of *Opry* history: "When George D. Hay first started the *Opry* there was some singing, but most of the numbers they featured were instrumental. I was possibly the first one that came there with what they call a voice."[2]

But who, in fact, *was* the most popular act on the *Opry* when Acuff joined in 1938? It was no string band or rustic ace fiddler, but rather a trio of college-educated harmony singers from Chicago: The Vagabonds (Figure 1). With only spare guitar accompaniment, they sang mostly well-known sentimental ballads, such as "Red River Valley," and "heart songs," such as "When It's Lamp Lightin' Time in the Valley." Like other WSM radio station staff bands, the Vagabonds performed on a number of pop music programs as well as on the *Opry*. Unlike the Jack Shook Orchestra, who donned rustic outfits to perform on the *Opry* as "Smiling Jack and His Missouri Mountaineers," the Vagabonds changed neither their moniker nor their costumes. They always appeared on the *Opry* stage in matching casual, collegiate outfits.

Figure 1. The Vagabonds in a mid-1930s model soft-shell publicity
photo. Courtesy of the Country Music Foundation, Inc.

The Vagabonds were not an aberration. Rather, they were part of a drift
toward a softer, popular music sound, one that was clearly heralded by
a number of important additions to the 1930s *Opry* roster, including the
Pickard Family. Their mix of old favorites included comedy ("Froggy Went A-
Courtin'"), tearjerkers ("The Little Rosewood Casket"), dance tunes ("Turkey
in the Straw"), and religious songs ("I'm Gonna Walk the Streets of Glory").
Still and all, the Vagabonds were different enough from the carefully nurtured
"friends and neighbors" image of the *Opry* that its impresario, George D. Hay,
devoted several paragraphs of his 1945 fan-oriented *Story of the Grand Ole
Opry* to demonstrating that the group actually did conform to the *Opry* image:

A NEW turn in the *Opry* road was reached in 1931 when the Vagabonds . . . joined the company. . . . [Each member of the group was] the son of a minister of the gospel, and the boys were thoroughly familiar with sacred numbers and heart songs. . . . Their backgrounds varied somewhat from the other members of the company, in that they received more formal education. . . . [Thus] they could hardly be called "country boys," but they loved folk music, [and accompanying themselves] with a mellow home made guitar . . . their voices blended so well and their enunciation was clear. . . . The Vagabonds told a story with each song.[3]

Then, on 19 February 1938, Roy Acuff, a skinny, fiddle-playing, nasal-voiced rustic singer stepped up to the *Opry* microphone, and his immediate success brought to an end the *Grand Ole Opry*'s drift toward softer sounds. Not only did Roy Acuff and his band win enough audience approval to stay on the *Opry*, but in October 1939, when the NBC network began to carry a thirty-minute segment of the *Opry* each week, Acuff was named its host and thus became the first acknowledged star of the show. Within a year he had become country music's best-known performer, variously hailed as the "King of the Hillbillies," the "Backwoods Sinatra," and the "Caruso of Mountain Music." Capping his rapid rise to prominence was Acuff's appearance on the cover of *Newsweek* in 1952.[4]

ONCE CONFRONTED with this glaring anomaly in the theory of country music's development from rustic to pop style, I began to see numerous other examples of the same sort in the standard accounts of its history. Indeed, the linear-development story runs afoul of the facts right from the beginning of recorded country music, when the old-time songs rendered in the rich operatic stylings of Vernon Dalhart became popular *before* the rougher vocalizations of Fiddlin' John Carson and the "blue yodels" of Jimmie Rodgers did. Bill C. Malone attributes this anomaly, with considerable justification, to the fact that the commercial record producers and radio broadcasters only gradually realized how great a demand there was for music that seemed more rustic or less polished.[5]

The same rationale cannot, however, explain the numerous exceptions to the linear-development theory that dot country music history right up to the present. To cite but one recent major case, the pop-like styles of Barbara Mandrell, Kenny Rogers, Lee Greenwood, Anne Murray, and Ronnie Milsap that were the most popular in the late 1970s and early 1980s were displaced at the top of the charts in the mid-1980s by the more traditional sounds of such artists as Randy Travis, Ricky Skaggs, and George Strait. Promoters and music critics sometimes even referred to these and other leading artists of the late 1980s as "traditionalists." More often, however, they labeled them "neotraditional," and the "neo-" is as important as the "traditional" in the characterization, for while these artists harked back to older lyrical themes, instrumental modes, and performance styles, they did so in ways that profoundly changed and updated the "traditional" elements for a contemporary audience.

Thus a reformulation of the conventional theory of country music's development might well begin by eschewing the word "traditional" because many elements of the so-called *non*traditional performance style are every bit as old as those considered traditional and have a historical continuity of their own. In effect, there is a performance tradition that connects Kenny Rogers with Vernon Dalhart, just as there is one that connects Randy Travis with Roy Acuff and Jimmie Rodgers.

Because these two kinds of performers differ as much in the way they relate to audiences as in their performance styles, those who appeal to the "rustic" tradition are labeled *hard-core* here, while those identified with the more pop-oriented, "parlor" tradition are termed *soft-shell*. The basic promotional claim made for hard-core country music is that it's authentic—made by and for those who remain faithful to the "roots" of country. The corresponding claim made for soft-shell country is that it melds country with pop music elements to broaden its appeal for the much wider audience of those less familiar with or knowledgeable about the hard-core style.[6]

WE CAN BEGIN TO UNDERSTAND the dialectical processes involved in the hard-core/soft-shell distinction by focusing on Roy Acuff's efforts to become a regular on the *Grand Ole Opry*. By 1937, he had already made a number of records and was performing regularly on radio in Knoxville, Tennessee, yet he had been unable to land even a guest appearance on the *Opry*—the institution with which his name is now so closely identified. His early failure and subsequent success can tell us much about the dynamics of neotraditionalism.

From 1934 on, Acuff traveled to Nashville one or more times annually to audition for the *Opry*, but to no avail. Given the *Opry* management's bias toward a soft-shell sound, their lack of interest in Acuff is understandable. His fiddle-playing was not up to that of the *Opry*'s best string band fiddlers, and his singing had none of the polish of other recent recruits, such as the Vagabonds, Robert Lunn, or the Delmore Brothers. They sang in the newly popular "crooning" style that had been made possible by advances in microphone technology. Like Bing Crosby, the greatest of the early crooners, these *Opry* performers sang quietly, but directly into a microphone, so their amplified voices sounded sonorous and their delivery intimate. Such intimacy was striking, particularly in comparison to the full-voiced sound of operatically trained singers like Enrico Caruso and Vernon Dalhart as well as the older *Opry* rustics like Uncle Dave Macon, who were used to projecting their unamplified voices in large halls.

On the advice of promoter Joe Frank, who had gotten to know Acuff when both were in Knoxville, the *Opry* managers invited Acuff to play a guest spot on the program in 1938, substituting for virtuoso fiddler Arthur Smith, who was being furloughed from the *Opry* to deal with his alcohol problem. Acuff nervously played a fiddle tune and then launched into his most popular piece, "The Great Speckled Bird." But, to be fashionable, Acuff sang it, as best he could, in the popular crooning style. This proved a disaster—Acuff himself said, "My voice sounded to me like a whining pup's"—and the band returned to Knoxville, expecting never to hear from the *Opry* management again.[7] Because the *Opry* still needed a temporary replacement for Arthur Smith (and for other, more complex reasons to do with *Opry* "politics"), Acuff and his band were invited back. This time, however, Acuff sang "The Great Speckled Bird" in the full-voiced, high-pitched, nasal, and emotional style he had learned while working without a microphone as a medicine show entertainer. The positive audience response was conveyed immediately via telegrams and letters, and Acuff was signed to fill the temporary slot on the *Opry* and to do a daily early-morning show. Much to the *Opry* management's dismay, Acuff's popularity continued to grow, and he was given even more radio exposure until, within a year of his first appearance, he had become the most highly acclaimed act on the *Opry*.

But while the *Opry* management certainly recognized the need to satisfy an unexpected audience demand, Acuff himself rapidly learned to emphasize in his performances the particular elements that evoked a positive response. He took great pains to sing each song with great clarity and raw emotion, often crying openly while singing such tragic/moralistic songs as "Wreck on the Highway." All of the early accounts of Acuff's appeal stress his appearance of sincerity. Perhaps not since Jimmie Rodgers, who had died five years earlier, had a country music performer so clearly injected such personal feeling into a song.

During Acuff's first months on the *Opry*, the hard-core elements of his act became consolidated. Musicians who championed the band's crooning, jazz-like sound left and were replaced by (more expert) musicians comfortable with the string band style. The most risqué and pop-oriented songs were cut from the band's repertoire, while additional old tunes, or old-sounding tunes, and religious songs were introduced. Acuff paid great attention to image as well. The band's name was changed from the "Crazy Tennesseans" to the "Smoky Mountain Boys," and its mixture of quasi-western and comedic outfits was replaced by a more consistent style of checked shirts and work jeans or the

Figure 2. Roy Acuff and his band strike a late 1930s hard-core rustic pose for a publicity photo. Courtesy of the Country Music Foundation, Inc.

coveralls appropriate for a hillbilly band of the era (Figure 2). One of the clearest demonstrations of Acuff's concern with image occurred in 1940 when he and the band were cast in the Republic Studio film *The Grand Ole Opry*. In keeping with the movie's "western" theme, the Smoky Mountain Boys were issued cowboy outfits. But when Acuff, who had been delayed getting to the dressing room, found them trying on the western garb, "he stood there" (as his biographer later recounted) "with feet wide apart, eyes flashing, and hands fisted. 'What's this all about?' he demanded of his troupe."

> "The movie folks told us to get into this garb."
>
> "Take it off! We'll wear our regular *Grand Ole Opry* clothes, or go back home."
>
> Then turning to the studio officials, he added, "We are just a bunch of country boys from Tennessee who have come out here to put on our little country show like we do back home, and we intend to do exactly that and wear our regular clothes." And they did. Reflecting on the incident in 1943, Acuff affirmed: "I am very annoyed when someone calls me a cowboy. . . . I don't intend for the public ever to see me as a cowboy."[8]

Acuff was also careful to accent the rural and small-town origins of band members in all their publicity and in the comments he made during performances. In some cases, however, Acuff found it less expedient to do so: When Rachial Veach joined the band, for example, she had never been far from her rural, central Tennessee home. She was unfamiliar with indoor plumbing, tall buildings, elevators, store-bought clothes, and the convention of regularly wearing shoes. These would all be natural fodder for country bumpkin comedy if a man were the butt of the jokes, but it would not work, Acuff decided, with a woman as the target because such humor would violate an unspoken Southern taboo against men's satirizing women in public.

Acuff also fabricated relationships among band members for the sake of the group's image. Veach was initially billed as "Rachial, Queen of the Hills," with two other band members billed as "Pap and Oswald, Rachial's Two Country Comedian Boy Friends." When fans expressed great concern that a young, single woman was traveling with a group of unrelated men, however, Acuff dropped this billing and created a comic sketch in which Rachial traded brother-sister quips with Pete Kirby, the Dobro player. To accent Kirby's protective role, Acuff dubbed him "Bashful Brother Oswald." Fans accepted "Oswald" as Rachial's big, protective, and personally circumspect brother, and this contrivance silenced the comments about a woman traveling with the band.

While he was creating a neotraditional stage image for himself and his band, Acuff was also changing the substance of string band music. Ostensibly a string band like those of the late 1920s, the Smoky Mountain Boys of 1938 actually represented what people *thought* a "traditional" string band was supposed to be. Most importantly, the strong audience response to Acuff's vocals effectively shifted the focus of attention in the string band. Rather than the typical performance consisting of ensemble instrumental work and virtuoso instrumental solos interspersed with occasional vocals by one or more instrumentalists, Acuff and the Smoky Mountain Boys featured strong vocals accompanied and supplemented by instrumental work. In the process, Acuff played fewer and fewer fiddle solos, and his singing became the center of attention. By 1943, the shift was complete: after hiring another hot fiddler, Acuff used his own instrument only as a prop.

The weight given to Acuff's vocals was reflected in the band's name. Earlier string bands were generally known by such collective names as "The Gully Jumpers," "The Fruit Jar Drinkers," "The Blue Sky Boys," "The Georgia Wildcats," and "The Crook Brothers," with no individual given prominence, but this band was called "*Roy Acuff* and *His* Smoky Mountain Boys." While the image of his group was clearly hard-core country, ironically, Acuff's innovative emphasis on vocal solos paralleled a shift that was occurring in popular music: dance bands led by such instrumentalists as Benny Goodman and Harry James were beginning to be displaced by ensembles that featured a vocalist, such as Frank Sinatra, Perry Como, Mel Tormé, or Dinah Shore. Another Acuff innovation was the introduction of the Dobro to the *Opry* string band. A steel-topped guitar played flat with a steel bar across the strings, the Dobro's whining yet mellow tone is redolent of the "Hawaiian" band sound that was extremely popular throughout the United States in the early part of the twentieth century. In 1938, the Dobro was still a relatively new instrument, yet its sound, full of sweeping glissandos, fit the nasal sonorities of Southern vernacular speech and singing, as well as country fiddle-playing. To cement the—then improbable—identification of the Dobro with hard-core country music, Pete Kirby, Acuff's Dobro player, was dressed in bib overalls and dubbed with the rube name of "Oswald."

While Acuff self-consciously shaped the Smoky Mountain Boys to fit the image of a country string band, he was also clearly intent on doing whatever it took to entertain an audience—including making himself the center of attention by making loud comments, balancing the bow of his fiddle on his nose, and doing tricks with his yo-yo while the band was playing. Later, in his autobiography, he justified those practices: "I figured I needed to keep everybody's attention, so I was always doing something, even if it was just moving around and talking to other performers. . . . I've always tried to keep things as lively and entertaining as possible on stage."[9] The style that Acuff devised for his band was thus influenced more by the consummate showmanship of such former vaudevillians as Uncle Dave Macon than by the dead-serious delivery of the early *Opry* string bands.

His consistent focus on being entertaining led Acuff to require by 1939 that every member of the band both be an excellent soloist and assume an identifiable persona that could be incorporated into comedy skits. This versatility made the band, unlike most others of the time, a completely self-contained entertainment unit that could tour and perform on its own rather than as one component of a larger package. In this context, Acuff essentially played "Roy Acuff, Master of Ceremonies and Bandleader," who was always trying to keep order among his boisterous set of hill-folk musicians. Acuff would dress for this role slightly better than the rest of the band, wearing slacks instead of jeans, with a sport shirt. He would play the personable host and act the role of the surprised and slightly shocked superego of the group during their more risqué skits, such as when an exchange of double entendres concluded with a huge, six-foot-long corn cob exploding out of a band member's pants, to the hysterical delight of the audience.

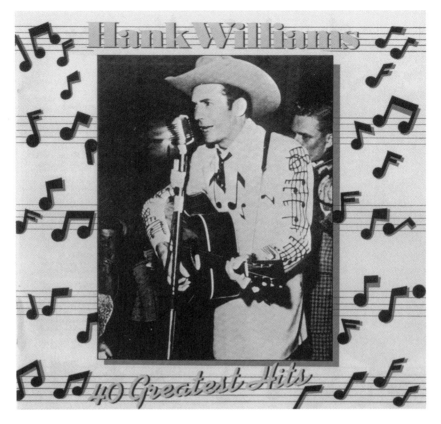

Figure 3. Hard-core paragon Hank Williams, who would die of drug complications in 1953, wrote great songs out of his own experience. *Hank Williams: 40 Greatest Hits* (Polydor CD 821 233–2); cover art and design by Richard Deagle.

Ironically, then, while Acuff had begun by trying to revive the old-time string band and bring sincerity back into singing, he ended up by becoming the prototype of the modern performer—singing ostensibly autobiographical songs and accompanied by his own band—the model of the country music ensemble that persists to this day. As Bill Malone has observed, with the advent of Acuff on the *Opry,* the star system was born.[10] His success facilitated the stardom of a whole new "sincere" generation of country singer-songwriters from Ernest Tubb, Kitty Wells, Hank Williams, Loretta Lynn, and George Jones right up to the present (Figure 3).

WHILE HARD-CORE COUNTRY MUSIC has received the lion's share of attention from archivists and scholars, soft-shell country has a distinctive aesthetic, recurrent features, and a history extending as far back as that of its counterpart. In what follows, I use "expression" as a generic term for a person, a musical rendition, a musical style, or some other representation of hard-core or soft-shell country music. When stripped of all contextual clues, an expression may be impossible to classify unequivocally as one type or the other. What factors provide clues? Those factors displayed in Table 1 may help us to differentiate between hard-core and soft-shell expressions (Figures 4 and 5).

Most expressions do not fall entirely to one side or the other of the dividing line between hard-core and soft-shell country music. Thus the scheme in Table 1 is probably most helpful in highlighting different emphases and trends or in showing that a given expression is hard-core in some ways, but soft-shell in others. It is best to compare an expression with others of the same period. Comparisons over time must be made with caution, however, because the conventions of singing, image-making, and so on can differ radically from one period to another. It is probably futile, therefore, to expect a definitive answer to the question "Who was more hard-core, Jimmie Rodgers or Hank Williams?"

FINALLY, WHAT CAN WE SAY about the hard-core/soft-shell *dialectic?* While one expression is usually predominant at any given time, and while the sequence of expressions is not mechanistically determined, it is possible to identify the forces—both aesthetic and commercial—that drive the dialectic. These forces can be tracked, for example, through the two decades from the early 1970s to the early 1990s.[11]

The "Nashville Sound," masterfully crafted by two producers, Owen Bradley and Chet Atkins, and promoted by the astute marketing efforts of the Country Music Association, had succeeded so well by the early 1970s that country music was enjoying more popularity than ever before. One indicator of this success was the rapidly growing number of radio stations playing country music, while another was the *Grand Ole Opry's* move from the storied but rickety Ryman Auditorium, in a seedy section of downtown Nashville, to a posh, air-conditioned theater in the newly opened, suburban, "American music theme park," Opryland. While much of the new appeal of country music was due to the relatively hard-core "folk" themes of Johnny Cash's weekly television show and the movie based on Loretta Lynn's autobiography, *Coal Miner's Daughter,* soft-shell country was the prime beneficiary of the music industry's promotional efforts. Numerous lush songs of seduction recorded by such artists as

Table 1. Hard-Core Versus Soft-Shell Country Music

|  | Hard-Core | Soft-Shell |
| --- | --- | --- |
| Speech | Southern or southwestern accent, "Southernisms," white Southern grammar; informal, self-deprecating manner (e.g., Ernest Tubb, Loretta Lynn, Randy Travis). | Standard American English, relatively unaccented, sometimes a melodious, slightly regional accent with all hard edges eradicated (e.g., Tex Ritter, Patsy Cline, Eddy Arnold, Vince Gill). |
| Singing Style | Untrained voice with nasal tone; meter often yields to lyrical demands of the story; rough harmonies; passionate delivery marked by raw emotion or personal conviction (e.g., Loretta Lynn, Marty Brown, Roy Acuff). | Trained voice with rich tone; studied interpretations of songs; smooth harmonies; meter in sync with instrumentation; songs sung, not emoted, with delivery conveying experiences and feelings shared with listener (e.g., Crystal Gayle, Red Foley). |
| Lyrics | Concrete situations, simple vocabulary, references to personal experience; wide range of emotions, with changes often charting a singer-songwriter's life experiences (e.g., George Jones, Johnny Cash). | General situation or specific situation described in general terms; mood-setting; third-person voice or, if first-person, invoking feelings shared by listener; repertoire reflecting singer's persona, which may change with shifting musical fashions (e.g., Red Foley). |
| Instruments; Instrumental Style (varies with era and/or instrument) | String instruments: fiddle, guitar (including Dobro), bluegrass banjo; rough, ragged, energized backbeat; drum, guitar, or bass; may musically refer to an earlier country style (e.g., George Strait's references to western swing); since 1975 includes rockabilly (e.g., Hank Williams, Jr.). | Strings, swooping pedal steel, brass, woodwinds, synthesizers; smooth, harmonious, even-four or waltz beat; appeals to recent pop styles, with an added, attenuated country accent (e.g., Chet Atkins). |

Table 1. Continued

|  | Hard-Core | Soft-Shell |
|---|---|---|
| Singer's Origins | South, Southwest; rural, farm or ranch; humble beginnings stressed; little education (or education downplayed); often from a family of musicians (e.g., Fiddlin' John Carson, Ernest Tubb). | Origins not stressed, except for "conversion to country" experiences (e.g., Ronnie Milsap, Kenny Rogers, Mary Chapin Carpenter); if raised on country music (e.g., Eddy Arnold, Bill Anderson), tendency to stress current refinement and distance from (rural, poor) youth (e.g., Anderson's "Po' Folks," with its wistful nostalgia for early life of poverty, stressing contrast with current circumstances). |
| Stage Presentation | Informal, friendly, accommodating, modest, personally revealing; connects with audience, refers to family and links to hard-core icons; establishes hard-core identity via stage banter about hunting, fishing, or housework, plus accent, vocabulary, grammar, and references to appropriate country roots (e.g., as Alan Jackson said of George Jones, "If you didn't know he was a star, you'd think he pumped gas somewhere"); "take me as I am, warts and all" stance sometimes manifested as a surly stage presence (e.g., Hank Williams, Jr.), more often as impression of a performer who could easily have been a farmer, truck driver, housewife, or hairdresser instead. | Formally packaged, distant, professional, unrevealing; like many pop artists, creates distance from the audience, then allows audience to share an intimate moment/song; often gives impression of someone who, if not in country music, would be in some other aspect of entertainment business. |

Table 1. Continued

|  | Hard-Core | Soft-Shell |
|---|---|---|
| Personal Life | Details widely known (even if partly fabricated) and often played out on stage: "lives the life s/he sings about" (e.g., George Jones and Tammy Wynette have sung—solos and duets—about their troubled relationship; Jones has also capitalized on his own reputation as "No Show Jones," a song about his often being too drunk to perform after his divorce from Wynette). | Privacy maintained as much as possible, not played up in music or promotion; indiscretions, bad habits often covered up via hypocritical self-righteousness (e.g., Red Foley). |
| Clothes/Hair Style (varies by era, sometimes by year, must be considered in relation to styles of the time, especially with respect to female stagewear) | Hillbilly, western-style leather, denim; males tend to wear the current version of hillbilly or western style, while females may be dowdy (e.g., Kitty Wells), gaudy (e.g., Dolly Parton), or in-your-face sexy (e.g., Tanya Tucker). | Tailored conventionally, like the mature popular singers of the time, with perhaps a touch of the current hard-core look; males may wear slacks and turtleneck sweaters (e.g., Eddy Arnold) or more formal wear (e.g., Jim Reeves); females often resemble middle-of-the-road singers of the time (e.g., Patsy Cline, Crystal Gayle, Barbara Mandrell, Reba McEntire), or they may be folksy but not folk (e.g., Emmylou Harris, Kathy Mattea). |
| Career Longevity | Most, if not all, of career spent in country music, due to personal commitment and/or difficulty of crossing over (gospel music an exception); more likely to die young as the life lived catches up with the life sung about. | Frequently crosses over (from or to) popular or easy-listening music; better able to move into such positions as music producer, publisher, etc. |

Figure 4. Patsy Cline never hinted at her lusty character or tumultuous personal life in her early 1960s, soft-shell crooner persona. Robert K. Oermann collection. Reproduced with permission.

Freddie Hart, Charley Pride, Charlie Rich, and Conway Twitty became big hits. (Twitty's 1973 hit "You've Never Been This Far Before" exemplifies these.)

In 1974, Australian pop/folksinger Olivia Newton-John was named Country Music Female Artist of the Year, and in 1975 another pop-folkie, John Denver, was named Entertainer of the Year. Many established hard-core country artists who were concerned about the drop in their generation's popularity formed the Academy of Country Entertainers to counter what they saw as the soft-shell bias of the Country Music Association. Meanwhile, national music critics were asking whether country music was dying or simply merging with what was called "adult contemporary middle-of-the-road" music. Clearly, soft-shell country was in the ascendancy.

Figure 5. In the mid-1960s, Loretta Lynn led country music's return to hard-core candor with her riveting, quasi-autobiographical lyrics and her disarming naturalness. Robert K. Oermann collection. Reproduced with permission.

In 1976, country music produced its first, certified million-selling album: *Wanted: The Outlaws*. Featuring Willie Nelson, Waylon Jennings, Jessi Colter, and Tompall Glaser, it was the harbinger of a hard-core renaissance. While Charley Pride, Ronnie Milsap, Crystal Gayle, and Don Williams, joined by Las Vegas favorite Tom Jones, continued to have hits in the late 1970s, Nelson and Jennings individually and jointly re-created the image of hard-core country music (Figure 6). Their #1 hits included "Good Hearted Woman (In Love with a Good Timin' Man)," "Lukenbach, Texas," "My Heroes Have Always Been Cowboys," and "Mammas Don't Let Your Babies Grow Up to Be Cowboys." The warning in the latter song was not about the occupational hazards of ranch life, but about those who follow the hard-drinking, hard-living, hard-loving "cow-

Figure 6. In this concept album, Willie Nelson re-created the hard-core image for the 1975–85 decade. *Red Headed Stranger* (Columbia CD); cover art and design by Monica White.

boy" way. This note of bragging mock-caution was echoed in a Jennings's #1 hit of 1980, "I Ain't Living Long Like This," which, like his Top 5 song, "Don't You Think This Outlaw Bit's Done Got Out Of Hand," indirectly referred to his widely publicized arrest for cocaine possession.

For his part, Willie Nelson staged a series of annual "picnics" in various Texas towns that brought older artists, including Roy Acuff, Tex Ritter, Earl Scruggs, George Jones, and Merle Haggard, together with newer hard-core artists, such as Hank Williams, Jr., Johnny Paycheck, Jerry Jeff Walker, Billy Joe Shaver, Kris Kristofferson, and the Charlie Daniels Band, and with such rock singers and bands as Leon Russell, Poco, the Allman Brothers, and The Eagles.

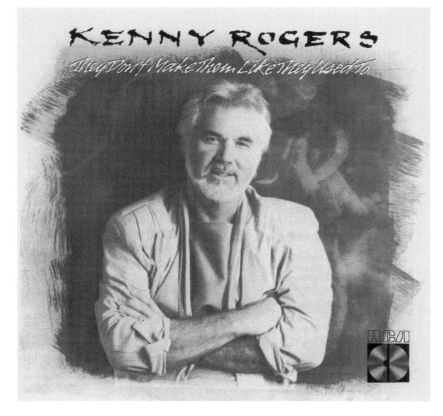

Figure 7. In the mold of Red Foley and Eddy Arnold, Kenny Rogers exemplified the relaxed soft-shell performer of the 1975–85 decade. *They Don't Make Them Like They Used To* (RCA 5633–2–R); photograph by Bernie Boudreau.

"Willie's picnics" helped to reconcile the then-contentious hippie and redneck elements of country music.

Propelled primarily by the Outlaw movement and a more general return to "rural straightforwardness," country music had reached an unprecedented popularity by 1980. Merle Haggard appeared on the cover of the jazz magazine *Downbeat;* Dolly Parton starred with Lily Tomlin and Jane Fonda in the movie *9 to 5; The Dukes of Hazzard* was a hit TV series; and Japanese bands played country music on the *Grand Ole Opry*. All this attention led Barbara Mandrell to exclaim, in a hit song, "I Was Country When Country Wasn't Cool." The apex of this country music wave occurred with the 1981 release of *Urban Cowboy,* a movie set in a Texas dance hall and starring John Travolta.

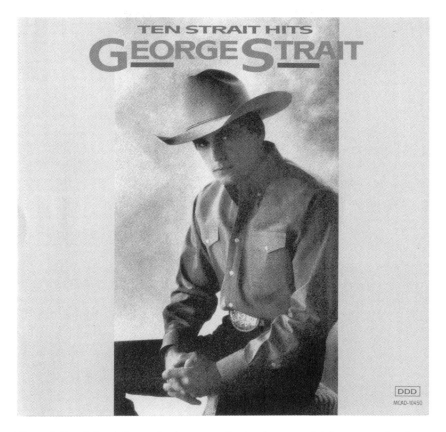

Figure 8. Ranch-bred George Strait was a 1980s hard-core model for a wave of early 1990s "hat acts." *Ten Strait Hits* (MCA MCAD–10450); photograph by Mike Rutherford.

While its hard-core imagery drew widespread attention to country music in the early 1980s, the main beneficiaries were once again those artists whose mode was soft-shell, including Kenny Rogers, Dottie West, Anne Murray, the Oak Ridge Boys, Lee Greenwood, and Barbara Mandrell (Figure 7). The latter hosted her own musical/variety TV show, as did Dolly Parton, who had transmuted herself from her original hard-core style. Country's popularity faded again in the mid-1980s, and many were asking whether real country music could survive all the Las Vegas/Hollywood glitter and glitz. The question was even broached by George Jones in his 1985 hit, which noted the passing of many, primarily hard-core country "Greats," asking, "Who's Gonna Fill Their Shoes?" A Bellamy Brothers song on the charts at the same time, "Old Hippie,"

Figure 9. Trisha Yearwood, in a 1992 billboard advertisement for *Platinum* [selling record] *Blonde* [hair], was the first country music artist ever promoted by a cosmetics company (Revlon) and given her own perfume, with the soft-shell name "Wild Heart." Photograph by Mary A. Bufwack. Robert K. Oermann collection. Reproduced with permission.

offered one possible answer: the baby boomer, raised on rock & roll, who had been driven to country music and homegrown weed by the Vietnam War, disco music, and hard drugs. This song identified the central audience for the next hard-core country wave in the late 1980s, a wave that had begun to gather strength even while soft-shell was at flood tide.

Although she had her first country hit, "If I Could Only Win Your Love," in 1975, Emmylou Harris nevertheless provided the model for the hard-core generation of the mid-to-late 1980s. Having earlier performed with Gram Parsons of The Byrds on the margins of rock and country, Harris was now combining a thoroughly modern sound with what were clearly folk sensibilities. Other significant new artists of the mid-1980s, while referencing an earlier country style, played in a manner that could be called "post-rock." In a sense, they were doing what Roy Acuff had done forty-five years before when he updated the string band.

Ricky Skaggs, an early associate of Harris, drew on bluegrass, as George Strait did on western swing, Randy Travis on hillbilly guilt themes, and Alabama on gospel harmonies (Figure 8). A number of acts mixed rockabilly energy with the honky tonk styles perfected by Ernest Tubb and Hank Williams. The most

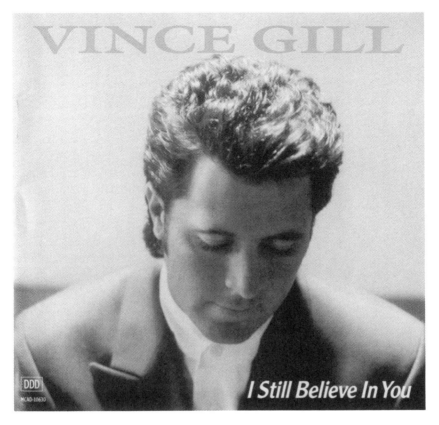

Figure 10. Vince Gill, would-be golf pro and bluegrass guitarist, became an early 1990s soft-shell crooner. *I Still Believe In You* (MCA MCAD–10630); photograph by Victoria Pearson Cameron.

successful conflations were those of Hank Williams, Jr. With numerous references to his father and his "family tradition," he showed how the redneck hippie was the natural descendant of the hard-core country legends. The career of George Jones, who had had his first hit in 1955, before some of these new artists were even born, underwent a revival in the 1980s, further cementing the links between new and older hard-core country music.

By the late 1980s, the hard-core expression had become so clearly ascendant that it was virtually a cliché. Record company executives, seeking well-defined types of male artists, competed to sign "hunks" and "hat acts," and by the early 1990s, country music was riding high again with such phenomenal successes as "hat act" Garth Brooks and "hunk" Billy Ray Cyrus. The range of acceptable images for female country music artists widened, as Mary A. Bufwack and Robert K. Oermann have pointed out, and, for the first time, women had more image options than men did.[12] It's also true that female artists were less successful on the whole than their male counterparts. This gender difference runs true to form because men have generally been dominant among hard-core artists, with women often doing better when soft-shell is more popular (though this is not always the case, as when Loretta Lynn and Tammy Wynette topped the charts with numerous quasi-autobiographical songs from the mid-1960s through the early 1970s).

In the early 1990s, soft-shell country artists were again the beneficiaries of hard-core country's popularity, with a number of distinctive women topping the charts in this soft-shell move: Kathy Mattea, Reba McEntire, Wynonna Judd, Mary Chapin Carpenter, and Trisha Yearwood (Figure 9). What is more, the biggest-selling male recording artist of 1992–93 (after Garth Brooks) was Vince Gill, a smooth-singing, hatless crooner cut in the soft-shell mold of The Vagabonds, Eddy Arnold, and Jim Reeves (Figure 10). Clearly, soft-shell country was again coming to the fore. How long will it be before music critics pronounce country music dead (again), and a new, young, hard-core country cohort starts tinkering with older sounds? The dialectic rolls on.

NOTES

1   The concepts "hard-core" and "soft-shell" were developed in discussions with three delightful groups of Freshman Seminar students in 1992 and 1993. I have benefited greatly from their insights as well as those of Hugh Cherry. Thanks also for the creative editing of Claire Peterson, Cecelia Tichi, and Candice Ward. An earlier version of this essay was delivered at the eleventh annual meeting of the International Conference on Country Music in Meridian, Mississippi, June 1994.

   The best academic history is Bill C. Malone, *Country Music U.S.A.*, rev. ed. (Austin, 1985 [1968]). The best popular history is *Country: The Music and the Musicians,* ed. Paul Kingsbury, Country Music Foundation (New York, 1988).

2   Quoted in Jack Hurst, *Nashville's Grand Ole Opry* (New York, 1975), 10.

3   Actually, Hay went completely over the top in fabricating the folksiness of their guitar. By this point in The Vagabonds' career, Curt Poulton's guitar was not homemade. Rather, it was a monogrammed promotional model, specially handcrafted by the Martin Guitar Company to Poulton's specifications (according to a letter in the Poulton folder, Country Music Foundation archives). See George D. Hay, *A Story of the Grand Ole Opry* (Nashville, 1945), 228–29.

4   Unless otherwise noted, this account of Roy Acuff's early years is based on his autobiography, *Roy Acuff's Nashville* (New York, 1983), and on Elizabeth Schlappi's

biography, *Roy Acuff: The Smoky Mountain Boy* (Gretna, LA, 1978), supplemented by my interviews with Schlappi and the late Roy Acuff.

5  Malone, *Country Music U.S.A.*, 61.

6  Most, if not all, forms of music probably have equivalent soft-shell and hard-core varieties. Thus, soft country is to hard country what semiclassical is to classical or what swing is to jazz.

7  Acuff, *Roy Acuff's Nashville*, 68.

8  Schlappi, *Roy Acuff*, 175–76.

9  Acuff, *Roy Acuff's Nashville*, 85–86.

10  Malone, *Country Music U.S.A.*, 205.

11  The following depiction of the dialectic is based primarily on Richard A. Peterson, "The Production of Cultural Change: The Case of Contemporary Country Music," *Social Research* 45 (1978): 292–314; Malone, *Country Music U.S.A.*, 369–415; Kingsbury, ed., *Country*, 374–567; Tom Roland, *Number One Country Hits*, (New York, 1991); and my current work-in-progress, *Fabricating Authentic Country Music: Fiddlin' John Carson to Hank Williams*.

12  Mary A. Bufwack and Robert K. Oermann, *Finding Her Voice: The Saga of Women in Country Music* (New York, 1993), 480–81.

# "The Sad Twang of Mountain Voices"

*Thomas Hart Benton's*

Sources of Country Music

 —————————————————————— **Vivien Green Fryd**

In December 1934, *Time* magazine applauded Thomas Hart Benton as a Regionalist painter whose dynamic narrative, figurative paintings appealed to the Depression era's desire for intelligible images of down-home, everyday Americana.[1] Forty years later, the first book-length study of American Scene painting situated Benton in a Regionalist triumvirate that also included Grant Wood and John Steuart Curry, artists who, like Benton, created "rural and country views [often of the Midwest], nostalgic in spirit."[2] Just one year after the publication of this book, Thomas Hart Benton completed his last work of art, *The Sources of Country Music* (Figure 1), commissioned by the Country Music Foundation (CMF) in 1973 for the Country Music Hall of Fame and Museum in Nashville, where it is now prominently displayed.

As I will show, this six-by-ten-foot mural constructs country music as a national rather than a regional folk art in order to assure the industry and the public of its grassroots origins and to ensure the Country Music Foundation's continued commitment to old-fashioned forms of country music. The mural speaks to the urban elite and intelligentsia associated with "high" art as well as to the lower-middle-class urban and rural whites who identify with country music's folksy, rustic, and working-class messages. Here, in his last work and near the end of his life, Benton returned to his Regionalist roots, creating an artwork that crossed not only class boundaries, but also those between the high art realm and the middle class, and between geographic regions.

BENTON'S MURAL, an example of "high art," must be examined within the context of popular culture and, in particular, country music and its recording

Figure 1. *The Sources of Country Music* (1974) by Thomas Hart Benton. Oil on canvas, 72" × 120". Country Music Hall of Fame, Nashville, TN. Photograph by Smith Kramer Fine Art Services. Courtesy of the Country Music Foundation, Inc.

industry, which became formalized in 1958 when a group of industry executives formed the Country Music Association (CMA) as a means to make its product competitive with rock music. The CMA established the Country Music Hall of Fame, which was initially part of the Tennessee State Museum, housed in the basement of Nashville's War Memorial Building, and the first inductees were named in 1961. In 1964, the CMA formed the CMF as a nonprofit, charitable, and educational corporation to operate the Hall of Fame and a museum, which opened on 1 April 1967; it includes the Hall of Fame, which exhibits the plaques of elected members and displays materials related to the history of country music, as well as a library for scholarly research.[3] The CMA selected Nashville as the home for the museum because this city, which was already being called the country music capital of the United States by 1950, had become the national center for the country music industry.[4]

The museum's barn-like appearance (Figure 2) was intended to underscore the music's associations with rural America, while its exhibits, as a plaque on the outside of the building announces, aim to capture country music's "spirit," "soul," "history," and "songs . . . so that all may see and hear and learn of the heritage of musical Americana." The museum originally showed a 1974 film narrated by the prominent country music singer and cowboy movie star Tex Ritter. Emphasizing country music's evolution from rural/regional music to a

Figure 2. Country
Music Hall of Fame and
Museum, Nashville, TN
(Earl Swenson and
Associates, 1967).
Photograph courtesy of
the Country Music
Foundation, Inc.

multimillion-dollar recording industry, the film highlighted such performers as Faron Young, Danny Davis, and Jeanne C. Riley, all of whom had become successful, but who uniformly stressed their simple, country roots. The business aspects of the music's history were also emphasized, showing Nashville's role in the successful production of a modern country music that had its roots in the past. The museum's exhibits further highlighted "the history of country music and the careers of its great innovators," along with providing "a glimpse into the sights and sounds of modern country music."[5] One year after the museum's inauguration, the *New York Times* declared it "the industry's shrine and showplace."[6]

The CMF is governed by a board of trustees who come from the music industry, and it was this group that commissioned Benton in 1973 to execute the mural for its then relatively new building. Two board members, Tex Ritter and Joe Allison (an artist, art collector, songwriter, record producer, and Capitol Records executive in Nashville), first suggested in the late fall of 1972 that Thomas Hart Benton, "the distinguished American painter . . . [and] America's greatest muralist," should make a country music mural.[7] Accordingly, in January 1973, these two men, along with Norman Worrell, executive director of the Tennessee Arts Commission, visited the artist in Kansas City. Worrell accompanied the two CMF board members because the foundation recognized that public and private funds would need to be raised, and in fact the project was supported by grants from the Tennessee Arts Commission and the National Endowment for the Arts.[8]

It is not surprising that the CMF commissioned this well-known Regionalist artist. His familiarity with country music dated to his childhood in Missouri, where he grew up listening to his grandfather's fiddling. His fascination with this type of music was rekindled during his travels through the Ozarks, the Smokies, and Virginia in the 1920s. This latter experience resulted in such works as *Lonesome Road* (1927), which illustrates a well-known folk lyric; *Country Dance* (1928), which shows dancers and fiddlers; *Jealous Lover of Lone Green Valley* (1931), a visual representation of a ballad; and his 1931 lithograph *Coming 'Round the Mountain,* based on the title of a country western song.[9] (The list of such works is extensive, indicating that folk music remained a lifelong interest.)

Benton's family life involved music on many levels. His wife, Rita Piacenza, played the guitar and sang, while his children, T.P. and Jesse, played the flute and guitar, respectively. In fact, what began as an amusement in 1931 for his four-year-old son—playing the harmonica—became for Benton a hobby and a passion as important as his painting. Between 1932 and 1934, Benton formed a string band of students (among them Jackson Pollock), musicians (Carl Ruggles, Charles Seeger, and Henry Cowell), and businessmen from the recording industry (Frank Luther and Carson Robison), bringing hillbilly music to Greenwich Village audiences. He also convinced the future ethnomusicologist Charles Seeger to abandon experimental music for hillbilly and African-American music, and he devised his own notation system for harmonica as well as a part system for old music and American folksongs.[10] In Kansas City, where Benton moved in 1935, he again drew together musicians who were art students, Ozarkians, and members of the city's symphony orchestra. At the same time, Benton continued his walking trips in the rural United States and collected, in his own words, "quite a batch of unusual and entertaining songs"; he compiled at least 130 hillbilly and fiddle tunes that proved crucial to the documentation of America's folk traditions.[11] Finally, Benton and his son recorded a three-record, 78 rpm set with Decca, *Saturday Night at Tom*

*Benton's* (1941), "a folksong revival statement" that, according to one musicologist, "made Americans aware of their folk heritage in music."[12]

"Benton warmed to the subject [of the mural] immediately," according to a report from Country Music Foundation executive director William Ivey, and decided that it "should show the roots of the music—the sources—before there were records and stars." "This idea of Benton's," Ivey continued, "that the painting should emphasize the folk cultures which produced country music, became the guiding theme of the project."[13] Benton elaborated in a letter of 18 December 1973 to Ivey, saying that he wanted his depiction of the "general theme [of] 'The Origins of Country Music'" to include images of pioneer fiddlers and square dancers, hymn singers, and ballad, blues, and cowboy singers. He also asked when the five-string banjo and guitar had been introduced into Appalachian string music, making it clear that although he wanted control over the mural's form, its subject matter was open to discussion.

Bill Ivey's reply to Benton (26 December 1973) provided a brief summary of the standard accounts of country music's history, in which British influences as well as indigenous forms of American folk music are acknowledged.[14] Ivey situated country music primarily in Anglo-American folksong, specifically, British ballads and songs brought by early settlers to the mountains of the American Southeast, which were sung rather than played on instruments. Fiddlers played for dancing between song interludes. Hymns sung by white Appalachians and such ballads as "The Wreck of the Old 97" were also part of this tradition. According to Ivey, the blues of African Americans and the cowboy songs of the Southwest, accompanied by the five-string banjo (in the late nineteenth century) and by the guitar (in the first decade of the twentieth century), similarly expanded the oral tradition as it spread beyond Appalachia. Ivey suggested that Benton's mural include the following: the heritage of white Protestantism, represented by "the image of a singing congregation" and a church in the country; a cowboy; a "Negro"; and "a transmitting tower, microphone, early recording session or radio show" to indicate the importance of radio and the recordings of the 1920s that professionalized the industry.

Apart from requesting some minor changes, the board of trustees approved Benton's initial sketch, which fused his own ideas (as outlined in his 18 December letter) and those offered by Ivey (Figure 3). The board suggested that the central motif of a country dance be replaced by singers, since "singing remains the heart of the tradition." They also recommended that a railroad be included. As Ivey explained in a letter to Benton (28 January 1974), "Several people felt that ballads and songs about trains were very important in early country music, and also that the railroad as a romantic lifestyle image had an impact on the

Figure 3. "The Sources of Country Music" (1973) by Thomas Hart Benton. Drawing, 7 ¹³/₁₆" × 12 ⁵/₈". Photograph courtesy of the Country Music Foundation, Inc.

music similar to the cowboy." The board apparently approved of the remaining sections, which represent (in counterclockwise order) a woman with a dulcimer, an interior of a church with singers, another church on a hill, a cowboy on horseback, an African American with banjo, and, in the right foreground, a table with a fiddle, guitar, banjo, and some open books.

The final mural retained Benton's original concept of dividing the composition into vignettes incorporating different figural groups, a method that he had established early in his career with *The Arts and Life in America* (1932) for the Whitney Museum of American Art. In *The Sources of Country Music,* the dancers and fiddlers remained the central focus, "not only because they suggest musical movement better than static figures," Benton explained in a letter of 5 February 1974, "but because I feel pretty sure that traditional country music, from Post Civil War time to World War I was more largely maintained, as a public factor, by the country dance than by ballad singing." This multifigure scene in the mural's middleground is framed by two larger-scale figures in the foreground: a woman playing a dulcimer and a cowboy playing a guitar. Behind the pink-clad dulcimer player is another woman, dressed in green and singing. Above these two females is a choir on an elevated stage. Running along at a diagonal from left to right are railroad tracks and a train. Beyond these is a church on a hill, while to the right is a riverboat "in proximity to the Negro blues singer," a seated black man playing a five-string banjo. The composition is enlivened by the counter-thrusting diagonals of the floor boards in the foreground, the numerous instruments (fiddles and bows, dulcimer, guitar, and banjo), the log upon which the black blues singer is seated, the choir's stage, the railroad tracks and parallel telephone poles, and the light projected from the train's headlight. The stage's base, the church steeple, and the boat's chimney stacks form the only stable vertical lines, while the curvilinear, undulating contours of the figures, objects, and landscape form the rhythmical cohesion that is typical of Benton's work. These compositional devices establish a sense of stability amidst explosive energy and movement, suggesting both the permanence and the powerful rhythms of the music.

BENTON MUST HAVE BEEN PLEASED by the CMF's stipulation "that none of the characters in the painting resemble any music personalities."[15] This allowed him to emphasize country music's evolution from a folk music traditionally practiced by amateurs. The CMF board and Benton apparently agreed that they should refrain from commemorating or glorifying a specific star, and Benton clearly wanted to bypass the commercialization of the industry that began in the 1920s.

The stipulation that Benton depict generalized rather than specific performers also enabled him to follow the working methods that he had established in the 1920s. He would typically sketch scenes from everyday life rather than use models in the studio, then transform his people into exaggerated stereotypes to create "archetypal anecdotes" that were not only faithful to contemporary perceptions of real life, but also appealed to a broad national audience.[16] Many of the figures in his last mural derive from earlier sketches of various folk musicians, such as Homer Leverett of Galena, Missouri, or Dudley Vance, a Tennessee fiddler who persuaded Benton that the commercialized Tin Pan Alley tunes and recorded hillbilly songs lacked authenticity.[17] The artist not only relied on earlier sketches executed during his travels throughout the United States in the 1920s, but also returned to the Ozarks in 1974 to find newer models of "country musicians [who] were not necessarily of the nationally advertised variety," such as Chick Allen, a jawbone player, and a student at the School of the Ozarks who was transformed into the mural's dulcimer player.[18] Besides reviving his interest in this folk tradition, the commission enabled Benton to reestablish the agrarian imagery so evident in such works as *Homestead* (1934), *Cradling Wheat* (1938), and *July Hay* (1942) by firmly situating the sources of country music in an agrarian economy signified by, for example, the clothing of the mural's figures.[19]

Figure 4. Monogram Pictures presents Tex Ritter in *Song of the Buckaroo* (1938). Photograph courtesy of the Country Music Foundation, Inc.

There is, nevertheless, one person in the mural who resembles a specific individual—the cowboy on the right, whose height, location on a low hill, and relative isolation all contribute to his prominence. This singing cowboy, with his guitar, holstered gun, boots, and the saddle upon which he steps, alludes to Tex Ritter, proclaimed by the president of the Tex Ritter Fan Club as the "hero in sixty Hollywood Westerns and patron saint of Country Music."[20] Ritter had been a popular country western singer, a regular performer on the *Grand Ole Opry,* and a Hollywood actor in such films as *Song of the Gringo* (1936), *Song of the Buckaroo* (1937; Figure 4), and *Prairie Gunsmoke* (1942); he sang the famous theme song in *High Noon* (1952). He also served as president of the Country Music Association in 1963 and 1964, when he spearheaded fund-raising efforts for the Country Music Hall of Fame and Museum, and was the first chairman of the CMF board in 1966. Elected in 1964 to the Country Music Hall of Fame as "one of America's most illustrious and versatile stars of radio, television, records, motion pictures, and [the] Broadway stage," Ritter was only the second living artist to be so honored (Figure 5).

Figure 5. Country Music Hall of Fame plaque for Tex Ritter, inducted 1964. Photograph courtesy of the Country Music Foundation, Inc.

Ritter was also involved in national politics. He brought such country music stars as Johnny Cash and Merle Haggard to the White House under Richard Nixon's administration and made an album of Nixon's speeches, which Ritter narrated: *Thank you, Mr. President* (Figure 6). He also campaigned on behalf of Howard Baker, Barry Goldwater, and Ronald Reagan, and, in 1970, Ritter ran for the U.S. Senate, losing to William Brock in the Republican primary for the seat of Senator Albert Gore. Identifying himself as a middle-of-the-road Republican, Ritter campaigned against Gore's populist platform, which he called "liberal left wing," and condemned the Democratic Party's "socialism," tracing it to Roosevelt's New Deal and the "spend, spend, spend" era it had inaugurated.[21] He

Figure 6. Tex Ritter with President Richard M. Nixon (c. 1969). Photograph courtesy of the Country Music Foundation, Inc.

favored Nixon's plan for ending the Vietnam War; the invasion of Cambodia; the support of Israel as a means to buttress anticommunist activity in the Middle East; prayer in the schools; and strict constructionists on the Supreme Court; but he also favored environmental programs, better highways, and increased Social Security benefits.[22] The Republican Party exploited Ritter's popularity as "America's Most Beloved Cowboy" in furthering Nixon's efforts to undermine Southern support for such Democrats as Gore.[23] Ritter's mix of conservative and more liberal positions seemed one way of appealing to those voters.

Given that Ritter had convinced Benton to come out of retirement to execute a mural for the Country Music Foundation, Ritter's politics must be considered in the light of Benton's own background. The son of a Missouri congressman as well as the great-nephew and namesake of Missouri's first senator, Benton was an artist whose work had consciously promoted the liberal Democratic and populist ideology of his upbringing and the New Deal politics that Ritter deplored. As Erika Doss has demonstrated, by the end of the 1930s Benton had abandoned his Regionalist style for more fanciful renderings of classical myths and biblical narratives as a result of his realization that he could no longer promote the failed New Deal ideology. His disappointing experiences with the advertising industry at the end of the 1930s and during the 1940s, along with the rise of fascism and the Second World War, consolidated Benton's rejection of both the Regionalist style and the progressive ideology. His more conservative, anti-Communist positions of the 1970s thus made him sympathetic to Ritter's campaign platform.[24] Clearly, then, the rapport that immediately developed between these two men, one an artist and amateur musician and the other a musician and movie star, resulted from their shared interests in country music and conservative politics.

When Ritter died in January 1974, before the mural's completion, Benton and Ivey agreed to pay him tribute by alluding to him in the figure of the cowboy singer, which would be "not a portrait but a reminder." A comparison between Benton's generalized "reminder" in the mural and photographs of Ritter indicates that the artist relied on Hollywood publicity photos of the 1930s singing cowboy to create a youthful, generic, and idealized type (Figure 7).[25] Benton must have enjoyed working once again with movieland material, the subject of his 1937 painting *Hollywood,* commissioned by *Life* magazine. Earlier, between 1913 and 1918, Benton had designed sets and done carpentry, scene painting, advertising, and historical research for Hollywood westerns and some two-reel melodramas produced in New Jersey.[26] Although Benton did not make any sketches of Ritter from his films while he was in Hollywood during the summer of 1937, he must have been familiar with this newly acclaimed cowboy movie star who had begun acting only the year before, but who made eight movies in 1937 and 1938 alone. Later, in 1954, Benton sketched a group of dancers from a production of *Green Grow the Lilacs,* a play for which Ritter had been an understudy in 1930, and it was on this drawing that Benton based the central dancers in his mural.

The singing cowboy figure indeed became prominent in the final work. Benton's earlier sketch (Figure 3) had shown a smaller cowboy on horseback off to the right and in the distance, facing away from the viewer. This faceless riding cowboy is neither singing nor playing an instrument; instead, he gazes over an expansive western landscape dotted with cattle that extends to the church on the hill. By foregrounding the cowboy, who sings, plays a guitar, and is stand-

Figure 7. Tex Ritter with White Flash (n.d.). Photograph courtesy
of the Country Music Foundation, Inc.

ing in the mural, Benton emphasized country *western* music and its mythic
cowboy associations.

Tex Ritter, despite being "the most believable of all the singing cowboys,"
had never been on a cattle ranch except in the movies.[27] Originally from Mur-
vaul, Panola County, in east Texas, Ritter majored in political science at the
University of Texas and then spent two years at Northwestern University School
of Law before going into show business. As a singing-songwriting cowboy, he
wrote a hybrid western music that derived from a number of sources, only
one of which was the Southwest. He sang in a "rough-hewn" voice that had
"the echo of the plains in its timbre" and wore western clothes and pointed-

toed boots throughout his life.[28] Ritter joined Gene Autry and Roy Rogers in Hollywood, where they formed a trio of country western celluloid stars who appealed to a wide audience in the United States during the 1930s and 1940s.[29] Benton's mural contributed to this mythic image of Ritter and of cowboys in general as central to country music, thereby promoting country music singers, the country music industry, and Hollywood during a period when the popularity of western movies had waned.

It is no wonder that Ritter and Benton hit it off so well when they met in 1973. They were, after all, kindred spirits who shared an interest in folk ballads, conservative politics, experiences in Hollywood, and, as will become evident, certain beliefs about African-American contributions to country music. Ritter's conviction that country music "reflects the hopes and dreams of everyone, as well as everyone's fears and failures," and that these constitute "a common meeting ground," in fact, conformed to Benton's lifelong goal to create art for the common man.[30]

THE FIGURE MOST CLOSELY associated with the cowboy in the composition of Benton's mural is the African-American banjo player, whose pose aligns him with the foregrounded cowboy, as does his hat; the angles formed by their hats and instruments and by their bent arms and knees also reiterate one another. This singing man, seated on a log, underwent major changes from Benton's initial drawing to the final work. In Benton's earlier conception, the standing, front-facing black man in the foreground wears tattered clothing with ripped sleeves and a patch on his pants, resembling the photographs (and constructed persona) of Leadbelly, an ex-convict from the backcountry of Louisiana who was discovered and promoted by the Lomaxes in the 1930s. The frontispiece to their 1936 book, *Negro Folk Songs as Sung by Lead Belly,* shows Leadbelly in overalls and bare feet, singing with his mouth wide open and head back, not unlike Benton's drawing (Figure 8).[31]

In Benton's mural, the black man became less prominent with his relocation to a middleground, seated position behind the monumental standing cowboy. Wearing a farmer's blue-jean overalls rather than torn clothing, he no longer suggests poverty but employment, perhaps as a cotton picker in the rural South. Unlike the Ritter-alluding cowboy, the black man has been transformed into a generic type, thereby avoiding the glorification of any specific individual. The man's enormous mouth and large lips are less exaggerated than in the initial sketch, but both versions invoke the stereotypical African American with an innate love of music. This stereotype is reiterated by the gyrating group of African Americans along the riverbed in the background. Their arms

Figure 8. Leadbelly. Photograph by Herbert Peck. Reproduced from
*Negro Folk Songs as Sung by Lead Belly* by John A. and Alan Lomax
(New York: Macmillan, 1936).

raised, they sing and dance in an almost frenzied manner, in sharp contrast to
the more sedately postured white church choir in the left middleground. The
pose of the black woman in yellow, however, corresponds to that of the white
preacher, but where her posture suggests spontaneity and joy, his seems more
indicative of deliberation and control.

I want to go one step further in analyzing Benton's representation of African Americans by noting that they are marginalized and isolated in the mural.
Those on the shore of the river are small in scale, distantly located, and separated from the rest of the composition by the intervening railroad tracks. The
telephone pole and the tree frame this group as well as the seated banjo player,

who is similarly situated in an inscribed space (defined by a contour that leads from the tree and along the cotton bag to the left-hand foliage and telephone pole). Benton had originally placed the black man in the same plane as the white dancers, uniting them by a frame that separates the foregrounded group from the cowboy and the church choir. In the mural, while the white men and women form separate vignettes, they are nevertheless unified by their common location in the same foreground and grey space and by the U-shaped composition that connects the church choir to the cowboy, thereby suggesting a sense of community from which the blacks are excluded.

Benton and Ritter agreed from the outset that the contributions of blacks had to be among those recognized as "sources of country music." As Ritter explained in a 1973 interview, he and Benton both felt that "the old Methodist group camp meeting songs, and the Black Blues had a great effect on many of our artists."[32] In commenting on Ritter's remark, Richard A. Peterson observed that both Ritter and Benton downplayed the importance of black vocals and instrumentals by emphasizing their roots in spirituals rather than their influence on nearly every country music star from Jimmie Rodgers to the Carter Family, Hank Williams, and Chet Atkins.[33] This view is similarly suggested in the mural by the compositional means that Benton used to isolate and de-emphasize the African Americans.

The banjo-playing black man is not entirely isolated from the other figures, however, with some linkage provided by the colors of his clothing, his rhythmic contours, and his profile; he is thus configured ambivalently, both included and excluded in a fashion that reflects the status of blacks in the country music industry. Benton's marginalization of the African Americans corresponds to the "outsider populist" position accorded in the 1930s to such black singers as Leadbelly, who were promoted (and exploited) as common men and authentic folksingers, and to the unique position today of Charley Pride, who remains the only black country musician to have succeeded in the industry, becoming a star despite such obstacles as the refusal by some disc jockeys during the 1960s to play his records.[34] This tendency to diminish the importance of African Americans in the evolution of country music has been more recently manifested in a Country Music Hall of Fame and Museum exhibition that showcases Johnny Cash as well as Elvis Presley (through a film and the display of Presley's golden Cadillac and piano) without acknowledging the Southern black musicians who contributed to their styles.[35] As Bob Millard concludes in an article on Charley Pride, "For all the blues and minstrel influences in the roots of traditional country music, the genre's stars, those who have been at the top of the sales and box-office heaps, have generally reflected the color and culture of its primary purchasing audience: whites with rural roots."[36]

THE INSTRUMENTS DEPICTED in *The Sources of Country Music* associate blacks, women, and men with historically distinct roles and musical genres. The black man's long-necked, five-string banjo refers not to the old minstrel type played in Dixieland jazz and vaudeville, but to the bluegrass instrument, suggesting his contribution to this genre. The two women standing on the left, one of whom sings, while the other plays a dulcimer, represent the role of women in preserving Appalachian folk ballads; indeed, the dulcimer is the instrument traditionally associated with mountain women.[37] These women, along with the female choir singers, are situated on the left periphery of the composition, both a part of, yet separate from, the central scene of white dancers and fiddlers. Appropriately, the fiddlers in the mural are male, for in rural America until the 1930s only men performed with this instrument, which is strategically located in the central foreground demarcated by a bottle of spirits (called the "devil's box," the fiddle often established a festive atmosphere that included drinking and dancing).[38]

Given his gendered treatment of country music in the mural, it is hardly surprising to learn that Benton constructed himself as a macho, hard-drinking, cursing, rugged man, well-known for homophobic pronouncements that were apparently intended to mark him as the opposite of the museum world effetes, whom he called "pretty boy[s] with delicate wrists and a swing in [their] gait."[39] Benton denied his education, upper-middle-class status, and political background in order to identify himself with the macho culture of rural America, as pictured in the mural, where women are either led by men (the choir conductor, the dancers) or are standing off to the side of this male-dominated world. Not surprisingly, Benton, Ritter, and Worrell began their discussions about the CMF commission over "some good ole Jack Daniels," as the men proceeded to "hit it off with some salty language."[40]

His *Sources of Country Music* allowed Benton to reaffirm his own highly gendered vision of country music. As a result, he either consciously or unconsciously exposed and documented women's marginalized position in the field, which was already being seriously challenged during his lifetime. As Mary A. Bufwack and Robert K. Oermann have recently shown, women first participated in the country music industry during the Second World War, when they entered the workforce in general, and became even more prominent and outspoken during the women's liberation movement of the 1960s, just one decade before Benton created his mural.[41] Rather than document the changing status of women in the industry, however, Benton affirmed his own memory of women as marginal figures in the early days of country music.

THERE IS ONE OTHER OBJECT depicted in the mural that bears close examination: the railroad train in the middleground and just off-center in the composition—a prominent position. Although Benton had not originally intended to include any railroad images, when Ivey informed him that some members of the CMF board felt the train was indispensable to a depiction of country music's origins, he agreed that it was "too important to ignore" (letter of 5 February 1974). Consequently, he replaced the western landscape of his sketch with a locomotive that billows smoke as its headlight brilliantly shows the way. Benton certainly felt comfortable with this subject, given that his first childhood drawings were of railroad trains. As he recalled in his 1937 autobiography, "Engines were the most impressive things that came into my childhood. To go down to the depot and see them come in, belching black smoke, with their big headlights shining and their bells ringing and their pistons clanking, gave me a feeling of stupendous drama."[42] This description is indeed faithful to the image in Benton's last work, down to its belching black smoke and shining lights. Not surprisingly, trains are to be found in a number of other works by Benton, among them *Bootleggers* (1927), *America Today: Instruments of Power* (1931), *The Engineer's Dream* (1931), and *The Wreck of Ole '97* (1943; Figure 9). The latter work illustrates "the most seminal hillbilly event song" (according to Bill Malone), which recounts the fatal crash of the Fast Mail of the Southern Railway in 1903.[43] Benton turned to another famous train for his model in *The Sources of Country Music*: the Wabash Cannonball, which was immortalized as a symbol of death in two folksongs, "The Wabash Cannonball" and "Casey Jones" (the latter song was "one of the nation's favorites through much of the first half of the twentieth century").[44] Benton took great pains to accurately portray Engine No. 382, driven by Casey Jones when he crashed in 1900. (Since this one had been scrapped, Benton used a close copy, Engine No. 635, but retained the number "382," which is clearly visible on the mural's train.)[45] The locomotive in Benton's last work departs from these trains and the songs that immortalized them as technological disasters, however, since no wreck seems to be imminent.

The cowboy and the railroad train are the most prominent images, not only representing two major themes in country music, but also symbolizing the American past and present. The contemporary locomotive accorded with Benton's assessment in his autobiography of the train as "the prime symbol of adventurous life" for "our western people" and as a "symbol of change" that "had

Figure 9. *The Wreck of Ole '97* (1943) by Thomas Hart Benton. Egg tempera on gessoed masonite, 28 1/2" × 44 1/2". Hunter Museum of Art, Chattanooga, TN. Gift of the Benwood Foundation. Photograph courtesy of the Hunter Museum of Art.

the power to break down the barriers of locality." [46] The seeming onslaught of the train's movement across the painting can be read as a harbinger of change, perhaps alluding to the transformation of the country music industry, to which Benton chose not to refer directly. If the foreground is filled with a multitude of figures who perform folk ballads and dances, the train represents what is approaching—a more modern, commercial music industry. This harbinger of change and progress is both pushed into the distance and made to rush forward, suggesting an ambivalence about its impact on country music, but also a sense of inevitability, as the dulcimer-playing singer and the cowboy face toward the more centrally situated locomotive. The group of dancers in front is, in fact, located below the tracks so that the train is elevated and made more prominent as it thrusts forward into the smaller, self-contained, more privatized worlds of the black musician, the choir, and the square dancers.

The train must also be viewed within the context of the steamboat, whose twin chimneys similarly billow smoke on the distant river. When Benton wrote to Ivey in February 1974 to say that he agreed the train was indispensable to his mural, he also announced that he had decided to add a "riverboat in proximity to the Negro blues singer." Benton clearly associated the steamboat with the South and with African Americans, as is evident in such works as *Cotton*

*Loading* (1928), *America Today: Deep South* (1931), and *A Social History of the State of Missouri: Pioneer Days and Early Settlers* (1935–36). In these paintings, as in *The Sources of Country Music,* the boat is coming toward the shore to load cotton picked by blacks, invoking Benton's nostalgic reminiscences of watching the *Tennessee Belle* in New Orleans as it belched "smoke in the path of the setting sun, a perfect picture from the past."[47]

The foregrounded singers and dancers as well as the backgrounded steamboat located at the vanishing point both symbolize the past, while the locomotive in the middleground signifies the modern era. The CMF did not interpret the train and steamboat images in this manner, however, merely explaining them in a news release as representations of "non-musical influences."[48] More specifically, according to the CMF, they represent "the influences of occupation and technology upon the themes of country music."[49] These statements suggest that even if Benton had intended the train and steamboat to refer to the more modern aspects of country music, by the time the mural was completed, the CMF wanted to downplay this allusion.

THE CMF WAS ANXIOUS to express its commitment to tradition—to the music's folksy, "authentic" roots—during the 1970s when the industry was experiencing a crisis. The CMA had begun to be successful in its efforts to counter the popularity of rock & roll by convincing many radio station managers to adopt a full-time country music format that would appeal to a broad constituency of rural and urban, young and old listeners alike. As one radio consultant stated in a news release aimed at advertisers:

> *Modern* country music has no relationship to rural or mountain life. It is the music of this *Nation,* of this country, the music of the people. You find no screech fiddles, no twangy guitars, no mournful nasal twangs in the *modern* Nashville Sound of country music.

As a result, new country stations began to promote performers whose music could "cross over" from country to rock. Roy Acuff, Ernest Tubb, and Tex Ritter, among others, stopped trying to record "hits" because they recognized that their live-show performances and records no longer appealed to broad segments of the country music audience, who wanted the more popular Nashville Sound.[50] By the mid-1970s, however, even this reconstructed country music was losing its appeal.

At the same time, a revolt occurred within the industry when, on 5 November 1974, about fifty established country music entertainers met to form the Academy of Country Entertainers as an alternative to the CMA. These performers were united in their opposition to the dilution of country music and, more specifically, to the inequitable selection process for the annual, nationally televised CMA awards, which had resulted in Olivia Newton-John's being named Country Music Female Vocalist of the Year in 1974.[51]

Benton's mural helped the industry reestablish its commitment to traditional country music, as well as to a more traditional definition of country music. As Bill Hance, a reporter for the *Nashville Banner,* commented about the controversy, the fact that people protested against Olivia Newton-John as a "crossover" from pop to country indicated that there were "no concrete definitions of 'country.' " "What is a country entertainer?" queried this reporter, who provided some answers from fans: "sorrow and sequins," "twang twang," the *Grand Ole Opry*. He then explained that "country" really meant the period before 1935 when the guitar, banjo, and fiddle were the only instruments used.[52] It was this type of country music that Benton made the basis of the genre in his painting (indeed, he represented these three instruments along with the dulcimer), and it corresponded to the rural "hillbilly" image that George D. Hay, shaper of the *Grand Ole Opry,* created to signify "old-time music," beginning in 1926.[53] That the CMF still wants to reinforce this image is evident in a recent brochure proclaiming, "With all its many forms . . . country music has never forgotten the legacy of its origins or lost its down-home flavor." [54]

This attitude is also evident in the Hall of Fame's current exhibition, which is organized around the distinct styles or subgenres of country music—bluegrass, western swing, cowboy music, honky tonk, Cajun, and contemporary—with labels identifying each category and explaining how each evolved (noticeably absent are African Americans and their important contributions to the genre). The exhibition begins with "*The Grand Ole Opry:* On the Air," showcasing the significance of radio to the commercialization and modernization of the industry, but it concludes with Benton's mural, thus reinforcing country music's roots. Significantly, Tex Ritter's narrated film from the 1970s, which emphasized the modern Nashville Sound, is no longer shown.[55] Instead, one sees a video of Elvis Presley's television appearances during the 1950s and another one about various country musicians on television and in the movies. This latter film highlights traditional singers, such as Jimmie Rodgers, Gene Autry, and Hank Williams, who represent bluegrass, cowboy music, and western swing, respectively. Only a clip of Patsy Cline performing in 1957 refers to the Nashville Sound.[56]

Benton himself would have identified with the country music industry's image-making efforts. Just as "Judge" George D. Hay was responsible for changing the "look" of male *Opry* performers, replacing their dark suits, white shirts, and ties with bib overalls and neckerchiefs, Benton (along with Grant Wood, his friend and fellow Regionalist) dressed in similar garb to present himself as a down-home country boy who could identify with rural Americans. Although Benton was born in Missouri, his father was a prominent, upper-middle-class politician, and Benton himself was well-educated, having studied at the Chicago Art Institute and the Académie Julien in Paris, where he learned French and read literature, philosophy, and works on aesthetics.[57] Benton repudiated his early immersion in the abstract idioms he had learned and practiced in Paris and New York by returning to the Midwest and shifting to realism and narrative subject matter during the 1920s. As he admitted in 1951, Grant Wood, John Steuart Curry, and Benton himself had accepted their hillbilly roles as Regionalists, despite the fact that "the three of us were pretty well educated, pretty widely read, had European training, knew what was occurring in French art circles and were tied in one way or another to the main tradition of western painting."[58] In short, Benton's artistic transformation from avant-garde to Regionalist, Midwestern folk imagery, and his self-transformation from the highbrow intellectual to the down-home, rural, manly man, was concurrent with the *Grand Ole Opry's* image-shifting promotion of country musicians as hicks, a convergence of which he must have been aware while he worked on the mural.

BENTON'S INSISTENCE upon predating the sources of country music to the period before its commercialization in the 1920s was consistent with his desire to emphasize American "folk patterns," folk practices, and local customs in his art.[59] It was also consistent with the CMF's desire to associate itself with old-fashioned country music. As a news release about the festivities that marked the unveiling of Benton's mural announced, "What you will see represented here today is not the country music of today—that complex musical form which reaches far into American popular music, but rather the musical and cultural forces which were present in the Southeast when country music began."[60]

Benton's own experience with country music was mainly limited to Appalachian folk music, specifically, the repertoire of traditional ballads that were performed from the 1920s through the 1970s in a crescent-shaped area that extended west from the northeast Appalachian region—music that endured even when the urban centers and markets were beginning to appropriate the commercial country music known as the Nashville Sound.[61] In other words, Benton's folksy image of country musicians, which was based on his Appalachian experiences in the 1920s and again in the mid-1970s, supports contemporary evidence that this area remained a stronghold for old-fashioned country music at a time when, as one music critic concluded in 1971, country music had become "city music" because it sold to an urban audience.[62]

Benton's foregrounding of fiddlers and dancers, in fact, reflected the rural music practices that he observed and loved. The artist clearly felt that the modern, urban Nashville Sound had little in common with the Appalachian folk songs he had listened to as a youth and collected as an adult while traveling through the rural areas of America, concluding,

> Movie halls, phonographs, and radios wreck the old free play with music. Young singers, with references of canned music always at hand, sing in the standardized fashion of the cities, where a certain kind of rigid pattern for hillbilly music has been popularized. In the song festivals which have been revived in the Appalachians, urban expertness gets too much applause. The old timers are backing away.[63]

Benton also had this to say about hill country musicians in his autobiography:

> I like their plaintive, slightly nasal voices and their way of short bowing the violin. I like the modal tunes of the people and the odd interludes, improvisations, often in a different key, which they set between a dance tune and its repetition. I've played with, and for, the hill folks on a harmonica and have picked up unwritten tunes and odd variants of those which have found their way into music books. . . . The old music cannot last much longer. I count it a great privilege to have heard it in the sad twang of mountain voices before it died.[64]

Within this context, Benton's use of the train as a "symbol of change" must be reconsidered, for its ambivalent position, located in the mural's middleground but moving forward toward the viewer, suggests Benton's own regret at "the sad twang of mountain voices" being forgotten in the midst of country music's modernization. Benton's refusal to include any images of the recording industry, furthermore, reveals his abiding commitment to American individuals rather than to institutions (and their technologies)—ironically, given that he was commissioned by an industry organization when it wanted to reconstruct its own identity so as to appeal to a broader audience.

While the CMA and the CMF wanted to reaffirm their commitment to traditional country music, they also wanted to erase its negative associations among members of "high society." As Archie Green has demonstrated, even before the conflicts of the 1970s, many people in the country music industry had become uncomfortable with the music's 1920s-era self-identification as "hillbilly," recognizing that it had become associated with "poor white trash." George D. Hay, for example, was claiming by the 1940s that "we never use the word [hillbilly] because it was coined in derision. Furthermore, there is no such animal. Country people have a definite dignity of their own and a native shrewdness which enables them to hold their own in any company."[65] This eschewing of the "hillbilly" image resulted in new terminology: by 1949 *Billboard* identified non–pop music hits as "country" or "country western" in order to capitalize on the glamour of the movie cowboy and mythic West.[66]

When the CMF commissioned the Benton mural, it was hoped, as Bill Ivey noted in an April 1973 memo to the board of trustees, that Benton's painting "would bring a 'fine-arts' dimension to exhibits in the Country Music Hall of Fame and Museum." Over and over again, the CMF asserted that the commission represented the perfect marriage not only between the arts (music and painting), but also between popular and high culture.[67] The setting in which the mural is displayed, however, emphasizes its high-art status. Situated in a separate room with bright lights and white walls, the mural and Benton's preliminary drawings for it appear to be precious art objects, reverently displayed in a hushed environment, in sharp contrast to the rest of the museum's crowded exhibits, many of which include competing sounds of music and narration. Only Benton's voice occasionally disturbs the hushed environs of his mural as he explains his procedures and the subject matter of the mural in a video that also features a sound track of instrumental and vocal folk music.[68]

Ironically, the CMF commissioned a work of "high art" that was considered provincial in New York circles at a time when modernism reigned. By the mid-1940s, in fact, Benton's Regionalist style had already been relegated to the status of kitsch for popular consumption by the influential critic Clement Greenberg, who considered Benton's work inferior to the epic, universal, and tragic avant-garde paintings of such abstract expressionists as his former pupil Jackson Pollock.[69] By 1951, James Thrall Soby had announced the death of Regionalism in the *Saturday Review of Literature,* while Benton himself bitterly observed that "the bandwagon practitioners . . . left our Regionalist banner like rats from a sinking ship and allied themselves with the now dominant internationalisms of the highbrow aesthetes."[70] In short, Benton's art had already been dismissed by the very high culture with which the CMF wanted to be associated.

During the 1970s, when Benton undertook his last commission, scholars began to publish studies of American Scene painting and of folk music. Matthew Baigell, for example, wrote three books about Benton between 1971 and 1975, identifying him as the most "visible" American Scene artist of the 1930s.[71] In 1975, James Dennis published the first monograph ever written on Grant Wood.[72] As for country music scholarship, Bill C. Malone's *Country Music U.S.A.* was already in print by 1968, and Douglas B. Green's *Country Roots* appeared in 1976. Benton and folk music, in fact, both garnered public attention through the CMF commission and the scholarly publications that appeared during a period when art was becoming so diversified by such movements as body art, performance art, decorative painting, and New Image art, among others, that there seemed to be no dominant style or discernible star system.[73]

Certainly, the CMA and the CMF had a different view of high culture than that of the New York art world. They did not want to be associated with the avant-garde styles that prevailed there, but rather to improve country music's "poor white trash" image and, by so doing, bring back into the fold those who had abandoned country for pop/rock and crossover music. These organizations therefore used Benton's art, which belongs to neither high art nor popular culture, as a means of attaining a middle-class, middlebrow identity for country music and of encouraging the music's audience to identify with it as such—to identify themselves neither as elitists nor as backward hillbillies, but as members of the American mainstream. For the CMF, Benton's work was not kitsch but high art, and, as such, it made country music—a popular art form—respectable.

*The Sources of Country Music* enabled Benton, on the other hand, to play one last Regionalist song of tribute to democratic pluralism. As Benton asserted,

> I'm doing this mural because it's a public job. A lot of people will see it. It will last. I like public jobs. When I do a painting that somebody buys in order to make money on it, that's a commodity job.[74]

Benton is referring here to his earlier experiences with such corporate entities as Lucky Strike and *Life* magazine, for which he created advertisements during the late 1930s and early 1940s. As Erika Doss has shown, Benton became disillusioned with corporate patronage when he realized that he could not promote the New Deal ideology. He subsequently produced mainly fanciful panel paintings, hoping to find public arenas other than museums, which he felt appealed only to highbrow, snobbish members of the intelligentsia. As Benton put it, rather bombastically, in 1941 (when abstract art first began to replace American Scene painting as mainstream art), "I'd have people buy the paintings and hang 'em in privies or anywhere anybody had time to look at 'em." He continued, "Nobody looks at 'em in museums. Nobody goes to museums. I'd like to sell mine to saloons, bawdy houses, Kiwanis and Rotary clubs and Chambers of Commerce—even women's clubs."[75] Perhaps more seriously, Benton stated in 1951, "I believe I have wanted, more than anything else, to make pictures, the imagery of which would carry unmistakably American meanings for Americans and for as many of them as possible."[76]

Benton's much publicized search for a public space that would reach a general audience of upper- and lower-class Americans finally ended when the CMF commissioned *The Sources of Country Music*. And, by 1975, country music was reaching a wider audience as well: "Country music [had] broken away from its earlier ethnic and regional confines to be embraced by a broad segment of mid-life working- and lower-middle-class whites." The music had indeed become "an excellent example of . . . working-class cultural expression."[77] Since Benton himself wanted to create a mural that all Americans could see and appreciate, the audience for country music (which was also likely to patronize the Country Music Hall of Fame and Museum) constituted his ideal audience, as did workers at the Nissan Motor Manufacturing Corporation in Smyrna, Tennessee, who ate lunch in front of his mural for two weeks in March 1988 when it was on loan to the plant. It could be argued that, with his last work, Benton finally realized his lifelong goal to create realistic, narrative art for the general public that would be jointly funded by members of the business community and by the state and federal government, without compromising his style, subject matter, or ideological beliefs. Benton succeeded in documenting the "folk patterns" of American life for "genuine spectator participation," a goal that he had articulated long before in his autobiography and one for which he found the perfect vehicle—country music—at the end of his life.[78]

NOTES

Conversations with the following people contributed greatly to my nascent understanding of country music: John Knowles, Curator of Education, CMHFM; John Rumble, Historian, CMHFM; Alan Stoker, Audio Restoration Engineer, CMHFM; and Richard A. Peterson, Vanderbilt University. I am especially indebted to Professor Peterson for sharing his published and unpublished scholarship with me; to Ronnie Pugh, Head of Reference, CMF Library and Media Center, for assisting me in my research; to Erika Doss, whose thoughtful comments contributed to the clarification and elaboration of some ideas; and to Cecelia Tichi, who encouraged me to work on this project and provided insightful commentary.

1   "U.S. Scene," *Time,* 24 December 1934, 24–25.

2   Matthew Baigell, *The American Scene: American Painting of the 1930s* (New York, 1974), 55.

3   For information about the Country Music Foundation, see "History of Country Music Hall of Fame," CMF Library and Media Center, 1971; and "Country Music Foundation: The First Decade," *Record World,* 19 October 1974, 4: 42–43.

4   See John Lomax III, *Nashville: Music City U.S.A.* (New York, 1985), 7.

5   "Country Music Foundation," 42. I have been unable to learn more about the museum's exhibits prior to the building's expansion in 1976. There are no records of these exhibits, and no one I interviewed remembered their contents.

6   Fred Travis, "A Barn-Style Museum for Country-Style Music," *New York Times,* 7 January 1968, section 10, 15.

7   "Country Hall of Fame Mural is Thomas Hart Benton's Last Work," news release, Country Music Foundation, CMF Library and Media Center, n.d. According to William Ivey, Joe Allison had the idea of "a great painting about country music by an important painter," but Tex Ritter persuaded the board of trustees to commission the work. Interview with William Ivey, 13 October 1993, Nashville.

8   The Tennessee Arts Commission provided $5,000, and the National Endowment for the Arts $20,000, toward the $50,000 that would be needed. See "Country Music Foundation Receives NEA Grant for Benton Mural—Project to Honor Tex Ritter," news release, Country Music Foundation, CMF Library and Media Center, n.d.

9   For a discussion of Benton's musical background and his images of musicians, see Archie Green, "Thomas Hart Benton's Folk Musicians," *JEMF Quarterly* 12 (Summer 1976): 74–90; "A Suggested Museum Show," *JEMF Quarterly* 15 (Fall 1979): 157–65; and "Tom Benton's Folk Depictions," in *Thomas Hart Benton: Chronicler of America's Folk Heritage,* ed. Linda Weintraub (New York, 1984), 33–68. See also Ray M. Lawless, *Folksingers and Folksongs in America* (New York, 1960), 12; and "Thomas Hart Benton's Jealous Lover and Its Musical Background," *Register of the Museum of Art* (June 1961): 32–39.

10  Green, "Benton's Folk Musicians," 85. See also Alan C. Buechner, "Thomas Hart Benton and American Folk Music," in Weintraub, ed., *Thomas Hart Benton,* 69–77.

11  Buechner, "Benton and American Folk Music," 71.

12  Green, "Benton's Folk Musicians," 85. See also Buechner, "Benton and American Folk Music," 74.

13  William Ivey, *The Making of "The Sources of Country Music,"* brochure, Country Music Foundation, CMF Library and Media Center, 1975.

14  Such accounts include Bill C. Malone, *Country Music U.S.A.,* rev. ed. (Austin, 1985 [1968]); and Douglas B. Green, *Country Roots* (New York, 1976); see also *The Country Music Hall of Fame & Museum* (Nashville, 1992). Benjamin Filene discusses the construction of the folk music canon during the 1930s in "'Our Singing Country': John and Alan Lomax, Leadbelly, and the Construction of an American Past," *American Quarterly* 43 (1991): 602–24.

15  Portion of Minutes, CMF board meeting, 11 April 1973, CMF Library and Media Center. Benton admitted in his letter to Ivey of 5 February that he did "not like to *point up* celebrated individuals in [his] paintings."

16  See Erika Doss, *Benton, Pollock, and the Politics of Modernism from Regionalism to Abstract Expressionism* (Chicago, 1992), 123.

17   For a detailed discussion of the sketches that Benton used for the mural, see Karal Ann Marling, *Tom Benton and His Drawings: A Biographical Essay and a Collection of His Sketches, Studies, and Mural Cartoons* (Columbia, 1985), 1–12.

18   See Robert Sanford, "Sketch of Benton in Ozarks," *St. Louis Post-Dispatch,* 24 January 1975, 3D. See also Marling, *Tom Benton and His Drawings,* 1–6.

19   See Richard A. Peterson and Paul Di Maggio, "From Region to Class, the Changing Locus of Country Music: A Test of the Massification Hypothesis," *Social Forces* 53 (1975): 498.

20   Jim Cooper (president of the Tex Ritter Fan Club), in his excellent summary of Ritter's life, "Tex Ritter in the Twilight Years," *JEMF Quarterly* 8 (Summer 1977): 79. See also Johnny Bond's more personal, full-length biography, *The Tex Ritter Story* (New York, 1976).

21   "Tex Terms Self Mid-Roader," *The Tennessean,* 20 January 1970, 4; "Gore Too Far Left," *The Tennessean,* 9 March 1970, 13; and "Ritter Rips Nixon Critics, Backs Veto," *Nashville Banner,* 28 January 1970, 30.

22   "Ritter Gives War, Home Views," *The Tennessean,* 12 July 1970, 10-A; "Ritter Hits Anti-Nixon Protestors," *Nashville Banner,* 11 May 1970, 6; "Ritter Urges Sale of Jets to Israel," *The Tennessean,* 18 June 1970, 5(?); and "Ritter Urges Hike in Aged Benefits," *The Tennessean,* 7 May 1970, 7.

23   Colonel Andy Jackson, "On the Tenth Anniversary of Its Birth, The Fourth Anniversary of Its Home," *K-Buc Kicker* (April-May 1971): 7.

24   Doss, *Benton, Pollock, and the Politics of Modernism,* 147–229.

25   Ivey wrote in his 28 January 1974 letter to Benton of his "strong feeling that the mural will evolve as a memorial to Tex." Benton did in fact ask Ivey in his letter of 5 February to send early photographs of Ritter, and Ivey has confirmed that the photograph in Figure 7 is quite similar to the one he sent Benton. Interview with William Ivey, 13 October 1993, Nashville.

26   See Doss, *Benton, Pollock, and the Politics of Modernism,* 42–44, 147–220. See also Karal Ann Marling, "Thomas Hart Benton's *Boomtown:* Regionalism Redefined," *Prospects* 6 (1981): 106–9.

27   Malone, *Country Music U.S.A.,* 144.

28   Douglas B. Green, "The Singing Cowboy: An American Dream," *Journal of Country Music* 7 (1978): 27.

29   "Tex Ritter Dies; Victim of Massive Heart Attack," *Nashville Banner,* 3 January 1974, 8.

30   Cooper, "Tex Ritter in the Twilight Years," 84.

31   For information on the Lomaxes' construction of Leadbelly, see Filene, " 'Our Singing Country' "; and, for a more recent biography of Leadbelly, see Charles K. Wolfe and Kip Lornell, *The Life and Legend of Leadbelly* (New York, 1992). When asked if this photograph might have influenced Benton, William Ivey said that it was possible, especially since Leadbelly, like Pete Seeger and Woody Guthrie, represented

the type of American folksinger that Benton wanted to highlight. Interview with William Ivey, 13 October 1993, Nashville.

32  Richard A. Peterson, unpublished interview with Tex Ritter, 27 July 1973, Nashville.

33  Conversation of 17 June 1993.

34  On this analysis of Leadbelly, see Filene, " 'Our Singing Country,' " 611. Charley Pride's autobiography discusses the difficulties he experienced in the industry; see Charley Pride and Jim Henderson, *Pride: The Charley Pride Story* (New York, 1994).

35  Richard A. Peterson made this same observation in "Class Unconsciousness in Country Music," in *You Wrote My Life: Lyrical Themes in Country Music,* ed. Melton A. McLaurin and Richard A. Peterson (Philadelphia, 1992), 38.

36  Bob Millard, "Charley Pride: Alone in the Spotlight," *Journal of Country Music* 14 (1992): 18.

37  See Mary A. Bufwack and Robert K. Oermann, *Finding Her Voice: The Saga of Women in Country Music* (New York, 1993), 13.

38  Ibid., 14. Wayne W. Daniel has elaborated on the fiddle's negative associations in American culture, in "Fiddles, Fiddlers, and Fiddling in American Short Fiction" (paper presented at the International Country Music Conference, Meridian, Mississippi, 1994).

39  "Benton Sounds Off," *Art Digest,* 15 April 1941, 3. This statement led to Benton's dismissal as head of the Department of Painting at the Kansas City Art Institute. See *Parnassus* 13 (1941): 191; and *Art Digest,* 14 May 1941, 14.

40  Jerry Bailey, "Tom & Tex Worked Out New Hall of Fame Mural," *The Tennessean,* 29 March 1974, 63.

41  Bufwack and Oermann, *Finding Her Voice,* xi.

42  Thomas Hart Benton, *An Artist in America,* rev. ed. (Columbia, MO, and London, 1983 [1937]), 13.

43  Malone, *Country Music U.S.A.,* 61.

44  For this assessment of "Casey Jones," see Norm Cohen, *Long Steel Rail: The Railroad in American Folksong* (Urbana, 1981), 134. Henry Adams identifies the train as the Wabash Cannonball in *Thomas Hart Benton: An American Original* (New York, 1989), 340.

45  Henry Adams, *The Sources of Country Music,* brochure, Country Music Foundation, n.d.; see also Adams, *An American Original,* 341. On a preliminary drawing of the train for the mural, Benton wrote that he had consulted a photograph in the *Yazoo City Miss. Herald,* 30 April 1970.

46  Benton, *Artist in America,* 70–71.

47  Ibid., 136. *Cotton Loading,* in fact, illustrates this earlier experience and is invoked in Benton's last mural, where the same boat billows smoke as it approaches the shore.

48  "Country Music Hall of Fame Unveils Final Benton Mural," news release, Country Music Hall of Fame and Museum, CMF Library and Media Center, n.d. This is reiterated in Ivey, *Making of "The Sources of Country Music."*

49   *Country Music Hall of Fame & Museum,* 9.

50   See Richard A. Peterson, "The Production of Cultural Change: The Case of Con-
     temporary Music," *Social Research* 45 (1978): 292–314.

51   See Teddy Bart, "Country Artists Purely Motivated But Misguided," *Nashville Ban-
     ner,* 19 November 1974, 9. See also Jerry Bailey, "Artists Fear Country Music Identity
     Loss," *The Tennessean,* 9 November 1974, 1–2.

52   Bill Hance, " 'Twang' Goes Country Music, Into a Little Argument," *Nashville Ban-
     ner,* 15 November 1974, 21.

53   Richard A. Peterson and Paul Di Maggio, "The Early *Opry:* Its Hillbilly Image in
     Fact and Fancy," *Journal of Country Music* 4 (1973): 43–44. See also Richard A.
     Peterson, "La Fabrication de l'authenticité la country music," *Actes de la recherche
     en sciences sociales* (June 1992): 3–19.

54   *Country Music Hall of Fame & Museum,* 7.

55   According to Alan Stoker, the museum's audio restoration engineer, the film was
     shown between 1974 and 1976. William Ivey said that the film is not shown now
     because it is "no longer current" in terms of the stars it highlights and the statistics
     it reports. Interview with William Ivey, 13 October 1993, Nashville.

56   For a discussion of some of these exhibits, see Charles F. McGovern, "Real People
     and the True Folk," *American Quarterly* 42 (1990): 478–97.

57   Benton, *Artist in America,* 378.

58   "Hic Jacet Regionalism," *Art Digest,* 1 October 1951, 26.

59   See A. Green, "Benton's Folk Musicians," 75: and "Suggested Museum Show."

60   News release, Country Music Hall of Fame and Museum, CMF Library and Media
     Center, 1974.

61   See Richard A. Peterson and Russell Davis, Jr., "The Fertile Crescent of Country
     Music," *Journal of Country Music* 6 (1975): 19.

62   Marc Landy, "Country Music: The Melody of Dislocation," *New South* 26 (1971): 67.

63   Quoted in Buechner, "Benton and American Folk Music," 75.

64   Benton, *Artist in America,* 113.

65   Quoted in Archie Green, "Hillbilly Music: Source and Symbol," *Journal of Ameri-
     can Folklore* 78 (1965): 204–28.

66   Cohen, *Long Steel Rail,* 31; D. Green, *Country Roots,* 107.

67   See, for example, "Thomas Hart Benton," news release, Country Music Foun-
     dation, CMF Library and Media Center, n.d.; and "Country Music Foundation
     Receives NEA Grant for Benton Mural."

68   *Thomas Hart Benton's The Sources of Country Music.* Video by John Altman and
     Mary A. Nelson, 1974.

69   Nor has Benton's reputation improved in some circles. See Hilton Kramer, "The
     Benton Affair," *Art & Antiques* (Summer 1987): 113–14, in which this critic iden-
     tifies Benton as "a *failed* artist . . . a minor figure" whose "kitschy illustrational
     style . . . [isn't] worth the materials used to execute [it]."

70   For a discussion of Soby's essay, see Doss, *Benton, Pollock, and the Politics of Mod-*

*ernism,* 376. Benton is quoted in *A Thomas Hart Benton Miscellany,* ed. Matthew Baigell (Lawrence, KS, 1971), 109.

71  In addition to Baigell's *Thomas Hart Benton Miscellany* and *American Scene,* see Matthew Baigell, *Thomas Hart Benton* (New York, 1975).

72  James Dennis, *Grant Wood: A Study in American Art and Culture* (Columbia, 1986 [1975]).

73  *Making Their Mark: Women Artists Move into the Mainstream, 1970–85,* ed. Randy Rosen (New York, 1989).

74  Sanford, "Sketch of Benton," 3D.

75  In response to these (then scandalous) pronouncements, Billy Rose volunteered to exhibit Benton's *Persephone* in his popular Diamond Horseshoe nightclub. The painting hung on loan in the night club for a month in 1941. See "Blast by Benton," *Art Digest,* 15 April 1941, 6.

76  As quoted in Baigell, ed., *Thomas Hart Benton Miscellany,* 38.

77  Peterson and Di Maggio, "From Region to Class," 503; Peterson, "Class Unconsciousness in Country Music," 36. Peterson argues that country music lyrics both evoke and undermine working-class consciousness by promoting the status quo and thereby fostering "class un-consciousness, a fatalistic state in which people bemoan their fate, yet accept it" (36, 60).

78  Benton, *Artist in America,* 319.

# Mecca for the Country Music Scholar

❦ ─────────────────────────────────────── **Ronnie Pugh**

Downstairs in one of America's most famous tourist attractions, Nashville's Country Music Hall of Fame and Museum, is housed an unmatched collection of research materials that documents country music's past. Tourists never see it, and the local community doesn't know much about it. But country music scholars, critics, historians, and serious fans the world over not only know about the Country Music Foundation Library and Media Center, but regularly use it. A full-time staff of eight professionals and one paraprofessional, along with an assortment of student interns and volunteers, maintains the collection and assists those who use it—whether they come in person or send inquiries by phone, mail, or fax.

Over the twenty-plus years of its existence, the CMF Library and Media Center has amassed the largest collection of materials related to a single genre of American popular music. From the library's inception, certain collecting priorities were established and are reflected in the current breakdown of holdings. The collection of recordings, in many ways the library's showcase, now exceeds 150,000 items—78s, 33s, 45s, CDs, tapes, and recorded radio shows—and is kept under lock and key in customized cabinets. Other libraries have more recordings, but none that specialize in a single type of music. Given that specialization, the emphasis placed upon this collection is hardly surprising.

Documentary-makers all over the world rely upon the CMF's holdings of films and videotapes, which now number approximately 5,000, with about 500 additions (mostly new music videos) made each year. Lab fees are charged for listening, viewing, and for any permissible duplicating, which can be done in a wide range of tape formats. Print publishers are the main users of the more than 30,000 photographs kept in the library's vault. This collection, consisting almost entirely of 8 × 10 black and white prints, spans the history of country music and includes promo poses and candid shots of all major and most minor stars. Donated company files, stocks purchased from individual photographers, and items culled from fan scrapbooks continue to swell this collection, which is sorted into artist/subject files. (Reproduction and one-time user fees, while comparable to what other archives charge, are pegged to companies with large budgets and may be prohibitive for individual purchasers). Both publishers and museums use the library's collection of show posters, "one-sheets," and album artwork, which currently includes over 1,000 items. Most of these colorful flat items have been photographed for ease of selection with minimum handling.

The CMF collection also includes basic print materials, such as newspaper clippings gathered from papers all over the United States, especially between 1970 and 1990. Covering all aspects of country music, these clippings now number in the hundreds of thousands, filling some 1,300 subject files. The book collection, though relatively small, includes 10,000 titles and continues to grow. The number of periodical issues now held exceeds 4,500, while over 300 titles are currently received, constituting a large share of the library's ongoing acquisition costs. The number of songs in the sheet-music collection (one of the better-catalogued holdings) exceeds 7,000, boosted by a recent donation from *Country Song Roundup* magazine, and this collection is a valuable resource for a growing number of lyric analysts.

The holdings described above amount to a collection of consumer items that anyone with enough money, time, or diligence might have found and purchased for a personal collection. But with its industry-wide support and prestige, the Country Music Foundation has also been able to acquire valuable primary source materials from companies, writers, performers, and scholars. For example, early on, the foundation began an oral history project, and the library vault now holds taped interviews with hundreds of country music "greats" and "near-greats." Singers, songwriters, disc jockeys, music publishers, and many other significant figures have consented to be interviewed through the years under CMF auspices, and, in other cases, journalists have donated tapes of their own interviews to the foundation. Although most of these tapes are not yet transcribed or indexed, listening facilities are available upon advance request, and brief excerpts may be quoted in published works if proper credit is given.

The scrapbooks and personal papers of some key industry figures are also part of the foundation's primary source material holdings. A few months after

Roy Acuff's death in 1992, a set of scrapbooks kept over several decades by his wife, Mildred, was donated by their son, Roy Neill Acuff. These volumes of photos, clippings, awards, commendations, fan mail, and handwritten song lyrics augment the special Roy Acuff Collection that California collector and Acuff biographer Elizabeth Schlappi gave the CMF in 1977. Dozens of other artists' scrapbooks have been donated to the CMF over the years, including those of T. Texas Tyler, Claude Casey, Pee Wee King, Cliff Carlisle, and the Duke of Paducah. Many of these priceless scrapbooks are now on microfilm, but hard copy can also be made available to researchers. The largest fan collections of material on individual country artists, comparable to Schlappi's Roy Acuff Collection, are the materials on Marty Robbins and the Oak Ridge Boys donated by Barbara Pruett, and Dorothy Gilbert's donation of her many scrapbooks of memorabilia from Merle Haggard's career. "Ranger Doug" (Douglas Green) of the Riders in the Sky continually donates career papers when he cleans house: the CMF already has ten or so boxes stuffed with contracts, letters, photos, and publicity blurbs, with undoubtedly more to come. (Would that the careers of all prominent country artists had been as conscientiously documented.) Personal papers of bandleader Shelley Lee Alley and of Washington, DC, promoter/impresario Connie B. Gay were donated posthumously by members of their families; the Gay Collection, the largest posthumous donation of personal papers, is particularly accessible owing to a CMF archival pilot project.

Discographers can also find a wealth of data in several primary source collections of the CMF. Studio logbooks, loaned to the CMF for copying by several prominent Nashville session musicians, provide the historian with recording information from the 1950s to the 1970s. Several major recording companies have furnished the library with microfilm or photocopies of all or part of their logs for country music recording sessions: Decca, Columbia, Capitol, and RCA (with the most complete session logs of all). The files of several important smaller companies (Starday, King, and Four Star, among others) have been microfilmed over the years and are available to researchers. Nashville's American Federation of Musicians (A.F. of M.) has faithfully donated recording information (master sessions, demos, and radio, film, and TV work) on Nashville from 1970 through the mid-1980s, with more to come as they clean house periodically.

With a collection of this magnitude and a staff that stands ready to help, the CMF Library and Media Center has become something of a mecca for scholars drawn to this American musical art form. The library is open Monday through Thursday (except for holidays), with service hours from 10 A.M. to 5 P.M.

(CST/CDT). No museum admission fee is required, but appointments must be made for in-house use of library holdings, and hourly fees are assessed for any research or duplication work done by the staff. Scholars can write for further information to the Country Music Foundation Library and Media Center, 4 Music Square East, Nashville, TN 37203; telephone (615) 256–1639; fax (615) 255–2245.

# Country Music, Seriously

*An Interview with Bill C. Malone*

 **Cecelia Tichi**

*Since the 1960s, Bill C. Malone's name has been synonymous with country music studies. His lifelong "love affair" with the music resulted first in the 1968 publication of the seminal* Country Music U.S.A. *(rev. ed. 1985), which mapped the social history of the music and remains the foundational encyclopedic study. In 1975, he coedited (with Judith McCulloh) a collection of essays,* Stars of Country Music *(rpr. 1991), and his most recent book is* Singing Cowboys and Musical Mountaineers: Southern Culture and the Roots of Country Music. *Bill C. Malone is Professor of History at Tulane University.*

CECELIA TICHI: If I could ask you, Bill, to talk autobiographically about your developing interest, not just as a hobbyist, but as a professional historian of country music. I happen to know because I teach at Vanderbilt that you were a boyhood friend of our chancellor, Joe Wyatt—

BILL C. MALONE: —Right—

TICHI: —who recalls your having a passion for that music as far back as, was it fourth grade?

MALONE: Yeah, as far back as I can remember. I grew up in a household where music was always present. We were either listening to our little battery radio, after 1939, or hearing my mother and older brothers sing. My mother sang mostly fragments of songs, gospel songs, sentimental songs like "The Letter Edged in Black" and "Two Little Orphans," that sort of thing. And when we got the radio, we started to listen to the local shows and to the *Grand Ole Opry*. So as far as I can remember, I've always had a passionate love of music, and I never thought that there was conceivably an academic way to even approach it. But I went to the University of Texas at Austin, and I sang all the time—you know, sang at parties, and in the late 1950s started going out to a now-famous honky tonk called Threadgills a couple of times a week, so finally my supervisor said to me, "Why don't you turn this interest into a topic?" He was a business historian, among other things, and he wanted a history of Nashville publishing. But I seized the opportunity, and once I got into the study, then I moved into a more general history, with his blessing—you know, he let me go the way I wanted to, in part because he knew nothing about the subject—although he knew it was important, he knew it had interest.

TICHI: So you're saying that your doctoral dissertation advisor understood the importance of the music. He wasn't questioning that subject, as a dissertation advisor might have in some other department, or at some other university.

MALONE: But mainly as a business history. Country music was beginning to boom at that time, although of course rock & roll had come in and given it a blow. But nevertheless, country music was still a very powerful economic entity, and he thought it would be worth a good business study. But I moved it to a more general cultural and musicological study.

TICHI: So you kind of came in under the camouflage of business history—

MALONE: —Right—

TICHI: —but you are also recounting a life in which the absence of country music would have been unthinkable—from your family to the radio, it was a part of your environment.

MALONE: It filled many of my waking hours. We woke up to country music every morning. When you turned on the radio, it was on some sort of country show, either with disc jockeys or maybe a live show. While we were still out on the farm, when Daddy came in from work, we would listen to Bob Wills, the Chuck Wagon Gang, or maybe the Stamps Quartet, and then I'd listen to the shows in the afternoon, and of course we never missed a *Grand Ole Opry*. Music was a constant presence, and I used to buy the *Country Song Roundup* and cut the songs out—I wish I hadn't; I wish I'd saved them now.

TICHI: [Laughs.]

MALONE: Before that, my mother had done something similar. There was a paper, a newspaper, circulated widely throughout east Texas called the *Semi-Weekly Farm News,* and it was published by the *Dallas Morning News*. And, I guess since almost the turn of the century, it had a young people's page, where requested songs were published. And my mother would generally clip those songs out and paste them in an old grammar book or history book, or something like that. I think a lot of people did that. And so she saved those old songs, in a way kind of similar to what I did later with the *Country Song Roundup*.

TICHI: My goodness, you had in your mother a research assistant, unknown to you at the time.

MALONE: Yes.

TICHI: Now, you know, I've heard so many scholars say that it took them many years, even decades, to make the personal connections with their scholarship. The scholarship seemed very far afield at the time they were undertaking it, whatever those projects were, of their deepest personal concerns. For you, it sounds as though your environment of country music and your developing knowledge of that music, sort of biographically, was much more, almost—I'll say *natural,* knowing that that word is a dangerous word to use—but that you didn't feel, as a historian-in-training, that you ought to undertake a research project markedly far afield of your personal passions. Is that right?

MALONE: In the beginning, that was true. Later on, when I was trying to get a good, tenured job, I was encouraged to go into something else. In the beginning, I think, for good or ill, I associated country music with growing up on the tenant farm there in east Texas, and what I saw of value in the music I associated with my family and their culture.

TICHI: Yes.

MALONE: But as time went on, I became much more sophisticated, I think, and I began to see the ways I probably oversimplified the culture and distorted it—romanticized it, for sure. But when I came to Tulane University, in the early 1970s—

TICHI: —Where had you—may I ask, that wasn't your first teaching—

MALONE: —That was my third job.

TICHI: Would you recount, a little bit, the road from your dissertation into teaching, and the receptivity that you found, or the lack of it, as you started your first job search?

MALONE: Well, before the dissertation was finished, I went down the road from Austin about thirty miles and began teaching at Southwest Texas State College, where LBJ got his degree.

TICHI: Right.

MALONE: And I stayed there for five years, and the dissertation was finished during that time. And then I went to Murray State in Kentucky, then Wisconsin State. Then, at Tulane—I came as a visiting professor and was trying hard to get into a vacant cultural history position here—I was advised by a couple of people who were in my corner that I ought to get out of country music, that I ought to publish something else, just to demonstrate that I had more serious interests.

TICHI: Good Lord.

MALONE: I remember one of them saying that once you've done that, then you can go back to what you want to do, but first establish your credentials. He was saying, of course, immediately too, that that would be a good way of getting this job and getting tenure. But country music has continued to be a tremendous interest—if I had taken that warning, I don't know if it would have continued to be such an interest, in different aspects of it, opportunities to give speeches, and lectures—

TICHI: —That's right; I have heard by word of the grapevine that when you lecture, you—don't you bring your guitar? I know you sing.

MALONE: Usually. I like to give lectures and illustrate them with songs. Occasionally, that can be with a tape, particularly if I want to inform the listeners of how country music sounds today, and how contemporary people are treating certain themes—that can be with a tape. But almost always I do songs of my own, and my wife and I also give performances; she plays the mandolin, and we play for clubs, old folks' homes, that sort of thing. We get a lot of enjoyment out of that.

TICHI: Yes. Did you learn to play guitar while you were growing up? Was that part of your household life?

MALONE: My two older brothers played the guitar, but I never learned when I was a child. I didn't learn until I was at the university. When I first went down and sang for parties, I really—I wore out guitar players. I remember I had two real good friends, Tom Crouch and later Willie Benson, who used to play for me for hours and hours.

TICHI: Aha.

MALONE: Just doing one song after another. And all the while, I was trying to learn a few chords. Unfortunately, I discovered the capo and found out that you could play complicated chords simply with that, so I didn't learn as much as I should have. I wish I was a better guitar player than I am, but I'm good enough to accompany most of the songs that I do.

TICHI: I'm sure. What cachet—a scholar who can perform part of a lecture musically! That just sounds wonderful to me. Let me turn to your relation to students. Obviously, you got that job at Tulane; obviously, in the various history departments in which you have taught, the historians of the Middle Ages or the Enlightenment all joined in to welcome you, or at least to put up with you, in the departments. I want to ask about, and I know our readers will be interested in, the courses you teach in country music.

MALONE: I've taught country music as such at least a couple of times, but I'm really kind of hesitant to teach it, in part, I think, because—I guess this may sound funny or harsh—but I think it attracts the wrong kind of students, along with the good ones. It attracts an awful lot of people who think it's just going to be, you know, an easy course, just sit around and listen to a few songs—not do much beyond that and get a good, easy grade. But I'm a pretty tough teacher, and I think I take the subject so seriously that if I don't get the kind of response I want, or if I think the subject doesn't receive the kind of seriousness it deserves, it bothers me, and I guess it shows. I'd really rather teach country music on a non-credit basis, for people to take it who want to take it, and not worry about exams and the pressure. Other than that, I do have a course called "Southern Music," and although it has some of the same problems, I teach that almost every other year, and I deal with all the American styles that had their origins in the South: everything from jazz to blues, gospel, country, even protest music. So I'll be teaching that this semester on Monday evenings.

My favorite course, though, is one called "Southern Folk Culture," because, over the years, as I gradually learned more and more about the music, and about its relationship to working people and to American culture as a whole, I began to see the music as just one part of a much larger Southern folk culture. And, of course, I can talk about religion and work and politics and folklore, as well as music. So I also teach that almost every year. It's my favorite course, by far.

TICHI: But if I hear you right, you're saying that in a course on Southern culture, you're able to provide the context, all the contexts, for this music so that the music has meaning for the students beyond anything that would be possible simply by playing a series of songs in class and making observations about them, no matter how systematically. Is that right? You're really trying to give the students the cultural foundation for what they're hearing.

MALONE: And give them the context for it—tell them that the music is one way that people have had for defining themselves and informing the rest of the world about themselves.

TICHI: Let me ask you what you would advise as a—I'll say a kind of training ground for a would-be, or an aspiring, I should say, historian of country music like yourself. Is it possible, I guess the question is, for somebody from, say, New Jersey, to come along, develop this interest, and develop a professional relationship to it? And what would that pathway be, here in the 1990s?

MALONE: Well, I don't remember where you're from, but I know that you've already demonstrated that you don't have to be from the South—

TICHI: [Laughs.]

MALONE: —and from a so-called country music culture to understand it, although, of course, you take a very different approach from what I do.

TICHI: Yes.

MALONE: I think you need, first of all, to respect the people who perform it and listen to it. I think the music suffered for many years because people just could not take it seriously. It seemed to represent a degenerate, illiterate culture, and although there's some truth to that, that's not all there is to the story. There's both strength and virtue along with the weaknesses. But when people come with an open mind and respect the beliefs and values of people who may be different from themselves, who may in fact have ideas that are occasionally radically different from their own, if a person tries to empathize with them—and then once they do, once they get to the subject—they're also going to find more commonality than they suspected. I think you're right on target in your book, when you say that country music addresses the same problems, the same themes, that the greatest writers in America have addressed over the years.

TICHI: Thank you for that compliment. If, say, a graduate student had this relation of respect to the music, would you advise them simply to start listening, to listen as far back as they can, to just—of course, read your work and the available work—?

MALONE: —Listen to as much of the professional music as you can, and an awful lot of it is available back to the 1920s, not nearly as much as there should be, not nearly as much, say, as blues. But in addition to that, I think you need to go out and just hear the music being performed, out in the honky tonks and the churches, in the VFW halls and American Legion halls, where people meet every Saturday night and just jam. There's an awful lot of them that haven't been explored to any great degree, not simply in the South, but all over the United States. There are people who've been meeting, in some cases maybe twenty, thirty years, regularly, just at somebody's home or down at some public meeting house. They tend to sing songs that they grew up with, but little by little the modern songs move in too. But I think that the aspiring student could learn an awful lot from this. And certainly, get away from Top 40 radio and from the television videos, and just really go out among the people themselves, and see what the so-called amateurs are singing, and what they're listening to.

TICHI: Now some readers are going to wonder why Top 40 radio isn't enough, or why not watch country music television videos. I know some readers will feel that they themselves are listening to the country stations in their home areas, they're watching TNN and CMT—

MALONE: —Well, they're not getting a wide enough exposure to the music. I think that what they hear on Top 40 radio may be good, and the issues that are addressed are certainly relevant, but they're not getting the whole picture if they're not also hearing the older singers like Merle Haggard, George Jones, Gene Watson, people like that. Did you read the article the other day in the *New York Times?*

TICHI: Yes, I did.

MALONE: I forget which one it was—whether it was Jones or Haggard, who said, "Don't drive us all to Branson."

TICHI: Yes, and I've forgotten which, too, but it was that article that had "Greybeards" in the headline, and it, of course, made the point that I think some of our readers might not be aware of, that the enduring major figures in country music do not these days get a hearing on the radio at all; they just don't get played, they're not on the playlist. And that Branson [Missouri] itself, as the reporter acknowledged, has a kind of dinosaur-park taint to it; it's known as almost a quarantine area for older country music performers, but especially those, we would say in this context, who just don't have access to the radio playlists. Very bad situation, right now. So you're saying that somebody with a really serious interest in this music, who might want to make a statement about it, has got to go around the radio—not turn it off, but find all of the musical resources that lie to the left, right, front, and back of radio.

MALONE: Or he or she, that is, the aspiring student, is going to find just how powerful Top 40 radio is, when the student goes to a small barn dance in, say, Quitman, Texas—let's call it the Saturday Night Hoedown—they're going to find a lot of young people there trying very hard to sound just like Garth Brooks or Reba McEntire. So even when they go out into the hinterlands, they're going to find just how powerful Nashville and Top 40 culture are. But they're also going to find people who are still trying to sing like Hank Williams, who sing nothing but Hank Williams, or Jimmie Rodgers. But you need to hear it all.

TICHI: You have to get out there, hear it.

Let me turn to your work. You, of course, are the author of the landmark study *Country Music U.S.A.* (1968). You also revised it in the early 1980s, is that correct?

MALONE: 1985.

TICHI: Right. And potentially, the book might undergo one more revision or so—I mean, you could—

MALONE: I hope to have the opportunity. As far as the average fan is concerned, you know, it needs to be revised right now because, when I was writing the 1985 revision, Randy Travis and Reba McEntire hadn't even moved out of obscurity, or were just beginning to. There's such a long period between the time when you submit a manuscript and when it finally comes out that, when you're dealing with popular culture, trends fade away, and performers fall by the wayside, and new ones appear. So I guess a lot of modern fans would be very disappointed if they picked up that revision because they wouldn't see this whole body of neotraditionalists in there, you know, like Alan Jackson and Garth Brooks.

TICHI: All right. These sound like note cards or databases for an imminent revision. I know your many admirers are going to appreciate hearing that you may well undertake yet another revision. But what's interesting is that *Country Music U.S.A.* is a book that can undergo another revision without disturbing its fundamental mapping; that is, it's the book that, in a literal sense, puts country music on the map, region by region, genre by genre. And updating it involves bringing newer artists onto the map, into the geographical area, but the encyclopedic, comprehensive nature of that book is undisturbed. Now your newest book, just out in the last year, *Singing Cowboys and Musical Mountaineers,* seems to me to have in it some arguments that will disturb, I'll say "traditionalists." It seems to me there are two things you do that I would ask you to reflect on. One is that you've done a good deal of archival research that shows that many of the songs we thought to be public-domain songs, preserved purely in folk culture, in the remote areas of the Appalachians and throughout the South, are in fact authored songs that were brought into those remote areas by touring companies and itinerant performers, and which were sustained in those remote areas—not public-domain songs at all, but published songs, with identifiable songwriters. Now, once you do this kind of historical research, it seems to me, you pose a fundamental challenge to some of the most beloved ideas about folk culture that some folklorists have sustained for a long time. So that's one area. And another is that you point out that some of the writers who would like to think of themselves as historians and scholars of this music have participated in romanticizing it, have become more a part of the creation of symbols than of the establishment of hard data on this music.

MALONE: And I think that we all—and by "we" I mean people who first went into the study of the music—I think we all did that to a certain degree. I know that, as I said earlier, I associated this music with growing up in east Texas, and with the kind of culture that I am a part of. But from the very beginning, I was also guilty of such romanticization. I guess that was fed by movies and popular culture, reading books like *The Little Shepherd of Kingdom Come,* and *Trail of the Lonesome Pine.* I had visions of remote mountain valleys where people still held to ancient folkways, and I think somewhere, I don't remember whether I said this in the first edition of my book or not, I said something about the music's being "as old as the hills from whence it came."

And, of course, now I know that the music came from many, many different sources, from all over America as well as Great Britain, but I know that, to a certain degree, I still have a little bit of the romanticism that affects my work as well as that of other scholars. So, lastly, I'd like to say that these criticisms are directed at my work, and at that of other writers who may come along. And it's very hard to strip away these illusions that are so dear to people, and to me too. I think it's time we all learned that it's not really the repertoire of folk music, of country music, but it's the way it's performed, the kind of style preserved and projected, first by the Southern folk, and later by country musicians. If they heard a good tune, they absorbed it. If it fit their interests, if it fit the values of their community, they absorbed it, whether it was a British ballad or local black blues, or came from a brass band—if the song was good, they accepted it, and then they performed it in their own way. And it might come out very different from the way it was originally published, originally performed, but it became part of the new culture.

TICHI: That's a very important position to take, it seems to me, because it's clear that you are saying we need revisionism, we need to scrutinize our own earlier work to see whether we ourselves have not participated in a kind of mythmaking about the music. But the alternative—and I think this is crucial—the alternative is not an iconoclasm in which, say, discovery of songwriters whose names ought to be affixed to some of what we thought of as the folk traditions—those discoveries of authorships, say, ought not to lead us into a mentality of iconoclastic exposé, but that scholars and analysts and critics, rather than going "Aha!" or "Gotcha!" to country music, need to redirect their attention, as you're putting it, to styles of performance, and cultural assimilation, and that there, in those areas, lies the appropriate focus for scholarly efforts. I think so much scholarship currently involves itself at the level of iconoclasm—loosely, in the popular press, "deconstruction" is the term—and one is left with a kind of rubble, but not with a redirection. And you're talking about how country music specialists and scholars and critics and partisans—and I could just go on in synonyms of certain kinds—but how this group can sustain its interest by redirecting it. Is that right?

MALONE: Right. To get a clearer picture of the whole universe. Another purpose being not to destroy any scholarship, or really any preconceptions. You destroy neither the idea of folk culture nor country music's distinctiveness by demonstrating just how rich those cultures have been, and how widely they have borrowed over the years.

TICHI: I want to ask you to speculate for a minute on a question that came up recently in my own university. What it's about is why other folk traditions, especially black blues, have been so interesting to scholars, and why country music—and this goes back to what we were talking about a little bit earlier—why it has met with resistance—resistance now on the part of, let's say, intellectuals, or those who think of themselves in those terms.

MALONE: Particularly Southern intellectuals.

TICHI: Yeah. I guess I'm coming around to asking, is it that black blues seems exotically different and therefore intellectuals will gravitate to it, but that country music seems to come out of poor white traditions and they're frightening, they might be contagious, you know? Why is one music so attractive to self-defined intellectuals, and the other so repellent to them, or to many of them?

MALONE: Well, I think you've put your finger on part of the answer. I think that black blues has been perceived as an exotic art form, the product of an oppressed people, you know—it's a correct perception. That music as well as other forms of black music have been vehicles by which oppressed people have sustained a sense of community and have explained themselves to the rest of the world; and it enabled them to survive in a hostile environment. I think by recognizing the music, you also recognize the legitimacy of black culture and its importance in American life. Country music, on the other hand, I think has always been perceived as music of a white culture that is really not necessarily a minority culture in American life, certainly not—too close, too reminiscent of the ills that have afflicted Southern life over the centuries and so have also afflicted American life as a whole. Associating the music with white folk culture also associates the music with racism and bigotry and ignorance and cultural degeneracy, the whole range of ills that have been identified for the last couple of centuries. I think Southern intellectuals, particularly Southern liberal intellectuals, have been very embarrassed by the music because it is so close, and it's so real, and, I don't know, maybe it reminds them not only of the dirty, unwashed white people around them, but maybe of some of their own relatives. Kind of a rambling answer, but . . .

TICHI: No, I think it's more of a comprehensive answer.

MALONE: You know, as I said in the book [*Singing Cowboys and Musical Mountaineers*], the music of the white South was always ignored over the centuries. Travelers and other observers occasionally saw it; sometimes they would even attempt a little bit of a description, particularly of country dances, but I think you can always tell from their descriptions that they were really—that they didn't quite take those people seriously, and therefore couldn't quite take the music seriously either. And so, over the centuries, the music was ignored, and suddenly when it was "discovered," it was those romantic groups on the fringe of the South that were emphasized—the cowboys of the far western plains, or the mountaineers of the Appalachians—the most romantic elements, both groups supposedly representing a kind of freedom and liberation that the rest of American society was losing. So it was tempting to believe that the mountaineers had preserved a great corpus of songs that were brought from Great Britain and that the cowboys, through their liberated lifestyle, were responding to that great expansive landscape of which they were a part, creating musical forms which demonstrated the kind of individualism that Americans once thought they had—individualism and liberation which moved over into styles of music like western swing. And while those two groups were being romanticized, all the rest of the Southern whites were being ignored, as if there were no music whatsoever between the mountains of Kentucky, let's say, and the plains of Texas—that whole hinterland that eventually produced Hank Williams and Jimmie Rodgers and a great body of the best musicians in America.

But I think it goes back to historical causes deeply rooted in American life. We remember those poor whites in the South, who lived in the vast interior of the South, who were never going to make anything of themselves, all the years they remained poor and illiterate, and that was seeming proof that they had no strengths and no virtues, so it was inevitable that their music would be terrible too. And then in the Civil War, those people went off and fought under the leadership of their upper-class "captains," whether they owned slaves or not, and the mountaineers supposedly resisted the war and resisted secession, which makes them even more appealing to the romanticists.

TICHI:  Yes.

MALONE:  I hope you're able to decipher all this.

TICHI:  Oh, yes. Well, it's a wonderful capsule of history, and it leads to a question of whether you think the music of this culture is undervalued even to this day, even as we're surrounded—and this is a more general question; it's a little beyond country music—I get asked, "Do you teach country music?" And I say, "Well, I make it a part of everything I'm teaching now," and I realize the extent to which we confine ourselves to print knowledge and print information. Of course, the whole electronics revolution is challenging our monopolistic practices in relation to print, and I guess I hadn't planned to talk about this, but I'm feeling at this point that music has generally been undervalued as a source of knowledge and understanding.

MALONE:  I think it's undervalued even by people who love it, in many cases. That may be one reason why I'm sometimes reluctant to teach country music or Southern music—although I always go back to teaching them. Often, while I am teaching, young people are just not taking the subject seriously. It's something you listen to, you dance to, it's fun. You know, you buy records, but to treat it seriously—as if it's really important, as important as high art music, or high art literature—some people just cannot make the connection. Listen to it, love it, buy it, but don't ever admit that it has any importance beyond that, beyond a diversion.

TICHI:  As you say this, I'm recalling telling a couple of people how I would listen to a phrase, let's say a Merle Haggard phrase, maybe twenty times, re-

winding on a tape, to try to really hear what he'd be doing in a short phrase —
and people look at me as if that's the strangest thing they've heard recently.

MALONE: What a waste of time.

TICHI: Uh-huh [laughs]. But I don't know, might it be — I suppose if our music
schools opened themselves to a greater variety of music and weren't only such
bastions of European music, we might get a better hearing for country music in
a serious musical focus or treatment. Do you think that's ever going to happen?

MALONE: It seems to be happening a little bit. From time to time, I hear of
people in music schools who are trying to write on country music, or who
teach it. I don't know how widespread that is. That would be interesting, to
make a survey of music schools around the country and see if, and to what
degree, country music is taught or discussed. I don't know, has anybody ever
done that?

TICHI: It would be interesting. Could you imagine the ideal Center for the
Study of Country Music? What would be in that center? Obviously, people
who are impassioned about and committed to that music, but what kind of
disciplines would you see involved and what sort of facilities would it have?
Just imagine your utopian country music study center.

MALONE: Hmm. You're speaking of artifacts, research materials?

TICHI: Anything. Anything you want. Let's say the dean calls you in, or better
yet, the president of Tulane, and says, "Bill Malone, we want to realize your
vision of an ideal — the very best — Center for the Study of Country Music that
you can help us invent." What would you put on your wish list?

MALONE: Well, you'd have to have the recording library, for sure, going back
to the beginning: sheet music, songbooks, songsters, a selection of videos, old
movie scenes that deal with the music, gospel songbooks, pop sheet music,
song sheets. It would have to — the library of such a center would have much
larger holdings than just country music itself, mainly for the reason we've been
talking about — because the music did draw on so many different sources.

TICHI: Right. How about the faculty? Would you want them to be involved in
the school of music, history department, fine arts? What?

MALONE: They would have to know more than just the music. They would
have to be students of American culture in general, and of the South specifically. I certainly wouldn't want a faculty made up solely of musicians or

musicologists; I would want people who had a comprehensive understanding of the cultural context from which the music came.

TICHI: And would there be instrumentalists on staff to come in and demonstrate, as you do?

MALONE: You'd have to have instrumentalists, but I just thought of another thing I should have mentioned right at the beginning, and that's a literature of dance. We need to do a whole lot more on that in country music because the origin of so much of this music was in dance music, and that has really been a neglected aspect of the music. We're beginning to see more and more people interested in it, but that would be a significant part of any center's study.

TICHI: Okay, so dance, instrumentalists, library—and, obviously, colleagues who were mutually supportive and not—no scorn, no sneering. Okay.

Is there any issue that you would like to bring up, that I haven't asked you to talk about?

MALONE: I think you hit the main bases.

TICHI: All right, let me just quickly ask you about any revision you might do or a second volume of *Stars of Country Music,* in which you organized a group of people to write thorough, in-depth essays on different country music performers. Is a sequel to that project anything you might undertake?

MALONE: Well, from time to time, Dick Wentworth of the University of Illinois Press has mentioned doing a sequel or a revision. I think the main reason why he hasn't really stressed it greatly is because he's hoping that I'll finish my other book for him.

TICHI: I see.

MALONE: I think he's afraid to get me off on that topic again.

TICHI: [Laughs.]

MALONE: I'm so easily diverted. But I would change it significantly. I certainly would add certain people. I think Willie Nelson probably ought to be added, maybe George Jones, Patsy Cline. Hmm, right now I don't know who it would be.

TICHI: Okay, but you would make up a new roster.

MALONE: I'd also make some changes. I think I'd drop Johnny Rodriguez. At the time, he seemed like a good example of a young performer who was going to endure, but he didn't. And I think I would change some of the authors too; I think the Bradley Kincaid essay needs somebody who would take it a little more seriously than the earlier author did.

TICHI: Yeah.

MALONE: Maybe Ronnie Pugh on Ernest Tubb. Take advantage of some of the writers we didn't use before, or who have come along since the book came out.

TICHI: Right, right.

MALONE: Maybe include Bob Cantwell, for example.

TICHI: Yes.

MALONE: Who would be your favorite star, if you were to write one? Who would you choose?

TICHI: Well, if you do this volume, I want to do Emmylou Harris.

MALONE: Oh, yeah.

TICHI: All right?

MALONE: When we were over in Ireland, we found out that she is a really strong influence there. Supposedly, the best-selling record over there has been a collection called *A Woman's Heart.* Have you heard of that one?

TICHI: No.

MALONE: It includes Mary Black and her sister, and Maura O'Connell and some others. And you can hear the influence of Emmylou Harris all over it.

TICHI: That's very interesting. I know she performs over there with some regularity, and, of course, she and Nanci Griffith are both often there, lauding the pure Celtic tradition that they want to see as the fountainhead of country music.

MALONE: You know, if we do get around to doing that sequel, I'll keep that in mind, that you'll do Emmylou Harris.

TICHI: All right! But let me perhaps conclude with a question about what everyone's going to want to know about—the book you have in progress. Would you say something about that?

MALONE: Yeah, it's a book which explores more deeply, more comprehensively, the presumed Southernness of country music. That was one of the themes of *Country Music U.S.A.,* and it has been challenged by some people, but I still hold to it. I think that country music, as always, has a special relationship with the South. That's not to say that if the recording men like Ralph Peer had gone elsewhere, if they had spent most of their time in the Midwest, or the old North-west, maybe they would have found just as many musicians, and the music might have taken on a different cast, but they didn't. I think for a variety of rea-sons, both real and imagined, they came south, just like the folklorists did, and found a thriving music culture. So, from the beginning, the music took on a Southern cast, and when people first heard it, they heard musicians with South-ern accents and dialects, so the association was made there which has endured.

Anyway, in the book, I take certain topics—"Home and Domesticity," "Reli-gion," "Work," "Politics," "Rambling," "Humor," "The Frolic Tradition"—and by that I mean the whole dance tradition—and I go back as far as I can in Southern and, in a few cases, in British history to take up a theme and then bring it forward to as close to the present as I can, by doing a comprehen-sive and chronological treatment of each topic. And it will be informed by two theses: first, that the music has had a Southern cast to it, and second, that until fairly recent times, it has been essentially a working person's music, working out the preoccupations, myths, fantasies, values of working people. Hence the preoccupation with cowboys and mountaineers, because I think that the musi-cians wanted to find something that was more appealing, more romantic than their real backgrounds, which were in most cases those of carpenters, railroad workers, coal miners, and the like. But there was nothing in their pasts that they thought was really commercial, nor were there any models of success within their own communities that they could emulate—that is, until Jimmie Rodgers came along. That's basically it; I take up some of the themes of *Singing Cowboys and Musical Mountaineers,* but I go on, trying to treat all those topics in a very comprehensive way. I guess it's taken me so long to do it because I've had so much to learn, and I'm still learning. I'll get into a subject, and then I'll get cold feet about it, and I'll think, "Oh, I don't know enough about this. I need to read more; I need to do more research"—I have just let it drag on for too many years.

TICHI: I don't know, it sounds like the feeling that's endemic to scholarship, the cycle of feeling inadequate to the subject, but then it strengthens one's resolve—you know, "If not me, who?" So I guess on that note, I'm going to thank you for all this, and I should let you get back to work—now you make me feel guilty!

MALONE: Back to the computer. Well, thanks very much—

TICHI: —Oh, our thanks to you.

NOTE

The interview was conducted by telephone on 25 August 1994. We are grateful to Carolyn Gerber for transcribing it with excellence and efficiency.

# Reading the Row

**Christine Kreyling**

All good country roads lead to Music Row in Nashville. The physical center of the country music industry is actually not a "row" at all but a neighborhood of intersecting streets where stars and agents, publishers and producers walk between the sets that make the music of the heartland. The Row sits on the southwestern edge of downtown, divided from the central city by a railroad gulch and Interstate 40, by the trains and cars that have ferried so many country singers away from Home. Music City's Music Row includes parts of 18th Avenue and various intersecting Music Circles, but the heart of the Row is 16th and 17th Avenues South. The northern ends of these avenues have been signed as Music Square East and Music Square West, in tribute to their culture and their commerce.

Music Row is the Vatican of country music. Like the home of the papacy, the Row is both a workplace and a holy of holies, a financial power center that is also a focal point of faith. But the classically inspired structures of Vatican City, even though they were assembled over centuries, convey a message that is all of a piece. They suggest stability and permanence, hierarchy and order. The navel of Roman Catholicism has had hundreds of years to figure out how to conduct business-as-usual amid a swarm of fans. In contrast, Music Row has been a mecca for only decades, and in that short time its architecture has been hybridized to the point of schizophrenia.

The best way to experience Music Row is from the seat of one of the trolleys that regularly departs from the Country Music Hall of Fame at the head of Music Square East. Guides point out the studios of the stars to groups of music fans, whose heads swivel back and forth like the grandstand crowd at a tennis

Music Row. Photo courtesy of the Country Music Foundation.

match, straining to see the sights. This was once a traditional neighborhood, the home of Vanderbilt and Peabody professors. Even now the area retains the small land parcels, alleys, and sidewalks that characterized residential living before the advent of the automobile.

It makes sense that the quiet, residential character of Music Row's streets gave birth to a cottage industry with a reputation for intimacy and informality. In the minds of the people who work on the Row, the casual hominess of the workplace has become a necessary component of creativity. In the Music City myth, millions can be made while sittin' and strummin' on the front porch swing.

The first music enterprise on what would become Music Row began in the recording studio that Owen Bradley created in 1956 by knocking out the second floor of an old house on 16th Avenue. Subsequent recordings were made in Bradley's famous Quonset hut and within the low-rise concrete block walls of Studio B. Music was written in and published from the neighborhood's spacious turn-of-the-century houses—the kind with beveled-glass front doors approached by narrow sidewalks, and broad front porches shaded by large trees.

The look of the place continues to send out a mixed message—of good country people come to town but still longing for home. The view from a seat on the Music Row trolley is an amalgam of suburban office park, early twentieth-

Tex Ritter, Frances Preston of Broadcast Music Incorporated, and Jo Walker (now Jo Walker-Meador), Country Music Association director. Photo courtesy of the Country Music Foundation.

century neighborhood, and country kitsch, the architectural expression of a big business uncomfortable with the idea of big business.

## A STABLE OF STARS

The Country Music Hall of Fame is the holy barn of country music. Housing the Hall of Fame itself, a museum of country music artifacts, and the offices and library of the Country Music Foundation (CMF), it has long been the major tourist attraction on the Row. Indeed, word of the Hall of Fame's imminent departure for downtown has virtually forced the Row to reassess its future.

The Music Row Visioning Committee—a group of industry volunteers that in 1998 included Ed Benson, executive director of the Country Music Association (CMA); public relations executive and deal-maker Bill Hudson; Nashville Gas president and Music Row property owner Bill Denny; CMF director Bill Ivey; and guitarist-producer Steve Gibson—has fine-tuned a list of goals and guidelines for new development on or near the Row. The committee has presented its "visioning" document, prepared with the assistance of developer Bobby Mathews, to the Metro Nashville Development and Housing Agency. The committee does not seem much concerned with increasing the tourist presence on Music Row. Neither are the members saying much about building tall towers. Instead, they are talking about the continuation of the Music Row legend. They are talking about big corporate business conducted on a field of down-home dreams.

That business and belief are codependents in the country music industry is clearly in evidence at the Country Music Hall of Fame. It's easy to imagine the congregation of a country church gathering in the building's central hall of a Sunday morning, the light of God streaming through the curtain of glass and bathing their bowed heads. At the Hall of Fame, however, the heads of the faithful are bowed to get a better view of the exhibit labels that describe Elvis's gold-and-white Cadillac and the relics of country's other canonized saints. This is the architecture of sacrament, not of a multibillion-dollar industry. Built in 1967 and expanded a decade later, the building, according to CMF director Ivey, was inspired by the Cowboy Hall of Fame in Oklahoma City. "It was an early major architectural statement for the Row," says Ivey, "and an obvious symbolic choice."

In its early years the country music business was scattered all over Nashville. "Many recordings were made downtown," Ivey says, "at the WSM studios in the National Life building, or at Castle Studios in the old Tulane Hotel. And Acuff-Rose was in the suburb of Melrose. The neighborhood near Vanderbilt was attractive because it offered, for modest prices, big, old houses that could be converted to other uses. What's more, the neighborhood was close to downtown without being part of it." During the 1960s and 1970s, Ivey explains, "The hallmark of the industry was the adaptive reuse of residences, and that's still a subtext. Garth Brooks has his offices in two of them." One of the Row's continuing attractions is that it allows "operations with shoestring budgets to be in proximity to the bigger businesses."

TOURISTS R NOT US

Every morning finds country music's pilgrims wandering Music Row in search of stars, queuing up at the Hall of Fame, and boarding the trolley for the short ride to Studio B—the home of a thousand hits. "The Row is where the music is made," says Ivey, "where the industry has its offices and studios." Asked if his definition of Music Row includes the tourist haunts of Demonbreun Street, a six-lane thoroughfare connecting the Row to downtown that is lined with such novelties as the Hat Closet and the Car Collectors Hall of Fame, he replies "I don't think so."

In the minds of industry leaders, the business of making music is carefully segregated from the souvenir stands clustering on the Row's flank. "The days of the T-shirt shops probably need to go away," says Bill Hudson. "It's got to do with the image of Music Row." The Row's preferred image, says CMA's Ed Benson, "is a community of creative excellence, not a storefront industry. We appreciate the fans, and it's natural that they want to see where the music is made. But we don't want tourists visiting the office buildings. We don't have the facilities to handle them." There may be other motivations for keeping the tourists at arm's length. "There is a real sense of ambiguity about the tourists," says Metro Councilman Leo Waters, who lives in the neighborhood and operates a tourist brochure distribution service on Demonbreun. "Some of the music people are embarrassed by the gift shops. And I'm not sure that some wouldn't like to see 16th and 17th Avenues closed off to traffic entirely." Ivey says this sense of ambiguity is nothing new. "The industry has always had an ambivalent relationship with visitors out here," he claims. "The industry wants to connect to its fans, but they also want stars and executives to feel comfortable going to and from their place of work. So there hasn't been an overt attempt to appeal to tourists." He recalls attending meetings at which there was talk of installing signs on the Row to lead tourists to the sites of historic events. "There's never a real negative reaction" to the idea, Ivey says, "but there's no great enthusiasm either."

The Hall of Fame's trolley tours do interpret Music Row as a historic site, while giving fans a hint of what goes on behind the scenes. Ivey tells of fans leaving the trolley and heading off down the Row, where they knock at a door and ask, "I understand this is Garth's office. Is he here?" Such incidents only enhance the reputation of Music Row tourists as intruders. "No one has ever asked us to stop pointing out where Garth Brooks' office is," Ivey says, "but if someone did it wouldn't shock me." The trolley tours will continue after the Hall of Fame's relocation, but businesses near the Row that cater to the tourist trade are fearful that the museum's departure will spell disaster for their incomes. Ivey says that there are ways to mitigate the negative impact of the move. He talks about creating "a new attraction related to the history of Music Row on the site of the current Hall of Fame," and he insists that "there will always be a fascination with where the stars make music." But even Ivey admits that "the question is how great a concentration of tourist-related businesses will remain. There's a lot of pressure right now for more office and studio space."

THAT CAMPUS FEELING

There's a strong sense of insider vs. outsider on Music Row. The neighborhood, like the nearby campuses of Belmont and Vanderbilt Universities, is frequently described as a small community within a larger one. "How to preserve the campus feel of Music Row is the primary issue addressed by the Visioning Committee," says CMA's Benson, who sees the physical proximity of the various studios and offices as an asset to the entire country music industry, not just to those who work on the Row. "There is no Tin Pan Alley anymore, and Los Angeles has always sprawled. The Nashville music business is unique," Benson says. "People come here from New York and L.A., and they love the fact that they can schedule meetings on the hour and walk from one to the next without allowing for a lot of drive time."

On the other hand, it is difficult to maintain a campus feeling amid commerce and cars. Just ask the planners at Nashville's Vanderbilt University, which lies to the west of Music Row. At one time, the Vanderbilt campus was crisscrossed by public streets and faced outward to the surrounding neighborhood. As the character of the neighborhood changed from residential to commercial, however—threatening the university's ambience of thoughtful tranquility— Vanderbilt's planning gradually changed direction. The primary façades of the buildings turned to face interior quadrangles rather than the street. Many public rights-of-way were closed. Through traffic was actively discouraged. Monumental masonry piers, iron fences, and hedges of magnolia now mark the border between Vanderbilt and everything else.

The Music Row Visioning Committee has faced similar issues. They want to preserve the Row's pedestrian ambience. They want more parking and less traffic. And they want to chart out the future growth of an area where there is a finite amount of land, much of which is already densely developed.

GROWING UP OR OUT?

Traditionally, the average American city has had the option of growing up or out, and the given urb has usually availed itself of both skyscrapers and sprawl. Neither option seems to appeal to the citizens of Music Row. To grow upward would be citified. It would run counter to the antiurban impulse of country music. "People in the country music business," explains Benson, "don't necessarily like a high-rise building as an image for the industry."

Music Row's first and only high-rise, the nine-story United Artists tower, was constructed in the mid-1970s, Ivey says, as "a speculative office tower without a primary tenant. And the building struggled for a long time." For the music industry, he explains, "The idea of riding in an elevator was not appealing. That told future developers that the industry liked low-rise." Now, with the influx of music executives from New York and Los Angeles, there may be a bigger market for high-rise buildings, Ed Benson suggests. Property on the north side of Demonbreun, the street that intersects with Music Row without being quite part of it, might be ripe for such development. High-rise towers there "could satisfy a certain amount of the demand for new offices brought by immigrants 'from

New York and Los Angeles]," Benson says. Already there are rumors that one group of "immigrants" is planning to build a high-rise. "It is my understanding," says one longtime Row resident, "that BMG [a music label based in Germany] is looking at several pieces of land across Demonbreun—one of them the old Gilley's tavern site—for a 20-to-30-story tower. That whole area is zoned commercial, it's underutilized, and it has a great view of downtown." Still, there is one drawback, the Row resident notes. "No one wants to build a nice modern building, and sit looking at a hot dog stand." The tourist traps of Demonbreun are blocking visions of a glorious future for the country music industry.

The Visioning Committee expects that mid-rise buildings will continue to cluster on Music Squares East and West, gradually replacing the old houses that remain there. Some companies are so desperate for land at the north end of the Row that they are willing to pay above-market prices for it. According to a real estate agent who specializes in Music Row property, Capitol Records paid more than $60 a square foot for the property where its new headquarters is under construction. "That's a lot more than what the area is worth," says the agent, "but they wanted to return from exile on West End Avenue. And paying too much for land is a Music Row tradition. I heard that Warner Brothers didn't even deal for their property; they paid list."

Meanwhile, if the industry were to attempt to grow outward, it might find itself moving into neighborhoods where the music business would not be particularly welcome. Beyond the Music Squares and Music Circles, there are limits to what can be demolished and what can be built. Beyond Horton Street on 16th and 17th Avenues, to the south of the area known as Music Row, the planning commission recently passed a conservation zoning overlay that—if subsequently passed by the metro council—will mandate the retention of the residential character and scale of structures, if not the residential land use and the actual structures themselves. Benson claims that this zoning overlay is consistent with his committee's vision of the future. "We don't want to lose the small entrepreneurs, the start-up businesses. They're part of our creativity. The [independent labels] may prefer an old house, and south of Horton is an area that can still lend itself to that cottage industry feel."

Meanwhile, Vanderbilt lies to the west of Music Row. And to the east lies an enclave of middle-class African Americans, living in homes wedged between the Row and Interstate 40. To tangle with any of these neighborhoods would be to stir up a hornet's nest of political problems. If the music industry is to spread out, it must make the jump north across Demonbreun Street. And now, more than ever, it must deal with cars.

BRILEY'S BOULEVARD

Every day during rush hour, commuters hurtle through Music Row along 16th and 17th Avenues, heading downtown from homes on the western side of Nashville and back again. "I think the only reason that pedestrians haven't been killed crossing the street," says Bill Ivey, "is because it is so obviously dangerous that people on foot are extraordinarily careful. It's safe for all the wrong reasons." At present, Magnolia Boulevard—a connector that diverts cars away from 21st Avenue and the neighborhood commercial center of Hillsboro Village—funnels traffic through the Row to Demonbreun Street on the way to downtown. Eventually, the Demonbreun traffic will arrive downtown via the proposed six-lane Franklin Street corridor. In the early planning stages of the corridor some consideration was given to a traffic pattern that connected Franklin Street with Magnolia Boulevard via 12th Avenue South rather than via Demonbreun Street. This now-discarded option still appeals to many denizens of Music Row because it would divert the commuters around them. But that solution to Music Row's traffic problems would be highly controversial, for it would channel primarily white commuter traffic through a primarily black neighborhood.

Ironically, the traffic problems on the Row are the result of efforts to encourage the music business. In the late 1960s, according to then chairman of the planning commission Farris Deep, representatives of the music business approached Nashville Mayor Beverly Briley with a futuristic vision of their own. Their goal was to stimulate the growth of the industry with a little help from friends in city government. Ultimately, Briley gave Nashville's metro council a proposal for a six-lane boulevard running all the way from 21st Avenue west of Hillsboro Village to Demonbreun Street. Illustrations in the country music journals of the day show a Music Boulevard lined with starkly modern high-rise towers elevated on piers. It was Le Corbusier's plan for Paris come to Nashville.

The primary purpose of the boulevard was not to make it easier for commuters to get from the west into downtown. It was an attempt to give the music business a prestigious address, the sort that any corporation would be proud to print on its stationery. The new boulevard would have required the demolition of a great deal of the residential fabric that the music business was beginning to infiltrate—everything east of the alley that runs between 16th and 17th Avenues. Briley's Boulevard was one part of a still-controversial urban renewal plan that ultimately devoured all the residential neighborhoods south of Vanderbilt University to Blakemore Avenue.

James Hamilton, who represented the Music Row area in the metro council

# Metro Mayor to Present Annual "Metronome" Award

### . . . for the most outstanding contribution to the development of Music City, U.S.A.

No award will be given the music industry with more appreciation than the golden "Mayor's Metronome". It is an annual award, presented each year to the individual adjudged to have contributed most to the development of the music business in Nashville. Metropolitan Mayor Beverly Briley presents the Metronome on behalf of the Music City citizens, appreciative of the tremendous importance to the city of the $65,000,000 music industry. And the mayor pledges that, to the pace of the Metronome, the city will continue to provide a healthy climate in which the music business can continue to grow.

METRO METRONOME
Presented to

for the outstanding contribution to the development of
MUSIC CITY, U.S.A.
19 65
Beverly Briley, Mayor

Mayor Beverly Briley, assisted by Tex Ritter and others, changes the name of 16th Avenue to Music City Boulevard (1965). Photo courtesy of the Country Music Foundation.

and who lived in an antebellum house that still stands at the head of Music Square West, strongly objected to the plan as an intrusion that would destroy the character of the area. An active neighborhood opposition formed to support his stance. "I had just moved back to Nashville," remembers neighborhood activist and Vanderbilt lobbyist Betty Nixon, "and I immediately became embroiled in the fighting because I lived nearby. It was the boulevard issue that involved me in politics, that ultimately got me into the metro council." According to Nixon's recollection, "The music industry supported the boulevard idea." But she adds this note of caution: "You have to remember that Nashville wasn't Music City USA at this point. Briley's vision was to give the industry a strong business presence."

Only part of Briley's Boulevard was ever completed, the curious six-lane hyphen between the four lanes of 21st Avenue and the three lanes of Music Squares East and West that is called Magnolia Boulevard. The blame for the defeat of the plan lies with greedy land speculators, although neighborhood activists are happy to take credit for short-circuiting Briley's master building. Once the plan for the boulevard was made public, says Farris Deep, "there was excessive land speculation that drove up the costs of acquisition for a public right-of-way." As a result, the Tennessee Department of Transportation came up with an alternate plan: 16th Avenue would be one-way heading downtown, and 17th Avenue would be one-way heading westward. The planning commission agreed with the TDOT's alternative, and not merely because it was cheaper. Deep says the commission "basically felt that it would be difficult for pedestrians, for tourists to cross six lanes." Property owners on the Row were disappointed. "They had invested in the land at a high price," Deep recalls. "At the same time they made the mistake of pushing for a massive rezoning at the northern end of Music Row that flooded the market with commercial property and further reduced its value. They just went too fast."

So do the commuters on Music Row. And for the people who do business there, parking is an increasing problem. Unlike the distant suburbs, Music Row does not have acres of farmland that can be developed for surface parking. And underground parking is hardly an affordable option. When you dig down eight feet on Music Row, like most everywhere else in Nashville, you hit bedrock. Meanwhile, Ed Benson argues that multilevel garages would mitigate "the campus feel" of the Row. Once again Music Row is trapped on the fence between practicality and ideology, refusing to jump.

LOBBYING FOR POWER

The buildings belonging to the American Society of Composers, Authors and Producers and to Broadcast Music Incorporated are home to the not-for-profit power brokers of the country music industry. These are the agencies that protect the rights of the songwriters. Ironically, the buildings of these two not-for-profits are the slickest on the Row, the buildings that speak the most unabashedly corporate language.

The ASCAP building is all precast concrete and reflective glass, with an interior in black and white, chrome and marble. Designed by Tom Bulla, Music Row's unofficial architect-in-residence, and with interiors by Keith Lightsey, it features an atrium and a red-and-white leather conference room that offers a splendid view of the old Hank Williams ranchburger and the endless stream of traffic fighting its way through the intersection-from-hell at the top of Demonbreun Street. "ASCAP is based in New York," explains Bulla, "and there was a real New York influence. It may be a branch, but it's still on a grand scale." A grand scale on a corner lot resulted in a building with three primary frontages—one for the parking lot to the side, a curving façade at the intersection, and another for the street. Sort of like the three faces of Eve.

BMI first established its presence on the Row with a low-slung, modernist brick building on a small lawn that borrowed much from the suburban ranch house. When a portico and a new wing were added, they spoke much the same language. Now the brutalist addition by Earl Swensson Associates quashes suburb-speak into numb silence. What the new BMI building tells us is how difficult it is to deal with multilevel parking aboveground while maintaining the scale of the Row. The new—with all flags flying—is devouring the old in a battle of styles that the ruthless concrete interloper cannot fail to win.

The ceremonial entrance to the BMI building is located on Music Circle North. It leads into a lobby that is a grand exercise in pretension. The oversize scale and roughly stuccoed piers and walls suggest the Baths of Caracalla, while the fieldstone floors go native. An inscribed quote from John Dryden dwarfs the workers at the reception desk:

> What passion cannot music raise and quell?
> The trumpet shall be heard on high,
> The dead shall live, the living die,
> And music shall untune the sky.

We've gone from Butcher Holler to the Second Coming.

ASCAP and BMI are about music as power. But it is Sony Music Publishing, on Music Square West right behind ASCAP, that most clearly reveals how a country music company displays and disguises its economic clout. The building's exterior has an undistinguished, office park look; it consists of warm brick and cool reflective glass—the standard building materials on much of the Row—jostling for supremacy. Near the sidewalk, four Sony bird feeders play host to doves and sparrows, whose coos and twitterings are lost in the sounds of traffic rushing by. "The absolute premise" of the interior of Sony Music Publishing, according to architect Tom Bulla, "was to make it homey." There are fireplaces in the lobby and in the conference room. There are wood floors, antiques—authentic and pseudo—area rugs and tapestries in rich colors. The office of CEO Donna Hilley has the look of a traditional living/dining combo, and there are no fluorescent lights anywhere. This is corporate office space making like a sorority house.

Other recent additions to the Row have a similar effect—so unsettling to outsiders—of the casual making of millions. "Brick says tradition," Bulla explains. "With the Opryland Music Group, there was no consideration of anything else. The new Capitol Records building will also be brick, he promises, and it will have "windows that open, even if they have to be motorized." On the Row, Bulla says, "everyone wants the warm feel of a home. I ask a client on the Row about studio space needs, and we end up talking about French doors. Music Row is very peculiar, because it's all about being part of the old Music Row—and that was houses."

When Warner/Reprise built its new home on Music Row, the self-conscious demand was for a "studied casual" work style. "We had lived in a building on Division Street that was once Dr. Barr's Infirmary and was later a home for unwed mothers," explains Eddie Reeves, Warner/Reprise VP and general manager. "It was like an old fraternity or sorority house, where people could put their feet up on the tables. We wanted to keep that residential feel in the new place—but of course we didn't, and probably couldn't, totally accomplish it." What architect Seab Tuck did accomplish for Warner Brothers is a building finely detailed in materials of gray brick, dry stack limestone, wood—in both natural and black stains—steel, and glass. Just inside the door, the sense of entrance is marred by a blank wood panel. It was supposed to display the logos of the various labels housed in the building, a welcome by the members of the Warner corporate family. But there have been so many buyouts and takeovers that the plaques have never been hung. The great hall on the building's second level features exposed wooden rafters and black leather furniture, and the hall opens into a conference room and terrace high in the treetops. "I was told that [Warner/Reprise] needed almost 40,000 square feet for close to 100 em-

Reba McEntire's Starstruck
Entertainment building.
Photo courtesy of the
Country Music Foundation.

ployees," says Tuck, "but that they wanted it to feel like a house." What Tuck's client got was the effect of an upscale resort hotel, which is probably as close to home as an architect can get when he's making this much space for this many people. Wide rather than high, the Warner/Reprise headquarters has a mass that is not exactly neighborly.

If you want to create a sense of family in 40,000 square feet of Class-A office space, it doesn't take a house; it takes a village. Otherwise you get a building with a split personality. Nowhere is that schizophrenia more in evidence than in "Reba's building." Reba McEntire's Starstruck Entertainment is housed in a brand-new monument that is the architectural equivalent of big hair. The structure is a decidedly odd combination of expensive and cheap, down-home and city slicker. The conspicuous consumption of the granite surrounding the major openings in the façade is undercut by walls of spray-on concrete. The gabled profile has a long history on houses, but at this scale it suggests the latest Kroger's supermarket makeovers. The green reflective glass windows and vaguely Wrightian postmodern light standards say this is the 1990s, or maybe the 1980s. The dry-stack fieldstone walls, alongside which graze a bronze mare and foal, transcend time—and architectural sense—entirely.

The Row does make sense, however, in its own way. Take the landscaping. Country music may be an industry, but it is not an industry that works amid bland corporate vegetation. In the summer there are real flowers blooming

Detail of Reba McEntire's building. Photo courtesy of the Country Music Foundation.

here, annuals and perennials. Beside Reba's building grows an old-time favorite—portulaca—the flower many remember from their grandmother's garden, the flower that grows in tin pie pans beside trailers on the back roads of the Deep South.

That small memory of gardens past is exactly the point. "Country music is about family values and everyday life," says Eddie Reeves of Warner/Reprise. "Its stars pride themselves on being regular people who speak plainly." Music Row's architecture, however, is hardly plainspoken. It is a confusing expression of the tension between modern commerce and country culture.

### SING ME BACK HOME

Bill Ivey is right when he says that country music found a home where it did because the area that is now Music Row offered relatively inexpensive land and buildings that were close to downtown. But there is more to it than that. A fledgling cottage industry gravitated to a residential neighborhood because it felt at home there. "Country music puts home's enveloping love and kindness against materialism, social status, hurdles of hierarchy, and all sorts of false value systems," writes Vanderbilt professor Cecelia Tichi in *High Lonesome*. "Repeatedly, country music positions the home directly against the opposing values represented by urbanism."

In many ways, country music continues to defy the realities of social change.

The Nashville music industry, however, must plan for its physical growth, taking into account the urban fact that it will inevitably have to deal with more workers, less space, and more cars. The goals developed by the visioning committee offer a compromise between the belief system of country music and the industry of country music.

# The Metric Makings

# of a Country Hit

Jocelyn Neal

Mention country music in most any audience and jokes will abound about everything from the lyrics to the instrumentation to the cowboy hat and boots required to appreciate such music. Undeniably, country music is an established part of American popular musical culture. It is a native art form that has evolved in conjunction with sociological changes, linked throughout its development to partner dancing and American folk dance. Country music carries many unchanging associations: beer, women, lost love, and especially dance halls. Musically, there is a pervading misconception that the genre relies on three-chord harmonic progressions and repetitive structural regularity. Investigation into the actual structures of the music reveals instead some unusual patterns.

The body of literature on country music includes scholarship on the history, cultural influences and interactions, and social and literary value of the music. There is a conspicuous absence of concrete musical analysis, however. The problems facing such an approach are significant. First, country music's terminology and methods of communicating musical ideas differ from those of classical music, where most musical analytical efforts are focused. Furthermore, the oral and improvisatory traditions in both country music and dance result in few artists with sufficient analytical vocabulary to communicate what they intuitively create. But country music is after all music, and scholarship in the field would be remiss not to address the musical aspects of the genre in a thorough and formal analytical manner.

Within the symbiosis of country music and dance, the structural prototype of the country song is revealed as just that—merely a prototype from which most music and dance departs. The harmonic structures involve occasional complex harmonic sequences and unconventional chord progressions. The default pattern of rigorous four-bar phrases and hypermeasures is not pervasive in the majority of the music and dance. This discussion addresses the musical structures found in popular country music, the fundamental patterns of country dancing, and the evolution of a country dance. Finally, the mutual influences of country dance and music on one another define the metric parameters of hit country songs.

## METRIC, HYPERMETRIC, AND PHRASE STRUCTURE ANALYSIS

Research in the field of music theory in recent years includes interest in the metric structure of music, in particular the interaction of phrases and metric structures.[1] Beginning with a prototype structure of four-bar phrases, pieces are built on basic four-bar metric units. Multiple layers of metric structures emerge as the piece is built up from short motives, longer phrases, periods, and sections. Hypermeter is created by regular metric pulses at the level of the measure, and four-bar hypermeasures are commonly generated by a strong sense of downbeats every fourth bar. In the most straightforward structure, four-bar melodic phrases occupy four-bar hypermeasures. Composers can alter these structures, resulting in artistically interesting expansions and overlaps of phrases that alter the hypermetric structure. The same techniques present in Bach's and Brahms's music appear in country music. Analysis of these structures provides insight into a country song's formal features and opens the song to additional levels of musical understanding.

One might question whether an underlying pattern of four-bar phrases and regular hypermeter is a valid prototype for country music. The very notation system used to chart songs in Nashville, however, confirms such an assumption. In his book *The Nashville Number System,* Chas Williams points out that the four-bar hypermeasure is the prototypical structure when he states, "There are usually four measures per line. . . ."[2] The notation system itself is laid out around that structure, with methods to allow flexibility when the song demands. So at some level, the stereotyped song structure is very much alive in country music.

## INFLUENCES OF COUNTRY MUSIC'S HISTORY

Country and western music finds its musical and structural roots in a hodge-podge of folk styles from all over the world, melded in a primarily oral tradition. Celtic fiddle tunes, western swing, and big band sounds are all part of the genre. As the recording studios discovered the commercial potential of country music, additional crossover instrumentation and styles were joined

```
4+4    4+4+4+4    4+4+4+4    4    4+4+4+4    4+4+4+4    4
[intro]  [verse]    [chorus]   intld  [verse]    [chorus]   tag
```

Figure 1. Hypermetric structure of Patsy Cline's "Faded Love" (John Wills and Bob Wills). The top line counts the number of measures, while the bottom line shows the structural sections.

to produce the sound. Influences of rock & roll, jazz, mariachi music, blues, western swing, and just about every other type of American music appear in the current brand of country music.

The relevance of country music's history to this topic is that much of it developed from musical traditions designed as dance music which relied on regular, predictable musical metric structures. This music was built on four-bar phrases, 16-bar choruses, 32-bar sections, etc., which matched the needs of the square dance callers, folk dance traditions, and oral heritage of the music. The music as art was of almost secondary importance to the music as dance accompaniment, whose patterns relied on these hypermetrically regular structures.

CURRENT COUNTRY MUSIC

Today, country music serves two diverse markets: the dance hall and the radio format. The radio market seeks songs for their artistic quality, while the dance hall looks for "danceable songs," a term to be discussed shortly. The audience for the two markets overlaps, but the needs of each differ. Nonetheless, almost all of the songs that are successful in one venue are at least moderately successful in the other, so most hit country songs must find a way to combine artistic excellence with the demands and specific requirements of a hit dance tune.

As mentioned, the prototype country song is built on 16-bar verses and choruses, with interludes, introductions, and tag endings also relying on four-bar hypermeasures and four-bar phrases. Phrases may occasionally extend beyond the end of the hypermeasure without disrupting the metric structure, such as when the vocalist ends a line on the beginning of the instrumental phrase. An anacrusis, or "pick-up" note(s), does not alter the basic structure of the phrase and hypermeasure. This prototype structure can support a song that feels basically balanced and complete. Figure 1 shows the metric structure of Patsy Cline's version of "Faded Love" (John Wills and Bob Wills), which falls into this category of complete structural regularity. The chart shows the number of measures in each section of the piece, grouping them into hypermeasures.

Bracketed sections show higher levels of duple regularity (four hypermeasures forming a section). Note the complete regularity at all metric levels up to the four-bar hypermeasure. The tag ending involves a ritardando and fermata, which slow the hypermeter but do not disturb its pattern.

Duple metric structures pervade this song at several different levels: the duple meter (time signature), quadruple hypermeasures, two- and four-hyper-measure groups for introduction, verses, and choruses. Songs which follow this steady pattern of uninterrupted four-bar hypermeasures will be referred to as "square." Square structures are not uncommon, but approximately two-thirds of all hit country tunes today deviate from this pattern. There is no uncontroversial way of measuring the success of a tune, but for purposes of this discussion, *Billboard*'s Hot Country Singles chart serves as a reference.

Common in today's hit songs are three different degrees of hypermetric structural anomaly. Many songs include composed-out fermatas, which effec-tively add a half-bar to the length of the group. Lee Greenwood's "God Bless the USA" (Lee Greenwood) is a prime example of this technique's application. In the final chorus he adds a cymbal crash that inserts an extra half-bar into the middle of what would have been a four-bar phrase. This phrase expansion high-lights the emotional and patriotic climax of the song. Note that this composed-out fermata does not alter the underlying metric pulse of the tune because it maintains the integrity of the half-bar unit, which defines the metric pulse. In both live and recorded performances, country musicians perform the length of fermatas as some multiple of the basic pulse unit to preserve this integrity.

An even more common technique employed by some country musicians is phrase overlap or extension that evokes hypermetric reinterpretation. Fre-quently the vocalist will finish a phrase (the fourth bar of a four-bar hyper-measure) at the same time that the instrumentalist will begin an interlude (the first bar of a four-bar hypermeasure). The overlapping phrases cause the same bar to act as both conclusion and downbeat, a dual interpretation or "reinter-pretation" of its identity in the hypermetric structure. Equally common is the insertion of extra time between the end of the vocalist's phrase and the begin-ning of the next section. These phrase expansions let the music breathe and allow the musicians to completely wrap up one musical idea before jump-ing into the next. Expansions also allow the vocalist time between completing a verse and beginning the following chorus, an essential structural feature if there are pickup notes to the following section that could not be sung or played while finishing the previous section. Many such overlaps involve two-measure units. Others involve one measure, resulting in three- or five-bar met-ric groups, sometimes even with extra half-bars as extensions or expansions.

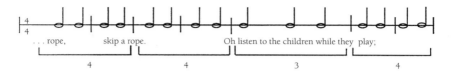

Figure 2. Hypermetric structure in Henson Cargill's "Skip a Rope" (Moran, Tubb).

Mindy McCready's "Guys Do It All the Time" (B. Whiteside, K. Tribble) uses five-bar units (phrase expansions). One such expansion occurs in the third phrase of the chorus. These types of irregularities are not a new addition to country music. The 1951 hit by Lefty Frizzell, "Always Late with Your Kisses" (L. Frizzell, B. Crawford), has an extra half-bar in certain phrases, again allowing breathing room in the music.

Sometimes these metric irregularities are an integral part of the tune's construction. One example is the major 1967 hit by Henson Cargill, "Skip a Rope" (Moran, Tubb). The chorus begins with a pattern of 4+4+3+4 half-bar units, sketched in figure 2.[3]

These expansions and overlaps allow freer expression and artistic creation in the music. Cargill's "Skip a Rope" links metric structure to expression of the text, skipping rope across the metric patterns. Seldom is the connection this explicit. Overlaps tend to provide momentum, propelling the music forward or building excitement. Expansions unlock the predictable and constant metric structure, highlighting sections of a song or merely allowing the music space for expression.

A survey of eight different three-hour blocks of radio airplay provides a sample of what the radio audience is currently listening to. Over an average three-hour period, only 31 percent of the songs played are square. The other 69 percent involve at least one of the irregular metric structures just described. These patterns are a feature of nationally marketed commercial country music. For comparison, among regional country bands that are yet undiscovered by the national market, the percentage of irregular tunes is less than half.

The percentage of tunes with irregular metric structures is even higher among the tunes that register on Billboard's Hit Country Singles chart. Table 1 shows a sample week's top 15 singles, listed by type of metric structure. This collection is for the week ending 7 September 1996. Almost three-fourths of these tunes exhibit some type of nonduple metric hierarchy. These numbers are representative of the whole spectrum of top country hits over the last few years.

Of course, to some extent different metric structures are characteristic of dif-

Table 1. Metric structures of the top 15 hit singles from *Billboard*'s Hit Country Singles chart.

|  | Artist | Song (Songwriters) |
|---|---|---|
| *Square* | | |
| 6 | Brooks and Dunn | I Am That Man (T. McBride, M. Powell) |
| 10 | Lone Star | Running Away with my Heart (M. Brit, S. Hogin, M. D. Sanders) |
| 13 | Faith Hill | You Can't Lose Me (T. Bruce, T. McHugh) |
| 15 | Trisha Yearwood | Believe Me, Baby, I Lied (K. Richey, Angelo, L. Gottlieb) |
| *Phrase Overlaps and Extensions* | | |
| 1 | Tim McGraw | She Never Lets It Go to Her Heart (T. Shapiro, C. Waters) |
| 2 | James Bonamy | I Don't Think I Will (D. Johnson) |
| 4 | Rick Trevino | Learnin' As You Go (L. Boone, B. Lawson) |
| 8 | Bryan White | So Much for Pretending (B. White, D. George, J. Tirro) |
| 11 | Billy Dean | That Girl's Been Spying on Me (M. T. Barnes, T. Shapiro) |
| 12 | Mark Wills | Jacob's Ladder (T. Marin, C. Sweat, B. Sweat) |
| 14 | Pam Tillis | It's Lonely Out There (B. DiPiero, P. Tillis) |
| *Irregular Metric Groups: Five-bar units, half-bar units, etc.* | | |
| 3 | Mindy McCready | Guys Do It All the Time (B. Whiteside, K. Tribble) |
| 5 | Garth Brooks | It's Midnight Cinderella (K. Williams, K. Blazy, G. Brooks) |
| 7 | George Strait | Carried Away (S. Bogard, J. Stevens) |
| 9 | Ty Herndon | Living in a Moment (P. Bunch, D. Johnson) |

ferent styles of country music. Blues patterns have intrinsic phrase structures; bluegrass is much less structured. While further codification of these patterns is outside the scope of this analysis, the phrase overlaps and expansions, metric reinterpretations, and irregular structures show up across all styles of country music. The single most striking feature of all the country music surveyed is that none of the tunes involves the addition or omission of a single beat. This characteristic is a result of the dance requirements placed on the music.

If today's definition of "danceable" music still required square metric structures, two-thirds of today's country hits would not qualify. Yet the requirements of country dance still regulate the music at the level of the half-bar. The recent increased popularity and influence of country dance indicates the necessity of such an investigation. Sixty-nine million households currently receive The Nashville Network's two dance shows, filmed in Nashville and Knoxville. Dance instructors are not only teaching traditional country dances but also are

Table 2. Duple-meter partner dances and the metric lengths of their basic patterns.

| | |
|---|---|
| *Most Common* | |
| Two-Step (Texas Two-Step) | 6 beats |
| East Coast (Country) Swing | 6 beats |
| Polka | 4 beats |
| *Less Common* | |
| West Coast Swing | 6 beats |
| Country Cha-Cha | 8 beats |
| *Rare* | |
| Whip | 6 beats |
| Hustle | 3 beats |

continually choreographing new ones. Clubs, teams, and classes are appearing even in unlikely geographic areas. Somehow this evolving, prominent art form remains intimately linked to the music in rhythmic and metric ways.

CURRENT COUNTRY DANCE

Today, two different styles of dance grace the floor in country dance halls. The first is unchoreographed or freestyle partner dancing. The second is choreographed line dancing. The partner dances are the direct descendants of the popular dance patterns from the early part of the 1900s and today consist of four different dances: two-step, polka, swing, and waltz. Other dances appear occasionally including West Coast swing, whip, hustle, and cha-cha. Table 2 lists the common freestyle partner dances and the number of beats occupied by their basic patterns. These freestyle partner dances consist of a basic pattern of steps, on which the man leads the woman through variations.

There are very specific metric requirements for "danceable" music, defined and enforced by the human body. First of all, a person has two feet—enforcing a duple nature on dance music. Even waltz, danced to triple music, is not immune to these duple requirements. However, waltz patterns deal with meter in very different ways, and because of the confines of this discussion, waltz will not be addressed.

Just like music, each dance pattern has an intrinsic hierarchy of strong and weak beats that cannot be violated. Violation of the strong and weak beat patterns in dancing results in so-called out-of-time dancing. However, the hierarchy of strong and weak beat patterns does not necessarily correspond at every level to the strong and weak beat pulse of the music. Dance teach-

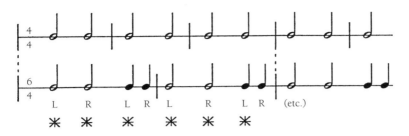

Figure 3. Metric comparison of basic two-step music and dance patterns.

ers frequently talk not about measures or meter, but rather just a strong-weak "Bum-Bip" pulsation in the music. This "Bum-Bip" pulsation is at the hierarchical level in the music that is a quick walking tempo—roughly 120 to 160 beats per minute. All dance patterns are then constructed around this strong-weak pulsation. Because the steps are taken in relation to this pulse, and the steps involve the left-versus-right nature of the human body, this two-beat unit can never be violated in danceable music. Basically, this unit is the amount of musical metric time required to get from the left foot to the right foot. For this discussion, the notational convention will be that a combined unit of strong-weak beats equals a half-bar in common time.

This half-bar unit of time is the only hierarchical level that must be the same between the dance patterns and the music. Above that level, the two art forms need not align, and, in fact, most of them do not. Let us start by examining the basic dance pattern for the common freestyle partner dances, which are two-step, swing, and polka. Figure 3 shows the metric placement of the man's feet in two-step.

The top line of figure 3 shows a basic metric structure of a two-step song, with barlines indicating measures. The bottom line shows the rhythmic pattern of the man's steps. Barlines mark off each completion of the basic pattern of the two-step. "L" and "R" indicate the man's left and right feet. The asterisks indicate the inherently strong beats in the dance pattern, which must fall on strong beats in the music (beats 1 or 3 in common time). The woman dances the same rhythm, but on opposite feet and usually going backward. Note that the basic pattern for a two-step requires six beats of music and involves four steps: two slow steps followed by two quick ones. The dashed lines in the example show places where the end of a dance pattern lines up with the end of a measure of music. These alignments occur every three musical bars—but keep in mind that three bars is not a usual metric unit of music! Because of these metric overlaps between the dance and musical patterns, a well-executed two-step

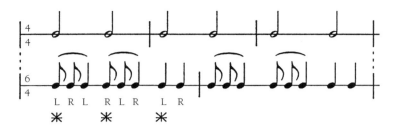

Figure 4. Metric comparison of basic music and dance patterns of East Coast swing.

Figure 5. Metric comparison of basic music and dance patterns of the polka.

seems to glide over the music above the framework of the meter. The dancers' physical acceleration at the end of each dance pattern falls in a different place on the music's metric landscape each time the pattern is repeated, interacting with the metric structure to add complexity to the combined patterns.

Of the other two most common partner dances (polka and East Coast swing), East Coast swing shares the same pattern of metric overlaps between the music and dance that occur in two-step. Figure 4 shows this pattern. In this style, eighth-notes are commonly swung. To maintain the intrinsic accents in the dance pattern, the half-bar unit must be preserved in this music. Note that the two patterns align every three musical bars.

Polka does not involve the metric overlaps and cross-phrasings. Figure 5 shows the basic metric pattern for the music and dance. Here the dance pattern is symmetrical and aligned with the musical meter.

These three dances make up almost all of the dance repertoire in the Southwest. Two of the three dances involve basic patterns that do not correspond to the duple hierarchy of the basic 4-bar hypermeasure, 16-bar phrase, or 32-bar chorus. Visualize a demonstration of East Coast swing, consisting of exactly four repetitions of the basic pattern. This will occupy twenty-four beats of music (six beats per pattern times four pattern repetitions), or six bars of common time music, and therefore the dance pattern will conclude in the middle of a standard-length phrase.

The physical phrasing of the dance patterns crosses over musical metric divisions such as the barline. As a result, the dance patterns have more rhythmic interest and complicate the interaction of dance and musical accents. If the dance is yet another instrument in the performance, the result is simultaneous different meters, or a kind of three-against-two hemiola.

The type of dancing found in dance halls varies by geography. In Texas, the Southwest, and much of the Northwest, one finds almost exclusively freestyle partner dancing. This is true in the big commercial dance halls and the local barn dances alike. Only a few old traditional line dances cross this boundary, specifically the Cotton Eyed Joe, Texas Schottische, and Four Corners. Otherwise, an evening out consists of all two-step, polka, waltz, and swing.

In Nashville and the Northeast, a different tradition prevails. Dancers use almost exclusively line dances and choreographed couples dances. In fact, many avid dancers in the Northeast can barely two-step at all. The line dances themselves vary from region to region, even dance hall to dance hall. The same line dance with the same name, danced to the same song might have some variation in footwork at the club across town.

Line dances are choreographed patterns, in lengths of usually 16 to 40 beats. The dancers dance the pattern over and over during the course of the song. No partner is required for many of them, so any number of men, women, or their combination form lines on the dance floor to execute the patterns. About a quarter of the line dances are choreographed for couples to dance together, commonly called couples dances.

The dance style discrepancy between the Southwest and the Northeast is readily explained by cultural differences. Country music, community dances, and cowboy traditions are still alive in the Southwest. In a community where dancing is learned while growing up, freestyle partner dancing traditions are easily assimilated. Children learn to two-step at the county fair. Country dancing has preserved much of the cross-generational dancing that died out in other musical styles. And a child who grows up two-stepping will continue to two-step, usually enjoying the creative freedom of a dance where the man can spin the woman whenever he wants. When an old man asks me to dance in a Texas dance hall, he usually has been dancing since he was old enough to wear boots.

In the Northeast, however, country music is less often part of a person's musical heritage. Most country dancers learned the art as adults or older teen-

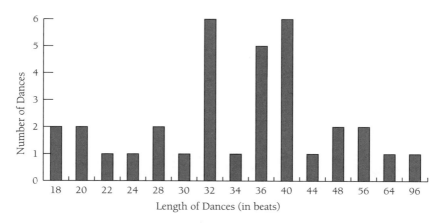

Figure 6. Length of dances found in Hilton Osborne's *Run to the Floor for Country Western Line Dancing* (Glendale, Calif.: Griffin Publishing, 1995).

agers. For this region, country dancing was imported as a packaged deal. The dances were specifically designed to be taught in class formats, participated in by any mix of men and women. Line dancing evolved into a marketing tool for the country music industry, to the point that now choreographed dances are released along with songs in a combined media blitz. This marketing technique has played a crucial role in the success of several well-known songs.

Line dances vary widely in length and complexity. A specific line dance is frequently danced to a specific song. Common features include a change of physical orientation somewhere in the pattern, either by 90° or 180°. Therefore, as the pattern is repeated during the course of the song, the dancer faces different directions in the room. It is the metric lengths of the dances, however, that is of the most interest in relation to the music. Figure 6 shows the lengths, in beats, of 34 dances described in Hilton Osborne's book on line dancing.

The first item of interest in figure 6 is that all of the dances are an even number of beats in length. It requires two beats, or a strong-weak combination, to take both a left and a right step. All the dances maintain body symmetry: if they start on a right foot, they end on a left foot so the pattern can then be repeated. This restriction mandates two-beat, or half-bar, metric continuity in the music in order for the strong-beat pulses to match in the music and dance. Of the thirty-four dances listed, only seven fit into the pattern of hierarchically duple lengths (16, 32, or 64 beats). In fact, Osborne's book does not include any 16-beat dances. For these seven dances, the dance pattern would repeat after a standard number of musical measures—4, 8, or 16—keeping the dance

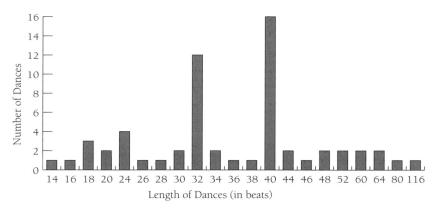

Figure 7. Length (beats) of sixty common line dances performed in local clubs.

pattern lined up with the prototype music. The nearly 80 percent of the dances remaining would not line up with standard 16- or 32-bar structures, that is, square verses in country music. These numbers match those found in other published sources of country line dances.

Line dancing is an art form primarily passed on person-to-person, and the dancers in the dance halls do not do a specific set of dances every evening. Instead, they have their favorites, which they might repeat, as well as many that are not recorded in published literature. Figure 7 records the pattern lengths for sixty line and choreographed couples dances used regularly in local clubs. Among these dances, 75 percent would not align with square country music.

When dancing any of these dances of irregular length, the dancer experiences the migration of the dance pattern across the metric grid of the music. Most of the dance patterns are punctuated with some sort of strong "cadence" in the form of clapped hands, stomped feet, kicks in the air, or some other identifiable gesture. If the dancer begins the line dance by clapping at the start of a verse of music, that clap will not return at the beginning of phrases, but rather it will shift hypermetric position throughout the song. This creates an audible situation of multiple meters, one in the music and one in the dance. Note that some of the dances involve pattern lengths far removed from the prototype 16- and 32-beat metric units. Forty-beat dances are common. These dance patterns, which are ten musical measures in length, preserve the two-bar hypermetric integrity of a tune. Other dances do not even preserve the metric integrity of the one-bar unit—note all those whose length is not divisible by four. These dances include the extremely common Electric Slide, Applejacks, and the couples dance, the Sweetheart Schottische. The Sweetheart Schottische is a 26-beat dance, which shifts its starting place by the half-bar as it moves across the hypermetric fabric of the music. The footwork consists of six 4-beat simple patterns plus a 2-beat pattern (total of 26 beats). In a demonstration of the Sweetheart Schottische, dancers could execute the pattern exactly once, requiring six and a half bars of music. If the dancers were to continue dancing, they would then immediately begin the pattern again. Picture this dance done to Garth Brook's "It's Midnight Cinderella" (K. Williams, K. Blazy, G. Brooks), a tune which itself contains several five-bar groups. So the dance pattern, requiring six and a half bars, is placed against a metric structure that varies in itself. No common alignment occurs during the course of the song except the first step taken, which can be placed at the beginning of a section. Also, note the nine-bar introduction to this tune, kicking it off with a phrase expansion.

THE RESULTANT INTERACTIVE PATTERNS

How do these dance patterns and today's music interact? In the world of partner dancing, there is a trend toward more square songs for polka and cha-cha, which are the regular duple-length dance patterns, and more irregular songs for two-step and swing, which are the irregular-length patterns. There is no strong correspondence between nonsquare tunes and irregular lengths of line dance patterns. In some cases, square tunes match up with square line dances. The Cotton-Eyed Joe is one such example. More commonly, however, the two are mix-matched. For example, the Kix Brooks and Ronnie Dunn tune "Boot Scoot Boogie" is a completely square tune, yet its line dance is 44 beats, or eleven bars long, and the dancers clearly punctuate the difference by clapping at the end of the dance pattern. Alan Jackson's "Chattahoochee" (A. Jackson, J. McBride) contains mostly four-bar groups, mixed with occasional metric groups of five and five and a half beats, while the line dance done to that tune is 28 beats, or seven regular bars long. The musical and dance meters never align during the course of the song. Figure 8 illustrates how the two structures interact in the chorus of the song. Note where the dance patterns end in relation to where the musical phrases end. The various units that function as hypermeasures, based on strong metric accents and structural patterns, are not all the same length.

RESPONSE FROM THE DANCE WORLD

I would prefer to say that the cross-phrasings and multiple meters that are created by these line dances are the conscious artistic result of the choreographers' work, but such is not the case. Most of the dance teachers and choreographers

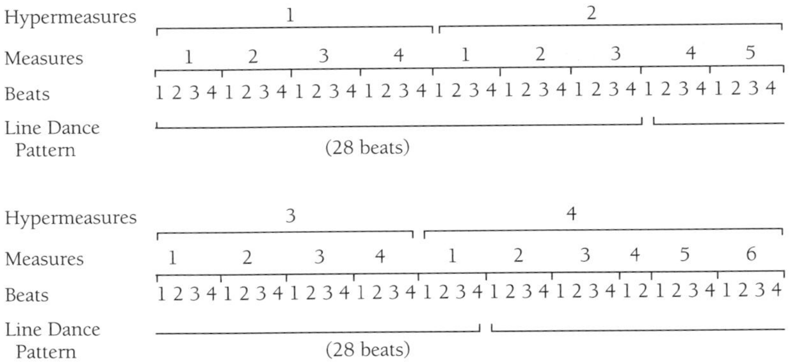

| Hypermeasures | 1 | | | | 2 | | | | |
|---|---|---|---|---|---|---|---|---|---|
| Measures | 1 | 2 | 3 | 4 | 1 | 2 | 3 | 4 | 5 |
| Beats | 1 2 3 4 | 1 2 3 4 | 1 2 3 4 | 1 2 3 4 | 1 2 3 4 | 1 2 3 4 | 1 2 3 4 | 1 2 3 4 | |
| Line Dance Pattern | | | (28 beats) | | | | | | |

| Hypermeasures | 3 | | | | 4 | | | | | |
|---|---|---|---|---|---|---|---|---|---|---|
| Measures | 1 | 2 | 3 | 4 | 1 | 2 | 3 | 4 | 5 | 6 |
| Beats | 1 2 3 4 | 1 2 3 4 | 1 2 3 4 | 1 2 3 4 | 1 2 3 4 | 1 2 3 4 | 1 2 3 4 | 1 2 | 1 2 3 4 | 1 2 3 4 |
| Line Dance Pattern | | | (28 beats) | | | | | | | |

Figure 8. Metric structure and line dance patterns in the chorus of "Chattahoochee."

I interviewed completely disregard any metric and hypermetric structures in music beyond the level of the basic pulse.[4] But even if the artistic creation of dances that are irregular in length is accidental, it is still a prominent and artistically valid feature of country and western dance. More important, without the constraint of worrying about metric groups and phrase lengths, good choreographers are free to design dances that move easily and stylishly. Scott Lanius, dance instructor at the Wild Horse Saloon in Nashville, reports that his most important consideration in choreographing a line dance is choosing steps that flow together well. These dances where style and flow are the primary considerations tend to end up as highly popular.

THE REQUIREMENTS FOR A COUNTRY HIT

For the musicians, the fact that country dance no longer requires square tunes opens up a wealth of compositional possibilities. The only unalterable requirement is a constant pulse at the level of the half-bar. Beyond that, the artists are free to shape the tunes as they choose. Nonduple metric structures certainly occurred in country music of the 1950s and before, particularly in the bluegrass tradition, but not in the same types of classifiable structures. Popular country music from the 1950s and 1960s occasionally makes use of these irregular structures. The more commercialized country music of today makes constant use of that freedom. Table 3 summarizes the metric patterns of today's music and dance.

Individual artists exhibit tendencies toward particular metric structures. Some artists, including Patsy Cline and Reba McEntire, seldom have indulged in such potential metric freedom. For others, including Alan Jackson, Garth

Table 3. Summary of metric patterns in current country music and dance.

| Dance and Music | Percentages with nonsquare or irregular metric patterns |
|---|---|
| Freestyle partner dances | |
| Common dances | 67 |
| All dances | 71 |
| Line dances | 75 |
| Survey or radio airplay | 69 |
| *Billboard* chart hits | 73 |

Brooks, and George Strait, most of their music takes advantage of the more irregular structures. There is a correlation between gender and structure in the artist's music. Preliminary findings indicate that female artists tend toward more conventional and traditional structures in their music. The most recent generation of female artists have started to break down these style differences. Further research is needed to define and explain these trends.

Perhaps the relationship between a song's success and its metric structure is a chicken-and-egg question. It may be that the more successful songwriters happen to use nonsquare patterns. Or songwriters who take advantage of hypermetric freedoms in their music end up with more commercially successful songs.

Of course, the role of the songwriter vs. artist in designing metric structure needs further investigation. Some songwriters consider the structure an integral part of their music, and the artists follow the songwriter's structure. In other situations the metric structure of the song is altered between the songwriter's version and the artist's released version. One such example is Barry and Holly Tashian's version of their own song "Two Ways to Fall" and the version that Ty England recorded, in which the metric and phrase structures of the song vary even in the introduction.

Wherever in the process of creating a song the metric structure is determined, the final situation is (1) many successful contemporary country tunes have nonsquare metric structures, (2) many common dances use patterns of irregular lengths, and (3) the irregular structures in both music and dance are possible because the two art forms evolved in tangent. As a result, the dance patterns do not restrict the music, and the music does not govern the dance patterns, leaving both music and dance free to stretch to new artistic heights. At the peak of the craft, country music and country dancing join to conquer the repetitive prototype of the four-bar phrase. And while hypermetric irregularity is no guarantee of success for a country song, it certainly places it in the company of today's hits.

NOTES

1   For an introduction to phrase and metric structural analysis, see William Rothstein's *Phrase Rhythm in Tonal Music* (New York: Schirmer Books, 1989).

2   Chas Williams, *The Nashville Number System* (Nashville: Williams, 1988), 22.

3   To simplify comparisons in this discussion, all music will be transcribed in common time where the quarter note is set at whatever value falls between approximately 120–170 beats per minute.

4   The exceptions to this trend appear in dances choreographed for stage or film performance by a trained team of dancers.

# "The Voice of Woe"

*Willie Nelson and Evangelical Spirituality*

 ——————————————————————— **T. Walter Herbert**

> I come to the garden alone,
> While the dew is still on the roses.
> And the voice I hear, falling on my ear
> The Son of God discloses.
> Refrain:
> And He walks with me, and He talks with me
> And He tells me I am His own
> And the joy we share as we tarry there
> None other has ever known
>
> He speaks, and the sound of his voice
> Is so sweet the birds hush their singing,
> And the melody that he gave to me
> Within my heart is ringing
> Refrain: And He walks. . . .
>
> I'd stay in the garden with Him
> Tho' the night around me is falling.
> But he bids me go, thro' the voice of woe
> His voice to me is calling.[1]

The distinguished gay critic Eve Kosofsky Sedgwick was charmed when she heard Willie Nelson sing "In the Garden" on her car radio, but she was also startled: "This blew me away. . . . Nothing had prepared me for a song in which the love and sensuality between two men could be expressed with such a pellucid candor, on AM shit-kicker radio or maybe anywhere."[2] This statement comes of lacking a down-home evangelical upbringing. If Sedgwick had grown up hearing male voices sing "Softly and Tenderly Jesus Is Calling," "Jesus, Lover of My Soul, Let Me to Thy Bosom Fly," or "Take My Hand, Precious Lord," she might well have been fascinated by Nelson's rendition of the hymn, but not particularly surprised.

For Nelson to convey male-male sexuality in "In the Garden"—or for listeners to find it there—is not a travesty of the religious tradition in which the song was produced. On the contrary, it is a gesture native to evangelical spirituality, where ambiguities and semantic doublings are routinely put in play. For example, the man in the garden clearly has two voices, the sweet voice that hushes the birds and the voice of woe bidding return to the world. Yet these two voices are intertwined with issues of sexual bliss and sexual sin. The garden in the song evokes the place of Jesus' tomb, where Mary Magdalene came with spices and ointments to care for his body; it also evokes the Garden of Eden where our naked first parents inaugurated all our woe, and it further evokes the Garden of Gesthemane where Jesus was betrayed by a kiss. Loving tenderness and the terrors of guilt are interdependent and interdefining within the evangelical consciousness at work in this text.

Still, discerning gay sentiments here may seem far-fetched, even satirical, since evangelical religion has been a formidable agent of homophobia in America and remains so today. When C. Austin Miles wrote "In the Garden" in 1912, the context of performance—in Nazarene, Baptist, and Methodist Sunday services—guaranteed that same-sex erotic sentiment remained unconscious, if it was provoked at all. It is also true that expressions of passionate intimacy between the believer and Christ stand in a long tradition, dating in America to John Winthrop's declaration in 1637 that Christ "would oft tell mee he loved mee. . . . I talked with him upon the way, hee lay down with mee and usually I did awake with him. . . . So sweet was his love to mee as I desired nothing but him in heaven or earth."[3] Such expressions of devotion are generally not considered to have erotic meanings, and when such meanings are felt to be present, they typically prompt sexual loathing. J. M. Cameron, a contemporary Christian scholar, responds to "In the Garden" as "a terrible degradation of religion not simply as a purveyor of the false and the unworthy but as a kind of nastily flavored religious Jello, a fouling of the sources of religious feeling."[4] Such pious disgust testifies to the sexual meanings of the song, but hardly to their sources in evangelical tradition.

Evangelical religion has been a powerful force in the cultural processes that have redefined gender and sexuality during the interval between Winthrop and ourselves. Winthrop lived in preheterosexual times, which prevailed before the polar conceptions of manhood and womanhood that typify the domestic ideal became a defining axis of social reality, with the attendant sharp opposition between same-sex and other-sex erotic susceptibilities. As an agent of homophobia, evangelical religion enforces compulsory heterosexuality, and it assumed these powers during the interval between Winthrop's seventeenth century and the early twentieth century, in the period before Willie Nelson was brought up Methodist.[5]

I want to propose that Nelson's version of "In the Garden" welcomes a gay reading because he creates for it a new context of performance that unearths a structure of emotional possibility that is native to the religious tradition that the song represents. Nelson generates this new context by achieving a distinctive appropriation of evangelical spirituality, not by repudiating it. He has produced a body of work and a public identity in which historic themes of evangelical religion come to life.

In reconstructing gender, evangelical religion reconstructed class, serving the interests of the middle-class elite that rose to dominance in the late eighteenth and early nineteenth centuries. At the core of this emergent ideology stands the mythic figure of the heterosexual self-reliant male. Successive waves of revivalism consolidated this manhood by enacting and reenacting its defining feature, that of individual moral agency: revivals portrayed the soul's essential act as that of making a decision for or against Christ.

For the elite, this ethos of ontological self-reliance generated a militant spirituality that expected triumph in the struggle against worldly evils, as in *Uncle Tom's Cabin* and "The Battle Hymn of the Republic." But Willie Nelson did not internalize a religion promising moral victory in this world; he grew up dirt-poor in Abbott, Texas. He is the product of a white rural Southern working class that is given the ideological role of endorsing their bourgois oppressors' creed. Alienated work, persistent hardship, and chronic financial vulnerability are interpreted in individualist terms; they are felt to be the consequence of personal failure, not of class exploitation. Nelson's music persistently sacralizes defeat; it centers moral consciousness on intractable moral dilemmas, such that the anguish of sin can only be solaced, never permanently removed. But Nelson's "voice of woe" is not—or not only—the voice of subservience to a reigning ideology; on the contrary, Nelson reshapes evangelical piety to articulate the integrity of the oppressed and to bid defiance to the oppressor.

◆⊰৯

Shotgun Willie sits around in his underwear
Bitin' on a bullet, pullin' out all of his hair
Shotgun Willie's got all of his family there.

Well, you can't make a record if you ain't got nothin' to say.
You can't make a record if you ain't got nothin' to say.
You can't play music if you don't know nothin' to play.[6]

THIS SONG WAS BORN in a seizure of anxiety, a crisis of the economic desperation that has haunted Nelson lifelong. Even in the midst of early success in Nashville, Nelson recalls, "I got so drunk and discouraged that I laid down in the street in the snow late at night in front of Tootsie's and waited for a car to come along and run over me. . . . I knew I could become broke and desperate again in the time it takes to snap your fingers. Anybody who went through the Great Depression—when broke and desperate described nearly the whole country and certainly the farm folks of Central Texas—grew up knowing financial security is an illusion."[7]

Evangelical religion teaches that broke and desperate drunks have only themselves to blame, but it also teaches that God will not despise the contrite heart. Spiritual empowerment is given to those who articulate their victimization as a confession of powerless need. The self-mockery of "Shotgun Willie" is just such a confession, and touches a bedrock inner reality for Nelson, from which creative energy springs. He wrote the song after walking out of an abortive recording session: "In my room I paced from corner to corner . . . the old sensation of need surging through me. Then I went into the bathroom and sat down. I saw a sanitary napkin envelope on the sink. I picked up the envelope and wrote out the lyrics." Returning to the studio with the envelope in his hand, Nelson recorded the song, which became the title song of a highly successful album that projected a new public identity for him, and a new voice. Nelson speaks of "Shotgun Willie" as "clearing my throat."[8]

At first glance, of course, there is nothing religious about "Shotgun Willie"; there's certainly nothing respectable about it. For a musician growing up in rural Texas the only places available to play were those notorious mortal enemies, the churches and the honky tonks. The split identity of country music reflects this situation: it originates in revivalist churches but finds its destiny in the precincts of sin. That Mickey Gilley, Jerry Lee Lewis, and Jimmy Swaggart are cousins dramatizes this polarity, as does the shape of Nelson's career before "Shotgun Willie" cleared his throat in 1973.

In the late 1950s Nelson was a successful Sunday school teacher in the Metropolitan Baptist Church in Fort Worth, when the preacher told him "either you
quit playing in beer joints or else you quit teaching Sunday school."[9] Willie responded with an analysis of the pertinent economic and class relations, noting
that the preacher was compelled to obey his wealthy parishioners in order to
make a living, while Nelson depended on the patrons of beer joints. Equivalent as means of survival, the work of the ministry and that of the guitar picker
were separated by an ideology of class dominance that was effectual even if—
as Willie noted—the parishioners and the beer joint patrons were often the
same people. So Nelson quit the church, since it meant "following the rules a
bunch of people had dreamed up to keep their subjects in line."[10] Yet as with
gender, so with class. Nelson's evangelical heritage afforded a basis on which
to unite these opposites, to become both a preacher and a beer-joint musician.

From the Reformation forward, evangelical religion has taught that ultimate
reality lies in the relation of the soul not to religious institutions, but to God. "I
had a powerful spiritual urge," Nelson says of the period following his departure from the church. "My inner voice told me the Methodists and the Baptists
didn't have a hammerlock on God . . . . I went to the Fort Worth Public Library
and began reading every book on religion I could find."[11] Nelson's rebellion is
premised on the conviction that his life is a personal pilgrimage toward spiritual integrity, and his inner voice is the voice of woe. It is a classic evangelical
paradox, exemplified as sharply by John Winthrop as by Willie Nelson, the man
of faith defiantly taking his stand on the spiritual authority of a sinful existence.
"The night life ain't no good life," Nelson soon declared, "but it's my life."[12] The
denizen of bars and honky tonks would become a witness to the power of God.

The album *Yesterday's Wine* (1971) announces the formation of this sacred
identity. "Perfect man has visited the earth already, and his voice was heard,"
Nelson declares at the outset of the album, "the voice of imperfect man must
now be made manifest."[13] The voice of imperfect man seeks a personal connection with the soul of every listener. "It's magic," says Poody Locke, Nelson's
stage manager. "If he's singing to one girl, or fifteen people in a hotel room,
or 200 people in a club or 50,000 people in a football stadium, these piercing
eyes will find the people and he sings straight to each one of them."[14]

It is the revivalist drama, the collective enactment of private experience
through the ministry of a public exemplar, a tradition running from Billy
Graham back through Charles Grandison Finney to Jonathan Edwards. The
paradox at work here is native to the culture of middle-class individualism,
which now features an "up close and personal" theater of intimate celebrity

in which all of our public figures must act. By the time of *Yesterday's Wine*, Nelson's multiple divorces and severe alcoholism were well-known in country music circles; within five years the "imperfect man" had become a superstar. He opened all his shows with "Whisky River," closed them with "Will the Circle Be Unbroken," and somewhere in the middle he always played "Amazing Grace."

❧

> After carefully considerin' the whole situation,
> And I stand with my back to the wall
> Walkin' is better than runnin' away
> And crawlin' ain't no good at all.
> And if guilt is the question and truth is the answer
> And I been lyin' to me all along'
> Then there ain't nothin worth savin' except one another,
> And before you wake up, I'll be gone.[15]

OBSERVE HERE the mental and emotional life of a sinful soul. The shock of the final line—"before you wake up I'll be gone—destroys the claim to moral credibility that is asserted by the preceding stanza. It turns out that "walkin'" is indistinguishable from "runnin' away," since she/he is going to slip out before her/his spouse awakes. As if that weren't sufficiently preposterous, the speaker solemnly declares that "runnin' away" will allow the couple to save one another. "After carefully considering the whole situation" thus becomes entirely ironic: the speaker is enmeshed in the situation and cannot size it up, or even see it from the outside. The realization that "I've been lying to me all along," does not mark a departure into truth-telling, but is said by a person who is manifestly self-deceived. This song, from *Phases and Stages* (1974), abundantly demonstrates Nelson's genius at voicing evangelical woe, the confusion and torment of a soul trapped by sin.

Failed love is a principal site of "woe" in Nelson's music, as in country music generally; it is also the principle place of solace, where angelic "little darlin's" and the "loose" women of the honky tonks play out their polar and complementary roles. Like their upscale urban sisters, these figures are twin victims of the feminization ordained by the gender system of the middle class, a figure of licit desire shoring up self-contained heterosexual male identity paired with a figure of its erotic dissolution. The honky-tonk angel, like other "fallen women," is the domestic angel in disguise, another supporting player in the melodramas of beset manhood. Nelson offers a subtle exploration of the resultant vexation, ecstasy, longing and murder in *Red Headed Stranger*. This "breakthrough" album carried him to superstardom, and it takes us back to Jesus as a male lover and the cruel logic of homophobia.

RED HEADED STRANGER is a drama of sin and salvation, which Nelson fashions by placing already existing country songs within an evangelical framework. When a man's redemptive "little darlin'" reveals that she has a mind of her own, and needs of her own, by leaving him for another man, a cycle of misogynist violence begins.[16]

> It was the time of the Preacher when the story began
> Of the choice of a lady and the love of a man
> How he loved her so dearly he went out of his mind
> When she left him for someone that she'd left behind
> And he cried like a baby and screamed like a panther
> In the middle of the night
> And he saddled his pony and he went for a ride
> It was a time of the Preacher in the year of '01
> Now the preachin' is over and the lesson's begun.[17]

The man is cast into an infantile desperation that his angel had assuaged, and he sets out on a murderous quest in which he kills his wife and her lover. Soon thereafter he is approached in a bar by a "yellow-haired lady"—another obverse of the submissive purity that his wife had violated—and he murders this woman when she dares to touch a horse that had belonged to the slain wife. The redemptive purity of the "little darlin'" is transferred, that is, to the horse, which the "yellow-haired lady" threatens to contaminate. The misogynist violence of the stranger enforces the moral structure of genders that is required by the self-reliant individual manhood that he embodies, and women pay its price in blood. Killing "bad" women and sex with "good" women become paired means of saving a man's soul, cognate forms of the solace that is necessary if a man is to bear his woe, and necessarily converging when the man comes into relationship with actual women. This composite image of man's sin and man's salvation recapitulates the feminization of Christ in evangelical religion, who is at once the source of tender mercy and marked for death. The sacrifice of women in *Red Headed Stranger* invokes this version of the sacrifice of Christ, the figure who saves the world by submitting to cruelty and forgives his tormenters as they crucify him.

The killing of fallen women and of gay men are gestures native to heterosexual male self-containment, and they evoke a likewise constitutional guilt.

This is true because the sexual loathing and homophobia that these gestures embody are cover emotions concealing and suppressing desire. The yearning of males for male-male intimacy is anathematized as homosexual perversion within the canons of masculinity that the "imperfect man" exemplifies by failing to fulfill them, yet it is also gratified by the Christ in the garden who "tells me I am his own."

Erotics and blood, the cleansing away of guilt, the confession of inescapable moral failure, and the vision of a feminized slain saviour all are at play in the old revival hymn that Nelson chooses to end his narrative of the redheaded stranger. Here the sinner experiences ecstasy in the confession of woe, confident that the Lamb of God will expiate the sin of the man who sheds her blood.

> Just as I am, without one plea
> But that thy blood was shed for me
> And that Thou bidd'st me come to Thee
> O Lamb of God, I come! I come!
>
> Just as I am, tho tossed about
> With many a conflict, many a doubt
> Fightings and fears within, without
> O Lamb of God, I come! I come! [18]

AFTER NELSON PROPOSED HIMSELF as "imperfect man" in 1971, one fan said "I'm worried about Willie. He thinks he's Jesus."[19] In the same year Nelson moved back to Texas, grew a beard and long hair, donned a headband and sandals, and joined the "outlaw" musicians in Austin at a new venue called the Armadillo World Headquarters. He swiftly assumed leadership in the creation of a new music that merged country with rock & roll, and brought together hitherto antagonistic audiences of "dopers and ropers," that is, the hippie drug culture and the rural working class. For this new constituency Nelson had a messianic charisma, in keeping with the radical spirit of the early seventies. In a nation whose conventional life and established institutions were tainted by racism, economic exploitation, and the war in Vietnam, there was a shared hunger for his "voice of woe"—the voice both harsh and caressing—with its shrewd analysis of guilt and gentle offer of solace.[20]

When this unchurchly evangelical identity culminated in 1975 with *Red Headed Stranger,* Nelson recalls, "there were people showing up at the ranch who thought I could lay hands on them and heal their crippled limbs."[21] The album was reviewed in the hip and sophisticated *Texas Monthly* under the title "Matthew, Mark, Luke and Willie."[22] Nelson had become a national superstar,

Willie Nelson. Photo courtesy of BMI Archives.

but he did not follow with material calculated to enlarge his mass audience. Returning to the religious sources of his newfound power, he recorded "In the Garden" along with fifteen other traditional gospel hymns in an album entitled *The Troublemaker,* whose title song is a further articulation of Nelson's identity as troubadour-preacher. The "troublemaker" is a no-account rambler, in long hair and sandals, who goes from town to town with a motley band of disciples stirring up the young folks to reject the establishment. The obvious reference to Nelson and Nelson's audience—composed of the jobless dropouts, Vietnam resisters and Vietnam returnees, hippies, and blue-collar workers, together with the larger population of college students who shared in their alienation—

becomes an allusion to Jesus and his followers in the closing lines as the troublemaker is led out to be crucified. Now virtually forgotten, Nelson's *The Troublemaker* sold 500,000 copies in the year after its release in 1976.

The performance context for "In the Garden" is a version of the Christian radicalism of the 1960s and 1970s that Nelson developed from the materials of his native religious heritage, and it challenges the gender structures that are intrinsic to conventional boundaries of class.[23] Nelson's long hair under the Indian headband projects an identification with the stigmatized and outcast, invoking the alternative sexualities not only of the dopers and ropers that he coalesced in his 1970s' audience, but also of Southwest Indians. Yet Willie with his flowing hair also invokes a ubiquitous icon of the Methodist piety that nurtured him, that of Salmon's head of Christ, a figure of male tenderness and intimacy.

Gay sentiments are not the only erotic sentiments activated by Nelson's version of "In the Garden," since women listeners are invited—here as everywhere—to make his voice their own. The prime biblical reference of the song is to the garden encounter between Jesus and the most sexually charged of New Testament figures, Mary Magdalene. Nelson's performance context reaches beyond the middle-class recasting of evangelical religion and removes the embarrassment provoked by the union of sexual desire with religious rapture, an embarrassment that has chronically afflicted Christian history from the time of Augustine forward. John Wesley was uneasy when his brother Charles wrote "Jesus, Lover of My Soul, Let Me to Thy Bosom Fly," because it smacked of sexual sentiments, and as this squeamishness became established as a defining feature of middle-class religion, it eclipsed the rich contrasting tradition of Christian eroticism illustrated in Leo Sternberg's recent book on medieval representations of Christ,[24] in Elaine Pagels's study of pre-Augustinian belief and practice, and most famously embodied in the traditional acceptance of the Song of Songs as a canonical depiction of the relation of Christ and the church.

As Curtis Ellison has observed, changing a gospel song to a country song can often be achieved by replacing the words "my sweet Lord" with "my sweet baby," a translatability that signals the amorous charge already implicit in "my sweet Lord."[25] The figure of Christ as a tender and intimate redeemer was produced in the feminization of Christianity that reshaped evangelical religion in the nineteenth century—and it answers to a yearning for male tenderness, felt by both women and men, but forced underground in men by the psychic protocols of heterosexualization and homophobia. In the posthomophobic performance context that Nelson has generated these buried erotic potentials are brought to the surface. Nelson's Southern white rural counterculturalism makes its protest against gender and class victimization by drawing on a taproot in evangelical Christianity and subverts opposing evangelical themes by which those victimizations were reinforced.

NOTES

1   C. Austin Miles, "In the Garden," *The Cokesbury Hymnal* (Nashville: The Cokesbury Press, 1923), 164.

2   Eve Kosofsky Sedgwick, *Epistemology of the Closet* (Berkeley: University of California Press, 1990), 141.

3   John Winthrop, "John Winthrop's Christian Experience," *The Heath Anthology cf American Literature,* ed. Paul Lauter et al. (Lexington, Mass.: D. C. Heath, 1990), ?, 203.

4   Cited in Sedgwick, *Epistemology of the Closet,* 142.

5   General information about Nelson's life and career is drawn from Willie Nelson, *Willie: An Autobiography,* with Bud Shrake (New York: Pocket Books, 1988).

6   "Shotgun Willie," Willie Nelson, *Shotgun Willie,* 1973, Atlantic Recording Corporation, SD 7262.

7   Nelson, *Willie,* 162.

8   Ibid., 163.

9   Ibid., 131.

10   Ibid.

11   Ibid., 132.

12   From "Night Life," one of Nelson's early hits. See Nelson, *Willie,* 109.

13   Ibid., 198. Imperfect man speech from *Yesterday's Wine.*

14   Ibid., 359.

15   "Walkin'," Willie Nelson, *Phases and Stages,* 1974, Atlantic Recording Corporation, SD 7291.

16   For a fine discussion of misogynist violence in country music, especially bluegrass, see Teresa Goddu, "Bloody Daggers and Lonesome Graveyards: The Gothic and Country Music," in this volume. For a fuller discussion of these issues in *Red Headed Stranger,* see my "Willie Nelson and Herman Melville on Manhood: *Pierre* and 'The Red-Headed Stranger'" *Texas Studies in Literature and Language* 35 (1993): 421–39.

17   "Time of the Preacher," Nelson, *Red Headed Stranger,* 1975, Columbia Records, C 33482.

18   Charlotte Elliott, in *The Cokesbury Hymnal,* 13.

19   Nelson, *Willie,* 198.

20   For a discussion of this period in Austin, see Jan Reid, *The Improbable Rise of Redneck Rock* (1974; rpt. New York: Da Capo Press, 1977).

21   Nelson, *Willie,* 253.

22   See *Willie Nelson Family Album,* compiled by Lana Nelson Fowler (Amarillo, Tex.: H. M. Poirot, 1980).

23   For a good discussion of religious radicalism in Austin during this period, see Doug Rossinow. " 'The Breakthrough to New Life': Christianity and the Emergence of the New Left in Austin, Texas, 1956–1964," *American Quarterly* 46 (1994): 309–40.

24   Leo Sternberg, *The Sexuality of Christ in Renaissance Art and in Modern Oblivion* (New York: Pantheon, 1983). Elaine Pagels, *Adam, Eve, and the Serpent* (New York: Random House, 1988). See also Peter Brown, *The Body and Society: Men, Women, and Sexual Renunciation in Early Christianity* (New York: Columbia University Press, 1988), and Daniel Boyarin, *Carnal Israel: Reading Sex in Talmudic Culture* (Berkeley: University of California Press, 1993).

25   Curtis Ellison, "Evangelical Religion and Country Music Performance," American Studies Association Convention, October 1994.

# "I'll Reap My Harvest In Heaven"

*Fred Rose's Acquaintance with Country Music*

◆~⑤ ——————————————————————— **John W. Rumble**

On 28 May 1942, *Grand Ole Opry* star Roy Acuff stood confidently before a microphone in a Hollywood recording studio. National magazines were lavishing attention on the handsome young singer and the popular radio show he headlined, but Nashville hadn't yet entered the commercial recording business. Most recording then took place in New York, Hollywood, or Chicago, and Art Satherley, kingpin of Columbia Records' country music department, had brought Acuff to the West Coast to make another batch of discs. On cue, the band sailed into "I'll Reap My Harvest In Heaven," whose words describe a faithful pilgrim ready to leave for a heavenly home. Acuff sang the verses masterfully, and tenor Pete Kirby joined him on emotionally charged duet choruses filled with piercing open intervals, soul-stirring in their intensity. So gripping was the performance that a listener might have imagined himself at a church service, somewhere high in the southern Appalachians. Like other songs that Acuff recorded at this session, "I'll Reap My Harvest" struck a responsive chord with thousands of country music fans during World War II—not just in the South, but throughout the nation.[1]

"I'll Reap My Harvest In Heaven" sounds as if it might have come from a hundred-year-old Protestant hymnal, but it actually sprang from the fertile imagination of Fred Rose, who first made his name as a Chicago pop songwriter. At the time of Acuff's session, Rose had just spent four years in Hollywood, where he had authored a string of hits for cowboy movie star Gene Autry. Most of these songs, however, resembled Rose's pop material. Writing for a folk-based recording artist like Acuff was quite a challenge, though "I'll Reap My Harvest" certainly proved Rose's ability to match song and singer. For reasons that Rose was keeping to himself, he used the pseudonym Floyd Jenkins for this number; even Acuff was unaware of the ruse at first. But by January 1943, when Columbia released Acuff's recording, the *Opry* star had been introduced to "Floyd Jenkins," and Rose had committed himself to country music. By this time the two men had organized Acuff-Rose Publications, a music publishing company whose appearance signaled Nashville's rise as Music City.[2]

"I'll Reap My Harvest In Heaven" symbolizes talents that let Rose reach rural Southerners—bedrock of the country music audience in his time—and broader national audiences, rural and urban. The lyrics reflect his spiritual consciousness, which enhanced his writing skills and helped him understand country music as a tradition-rooted idiom. In short, the song embodies a genius, craftsmanship, and sensitivity that made him Nashville's first outstanding country songwriter. In fact, from the founding of Acuff-Rose Publications in 1942 until Rose's death in 1954, few songwriters anywhere matched his achievements in country music. In addition to Acuff and Autry, a roster of country stars who performed Rose's material during that period reads like a who's who of the genre: Hank Williams, Bob Wills, Pee Wee King, Red Foley, Eddy Arnold, Jimmie Davis—the list goes on and on. Further, Rose linked the country and pop fields by teaching Tin Pan Alley songwriting techniques to country writers and by persuading pop artists like Patti Page and Tony Bennett to record country tunes. Singers across the musical spectrum continue to record such Rose standards as "Blue Eyes Crying in the Rain," "Deep Water," and "Low and Lonely."

Rose was also an editor par excellence. His revising of Hank Williams's songs has been widely chronicled, and for this alone Rose merits recognition as a creative force in twentieth-century American music. Insiders affirm that Rose also touched up Pee Wee King and Redd Stewart's "Tennessee Waltz" and many more hits for which he received no credit. As talent scout, he sponsored hopeful young singers—Hank Williams chief among them—and steered them to recording contracts with national companies. As Nashville's first independent producer, he supervised these artists in the recording studio. As publisher, he advocated for songwriters nationwide, and as a leader in the drive to make Nashville a music center, he advanced the South's full participation in national and international music circles. Admittedly, strong national currents of social and institutional change helped make Rose's success possible, as did the assistance of many individuals who helped create Nashville's music industry. Yet none of his contemporaries added more than he did or filled as many roles with such lasting results.[3]

Rose's appreciation of country music as a folk-derived art form embodying

America's individualistic, democratic, and religiously grounded culture helped him become one of the genre's most ardent spokesmen during the decade following World War II. Likewise, religious dedication led him to help others through musical gifts he saw as God-given. In tribute to this aspect of his character, friends and relatives had the title of "I'll Reap My Harvest in Heaven" inscribed on his tombstone. As a Christian Scientist, Rose did not subscribe to traditional concepts of heaven and hell, and certainly he lived to taste the financial rewards of promoting his publishing house, its home city, and country music generally. What the song title does imply is his faith-filled approach to life, his way of laboring patiently with confidence in the future, and his belief that, in the best of worlds, material gain should be the by-product of professional endeavor guided by higher values. Thus, Rose's influence persists not only because of his innate talents and strategic position, but because of his personality and profound sense of mission. The one-time pop writer took several years to learn the country music idiom, but after joining forces with Roy Acuff in 1942, Rose immersed himself in it with the zeal of the convert.

IN THE WORLD OF POPULAR MUSIC

Fred Rose came to country music from outside a tradition rooted most deeply in the rural South and more closely identified with the region in his day than in ours. Unlike Roy Acuff, Hank Williams, and other country boys who grew up with the music, Rose was a cosmopolitan, city-bred Midwesterner by upbringing if not by ancestry. Born Knowles Rose on 24 August 1898 in Evansville, Indiana, he was the son of Andrew Rose, a Scotch-Irish Indiana native born in 1872. Rose's mother, Annie West, was a Texan by birth, twenty-three years old when he was born. Andy and Annie were then living with Andy's parents, George Washington Rose, born in Tennessee, and his wife, Sarah, originally a Georgian. Both sides of Rose's family had working-class roots: Andy was a lathe operator, while the Wests were teamsters (later truck drivers).[4]

By the time he was ten years old, Fred Rose was singing for tips in St. Louis saloons. He and his sister, Effie Mae, were then living with their mother's clan as a consequence of family troubles. Evidently, Andy and Annie Rose separated soon after Fred was born. Andy stayed in Evansville with his daughter and shared George Rose's home as before, while Annie seems to have taken Fred with her to St. Louis. Fred and Effie Mae were left virtual orphans when their mother died about 1904, and neither youngster had an easy time of it. (Andy Rose seems to have taken no further part in raising his children.) "They were shuffled around from one relative to another," Rose's niece Artye explained. Extra mouths to feed burdened the Wests, and as Rose's son Wesley later said,

Fred "had to bring money home or he didn't eat." So Fred Rose left grammar school after the third or fourth grade. School had been an ordeal anyway, for classmates had mocked his crossed eyes. From then on, the spindly lad earned his keep by running errands, shining shoes, and performing in working-class taverns. Here he mastered the piano, absorbed musical impressions from other barrelhouse musicians, and assembled material for his first vaudeville routine, a singing newsboy act.[5]

Sometime during his teens, Rose struck out for Chicago, then on its way to becoming the nation's jazz capital. "Fred would play anyplace there was a piano," one of his Chicago buddies reminisced with a wink, remembering the city's rowdy nightlife. Often teaming with future bandleader Ben Trace, Rose mingled with audiences and musicians in rough-and-tumble clubs where jazz rhythms pulsed and liquor flowed freely despite Prohibition. Ben's brother Al reported: "They would work all the black-and-tan [racially integrated] joints, as they called them at that time, on the South Side of Chicago. They would play the white clubs on the near North Side and work until five and six o'clock in the morning. They made friends and were popular in all areas, yet I recall them telling me of brawls they would get into with drunks. So Fred started the music business the hard way."[6]

During the 1920s, Rose moved up the ladder by working vaudeville and minstrel shows, promoting tunes for various publishers, making rolls for player pianos, recording for the Brunswick label, and performing over Chicago radio stations KYW and WBBM. But his lasting recognition and greatest earnings came from songwriting. "Fred had a remarkable and natural talent," said Al Trace, who briefly lived with Rose and his wife, Della Braico (whom he had married in 1917), while studying drums and preparing for a career as a bandleader. Trace pointed out that Rose taught himself the piano and had no formal training, though the songwriter did learn to put down lyrics and simple melody lines for copyright lead sheets. Soon after Rose registered his first copyright, in 1919, top-notch entertainers were using his songs onstage and in the recording studio. As the 1920s progressed, recording acts like the Original Dixieland Jazz Band, the Cotton Pickers, and bands led by Jimmy Joy, Ted Fiorito, and Joe "King" Oliver popularized jazz stylings of Rose's "Sweet Mama, Papa's Getting Mad," "Mishawaka Blues," "Jacksonville Gal," "Red Hot Henry Brown," and "Deep Henderson." Top-selling crooner Gene Austin recorded " 'Deed I Do," and vaudeville star Sophie Tucker made "Red Hot Mama" one of her signature numbers. Around 1925, Rose worked briefly with bandleader Paul Whiteman, whose appealing—though diluted—style of jazz was a commercial sensation of the decade. The two musicians shared writing credits on "Flamin' Mamie"

(1925) and "Charlestonette" (1925), recorded by Whiteman's orchestra or other groups. In addition, Rose may have toured with Whiteman's group as a pianist. These and other hits helped Rose win election, in 1928, to the elite corps of the American Society of Composers, Authors, and Publishers (ASCAP), then the nation's only organization that collected performance royalties on behalf of the writers and publishers that it represented.[7]

Although ASCAP focused almost exclusively on the pop field, Rose was also in touch with country music, albeit obliquely. Two Chicago artists who performed his songs were Ford Rush and Glenn Rowell, mainline vaudeville stars and featured singers on the *National Barn Dance*. A Saturday night broadcast founded in 1924, this granddaddy of the barn dance genre was then America's most famous country show, and Rose's relationship with Ford and Glenn may have been his first brush with performers experienced in country radio. He and the duo copyrighted half-a-dozen songs together from 1928 to 1931, including "Little Silver-Haired Sweetheart" and "Tender Memories," titles suggesting the sort of sentimental tunes then well-received by country fans despite the singers' formal style and proper diction.[8]

In addition, Rose was living the kind of life that many a country musician has since made formulaic. "Before he got his religious tendencies," said singer Betty Poulton, whom he met in Nashville early in the 1930s, "he liked to drink a lot, and he spent money very, very prolifically. He told us that when he made his first fortune on a song called 'Honest and Truly'—and he was married to his first wife at that time—they went to New York, and they spent [a] whole royalty check, which must have been *thousands* of dollars, and they spent that in a three-week period." Drinking and profligate spending eventually shattered his first marriage and thus separated Rose from his first two children, Wesley, born in 1918, and Lester, born in 1920. Rose's freewheeling habits eventually undermined his second marriage as well, and when he later discussed domestic troubles with his flock of tyro country singers, he knew whereof he spoke.[9]

In 1929, however, Rose appeared to be settling down. That year his divorce from Della became final, and he married Helen Holmes of Monticello, Illinois. The birth of a son, Gene, in 1931, and a daughter, Patricia, in 1932, gave Rose a new lease on family life; meanwhile, extended visits from Wesley and Lester partially reknit earlier kinship ties. Coauthors routinely stopped by to work in the comfort of Rose's living room, but now he took more time to pitch horseshoes or give Wesley piano lessons. Radio income of $150 a week—a considerable sum in those days—financed a comfortable lifestyle filled with nights on the town hearing blues singers and Broadway shows—that is, until Rose "got drunk and fell off the piano stool during the program" at WBBM, as Helen candidly put it. It was 1932, and Rose's timing stank, for the music industry was spiraling downward with the failing national economy. And it was a long fall from a top-notch radio station to a mediocre restaurant where he hacked away for just $25 a week, a sum that forced the Roses from their comfortable suburban home to a cramped hotel apartment.[10]

Early in 1933, after a brief, unfruitful crack at the New York songwriting market, Rose got wind of an opening at WSM in Nashville, where he and his one-time radio partner Elmo Tanner had earlier traveled to see Tanner's family. Late in the spring, Fred and Helen Rose piled into a car with Charles Haines and Ray Ferris, a Chicago country-pop radio duo, and started South. The Roses' children stayed behind with relatives. When the four arrived in Nashville, Rose looked up the Vagabonds, a vocal group he had met in Chicago; by this time they were a high-powered WSM act. The influential trio set up auditions with Harry Stone, who had recently become station manager. Stone was pleased to hire more Chicago pop talent and scheduled programs for Rose and the Chuck and Ray team. Rose's pay would hardly be grand—about $7.00 a spot—but at least he would be back in radio, and he could use his show to advertise sheet music. After returning to Chicago long enough to store furniture and pick up their son and daughter, the Roses rented a furnished house in Nashville. By 21 June, Rose was on the air again, and within a month WSM was featuring "Freddie Rose's Song Shop," a middle-of-the-road pop program, four times a week. In Tennessee he would soon gain a knowledge of country music that helped point him toward his Nashville publishing venture.[11]

SAFE HARBOR

If Fred Rose had a country music heritage, he doesn't seem to have brought it from Chicago to Nashville. True, his mother and paternal grandparents were Southern-born, and there may have been a fiddler somewhere in his family tree. He even may have seen Chicago's *National Barn Dance,* a foretelling of country's growing popularity. Rose liked the South well enough, and visiting Elmo Tanner's family in Nashville had whetted his appetite for Southern barbecue and greens. But he hadn't been around his family of origin very long, and what musical ideas his St. Louis relatives may have given him remain a mystery. Early in the 1930s, country music was decidedly rural, imbued with Protestant Christianity and the sounds of a British-American folk past. Rose, by contrast, looked, talked, and acted like the Midwestern big-city boy that he was. His musical meat and drink was mainstream popular song—the secular music of America's urban white middle class, however affected by black styles. Merely by coming South, he embraced neither country music nor the region that gave it birth, and he kept his identity as a pop songwriter throughout the 1930s. Yet during these same years, Rose worked closely with country singers who sang his tunes onstage, cut them on records, published them in songbooks, and broadcast them on radio. These musicians borrowed freely from genres that Rose already knew, and they developed country-pop styles that he easily grasped. Radio shows and cowboy movies were spreading country music more broadly than ever, even though the depression temporarily blighted record sales. And as the music's economic clout impressed the commercially minded songwriter, spiritual awakening altered his values and prepared him for future work with highly traditional country artists.[12]

Whatever Rose's knowledge of country music in 1933, WSM was a great place for a down-and-out musician to land. Backed by its parent firm, Nashville's National Life and Accident Insurance Company, the station was then gearing up a national campaign to advertise newly drafted life insurance policies, publicizing Nashville and WSM artists in the bargain. This drive molded a commercial setting favorable to the Acuff-Rose alliance, united Rose and country performers in the same professional environment, and set important precedents for the Acuff-Rose partners, who would eventually reshape the city's booster tradition during the 1940s and 1950s. By the time that Rose hit Nashville, WSM had gained a coveted clear-channel license—one of only forty nationwide; a low broadcasting frequency of 650 kilocycles, which also maximized signal range; a signal strength of 50,000 watts, the legal maximum; and an 878-foot tower, the tallest in the United States. These advantages virtually eliminated nighttime interference from other stations and gave the Nashville outlet a tremendous wallop. WSM was now a powerful magnet for artists and announcers, and Rose had probably heard WSM programs booming into his Chicago stomping grounds.[13]

Not surprisingly, WSM's *Grand Ole Opry* proved essential to Rose's country music education. Organized in 1925 by then station manager George D. Hay, the show was well under way when Rose arrived in town. By 1932 the business-minded Harry Stone, who had taken over as Hay's health failed, was resolved to put WSM on solid financial footing and insisted that the *Opry* pay its way. About 1934, Stone began to divide the show into fifteen-minute segments that were sold to sponsors. Additionally, he organized the WSM Artists Service, or booking department, which sent performers into schoolhouses and theaters throughout the mid-South; he assigned the operation to his brother David. Radio talent fees and Artists Service publicity gradually helped tilt the balance of the *Opry* cast from semiprofessionals to full-time entertainers, who, like Rose, used radio to plug songbooks and show dates. The *Opry*'s diversifying ranks also made the program more accessible to Rose. The WLS *National Barn Dance* and Des Moines's WHO *Iowa Barn Dance Frolic* were threatening to drain the *Opry*'s talent roster and erode WSM's audience, so the Stones were hiring slick, vocally polished country acts to supplement the old-fashioned string bands that Hay favored and thereby broaden the *Opry*'s appeal. Advertising accounts were at stake, and there were insurance prospects to reach in cities like Pittsburgh and Detroit, where National Life was expanding its operations.[14]

The *Opry* performers known best to Rose belonged to this rising group of singing stars who were more open to pop influences than were many string band pickers. Two young musicians who gravitated Rose's way were Alton and Rabon Delmore, a pair of Alabama country boys who were helping to make duet singing the Southeast's "new" country sound. Early on, the Delmores had won second place in a local talent contest with Rose's "That's Why I'm Jealous of You," a song they probably learned from sheet music, recordings, or radio shows. To the two young Southerners, the cross-eyed, nearsighted Rose didn't look the part, but they were nonetheless thrilled to know "the first big time song writer we had ever met in the pop field," as Alton later wrote. Alton, a gifted writer himself, looked to Rose for guidance: "If there was any way he could help a beginner, he would do his very best." The veteran tunesmith helped the brothers edit several compositions and tried to place one of Alton's tunes with a Chicago publisher, who dragged his feet and ultimately refused it. In response, Alton continued, Rose "never did send that publisher another song just because he had broken up the promise he had made to two green country boys." The episode revealed on Rose's part a deep-seated concern for songwriters, arising from his own struggles, that became a hallmark of his Nashville publishing years.[15]

Rose's best *Opry* buddies, however, were the Vagabonds, a Chicago pop trio of the late 1920s who had moved on to St. Louis and Nashville. At WSM, Herald Goodman, Dean Upson, and Curt Poulton added hymns, sentimental favorites, and folk songs to their repertoire and worked on pop shows as well as on the *Opry*, where their mellifluous harmonies dazzled listeners accustomed to whoop-and-holler hoedowns. What's more, the Vagabonds' skillful promotion reinforced ideas that Rose later used in publicizing Roy Acuff. The three singers didn't pretend to be hillbillies, but they used folk and Southern images just the same. In 1932 the trio published a songbook aimed at *Opry* listeners, *Old Cabin Songs of the Fiddle and the Bow,* whose title identified the group with an extremely popular instrumental tradition even though they used only Poulton's guitar. George Hay almost certainly wrote the book's foreword, which highlighted the performers' humble origins as preachers' kids and characterized their songs as folk tunes "originated by the Pioneer Settlers in the mountains of the Southland." The Vagabonds' publishing outfit, the Old Cabin Company, was evidently the first established by any WSM act. Although the venture lasted only about two years, it gave Rose something to think about. *Old Cabin Songs* went through twelve printings by 1934 and sold "by the thousands," in Judge Hay's estimation. Finally, the Vagabonds not only showed Fred Rose how pop vocal stylings and adroit marketing could sell country music, but they exposed him to country songs. The singers became some of his closest pals after he and Helen parted ways late in 1933, and Helen, children in tow, returned to her family in Illinois. Marking the end of his second marriage, the breakup left Rose with too much time on his hands, so he found an apartment near Goodman's house and spent many of his idle hours with the group. Watching the act rehearse filled Rose's ears with traditional folk songs ("Froggie Went A-Courtin'"), Tin Pan Alley tunes that had entered folk tradition ("The Fatal Wedding"), and numbers that the trio had patterned on folk models ("Little Mother of the Hills").[16]

Personal appearances acquainted Rose with other performers who were crossing tenuous boundaries between country and pop. Working through the WSM Artists Service, he played shows in Kentucky and Tennessee during the mid-1930s, usually sharing the road with *Opry* stars Edna Wilson and Margaret Waters, creators of the comic rural characters Sarie and Sally, and Jack Shook, Napoleon "Nap" Bastien, and Dee Simmons, a WSM pop combo known as Jack, Nap, and Dee. Trained musicians with their own weekday programs, this trio also played in an *Opry* western band known as Jack and His Missouri Mountaineers, so mixing pop and country tunes in the same show was no problem for them. "We sang a lot of the Sons of the Pioneers songs, plus Freddie's songs," Shook explained. "We did nearly all of Bob Nolan and Tim Spencer's songs, like 'Cool Water,' 'Tumbling Tumbleweeds' . . . and all those things." Rose was now working shoulder-to-shoulder with country entertainers, and some of their music was beginning to rub off.[17]

CRISIS AND CONVERSION

During the mid-1930s, Fred Rose put down roots in Tennessee. On 27 March 1934 he married Lorene Harmon Dean of Nashville, whom he had met through Elmo Tanner's family. A widow with two teenage daughters, Lorene had substantial investments and owned a comfortable home in Belmont-Hillsboro, one of the city's better residential sections. Rose now had a relatively secure base of operations, though financially he still needed to work. Still, Harry Stone let Rose come and go as he pleased, and the restless musician was always ready to pack a suitcase on short notice. Sometimes a guest spot on a station in Chicago or Atlanta, for instance, would lead to a run lasting a month or more. "In those days," said Lorene, "everywhere he went they offered him a job, it looked like, and he'd work awhile and just didn't like it, and we'd leave. [We'd] always come back to Nashville." Rose's longest out-of town foray lasted many months. By June 1935 he was off for another run at Tin Pan Alley, and during this and subsequent New York trips, he began to revive his pop songwriting career. Soon his credits would include such hits as "Moon Rose," recorded by pianist-songwriter-stylist Thomas "Fats" Waller, "I'm Nuts About Goofy Music," by Jimmie Lunceford's orchestra, and "I Take to You," by vocalist Lena Horne.[18]

In addition, Rose made important country music contacts in New York, including Ray Whitley, a Georgian then starring on New York's WHN *Barn Dance* and beginning to make records for Decca. On 22 August 1935, Whitley recorded two of Rose's tunes, "Will Rogers, Your Friend and My Friend," and "Last Flight of Wiley Post," for the recently established American Decca label. The celebrated humorist and the ace pilot had perished in an airplane crash a week earlier, a tragedy that made worldwide headlines. Decca president Jack Kapp, formerly Rose's producer at Brunswick, commissioned Rose to create these "event" songs for Whitley's session. In a sense, they continued a 400-year tradition of British-American broadside ballads, which often coupled moral homilies with stories of remarkable occurrences. Street vendors in eighteenth-century England had sold ballads on paper sheets, or broadsides, and American peddlers hawked them at courthouses and fairgrounds into modern times. Recordings of commercially written event ballads, such as Vernon Dalhart's rendition of "The Death of Floyd Collins," profited from newspaper and radio news reporting, and they sold well during the 1920s. Music executives of the 1930s kept using songs like Rose's, but with only middling results.[19]

It was also in New York that Rose committed himself to Christianity. Up to this point, he had generally avoided churches because an aunt's narrow religiosity had set his mind against them as a youth. Before he left Chicago, though, Rose had begun to investigate Christian Science, a belief system first summarized by Boston religious leader Mary Baker Eddy during the later nineteenth century. Many believers seek the aid of practitioners, or healers, certified by the Church of Christ Scientist for their skill in metaphysical concerns. By the end of 1932, Rose was consulting a Chicago practitioner, possibly hoping that faith might remedy eye problems that physicians hadn't been able to cure.[20]

By all accounts, however, Rose's lasting conversion happened about 1935, during his prolonged stay in New York. At the time, Rose's spirits had plummeted, probably for a combination of reasons. He was getting his songs recorded, but big hits were eluding him. The burdens of near-blindness—evidently caused by untreatable cataracts—and two failed marriages probably weighed heavily, too. Drinking spells only made matters worse, and what private demons tormented him are anyone's guess. It was pop songwriter Ed Nelson who happened upon Rose near the Brill Building early one morning as Rose, depressed and pondering suicide, was reportedly walking dejectedly toward the George Washington Bridge, a considerable distance uptown. Nelson, a Christian Scientist, confronted him, ushered him to a Christian Science Reading Room, and gave him some books to study. Rose perused them as Nelson had advised, and the effects were immediate and unmistakable. "I turned back," Rose recalled in 1954. "I turned away from worry, fear, atheism, and hard drink to the religion and way of life that sustains me today." His transformation struck many who witnessed it. "He was a completely different person," said Jack Shook, for one. "He was just quieter, easier to get along with." From then on, Rose would set aside devotional time each morning, and in Nashville he would study with a practitioner and attend Christian Science services. Moreover, a large, extended family further increased his sense of stability. By the late 1930s his household included his wife, Lorene; Lorene's daughter Mildred; Mildred's son, Bill Collins; and Lorene's parents.[21]

Reordered values breathed new life into Rose's musicianship. From 1935 until 1938 he divided his time mostly between New York, Nashville, and Chicago, living music almost every waking moment. When he wasn't broadcasting, making personal appearances, or shopping his songs to music publishers, he composed and edited new material; he especially enjoyed songwriting, whether with Ed Nelson, who often came through Nashville, or with WSM musicians.[22]

Just as Nelson was prodding Rose to crank out more pop tunes, Curt Poulton was encouraging him to write for country singers. By 1936 Poulton was performing on the *Grand Ole Opry* and making personal appearances in Kentucky and Tennessee. He needed new material to establish himself as a solo act, and he asked Rose to help him write it. "There's an Old Easy Chair By the Fireplace," a nostalgic song reminiscent of Billy Hill's "Old Spinning Wheel," was one of their joint efforts. Its pop structure aside, the image of a vacant seat, unfilled by Father, brings back "sweet memories" and qualifies this number as a genuine country tearjerker.[23]

Rose and Poulton also wrote a western song about this same time—hardly surprising, since touring with Jack, Nap, and Dee kept Rose mindful of America's growing appetite for cowboy tunes. Advising Rose and Poulton was Poulton's wife, Betty, a versatile WSM artist in her own right. Early in 1936, Rose and the Poultons joined forces on "We'll Rest at the End of the Trail," a cowboy's reassurance to his trusty horse. Although the subject may seem earthy enough, this number musically soars in true Tin Pan Alley form. Its standard pop musical grammar employs a verse-and-chorus format and a release that falls in the third phrase of the chorus, where the melody peaks. "He was at our house," Betty Poulton remembered. "Fred said, 'What are the names of horses? . . . And I said, 'Gee, I think some horses you'd call Star.' . . . So here's the way Fred used that: 'If we feel like ropin' we'll hitch to a star . . . .'" Such gossamer stuff was the sure mark of a pop lyricist. Even so, "We'll Rest at the End of the Trail" hinted at a new direction for Rose's talent. Through Decca's Kapp, Rose gained several recordings of the song, including Decca renditions by pop idol Bing Crosby, cowboy film star Tex Ritter, and the Sons of the Pioneers—the nation's favorite western harmony group. The lesson of this hit was not lost on the pop tunesmith. Within two short years, Rose would be specializing in western material.[24]

TRANSITION TO COUNTRY MUSIC

The American West had produced authentic folk songs, of course, but the popular singing cowboy films of the thirties and forties left most of this folk legacy far behind. Indeed, most Hollywood buckaroos wore fancy outfits and warbled mellow tunes similar to Rose's pop numbers. The benefits for country entertainers, though, were enormous. Romanticized for decades in dime novels and films, cowboys symbolized freedom and self-reliance, thus providing serviceable alternatives to negative Southern hillbilly stereotypes. Everywhere, country musicians were donning western costumes, and some of these performers would show Rose a pathway to traditional country singers.[25]

The spring of 1938 found Rose in Hollywood, where dozens of writers were composing music for the flourishing film industry. Working with Gene Autry, America's leading cowboy hero, and Johnny Marvin, a musician from rural Oklahoma, Rose was crafting songs for Autry's Republic film *Gold Mine in the Sky* (1938). A WLS radio star of the early 1930s, Autry had known Rose in Chicago and had recently called on him in Nashville. "Gene came to our house," Lorene Rose remembered, "to get Fred to write him six songs for a new picture. So Fred wrote one while at the noon dinner table. Pee Wee King's father-in-law [Joseph "J. L." Frank] brought Gene out to our house at noon." Frank, an up-and-coming promoter then operating out of Nashville, had met Rose in Chicago early in the 1930s while booking Autry. In 1937, Frank had moved to Nashville to manage his newly organized *Opry* headline act, the Golden West Cowboys, fronted by accordionist Frank "Pee Wee" King; the next year, the promoter negotiated the band's contract for parts in *Gold Mine in the Sky* and set up Rose's first big Hollywood project.[26]

At first, Rose considered his 1938 Hollywood songwriting trip a vacation. It wasn't. "We went out for six weeks," Lorene Rose said, "and ended up staying there four years." Autry kept offering new assignments, and the Roses did spend most of the years from 1938 through 1942 in California, though they returned to Nashville periodically. Writing on location put Fred Rose at the center of California's lush country music landscape. There he saw stars like Tex Ritter and Ray Whitley, groups like the Golden West Cowboys, and California-based bands such as the Jimmy Wakely Trio and the Sons of the Pioneers, who often backed western stars onscreen, on radio, or in the recording studio. For example, Rose formed many friendships at live broadcasts of Autry's *Melody Ranch,* a long-running, highly rated CBS radio program that began in 1939 and featured many of the tunes Rose crafted for Autry's pictures, now the centerpiece of Rose's writing activity.[27]

Typically, Rose shared writing credits with Autry and Johnny Marvin, who doubled as general manager for Western Music, Autry's publishing company. "We worked well together," Autry asserted, "often sitting down and designing a song for a particular movie scene." As the star put it, Rose could write on demand and still produce songs that had "heart." And there was more: "I think that Fred Rose was the greatest song doctor that I ever knew in my life. . . . If you had a song that you were trying to work on and it just wouldn't go together, why, you could get with Fred and talk with him, and he knew how to doctor the song up and put it together and make a real song out of it. . . . He could write darn near any kind of a song you wanted." Collaboration varied from song to song, but Autry usually depended on Rose to complete musical ideas. "I . . . would get some ideas for songs, and then Fred would come along and work with me and finish 'em up," Autry said.[28]

Ray Whitley, Rose's Hollywood pal, agreed: "I'm not a bit hesitant to say that he was the master when it came to writing." Their admiration was mutual, however. Whitley himself was an able songwriter (he wrote Autry's theme, "Back in the Saddle Again"), an engaging performer, and an important influence on Freddie Rose. Friends since their 1935 New York recording sessions, the two musicians were reunited during Rose's first major Hollywood writing stint in 1938. Two years later, Rose and Whitley traveled to Tulsa, at the behest of Herald Goodman. After the Vagabonds had split, Goodman had organized the Tennessee Valley Boys and left Nashville for Tulsa, where he started KVOO's *Saddle Mountain Roundup* in 1939. Whitley guested on the barn dance during early 1940, when Rose was also on the scene with a KVOO pop program similar to his WSM *Song Shop.* Rose generally worked early morning spots, hard on the heels of Whitley and other country musicians, and watched the *Roundup* on weekends. As usual, the gregarious writer took a keen interest in his colleagues. In Tulsa his musical favorites were Bob Wills's Texas Playboys, kings of western swing and tops with legions of KVOO listeners. The bandleader's inventive style, with its strong pop and jazz components, fascinated Rose, and he and Whitley caught the Playboys' shows whenever possible. Wills befriended both musicians and sometimes asked them to Sunday dinner at his home. "We used to go out and eat chicken at his house," Whitley said, "and we knew his mother and dad and the whole family." [29]

In mid-1940, though, Rose went west again to continue his work with Whitley and Autry, living with Whitley and his wife, Kay, until Lorene could join him. Close bonds with the Whitleys nourished Rose's creativity and fostered a healthy blend of his personal and professional life. The Rose and Whitley homes became hangouts for performers of all descriptions, who often dropped in unannounced. A knock at the door might mean that Jimmy Wakely, Johnny Marvin, or Tex Ritter had come over to edit a song, savor one of Lorene's tempting recipes, or dip into one of Fred's huge pots of chili. Impromptu parties let everyone try his latest material before friendly audiences and do business on an informal basis. "All the cowboys would come," Jimmy Wakely said, "Gene Autry and sometimes Bob Nolan and Tim Spencer . . . and we'd have a lot of fried chicken and a lot of guitars and bass fiddles and everything, and a lot of picking and grinning. And when the party was over, Freddie Rose would sit down at the piano and sing some of the most sophisticated songs you ever heard in your life." Rose's sense of humor was just as ingratiating. He loved a good gag, and when the Whitleys were expecting their third child he surprised the couple with miniature diapers from a doll's wardrobe. "He just always came up with a snapper on any occasion," Ray Whitley said, laughing as he mentally relived those times.[30]

There were deeper moments, too. Rose studied Christian Science with Ray and Kay Whitley and attended Christian Science lectures with Kay, Johnny and Gloria Marvin, and Gene Autry's wife, Ina. "Fred was never overbearing with his desire to talk about Christian Science," Ray said, "but he would discuss it at the drop of a hat if he felt that there was a need for it." During these years of personal growth, faith lifted Rose's self-confidence and stiffened his resolve to deal with his visual handicap. "He tried, in his own way, to work it out metaphysically that he wouldn't have to wear glasses," Kay Whitley said. "And when he couldn't, then he conceded." Rose also struggled with smoking, drinking, and flashes of temper. The musician's hotheadedness could be amusing, Kay remarked, when he slammed down his Ping-Pong paddle after a lost point. "We used to call him Impetuous Peter," she said, chuckling. "He had a lot of things that he was trying to improve on."[31]

Songwriting, however, was one thing Rose had firmly under control, even though when he was scrunched up in a chair in the Whitleys' living room he didn't look like the talent he was. In slacks and a sport coat he was presentable enough, but his light brown hair was thinning at the temples. Since he could see only through portions of his eyes, he squinted much of the time and held song manuscripts within an inch of his face. And as Claire, the Whitleys' daughter, explained, a muscle defect let one eye wander: "He didn't even look directly at you; he had the mannerism of tilting his head at you." At 5' 8" and 150 pounds, "he was very small in stature and not impressive physically," Ray concluded. "But boy, once he started that brain to working, why, you really sat up and took notice. . . . Gene Autry called him Maggot Mind, because he said, 'Fred's mind is just like a maggot, just working all the time.'"[32]

Rose and Whitley made a good songwriting team. For two years the writers composed songs for features starring Autry, Whitley, Tim Holt, or Roy Rogers, who was then starting to challenge Autry's claim to the singing cowboy throne. Composing for films was fairly cut and dried, because scripts usually indicated the songs that each scene needed, but cowriting was fun, and movie plots were varied enough to keep the partners interested. As Whitley explained, collaboration turned what could have been a mechanical job into a learning experience for both men. "I said, 'Freddie, I'm not the songwriter that you are.' And he said, 'But Ray, you talk in titles . . . and titles are the most vital part of songwriting. You just give me a title, and I don't care if you write one line in the song, why, we'll split it. . . . I don't come up with the lines. The lines are given to me because I'm able to tune in. But the lines come from the Master himself . . . and I don't want you to feel sensitive about it at all.' . . . I used to be apprehensive about the deadline," Whitley continued, "but Fred had such complete confidence that he would wave aside any tensions that I might have." Whitley reported further on Rose's writing technique: "He would just keep going and going and going until he got everything down, and then he would swap lines around, and, of course, put the strongest lines in the strongest place where he thought it was needed."[33]

Rose could easily write for Gene Autry and his cohorts partly because they modeled themselves on pop vocalists, singing distinctly and from the chest, generally shunning the nasal twang of hillbilly singers. And this was just fine with Freddie Rose, pop tunesmith. Accordingly, he used pop structures and conventional love themes for many of his western numbers, with plenty of lyrics about horses and Texas moons thrown in for effect. At first, simple songs occasionally embarrassed him: "Don't you put my name on that silly tune," Rose warned Whitley on one occasion. With time, advice from Whitley, and the pull of the marketplace, Rose grew more comfortable with musical simplicity. "They are country tunes," Whitley told him, "and they've got to be simple for people to like them." Singing tenor, Rose helped cowboy bands make several motion picture soundtracks, and in the process he discovered that even the most basic songs could be beautiful when sung in two- and three-part harmony backed by well-played fiddles and guitars.[34]

Gradually, Rose began to test song patterns then typical of country music. He fashioned "Be Honest with Me," for example, with a three-chord harmonic progression. In contrast to his highly developed pop tunes, this song clusters around a five-note scale. The same simple four-line melody repeats in each verse, and there is no chorus whatsoever. A bridge is also conspicuous by its absence. But simplicity seemed to be what was needed. Gene Autry hit with this song on disc and featured it in *Ridin' on a Rainbow* (1941); the number received a 1941 Academy Award nomination in the category of best song in a musical film. Rose explored similar structures with "Tweedle-O-Twill," a novelty tune about a country boy "puffin' on cornsilk," written for Autry's *Home in Wyomin'* (1942). Columbia issued Autry's recording of this song in April 1942, and by early July it was taking off.[35]

Between 1938 and his 1942 army enlistment, Autry remained Rose's best channel to the record-buying public. The cowboy singer's tours across the Midwest and New England, together with his films and radio shows, further promoted Rose's tunes. Meanwhile, cowboy vocalists Jimmy Wakely and Roy Rogers were recording Rose's songs, and pop versions of "Tweedle-O-Twill" (the Merry Macs) and "Be Honest with Me" (Bing Crosby) put still more feathers in his cap. By the spring of 1942, Rose's country hits were coming thick and fast. *Billboard* praised Autry's renditions of "You'll Be Sorry" and "Tears on My Pillow" in April and May. Jimmie Davis, to be elected governor of Louisiana in 1944, clicked with "The End of the World" that summer. Autry's readings of "Take Me Back into Your Heart" and "There's a Rainbow on the Rio Colorado" set jukebox meters spinning in mid-year, and his "Tweedle-O-Twill" cut promised to be 1942's biggest country jukebox hit. "It's named as the top record in reports received from North, East, South and West, and appears to be sweeping the country," *Billboard* reported in July. In the meantime, Rose was starting to write very different songs for one of country music's most tradition-minded artists—Roy Acuff.[36]

EDGING TOWARD PARTNERSHIP

Although Roy Acuff, the son of an east Tennessee preacher, specialized in traditional songs, hoedowns, and hymns, vocal prowess let him incorporate a wide
range of new songs into his string band style. For instance, in a 1941 Chicago
session directed by Columbia's Art Satherley, Acuff recorded "Be Honest with
Me," evidently the first Fred Rose tune Acuff put on disc. This was basically
a standard love song, yet simple and straightforward enough to become one
of Acuff's yearning "heart" songs, and it spoke to men and women hungry for
emotional reassurance amid the dislocations of wartime. For his part, Satherley
had long since discovered Rose's songwriting skills. For three years the executive had been using Rose's tunes, first with Gene Autry, then with Bob Atcher
and Louise Massey, both smooth-singing network radio stars. Satherley often
called on Rose for help in the studio, and Rose first met Acuff at one of the
singer's early sessions, probably the "Be Honest with Me" session of 29 April
1941.[37]

Satherley set Acuff's next session for May 1942 in Hollywood. In preparation, the Columbia executive chose several Rose songs, without telling Acuff
who had written them. Shortly before the session, Satherley, his friend (and
eventual wife) Harriet Hares, and Rose visited Acuff in Nashville and played
him several selections on a small player-recorder. Rose had written some of
these tunes under the name Floyd Jenkins, but he didn't let on that the songs
were his. Acuff especially liked "Fire Ball Mail" and grew suspicious when he
asked Hares to sing the song, which she had claimed as hers, and she deferred
to Rose. Still, no one told Acuff the secret that evening.[38]

Rose had already used his countrified pseudonym on Bob Atcher's versions
of "Let's Tell Our Dream to the Moon" and "In the Echo of My Heart," recorded
for Columbia in January 1942 and released two months later. The following
May, about the time Satherley, Rose, and Acuff were holding their Nashville
powwow, Atcher cut two more "Floyd Jenkins" tunes, "Pins and Needles in My
Heart" and "Time Alone." In part, Satherley said later, he and Rose wanted to
head off other writers or publishers who might have wanted to lure Rose away
from him. Also, Rose may have been skittish about linking his real name with
Acuff's recordings. After all, writing for mellow voices like Autry's or Atcher's
was one thing; composing for Acuff—leather-lunged and unmistakably rural—
was another.[39]

Although the decisions behind Rose's nom de plume may never be completely unearthed, Rose clearly began to manage his own copyrights well before
the Acuff-Rose partnership became permanent. Early in 1942, "Floyd Jenkins"
and Columbia Records executed contracts naming "Jenkins" copyright holder

Fred Rose. Photo courtesy of BMI Archives.

of "In the Echo of My Heart," "Time Alone," "Let's Tell Our Dream to the Moon," "Pins and Needles in My Heart," "I'll Reap My Harvest in Heaven," and "Fireball Mail." Columbia was to pay Rose a royalty of 1 cent per recorded side for using each of the tunes on disc. Record companies often made such arrangements because they typically cost less than paying a publishing house under a standard mechanical license, which usually meant 2 cents per recorded side on full-priced recordings and somewhat less on budget lines.[40]

Significantly, Rose and Satherley split songwriters' royalties or copyright holders' royalties on some of the Floyd Jenkins songs. "I had a part of a few of the songs," Satherley later confirmed. It wouldn't be the first time a recording official and a writer struck a deal, nor would it be the last. According to Satherley, the arrangement transpired after he tried to help Rose out of financial straits and offered a publisher a sheaf of Rose tunes in hopes of getting Rose a $1,600 cash advance. When the publisher refused, Satherley explained, "There was a certain friend who loaned Freddie the sixteen or seventeen hundred dollars for those songs." Rose paid back the loan, Satherley said, from royalties earned on tunes that Satherley used in recording sessions with country artists like Acuff, Atcher, and Bob Wills. The "friend" was probably Satherley himself, whom Rose secretly cut in on the Floyd Jenkins songs to circumvent

Columbia's rule against A&R men having publishing companies. This probably explains Rose and Satherley's secrecy during their meeting with Acuff.[41]

Whatever Rose and Satherley were up to, the four Floyd Jenkins songs Acuff recorded on 28 May and 1 June 1942 marked Rose's arrival as a writer of tradition-oriented country music. True, Acuff's powerful singing was modernizing string band music, and he was every inch a showman. But he and his Smoky Mountain Boys symbolized traditional country with their acoustic instruments, their songs, and their name. Rose's songs provided foundations for stirring performances, and all four became wartime hits. In all likelihood, Satherley prompted Rose to craft the tunes with Acuff in mind. "I knew that Freddie could write material," the producer said in retrospect. "Whether it was for New York or Timbuctu, he could write it." Acuff agreed, speaking long after he learned about the Floyd Jenkins subterfuge. "He was quick to grasp the type of numbers that I could perform," Rose later confessed to self-doubts about coming up with Acuff-style material, yet he shaped these four songs with characteristic professionalism. Each is structurally simple, both lyrically and melodically. One of the four, "Low and Lonely," has three chords (I, IV, and V); the others, only two (I and V). Only "I'll Reap My Harvest in Heaven" has a chorus, the others consisting entirely of repeated verses. And only the chorus of "I'll Reap My Harvest" even hints at a bridge, or release. Yet lyric-melodic sequences and carefully constructed rhyme schemes knit each tune into a synergistic whole. In "Low and Lonely" sad words fuse with a bright melody to produce a toe-tapping number Acuff often used to open *Grand Ole Opry* shows. Likewise, "Fire Ball Mail" augmented Acuff's stock of lively, crowd-pleasing train songs. Rose's vivid images make the train come alive as it chugs by, "eatin' that coal" and swaying "like a hound waggin' his tail." The melody, peaking in the third line of each verse, let Acuff push his voice to its zenith.[42]

With "The Prodigal Son" and "I'll Reap My Harvest in Heaven," Rose expressed his high regard for spiritual values while varying religious themes of material that Acuff had previously recorded. Rose's spiritual numbers tend to be extremely positive, less melancholy and less otherworldly than such Acuff classics as "Great Speckled Bird" or "The Precious Jewel." Even so, phrases like "beautiful shore" (rhymed with "heavenly door") employ the vocabulary of Protestant hymns Acuff sang so earnestly. "I'll Reap My Harvest" describes an individual facing death with peace of mind, a standard subject of Christian hymnody. Confident that he will "plow a field up in glory," the speaker leaves his earthly crops to his neighbors, as his Maker instructed. "The Prodigal Son" presents similar ideas, using a melody and tempo deliberately imitative of "The Precious Jewel," whose melody Acuff himself had borrowed from the folk ballad "Hills of Roane County." Rose's song plays on a familiar biblical story to depict a person bound for a home on high. As the individual leaves, he encourages friends and family to love each other in this life and promises to meet them in the hereafter. Although neither "The Prodigal Son" nor "I'll Reap My Harvest" should be read as a literal statement of Rose's theology, both songs reflect his upbeat outlook on life, his sense of pilgrimage, and a spiritual sense that was helping him master country music's cultural and artistic formulas. "He got the feeling of it after he became a Christian," Lorene Rose emphasized. "He had all that feeling, all that sad stuff, you know. He liked it more, I think. At first, he couldn't get with it."[43]

With his Acuff songs, Fred Rose was moving beyond material he had written for Gene Autry, most of which merely added western lyric motifs to pop song constructions. Even "Be Honest with Me," a combination of conventional love words with simple melodic lines, and "Tweedle-O-Twill," essentially a novelty song, didn't represent hard-core country music as "Fire Ball Mail" or "The Prodigal Son" did. Acuff, no purveyor of cowboy kitsch, was down-home country personified, and writing for the *Grand Ole Opry* star brought Rose face to face with a folk-rooted artist and a tradition-based music. As a writer of jazz-oriented popular songs, Rose had encountered folk traditions before, though just how seriously he considered jazz's ethnic roots is impossible to say. At times he had superficially jazzed up pop tunes to exploit the popular trend, as other Tin Pan Alley writers had done. But now he had to deal with Southern culture in a way that Tin Pan Alley pop and minstrelsy, with their moonlight-and-magnolias imagery, had not. To write consistently for Acuff, Rose had to transcend both the country-pop songs he had produced for Autry and earlier sentimental tunes such as "There's an Old Easy Chair by the Fireplace." "I'll Reap My Harvest," "Low and Lonely," "Fire Ball Mail," and "The Prodigal Son" met the challenge head-on.

COMPLETING THE ALLIANCE

Sometime in mid-1942, Acuff approached Rose about starting a music publishing company. Rose's acceptance signaled a new phase of his career. He would no longer be a pop songwriter temporarily working the country market, but an entrepreneur who had entered the country field to stay.

Rose might well have started a country music publishing house in Hollywood, but he had returned to Nashville by the time of Acuff's business offer. Lorene Rose had wearied of late-night Hollywood parties, especially in quarters she didn't like. She also dreaded wartime civil defense blackouts and missed her family in Tennessee, who urged her to return for her own safety. "I just told him, 'I'm leaving,' " she related, "and he wasn't about to let me go and . . . stay there by himself." Rose was ready to leave, too. Hollywood seemed to be "going to pot," he had complained as the armed forces drained civilian manpower. Gene Autry's impending army enlistment made his future uncertain; no one knew how much longer he would remain a hitmaker. Besides, Rose could always mail songs to the West Coast or commute from Nashville if necessary.[44]

Equally important, restrictive royalty arrangements with Autry limited Rose's income just as a national country music bonanza was getting started. Early in their association, Rose sold Autry certain tunes outright for as little as $25 each. On other numbers that Autry published, Rose almost always split songwriters' royalties with Autry and other coauthors, and writers divided only 50 percent of a song's earnings, the other half going to Autry's firm. Western Music evidently gave Rose a modest draw, or monthly advance against future royalties, yet nothing spectacular. Rose didn't dwell on the past, and he drew upon religion in coping with music industry materialism, but he was no Pollyanna. As he entered his mid-forties, he almost certainly wanted a larger piece of the action.[45]

So in June 1942, Rose reestablished himself at WSM and worked there regularly for the next few months. Along with his pop numbers, Rose sang country songs, laying on "Tweedle-O-Twill" hard and heavy. Still, he was only marking time. Bigger things were in the offing.[46]

Acuff probably made his business proposition by early summer. The offer was exceedingly well-timed. World War II was reviving the economy, while urbanization, the intermingling of people from different regions in military service, and a climate of patriotism were widening country music markets. In addition, a new performance rights society, Broadcast Music, Inc. (BMI), begun by radio interests in 1940 as a rival to ASCAP, was opening new doors for country writers and publishers. Whereas ASCAP monitored only prime-time, pop-oriented, live network radio shows to determine which songs earned performance royalties, BMI also included independent stations and recorded-music programs that often featured country songs.[47]

Acuff was riding high on this country music wave. By now the star of the *Opry's* weekly network show, he earned some $200,000 in 1942. Most of these fabulous earnings then came from personal appearances, but Acuff and his wife, Mildred, were also selling songbooks hand-over-fist, sponsoring an *Opry* segment specifically for this purpose. "It was more *my* business to start, using his numbers," Mildred later revealed, "and pay him a percentage on the sales." Her initiative paid off in a hurry: soon her office assistants were lugging quarters to the bank by the bushel basketload, and the Acuffs quickly amassed the capital they thought they needed to back their publishing venture. While Nashville artists had been putting out songbooks since the early 1930s, the Acuffs were about to take the crucial step from a one-singer operation to a bona fide publishing house. Acuff-Rose Publications would assemble the songs of many writers in its catalog, and it would be the first Nashville country publishing firm to develop copyrights systematically through recording and broadcast media, as well as through sheet music and songbook sales.[48]

The Acuffs wanted to invest some of their income and protect Roy's copyrights, including original compositions, arrangements of traditional tunes and numbers purchased from other musicians. The artist was still smarting from his run-in with William R. Calaway of the American Recording Corporation (ARC), who had copyrighted for himself many of the songs recorded by Acuff at his first two sessions. Stung by the wily producer, Acuff had refused to record from March 1937 to November 1938, when Art Satherley, who became Columbia's country recording director after Columbia bought ARC, coaxed him back into the studio. Whether or not Satherley met Acuff's expectations, Columbia began to pay Acuff copyright royalties on certain songs as early as 1940. Did Acuff learn that Rose and Satherley had struck a bargain, or that Rose's copyright royalty rate on the Floyd Jenkins songs doubled his own? If so, did the discovery lead Acuff to start a publishing company and better the deal that Rose and Satherley had made? And did Rose, Satherley, and Acuff reach some agreement about the future of Acuff-Rose Publications? The answers to these questions may never be learned, but having a publishing house—especially one led by one of Satherley's top songwriters—was bound to improve Acuff's bargaining position in future dealings with Columbia, not to mention fattening his wallet.[49]

In any case, Northern publishers, bidding as much as $2,000 for each of Acuff's copyrights, opened his eyes to what owning a song could mean. "They was hearing the numbers that I was recording," Acuff said, "and how they were being played on the jukeboxes back in those days. They would come here and try to buy my songs, but I refused them. . . . I was as green as anyone, but I wasn't stupid enough just to sell all my songs to somebody in New York . . . ." The Acuffs needed someone to manage a publishing enterprise while they focused on Roy's demanding radio and road schedule. Rose seemed an excellent prospect. "He was the first one I considered," Acuff said later. "At this time [1942] I didn't know Fred too well. I just knew that he was capable." And as Mildred added, "[Roy] knew that Fred had connections. . . . He just liked him as a person, and I had a lot of confidence in him."[50]

At first, Acuff recalled, Rose thought Acuff was kidding, but evidently the proposal sounded better the more that Rose thought about it. The advantages of controlling the publishing rights to all his future compositions—and those of other writers—were presenting themselves more plainly all the time, as some of the numbers he owned, including "Fire Ball Mail," became hits. Additionally, Acuff's impassioned singing was turning Rose into a country music believer. Watching the entertainer reach fans was teaching Rose something that he hadn't yet fully learned. "It was at the *Opry* one night many years ago," he recalled in 1954. "Roy came out on the stage and sang 'Don't Make Me Go to Bed and I'll Be Good.' Real tears rolled down Roy's cheeks that night. Those tears stained his shirt. I felt I had discovered the real secret of country music."[51]

Soon Acuff and Rose talked again. Rose had no money to invest and allowed as much. "I'm not looking for that, Fred," Acuff reassured him. "I'm looking for someone that has ability." Acuff wanted his future partner to run the company. The *Opry* star would provide financial support and name recognition, along with radio and recording exposure for the firm's catalog. Mildred would assist with the office and serve as nominal partner in the Acuffs' behalf. But Rose was to be in the driver's seat: "You can carry it," Acuff told him. Before sealing the agreement, Rose conferred with Fred Forster, his Chicago friend and one-time publisher, who agreed to serve temporarily as distributor for Acuff-Rose sheet music and songbooks. Rose returned to Nashville enthusiastic about the new enterprise. On 30 October 1942, he formalized Acuff-Rose Publications, originally based on a handshake agreement with Acuff, as a partnership between Mildred Acuff and himself. (The arrangement would not only save Mildred inheritance tax headaches should anything happen to Roy, but it also allowed her to sign checks for the firm while Roy was on the road.) The company was capitalized at $50,000. For his contribution, Rose put up his personal song catalog. Any songs that Rose or Acuff composed after 1 January 1943, as well as all writing or publishing interests they held in songs created before that date, would be shared fifty-fifty. For their part, the Acuffs placed $25,000 at Rose's disposal in a local bank. As it turned out, Rose didn't have to draw on this sum, because income from hits that he and Acuff already had, plus a $2,500 advance from BMI, with which Acuff-Rose affiliated, proved sufficient for ongoing needs.[52]

Acuff-Rose Publications significantly altered the long-standing dependence of rural, folk-based Southern musicians upon urban cosmopolitan entrepreneurs. As the Acuffs had learned, these musicians had often been exploited, and many would continue to be. Nor would Rose and Acuff be immune to crafty businessmen whose maneuvers the Acuff-Rose team sometimes had to parry in kind in order to survive. But their own partnership rested upon mutual trust, and it was set up on equal terms. The Acuffs' initiative, and their belief in Rose, had called the new company into being. Although Rose's Chicago connections would help Acuff-Rose get started, the new country music operation was opening its doors in Nashville. What's more, it would be run by a Midwesterner who had adopted Tennessee as his home and was beginning to grasp what country music was all about.

As it turned out, the Acuff-Rose alliance marked a milestone in Nashville's musical history. Admittedly, Acuff-Rose Publications owed much of its livelihood to WSM performers who would soon support a thriving local recording industry, but neither WSM nor its corporate parent, National Life Insurance, took much interest in music publishing or recording, the endeavors that eventually made Nashville a full-fledged music town. For National Life, WSM remained a vehicle to sell insurance; by contrast, Acuff-Rose promoted songs and singers in their own right. With Rose in command, the company became the first of several publishing and recording enterprises that helped create Music City during the decade after World War II. And by increasing Nashville's influence within the music industry, Acuff-Rose helped change the course of America's regional, national, and international expansion. Indeed, the years from 1942 until 1954 would show just how far-sighted Roy and Mildred Acuff were in choosing Fred Rose as an ally.

NOTES

1  Arthur E. Satherley Notebook and Roy Acuff, "I'll Reap My Harvest In Heaven" (Okeh 6704), Country Music Foundation Library and Media Center, hereafter Satherley Notebook and CMF Library; *Billboard,* 1942–43, passim; U.S. Copyright Office Search of the songs of Fred Rose, typescript report to Wesley H. Rose, 28 March 1958, hereafter cited as Copyright Search, in author's files. Unless otherwise noted, all documents and copies of documents are in the author's files.

2  Satherley Notebook; Partnership Agreement between Fred Rose and Mildred Acuff, 30 October 1942, Opryland Music Group files.

3  Interview with Frank "Pee Wee" King and Redd Stewart, Louisville, Ky., 12 March 1977. Unless otherwise noted, all interviews were conducted by the author in Nashville and are in the author's files or in the CMF Library.

4  Telephone interview with Artye Rose, 19 November 1983; Local Certified Copy of Birth Record, no. 8948, City-County Department of Health, City of Evansville/Vanderburgh County, Ind., 15 September 1983; U.S. Census MSS, Vanderburgh County, Ind., 1900, Enumeration District no. 109, sheet 11; *Bennett and Co.'s Evansville City Directory* (Evansville, Ind., 1872–1900), passim.

5  Artye Rose to the author, 15 December 1977; interviews: Wesley Rose, 25 February 1977 and 8 March 1978; Johnny Sippel (telephone), 23 January 1978; Patricia Goodier, 10 March 1978; Helen Carter and Lester Rose, 27 February 1979; Helen Carter, Patricia Goodier, and Lester Rose, 16 May 1978.

6   Interviews: Lorene Rose and Mildred Wagoner, 10 April 1977; Elmo Tanner, 29 March 1978; Al Trace (self-interview), 10 May 1978.

7   Notarized photocopy of Certificate of Marriage, Fred Rose and Della Braico, 5 May 1917; Al Trace to the author, 8 May 1978; interviews: Al Trace; Elmo Tanner; Wesley Rose, 8 March 1978; Russell Sanjek, 16 March 1977; Fred Rose's Brunswick Records artist cards, CMF Library; *ASCAP Biographical Dictionary,* 4th ed. (New York: R. R. Bowker, 1980), 429. Artists who recorded Rose's songs were determined by cross-referencing Roger D. Kinkle's *The Complete Encyclopedia of Popular Music and Jazz 1900–1950,* 4 vols. (New Rochelle, N.Y., Arlington House, 1974), and Brian Rust, *Jazz Records 1897–1942,* 4th rev. and enlarged ed., 2 vols. (New Rochelle, N.Y., Arlington House, 1978), with the Copyright Search referenced in n. 1 above. Many of the songs cited here are credited to Rose and various coauthors. Although it is impossible to determine the precise roles of each author, the burden of interview evidence suggests that Rose's contributions were usually substantial.

8   Copyright Search; James F. Evans, *Prairie Farmer and WLS: The Burridge D. Butler Years* (Urbana: University of Illinois Press, 1969), 163, 215, 219; Bill C. Malone, *Country Music, U.S.A.,* rev. ed. (Austin: University of Texas Press, 1985), 69.

9   Interviews: Wesley Rose, 25 February 1977; Helen Carter, Patricia Goodier, and Lester Rose; Vervia (Betty) Poulton (self-interview), 25 April 1977.

10   Photocopy of Certificate of Marriage, Fred Rose and Helen Holmes, 27 May 1929; interviews: Helen Carter, Patricia Goodier, Lester Rose; Al Trace; Wesley Rose and Lester Rose, 30 March 1977.

11   Interviews with Elmo Tanner; Helen Carter, Patricia Goodier, and Lester Rose; Helen Carter and Lester Rose, 27 February 1979; Aaron Shelton, 1 September 1983; Vervia (Betty) Poulton (self-interviews), 25 Apr. and 20 May 1977; *Nashville Tennessean,* 21 June 1933; *WLS Family Album 1936* (Chicago: *Prairie Farmer* Publishing, 1935), 17.

12   Interviews with Elmo Tanner; Helen Carter, Patricia Goodier, and Lester Rose; Mildred Wagoner (telephone), 20 December 1983.

13   Powell Stamper, *The National Life Story* (New York: Appleton-Century-Crofts, 1968), 160–62; John H. DeWitt, Jr., "Early Radio Broadcasting in Middle Tennessee," *Tennessee Historical Quarterly* 31 (Spring 1972): 80–94; *Our Shield,* 11 October 1933, 13; *Broadcast News,* 12 November 1932, 30, 35. *Our Shield* was National Life's official magazine. *Broadcast News* was a local listener's guide to radio programming.

14   Interviews: Aaron Shelton, 1 September 1983; David Stone, 25 May 1983; *Broadcast News,* 7 May 1932, 7; Alton Delmore, *Truth Is Stranger than Publicity,* ed., with an introduction, commentary, and discography by Charles K. Wolfe (Nashville: Country Music Foundation Press, 1977), 59–62; Charles K. Wolfe, *Tennessee Strings: The Story of Country Music in Tennessee* (Knoxville: University of Tennessee Press, 1977), 54, 64–67; Timothy Patterson, "Hillbilly Music Among the Flatlanders: Early Midwestern Radio Barn Dances," *Journal of Country Music* (Spring 1975): 12–16.

15  Delmore, *Truth Is Stranger Than Publicity,* v–vi, 84–85. Delmore indicates that he and his brother met Rose before moving to Nashville, possibly on a trip that coincided with Rose's Nashville visit with Elmo Tanner.

16  Interviews: Helen Carter and Lester Rose; Vervia (Betty) Poulton, 20 May 1977 and 9 June 1978; *Broadcast News,* 12 November 1932, 19–20; *Old Cabin Songs of the Fiddle and the Bow* (Nashville: Old Cabin, 1932); *Old Cabin Songs of the Fiddle and the Bow,* 12th printing (Nashville: Old Cabin, 1934); George D. Hay, *A Story of the Grand Ole Opry* (Nashville: privately published, 1945), 28; Wolfe, *Tennessee Strings,* 61. *Our Shield,* 4 April 1933, 14, reported that Chicago's Forster Music bought the Old Cabin Company.

17  Interview with Jack Shook, 1 March 1978; *Rural Radio,* June 1938, 14.

18  Interviews with Mildred Wagoner, 8 March 1978 and 20 December 1983 (telephone); Lorene Rose, Mildred Wagoner, and Marie Baker, 17 October 1983; copy of Certificate of Marriage, Fred Rose and Lorene Harmon Dean, 27 March 1934; Copyright Search; Kinkle, *Complete Encyclopedia,* 2:1130, 3:1624, 1950.

19  Interviews: Mildred Wagoner, 8 March 1978; Ray and Kay Whitley, 8 June 1978; Ray Whitley's Decca artist cards; "Tragedy: Two Great Men Die Casually, Proving Pilots' Maxim," *Newsweek,* 24 August 1935, 18–19; Malone, *Country Music, U.S.A.,* 45–49, 64.

20  Helen Carter and Lester Rose interview; *Encyclopaedia Britannica* (Chicago, 1970), s.v. "Christian Science," by Rev. Charles Samuel Braden.

21  Interviews: Murray Nash, 2 October 1991; Jack Shook; Bill Collins, 5 September 1990; Lorene Rose, Mildred Wagoner, and Marie Baker; Mrs. John Duke, 1 March 1978; H. B. Teeter, "Mr. Country Music," *Nashville Tennessean Magazine,* 31 January 1954, 6.

22  Interviews: Lorene Rose and Mildred Wagoner; David Cobb, 18 August 1983; Vervia (Betty) Poulton, 8 June 1978; David Stone to author, 14 October 1977.

23  Vervia (Betty) Poulton interviews, 20 May 1977 and 9 June 1978; Nashville *Tennessean,* 7 November 1935; "There's an Old Easy Chair by the Fireplace," lead sheet in Curt and Betty Poulton Scrapbook, CMF Library; Billy Hill, "The Old Spinning Wheel" (New York: Shapiro-Bernstein, 1933). All sheet music and songbooks cited are in CMF Library.

24  Vervia (Betty) Poulton interviews, 25 April 1977, 20 May 1977, and 9 June 1978; Curt Poulton and Fred Rose, "We'll Rest at the End of the Trail" (New York: Select Music Publications, 1936); Decca artist cards for Bing Crosby, the Sons of the Pioneers, and Tex Ritter.

25  Malone, *Country Music, U.S.A.,* 137–75.

26  Interviews with Lorene Rose, Mildred Wagoner, and Marie Baker; Pee Wee King, 10 February 1989; Gene Autry (telephone), 3 September 1980; *Frankie and Johnny Marvin Folio of Down Home Songs* (New York: Southern Music Publishing, 1932), 2; Jack Burton, *The Blue Book of Hollywood Musicals* (Watkins Glen, N.Y.: Century House, 1953), passim.

27    Interviews with Lorene Rose, Mildred Wagoner, and Marie Baker; Jimmy Wakely and Ray Whitley (self-interview), February 1977; Johnny Bond to the author, 15 February 1978; *Variety,* 7 May 1941, 31.

28    Gene Autry interview; Johnny Marvin to Roy Acuff, 18 June 1941, Roy Acuff Scrapbook, CMF Library; Copyright Search; Gene Autry, with Mickey Herskowitz, *Back in the Saddle Again* (Garden City, N.Y.: Doubleday, 1978), 26.

29    Interviews with Ray and Kay Whitley; Ray Whitley (self-interview), March 1977. *Tulsa Daily World,* June 1939–March 1940, passim; Gerald F. Vaughn, *Ray Whitley: Country-Western Music Master and Film Star* (Newark, Del.: privately published, 1973).

30    Los Angeles *Examiner,* 14 September 1941. Interviews with Lorene Rose and Mildred Wagoner; Ray Whitley (self-interview), March 1977; Jimmy Wakely, interviewed by Douglas B. Green for Country Music Foundation, 25 June 1974; Ray Whitley, interviewed by Douglas B. Green for Country Music Foundation, 30 March 1975.

31    Interviews with Jimmy Wakely and Ray Whitley; Kay, Claire, Delores, and Judy Kay Whitley, 11 October 1981.

32    Interviews with Jimmy Wakely and Ray Whitley; Kay, Claire, Dolores, and Judy Kay Whitley; Ray Whitley, 30 March 1975.

33    Jimmy Wakely and Ray Whitley interview; Copyright Search; Vaughn, *Ray Whitley.* Gerald Vaughn generously cross-referenced copyright records with Jack Burton, *The Index of American Popular Music* (Watkins Glen, N.Y.: Century House, 1957), and Burton, *Blue Book of Hollywood Musicals.*

34    Jimmy Wakely and Ray Whitley interview. For examples of Rose's pop-western tunes, see *Songs Gene Autry Sings* (Hollywood, Western Music Publishing, 1942).

35    Gene Autry and Fred Rose, "Be Honest with Me," in *Songs Gene Autry Sings,* 4–5; Gene Autry and Fred Rose, "Tweedle-O-Twill" (Hollywood: Western Music Publishing, 1942); Satherley Notebook; *Billboard,* 8 August 1942, 67; Autry, with Herskowitz, *Back in the Saddle Again,* 26, 225; Kinkle, *Complete Encyclopedia,* 4:2031.

36    Autry, with Herskowitz, *Back in the Saddle Again,* 83; Merry Macs, Bing Crosby, Roy Rogers, and Jimmy Wakely Decca artist cards; *Billboard,* 11 July, 1942, 69 and April–August 1942, passim.

37    Interviews with Arthur E. Satherley (self-interview), 16 March 1978; Roy Acuff, 3 March 1977; Bob Atcher, 1 May 1987; Satherley Notebook; Elizabeth Schlappi, "Roy Acuff," in *Stars of Country Music: From Uncle Dave Macon to Johnny Rodriguez,* ed. Bill C. Malone and Judith McCulloh (Urbana: University of Illinois Press, 1975), 195–219; Mary A. Bufwack and Robert K. Oermann, *Finding Her Voice: The Saga of Women in Country Music* (New York: Crown, 1993), 89–92.

38    Roy Acuff interview, 3 March 1977; Satherley Notebook.

39    Satherley interview; Satherley Notebook.

40  Contracts covering the above-referenced songs, made between "Floyd Jenkins" and the Columbia Recording Corporation, Opryland Music Group files.

41  Satherley interview.

42  Interviews with Arthur E. Satherley; Lorene Rose, Mildred Wagoner, and Marie Baker; Roy Acuff, 3 March 1977; Satherley Notebook; John W. Rumble, comp., *Roy Acuff* (Alexandria, Va., Time-Life Records, 1983).

43  Lorene Rose, Mildred Wagoner, and Marie Baker interview; Rumble, *Roy Acuff*.

44  Interviews: Arthur E. Satherley; Lorene Rose and Mildred Wagoner; Lorene Rose, Mildred Wagoner, and Marie Baker; *Variety,* 10 December 1941, 1; *New York Times,* 28 July 1942.

45  Interviews with Gene Autry; Vic McAlpin, 14 May 1977; Johnny Bond to author, 15 February 1978.

46  Jud Collins interview, 24 March 1977; *Nashville Tennessean,* 13 June 1942.

47  Interviews with Roy Acuff, 3 March 1977; Russell Sanjek, 16 March 1977; Johnny Bond to author, 15 February 1978; Elizabeth Schlappi, *Roy Acuff: The Smoky Mountain Boy* (Gretna, La.: Pelican, 1978), 177; Malone, *Country Music, U.S.A.,* 177–79; Russell Sanjek, *American Popular Music and Its Business: The First Four Hundred Years,* 3 vols. (New York: Oxford University Press, 1988), III: 287, 322–23. Bond believed Acuff may have proposed the publishing partnership to Rose while filming *Hi, Neighbor* (Republic Pictures, 1942), which was made in May or June 1942, and that Rose returned to Nashville from Hollywood committed to the venture. Acuff recalled making the proposal at WSM.

48  Interviews with Mildred Acuff, 5 April 1978; Mildred Wagoner, 8 March 1978; *Billboard,* 6 March 1943, 7; Schlappi, "Roy Acuff," 275; Chet Hagan, *Country Music Legends in the Hall of Fame* (Nashville: Thomas Nelson, 1982), 38.

49  Roy Acuff interview, John W. Rumble and Charles K. Wolfe, interviewers, 16 March 1982; Contract between Roy Acuff and the Columbia Recording Corporation covering "Just to Ease My Worried Mind," 11 April 1940, Opryland Music Group files; Rumble, *Roy Acuff; Roy Acuff's Grand Ole Opry Song Favorites* (Nashville: privately published, ca. 1941).

50  Interviews with Roy Acuff, 3 March 1977 and 19 December 1978; Mildred Acuff.

51  Interview with Roy Acuff, 3 March 1977; Teeter, "Mr. Country Music," 7.

52  Interviews with Russell Sanjek; Roy Acuff, 3 March 1977; Lorene Rose, Mildred Wagoner, and Marie Baker; Partnership Agreement between Fred Rose and Mildred Acuff, 30 October 1942; Elizabeth Schlappi, *Roy Acuff,* 152. In 1943, Rose and the Acuffs set up an ASCAP-affiliated firm, Milene Music.

# Jim Crow and the Pale Maiden

*Gender, Color, and Class in Stephen Foster's*

*"Hard Times"*

 **Amy Schrager Lang**

The history of the rise of blackface minstrelsy in the United States has been written as a history of "blacking up," that is, as a history of the ways in which the performance of a fabricated and stylized blackness served the needs, both social and psychological, of discontented white workingmen. Insofar as this story is one of blacking up, it is a story of incipient class conflict enabled, displaced, or masked by the donning of racial disguise. I want to propose that the history of blackface minstrelsy is also and importantly about taking off that disguise, about the resumption of whiteness and, with it, the potential restoration of class harmony. Regarded in this way, the simultaneous emergence and popularity of the "vulgar" minstrel show with its predominantly white working-class male audience and the domestic novel with its genteel white female readership might be seen as standing in a new relation—standing, in fact, in something like the relation made concrete in another popular nineteenth-century form, the topsy-turvy doll, which held one way represents a black "mammy" figure whose long skirts, when the doll is inverted, reveal a white girl. Likewise, it seems to me, blackface minstrelsy and the culture of sentiment are joined, as it were, at the hip. "Hard Times," anomalous among Stephen Foster's songs in its direct attention to class interactions, provides one opening into the relationship between the plantation melodies for which Foster is most famous and the parlor ballads to which he was most devoted.

In 1864, at the age of thirty-seven, Stephen Foster died, alone and destitute, in a Bowery hotel. Contemporary accounts of Foster's last months abound, focusing primarily on his greasy clothes, his empty pockets, his "gentleness," and his alcoholism. One account was written by a New York reporter and temperance man, John Mahon. According to Mahon, Foster recalled the melodies of all his songs, but the only lyrics he remembered were those of "Hard Times," written in 1855—the song that other journalists claim to have heard Foster sing in the grocery grog shops that he frequented. While most likely too apposite to be true, Mahon's story is nonetheless suggestive, particularly so in light of Foster's role in refining minstrelsy.[1]

Foster began his songwriting career in the 1840s, just as the minstrel show began its meteoric rise to popularity.[2] "Oh! Susannah," among the first of his songs to be published, was an instant success on the minstrel circuit (albeit in pirated form). Over the next decade Foster produced approximately 180 songs. Of these, the most famous and the most widely circulated, though not the most numerous, were plantation songs like "The Old Folks at Home" and comic dialect songs like "Camptown Races." Embraced by the Christy Minstrels, the Sable Harmonists, and their like, Foster's "pathetic" plantation melodies, replete with images of freed or departed slaves mourning their lost days of servitude, are widely understood to have originated a shift in the emotional tenor of blackface performance. Figuring the slave as loyal, affectionate, "feminized" in the manner of Uncle Tom, these songs are, in fact, suffused with the same sentimental nostalgia that characterizes the larger group of songs Foster wrote for the parlor trade—songs like "Jeanie with the Light Brown Hair" and "Beautiful Dreamer."[3]

This similarity is no accident. There is convincing evidence that Foster valued his "poetic" compositions more highly than the "Ethiopian" melodies he wrote for the blackface minstrel shows. Early in his career his concern for his reputation led him to relinquish his rights in "The Old Folks at Home" to E. P. Christy of the Christy Minstrels, under whose name the song was published. In a later unsuccessful effort to reclaim the song ("Old Folks" did not bear Foster's name until 1879), Foster wrote to Christy (1852): "I had the intention of omitting my name on my Ethiopian songs, owing to the prejudice against them by some, which might injure my reputation as a writer of another style of music, but I find by my efforts I have done a great deal to build up a taste for the Ethiopian songs among refined people. . . . Therefore I have concluded to reinstate my name . . . and to pursue the Ethiopian business without fear or shame. . . ."[4]

While his publishers indiscriminately advertised "Massa in the Cold Ground" alongside "Jeanie" and "Come Where My Love Lies Dreaming," Foster worried at the distinction between the vulgar and the refined. The youngest son of a genteel and politically well-connected Pittsburgh family whose initial dismay at his association with the Christy Minstrels is manifest in its members' ambivalent accounts of the songwriter's life, Foster may have decided to pursue the "Ethiopian business" without shame, but even a cursory glance at the list of his published songs suggests that he increasingly wrote for the parlor trade. This preference for the refined is not surprising. Unlike Christy and the other men from middle-class urban families in the North who founded blackface minstrelsy, Foster, for all his struggles with respectability, did not rebel and leave home to join the circus or the theater.[5] On the contrary, rather than flee the parlor for the largely male arena of the minstrel show, he determined to bring the minstrel show home to the ladies.

The distinction that Foster draws in his letter to Christy between the "Ethiopian" and "another style"—the refined style of the parlor ballad—is not the one that governs modern discussions of his music. Instead, a tripartite division (likewise drawn from Foster) sorts the songs into the comic, the poetic, and the pathetic. This division distinguishes between musical forms and subjects, but it is not without secondary effects. Distributing Foster's blackface songs over three genres, the racial—not to say, the racist—content of his compositions is submerged: pathos is pathos, wherever it is found, and likewise poetry and comedy. It is perhaps a consequence of this analytic structure that the propensity of nineteenth-century performers and twentieth-century scholars alike to transport Foster's songs back and forth across racial lines goes largely unmentioned. No notice is taken when the parlor composition appears in the midst of a minstrel performance or when the frontispiece photograph of Foster's white parents is identified as "the old folks at home," as it is in their granddaughter's biography of Foster. Nor does the workinggirl in "Hard Times," misplaced as I hope to show her to be, require comment. Whatever its merits from a musicological point of view, the use of generic distinctions to organize Foster's songs confounds rather than addresses the already ambiguous relationship between songs whose subjects and singers are black and those whose subjects and singers are white. It masks what I would like to suggest is a fundamental connection between Foster's "vulgar" and his refined productions.

By contrast, Foster's simpler division between minstrel songs, on the one hand, and genteel ballads, on the other—a division that appears to follow racial lines—makes visible the overlapping social vocabularies of plantation and parlor. Despite his hopes for a refined audience and the admiring notices of his "Ethiopian" melodies in refined publications like *Godey's Ladies Book,* Foster's plantation songs, like others of their type, were performed in blackface for the entertainment of Northern urban working-class *men;* their lugubrious sentimentality, like their racist content, as others have argued, allowed for the expression of "the longings and fears and hopes and prejudices"—and the discontents—of that audience. Songs of the lost plantation, with its "natural" hierarchy of master and slave, as Eric Lott has argued, played to the fears of white workingmen of a shift in the domestic balance of power consequent on increased female employment and their own reduced opportunity.[6] Arguably, songs of the lost lady—like Foster's parlor ballads—played to analogous fears of domestic disruption, only in a different class register.

But if blackface minstrelsy developed in counterpoint to "languages of class [that] hinged on the quite vague definition of white workers as 'not slaves,'" as David Roediger has proposed,[7] sentimental parlor songs depend on a language of class in which middle-class women are "not black" and white women are not workers. If the "racial meanings" of blackface performance provided a "cover story" for the class struggles of white workingmen, the gendered meanings of parlor ballads, with their endless attention to lost—or absent or sleeping or dead—women, point to the fragility of an ideal of class harmony figured in the genteel white household. Both of these forms, the plantation melody and the parlor ballad, use social vocabularies of race and gender to answer an overwhelming anxiety over class conflict that afflicted white Americans at mid-century. Structured around fixities of race and gender, Foster's songs nonetheless offer a record of social instability, of disrupted relationships, of lost homes, that is itself entirely fluid.

> *Hard Times Come Again No More*
> Poetry and Music by Stephen C. Foster (1854)
>
> Let us pause in life's pleasures and count its many tears,
> While we all sup sorrow with the poor:
> There's a song that will linger forever in our ears;
> Oh! Hard Times, come again no more.
>
> Chorus:
> 'Tis the song, the sigh of the weary:
> Hard Times, Hard Times, come again no more:
> Many days you have lingered around my cabin door;
> Oh! Hard Times, come again no more.
>
> While we seek mirth and beauty and music light and gay
> There are frail forms fainting at the door:
> Though their voices are silent, their pleading looks will say—
> Oh! Hard Times, come again no more.
> Chorus.

There's a pale drooping maiden who toils her life away
With a worn heart whose better days are o'er:
Though her voice would be merry, 'tis sighing all the day—
Oh! Hard Times, come again no more.
Chorus.

'Tis a sigh that is wafted across the troubled wave
'Tis a wail that is heard upon the shore,
'Tis a dirge that is murmered around the lowly grave,—
Oh! Hard Times, come again no more.
Chorus.

A song like "Hard Times"—neither plantation song nor parlor ballad—takes on a special usefulness in exploring this terrain. We have no definitive history of the composition of "Hard Times," although accounts of the song's origins abound. Some biographers, including Foster's niece, claim that the song was written in response to the widespread closing of the cotton mills in Pittsburgh and Allegheny in 1854—closings that resulted in a dramatic and visible increase in unemployment in the area.[8] Others point to Foster's passing youthful encounter with Charles Dickens during the author's 1842 visit to Pittsburgh and see "Hard Times" as a direct allusion to the title of Dickens's 1854 novel about the life of labor in the north of England.[9] Morrison Foster, in his 1896 biography of his brother, cites "Hard Times" in his unconvincing effort to "authenticate"—and thus, presumably, legitimize—Foster's compositions by linking it to African American musical forms.[10] The melody of "Hard Times," Morrison Foster claims, was recalled by Foster from his childhood visits to the church of the Fosters' West Indian servant, Olivia Pise. Since Pise left the Fosters' service when Foster was three, this story seems implausible at best. Yet another account of "Hard Times" ascribes its inspiration, and sometimes its composition, to Charles Shiras, the poet and abolitionist whose relationship to Foster is the subject of considerable scholarly mystification.[11] Rather than resolving the issue of the song's provenance, these attempts to locate "Hard Times" in a particular social frame—a concern for the condition of labor, a commitment to sentimental form, or a lineage of "real" black music—only accentuate its instability.

Nonetheless, on the face of it, "Hard Times" seems simple. Explicitly about social class, it treats the relationship of wealth to poverty. Appealing to the conscience of his genteel audience, the singer—the maker of "music light and gay"—calls upon others like himself to pause amid "life's pleasures" and "sup sorrow with the poor" whose endless lament—"hard times come again no more"—serves as the song's refrain. Absorbed in their quest for "mirth and beauty," the prosperous must be brought to notice the "frail forms" of the poor "fainting at the door." The poor themselves, with their "silent" voices, can do no more than cast "pleading looks" in the direction of those who might rescue them from their fate; the singer, on the contrary, puts their plight into words, thus bringing the existence of the poor to the attention of his peers. The singer can make the poor visible; he can make their silent song audible and count their tears; but importantly, he does not even so much as intimate a social remedy for their condition. Such a remedy is, in fact, precluded and superseded by the particular figuration of the poor in "Hard Times."

If the first two stanzas of "Hard Times" are directed at establishing the existence and the proximity of the song's subject—the silent poor, standing at the door—stanzas three and four provide poverty with a specific social location. The quintessential figure of destitution, it turns out, is a "pale drooping maiden who toils her life away." This figure—whose demise, by implication at least, provides the subject of the second half of the song—has a complicated history. Most strikingly, she recalls the hapless female protagonists of the domestic fiction that reached its peak of popularity in the 1850s with works like Maria Cummins's *The Lamplighter* and Susan Warner's *The Wide, Wide World*. These novels focus, as a rule, on an impoverished young girl who, by dint of her innate gentility, a laborious commitment to Christian self-restraint, and the efforts of an altogether angelic "sister," is translated from the slums into the refined (but never aristocratic) precincts of the middle class. This translation is literally (or literarily) accomplished by the substitution of a vocabulary of material inequity into a vocabulary of gender: poverty is at once replaced and answered by femininity and the attendant prospect of mobility through marriage. Gender, in other words, provides the solution to a problem almost always first formulated as one of class. Foster's "pale drooping maiden" must, then, have a "worn heart" and a voice that sighs "all the day." She is neither stalwart working-class woman nor independent Bowery "g'hal she," despite her toil. Rather, she is the most lamentable case available to mid-nineteenth-century culture—and surely one of the most representable: the genteel maiden, whose "better days" guarantee her essential respectability. A virtuous woman fallen on hard times, she is poor but she is emphatically not *the poor*, whose representative female figure, the factory girl, was excoriated as morally degraded.

A frail and undoubtedly respectable maiden, Foster's subject is, in fact, conspicuously out of place in the world of toil. Lest we have any doubts, however, her misplacement is confirmed by her pallor. Not simply a maiden but a "pale" maiden, the figure of poverty is both female and white—and, it should be noted, virginal. If she proves her unassailable femininity by drooping, fainting, sighing, and pleading, she belies her poverty by her whiteness. Not, of course, that white women never toiled their lives away. Rather, in the representational scheme of things, white women did not remain white when they toiled. They were, one might say, "blacked up" by their labors.

Let me try to explain what I mean by pointing to another literary genre, the industrial novel. Fifteen years after the composition of "Hard Times," Elizabeth Stuart Phelps published a novel entitled *The Silent Partner.* Touted as one of the first American industrial novels, *The Silent Partner* treats the encounter between a mill owner's daughter and a mill girl. Simultaneously a protest at the exclusion of women and workers from partnership in the mills and at the silent partnership demanded of women in marriage, both the formal structure and the ideological imperatives of the novel require that the genteel Perley and the mill girl Sip be at once united by gender and divided irrevocably by class. This distinction is conveyed in part by the narrator's recurrent allusions to their color. As befits her name, Perley is white, her face pale, and her hands like "rice paper." Sip, on the contrary, is "brown." But this brownness immediately calls attention to itself, for girls like Sip who work in the weaving room are never brown. In fact, as the narrator carefully explains, weavers are marked by their bleached skin. Racially speaking, of course, Sip is white—in fact, a "Yankee"; her brownness is the visible sign of her poverty, of her membership in the sisterhood of toil.

When this extended context is kept in mind, the pallor of Foster's maiden seems as central to the inchoate vision of class harmony of "Hard Times" in which the well-to-do "sup sorrow" with the poor as blackface is to the plantation ballad. In fact, just as black slaves are and are not the subjects of blackface minstrelsy, so the factory girl is and is not the subject of "Hard Times." If blackface enables the expression of class antagonism, whiteface restores the prospect of harmony. Not surprisingly, perhaps, the slip that tells—the incoherence in "Hard Times" that calls our attention to the whiteness of its subject—is also (and necessarily) the one that blurs the racial identification of the song's protagonist. In the refrain to "Hard Times," the impoverished maiden addresses a personified "hard times." "Many days you have lingered around my cabin door," she says, "Come again no more."

This cabin, I would suggest, is a problem. We do not customarily find pale drooping maidens in cabins; in fact, we find Uncle Tom—or, more to the point, Aunt Chloe—there. The maiden of Foster's song, like her sisters in the domestic novel, seems more likely an urban figure. She might, for example, be one of the "thirty thousand virtuous women" (the unrelated) George Foster describes in his 1854 *New York in Slices,* women "reduced from affluence to . . .

keen want," "patient . . . starving, toiling, heart-broken, yet courageous."[12] Or, alternatively, she might be one of the "unfortunate sisters" represented in the workinggirl melodramas that dominated the Bowery Theatre and its like by the end of the 1850s, girls whose remarkable refinement is revealed as an inborn trait by the return of a long-lost but highly respectable and usually well-heeled parent. When the brown-faced Sip is considered, however, this slip from the parlor to the plantation suggests the permeable boundary between the two.

If the relationship between race and gender in a song like "Hard Times" is complicated by a consideration of contemporary fictional representations, that relationship is complicated even further by the appearance of "Hard Times" in a "Negro Extravaganza" of the same name produced in 1855 by one of the most famous of the early blackface minstrels, Dan Emmett. A skit of one scene, Emmett's "Hard Times" is written in dialect and meant to be performed entirely in blackface. It enacts the story of an impoverished black man who bargains with the devil and, through a legal loophole provided by his wife, bests him. The skit opens with the entrance of the stock character of Old Dan Tucker, "a sufferer by the pressure of the times," singing a fragment of Foster's song to himself. "Hard times! Hard times! an' worse a comin'," Tucker intones, "Hard times thro' my old head keeps runnin'; I'll cotch de nigger make dat song."[13] Tucker claims that he would sell himself "body an' soul, / For jist a peck ob fire coal," and immediately Beelzebub appears to sign a "contract" to just this effect: Old Dan Tucker will be his, body and soul, when once the sack of coal Beelzebub provides is burned. When his insufficiently disciplined son unwittingly burns the coal, Tucker is saved from being possessed by the devil through his wife's claim that she already owns him: "don't de law say what belongs to de woman belongs to herself, an' what's her's am her own?" Having given the hide of her father's dog to purchase a marriage license and her calf to pay for the wedding ceremony, she has so clear a title to Tucker that even Beelzebub is forced to recognize her claim.

Clearly, Old Dan Tucker is in the midst of hard times, but equally clearly, Foster's "Hard Times" is neither sung by a ragged black laborer nor written by one. Nor does it engage the issues of paternal authority, individual self-possession, or the legal rights of women on which the skit hinges. Playing to the anxieties of a white working-class male audience, Emmett's "Hard Times" records neither the tragic demise of the worn-hearted white woman pressed into labor nor the well-meant charities of the affluent. Instead, it addresses the helplessness of the white workingman hedged in by the master/devil who holds the contract that allows him to subsist, the disobedient son who thwarts his efforts to survive, and the wife who at once saves and unmans him. Presumably the familiarity of the audience with Foster's song allows for its presence in Emmett's skit, but interestingly that familiarity—including as it must have, knowledge of the song's subject—does not seem to have rendered it inappropriate. On the contrary, I mean to suggest, the allusion to Foster folds whiteness back into the blackface performance.

If the point of blackface in minstrelsy is, at least in part, to define—or even consolidate—the meaning of whiteness, the point of whiteness, I am arguing, is to establish class mobility. I am proposing, that is, that white workers, by insisting upon themselves as "not slaves" yet performing themselves as black, continually reasserted their whiteness and were thus able to be assimilated to a middle-class view of the essential (that is, the natural) harmony of class interests.

To wrench the topsy-turvy metaphor to my purposes, the flip side of the blackface representation of the white workingman is the figure of the pale drooping maiden in whom the problem of class—that is the experience of differentials of wealth, power, and prestige—is both focused and resolved by resort to gender. In the broadest sense, I am arguing that the erasure of class in a wide variety of cultural productions of the mid-nineteenth century is enabled not simply by the fact that race and gender are deeply implicated in class status; rather, race and gender are structurally able to substitute for class because the conjunction of attributes that define class position are rendered so intrinsic—that is, the poor are brown—or else so transcendent—that is, women are genteel—that they pass either below or above history. Where the contingency of social status is signaled—as it preeminently is in the very process of blacking up—the prospect of class conflict becomes visible; conversely, that prospect vanishes when the space between the attributes that are taken to constitute class and in which an explanation of their conjunction might be undertaken collapses, that is, when whiteness is restored as the permanent condition even of those whose real discontents are performed black.

On the one hand, then, I am proposing that we need to investigate the borders between cultural forms if we are to understand the representation of class in mid-nineteenth-century America. On the other hand (and this point is perhaps less clear in my discussion), I am suggesting that not only performers and audiences—the mechanic minstrels and their working-class male spectators, for example, or the parlor balladeers and their middle-class white auditors—but producers, themselves bearers of race, class, and gender—the genteel Stephen Foster, for instance—must be taken into account in uncovering the stories of class interaction in the United States.

I want to end with a word about the revival of "Hard Times" by performers like Emmylou Harris, Bob Dylan, and the Red Clay Ramblers. All of these modern versions of the song make concessions to contemporary taste. They all, for example, drop the final stanza. Harris's version in addition makes a series of smaller changes in usage: instead of "supping" sorrow with the poor, we are urged to "share" their sorrow; "mirth" becomes "love"; the maiden's would-be "merry" voice becomes a "singing" voice; the "pale drooping maiden" becomes a "pale young" maiden. But Harris's version makes one change that is, I would argue, substantive: that is, the elimination of the cabin, the one word in the song that could be seen as alluding back to plantation songs and thus potentially confuse the racial identification of the maiden—or invoke the racism of the composer.

The renewed currency of "Hard Times" is, I presume, bound to the omnipresence of the homeless in the United States—and perhaps more specifically to the phenomenon commonly referred to as the "feminization of poverty." In the face of recent dramatic increases in poverty and more particularly in the number of poor women, "Hard Times" is once again useful in recalling the middle class to sympathy. I would suggest, however, that the social logic that has returned "Hard Times" to view hinges as much on the whiteness of the female figure of poverty now as it did in the nineteenth century. Current public discourse about poverty, after all, precludes absolutely sympathy for the young black woman—represented [encoded] as the calculating (and always by implication promiscuous) "welfare mother" who reproduces for the sake of a pittance a week increase in her check. "Hard Times" can still engage our sympathies because it respects the terms of our prejudices: the "maiden" must still, I submit, be pale—must still, that is, mirror our middle-class selves—if we are to share her sorrow. The very fact that we can still be moved by "Hard Times"—though what exactly we are moved *to* remains unclear—may tell us something about the extent to which our thinking about class is still organized by vocabularies of gender and race.

NOTES

1   John Trasker Howard's 1934 biography of Foster, *Stephen Foster, America's Troubadour* (New York: Thomas Y. Crowell), details and discusses accounts of Foster's decline. See especially 306–46.

2   Thomas Rice "jumped Jim Crow" for the first time in 1831; the first blackface quartet, organized by Daniel Emmett, performed in 1843 at the Chatham Garden Theatre in New York.

3   William W. Austin's useful study of Foster's life and work, *"Susannah," "Jeanie," and*

*"The Old Folks at Home"*: *The Songs of Stephen C. Foster from His Time to Ours* (Chicago: University of Chicago Press, 1989, 2nd ed.), details the life histories of many of Foster's most famous songs, including their citation by other composers.

4   Howard, *Stephen Foster,* 196–97.

5   Alexander Saxton's "Blackface Minstrelsy and Jacksonian Ideology," *American Quarterly* 27 (1975): 3–28 details the individual histories of the founders of minstrelsy.

6   Eric Lott, *Love and Theft* (New York: Oxford University Press, 1993), 196ff.

7   David R. Roediger, *The Wages of Whiteness* (New York: Verso, 1991), 115.

8   Evelyn Foster Morneweck, *Chronicles of Stephen Foster's Family* (Port Washington, N.Y.: Kennikat Press, [1944] 1973).

9   See, for example, Austin, *"Susannah," "Jeanie,"* . . . , 161.

10   Morrison Foster's insistence on the authenticity of Foster's songs—that is, their origins in African American music—is not surprising in light of the fact that after Emancipation and into the 1950s Foster's songs were presented, first in concerts and then in songbooks and on recordings, alongside slave songs. This "adventitious connection," according to William Austin, greatly increased the prestige of Foster's compositions.

11   For example, William Austin speaks of Foster's relationship to Shiras, one of the "nice young men" of Foster's youth, in the following way: "Charles Perry Shiras was a more important part of Stephen Foster's life than . . . any teacher or classmate. Just how important can never be known, though there is always a possibility that further information may turn up to bring us closer to the full truth. . . . Morrison [Foster's] total omission of Shiras from his biography of 1896 suggests that Morrison knew both too much and too little to define the relation" (Austin, *"Susannah," "Jeanie,"* . . . , 168). Slightly later, Austin suggests that the record of the Foster-Shiras friendship is "tantalizing." "Whatever the extent of the friendship and collaboration," he goes on, "surely Stephen learned more from Shiras than from his own family about poetry and a career as a writer. The dream of 'Jeanie,' blended with so many dreams, could easily refer also to Charles" (Austin, *"Susannah," "Jeanie,"* . . . , 172).

12   George G. Foster, *New York by Gaslight and Other Urban Sketches,* ed. Stuart M. Blumin (Berkeley: University of California Press, [1850] 1990), 231–32.

13   Daniel D. Emmett, Hard Times: *A Negro Extravaganza—One Scene* (Chicago, 1874), unpaginated.

# Selected Discography

"The Alabama Flood." Blind Andy [Andrew Jenkins]. Okeh 45319.

"Answer to Weeping Willow." The Carter Family, *The Carter Family Country Music Hall of Fame Series*. MCA MCAC–10088.

"Appalachian Memories." Dolly Parton, *The Best There Is*. RCA CD 6497.

"Are You Sure Hank Done It This Way?" Waylon Jennings, *Are You Sure Hank Done It This Way?* RCA 61139.

"The Ballad of Hank Williams." Hank Williams, Jr., *The Pressure Is On*. Electra 5E–535.

"Before You Kill Us All." Randy Travis, *This Is Me*. Warner Brothers 9 45501–2.

"Billy Richardson's Last Ride." Vernon Dalhart. Brunswick 102; Al Craver [Vernon Dalhart]. Columbia 15098; Vernon Dalhart. Vocalion 5045.

"Blood Red and Going Down." Tanya Tucker, *The Greatest Hits Encore*. Capitol CDP 7 94254 2.

"Blue Moon of Kentucky." Bill Monroe, *Bill Monroe: Country Music Hall of Fame Series*. MCA 10082; Elvis Presley, *Remembering*. RCA pdc 2 1037.

"A Boy Named Sue." Johnny Cash, *The Essential Johnny Cash 1955–1983*. Columbia C3T 47991.

*The Bristol Sessions*. Various Artists. 2 vols. Country Music Foundation CMF–011–C.

"Brown Mountain Light." Tony Rice, *Tony Rice Plays and Sings Bluegrass*. Rounder CD 0253.

"Bryan's Last Fight." Vernon Dalhart. Columbia 15039.

"Can I Sleep in Your Barn Tonight?"/"Don't Let Your Deal Go Down." C. Poole. Columbia 15038.

"The Car Hank Died In." The Austin Lounge Lizards. Watermelon CD–1000.

"Cocaine Blues." Johnny Cash, *Johnny Cash at Folsom Prison and San Quentin*. Columbia CG 33639.

"The Conversation." Hank Williams, Jr., and Waylon Jennings, *Whiskey Bent And Hell Bound*. Warner/Curb 237-2.

"The Dance." Garth Brooks, *Garth Brooks*. Liberty CDP 7 908972.

"Dark as the Dungeon." Johnny Cash, *Johnny Cash at Folsom Prison and San Quentin*. Columbia CG 33639.

"The Death of Floyd Collins." Fiddlin' John Carson. Okeh 40363.

"The Death of Floyd Collins"/"Little Mary Phagan." Vernon Dalhart. Columbia 15031.

"The Death of Floyd Collins"/"The Wreck of the Shenandoah." Vernon Dalhart. Victor 19779.

"The Death of Hank Williams." Jack Cardwell. King 1172.

"Delia's Gone." Johnny Cash, *American Recordings*. American Recordings 9 45520-2.

"Delta Dawn." Tanya Tucker, *The Greatest Hits Encore*. Capitol CDP 7 94254 2.

"Dirty Old Egg-Sucking Dog." Johnny Cash, *Johnny Cash at Folsom Prison and San Quentin*. Columbia CG 33639.

"Down at the Twist and Shout." Mary Chapin Carpenter, *Shooting Straight in the Dark*. Columbia CK 46077.

"Eagle When She Flies." Dolly Parton, *Eagle When She Flies*. COL 46882.

"Eli Renfro." Del McCoury and the Dixie Pals, *Classic Bluegrass*. Rebel CD-1111.

*Elvis Presley: The Million Dollar Quartet*. Elvis Presley, with Jerry Lee Lewis and Carl Perkins. RCA 2023-2-R.

"Family Tradition." Hank Williams, Jr., *The Bocephus Box: The Hank Williams, Jr., Collection 1979-1992*. 3 vols. Warner Brothers 45104.

"The Fate of Kinnie Wagner." Al Craver [Vernon Dalhart]. Columbia 15109.

"Feelin' Better." Hank Williams, Jr., *The Early Years (1976-1978)*. Warner Brothers 25514.

"Five Minutes." Lorrie Morgan, *Leave the Light On*. RCA 9594.

"Flushed From the Bathroom of Your Heart." Johnny Cash, *Johnny Cash at Folsom Prison and San Quentin*. Columbia CG 33639.

"Folsom Prison Blues." Johnny Cash, *Johnny Cash at Folsom Prison and San Quentin*. Columbia CG 33639.

"From Hank to Hendrix." Neil Young, *Harvest Moon*. Reprise 9 45057-2.

"The Ghost of Hank Williams." The Kentucky HeadHunters, *Rave On!!* Polygram 314-512568-2.

"Girls with Guitars." Wynonna, *Tell Me Why*. Curb/MCA MCAD-10822.

"Good-bye Time." Conway Twitty, *Silver Anniversary Collection*. MCAD 8035.

"The Great Speckled Bird." Roy Acuff, *The Best of Roy Acuff*. Capitol 4XL-9406.

*Guitar Player Presents Legends of Guitar—Country Vols. 1 & 2*. Rhino R2 70718/23.

"The Hanging of the Fox (or Edward Hickman, the Slayer of Little Marian Parker)." Al Craver [Vernon Dalhart]. Columbia 15251.

"Hank." Jerry Bergonzi. Red 123249-2.

"Hank." Treat Her Right. RCA 9596-2-R13.

"Hank." Hank Williams, Jr., *Living Proof*. 3 vols. Mercury 314-517 320-2.

"Hank and George, Lefty and Me." Tommy Cash. Playback PCD-4501.

"Hank and Lefty Raised My Country Soul." Stoney Edwards. Capitol 3671.

"Hank Drank." Bobby Lee Springfield. Epic EK-40816.

"Hank, It Will Never Be the Same Without You." Ernest Tubb. Decca 28630.

"Hank's Song." Ferlin Husky. Capitol 2401.

"Hank Williams from His Grave." Paleface. Polydor 314-511217-2.

"Hank Williams Led a Happy Life." The Geezinslaw Brothers. Step One SOR-0052.

"Hank Williams Meets Jimmie Rodgers." The Virginia Rounders. Rosemay 1.

"Hank Williams Sings the Blues No More." Jimmie Logsdon. Decca 28584.

"Hank Williams Will Live Forever." Johnny and Jack. Victor 20-5164.

"Hank Williams You Wrote My Life." Moe Bandy, *Greatest Hits*. Columbia 38315.

"Hank Williams's Guitar." Freddy Hart. Kapp 694.

"Hank, You Still Make Me Cry." Boxcar Willie. Mainstreet MS-9308.

"Has Anybody Here Seen Hank?" The Waterboys. Ensign F2-21589.

"He Thinks He'll Keep Her." Mary Chapin Carpenter, *Come On Come On*. Columbia CK 48881.

"Heroes of the *Vestris*." Bud Billings [Frank Luther]. Victor 40021; Frank Luther. Brunswick 277; Tommy Wilson. Vocalion 5262.

"Higher Ground." Iris DeMent, *Infamous Angel*. Warner Brothers 45238.

"I Can't Take It No Longer." Hank Williams, Jr., *Living Proof*. 3 vols. Mercury 314-517 320-2.

"I Feel Like Hank Williams Tonight." Jerry Jeff Walker. Rykodisc USA RCD-10123.

"I Got a Little Bit of Hank in Me." Charley Pride, *I Got a Little Bit of Hank in Me*. RCA.

"I Remember Hank." Lenny Breau. Genes Compact CD-5006/12.

"I Swear." John Michael Montgomery, *Kickin' It Up*. Atlantic 82559.

"I Think I Been Talkin' to Hank." Mark Chestnutt. MCA MCAD-10530.

"I Walk the Line." Johnny Cash, *Johnny Cash with His Hot and Blue Guitar*. Sun Records CRM 2013.

"(I Would Have Liked to Have Been) Hank's Little Flower Girl." Little Barbara. Coral 64150.

"In Memory of Hank Williams." Arthur Smith. MGM 11433.

"In the Pines." The Louvin Brothers, *Tragic Songs of Life*. Stetson HATC 3043.

"Keep on the Sunny Side." The Carter Family, *Anchored In Love: Their Complete Victor Recordings 1927-1928*. Rounder CD 1064; The Nitty Gritty Dirt Band, *Will the Circle Be Unbroken*. EMI E4-46589.

"Kinnie Wagner." Al Craver [Vernon Dalhart]. Columbia 15065.

"Kinnie Wagner's Surrender." Al Craver [Vernon Dalhart]. Columbia 15098.

"The Last Letter." Jimmy Swan. MGM 11450.

"Left My Gal in the Mountains." Bud and Joe Billings [Carson J. Robison and Frank Luther]. Victor 40102.

"The Life of Hank Williams." Hawkshaw Hawkins. King 1147.

*Life's Like Poetry.* Lefty Frizzell. 12 vols. Bear Family Records BCD–15550–LI.

"Little Green Valley." Vernon Dalhart and Carson J. Robison. Victor 21547.

"Little Marian Parker." Blind Andy [Andrew Jenkins]. Okeh 45197; Al Craver [Vernon Dalhart]. Columbia 15218.

"Living Proof." Hank Williams, Jr. [*Hank Williams, Jr., & Friends.* Polydor 831575]; *Living Proof.* 3 vols. Mercury 314–517 320–2.

"Log Cabin in the Lane." Jim Eanes, *Twenty Bluegrass Originals.* Highland Music DLX–7909.

"Lonely Mound of Clay." Molly O'Day and the Cumberland Mountain Folks. Bear Family Records BCD–15565–BH.

"The Long Black Veil." Johnny Cash, *Johnny Cash at Folsom Prison and San Quentin.* Columbia CG 33639.

"Mama's Opry." Iris DeMent, *Infamous Angel.* Warner Brothers 45238.

"Mammas Don't Let Your Babies Grow Up to Be Cowboys." Waylon Jennings and Willie Nelson, *Waylon and Willie.* RCA 8401–4–R.

"Me & Hank & Jumpin' Jack Flash." Marty Stuart, *This One's Gonna Hurt You.* MCA MCAD 10596.

"The Miami Storm." Vernon Dalhart. Columbia 15100; Vocalion 5000.

"Midnight in Montgomery." Alan Jackson, *Don't Rock the Jukebox.* Arista 8681.

"New River Train."/"The Sinking of the *Titanic.*" Vernon Dalhart. Columbia 15032.

"The Night Hank Williams Came to Town." Johnny Cash, *Wanted Man.* Polygram 314–522709–2.

"Nobody's Child." Hank Williams, Jr., *Living Proof.* 3 vols. Mercury 314–517 320–2.

"The Ohio Prison Fire." Bob Miller. Columbia 15548.

"Old Man Death." Ralph Stanley and the Clinch Mountain Boys, *Pray for the Boys.* Rebel C–1687.

"Open Pit Mine." The Nashville Bluegrass Band, *Waiting for the Hard Times to Go.* Sugar Hill SH–CD–3809.

"Open Up Dem Pearly Gates." Bud Billings [Frank Luther] and Carson J. Robison. Victor 40115.

"Orange Blossom Special." Johnny Cash, *Johnny Cash at Folsom Prison and San Quentin.* Columbia CG 33639.

"Papa Loved Mama." Garth Brooks, *Ropin' the Wind*. Capitol C4 96330.

"Passionate Kisses." Mary Chapin Carpenter, *Come On Come On*. Columbia CK 48881.


"Ramblin' Man." Hank Williams, *Wanderin' Around*. Polydor 833 072.

"The Red Strokes." Garth Brooks, *In Pieces*. Pearl Records CDP–7–80851–2.

*Rhythm, Country & Blues*. Various Artists. MCA 10965.

"The Ride." David Allan Coe, *Castles in the Sand*. Columbia 38535.

"The River." Garth Brooks, *Ropin' the Wind*. Capitol C4 96330.

"Rodeo." Garth Brooks, *Ropin' the Wind*. Capitol C4 96330.

"Rollin' and Ramblin' (The Death of Hank Williams)." Emmylou Harris, *Brand New Dance*. Reprise 9 26309–2; Robin and Linda Williams, *All Broken Hearts Are the Same*. Sugar Hill SH–C–1022.

"The Rose." Conway Twitty, *Silver Anniversary Collection*. MCAD 8035.


"The Scopes Trial"/"The Santa Barbara Earthquake." Vernon Dalhart. Columbia 15037.

"The Shelby Disaster." Dan Hornsby. Columbia 15321.

"She's Gone." Marty Brown, *Wild Kentucky Skies*. MCA MCAD–10672.

"Singing Teacher in Heaven." Jimmie Skinner. Capitol 2401.

"The Sinking of the *Vestris*." Jimmie Black. Okeh 45275; Frank Luther. Brunswick 277; Victor 40026; Tommy Wilson. Vocalion 5262.

"Slow Hand." Conway Twitty, *Silver Anniversary Collection*. MCAD 8035.

"Standing in the Shadows." Hank Williams, Jr., *Living Proof*. 3 vols. Mercury 314–517 320–2.

"Standing Outside the Fire." Garth Brooks, *In Pieces*. Pearl Records CDP–7–80851–2.

"Stoned at the Jukebox." Hank Williams, Jr., *Living Proof*. 3 vols. Mercury 314–517 320–2.

"Storm at Sea." Ed Helton Singers. Columbia 15327.

"The Story of C. S. Carnes." Dan Hornsby. Columbia 15321.

"Sweet Is the Melody." Iris DeMent, *My Life*. Warner Brothers 9 45493–2.

"Sydney Allen"/"Frank Dupree." Vernon Dalhart. Columbia 15042.


"Take It Like A Man." Michelle Wright, *Now & Then*. Arista Records 18685.

"That Heaven Bound Train." Johnny Ryon. Coral 60148; Cal Shrum. Ranch House 10419.

"There's a New Star in Hillbilly Heaven." The Virginia Rounders. Rosemay 2.

"The Thunder Rolls." Garth Brooks, *Friends in Low Places*. Liberty C4 93866.

"The Tragedy at Daytona Beach." Blind Andy [Andrew Jenkins]. Okeh 45343.

"Tribute to Hank Williams." Joe Rumore. Republic 100.

"A Tribute to Hank Williams, My Buddy." Luke McDaniel. Trumpet 184.

*Trio*. Dolly Parton, Linda Ronstadt, and Emmylou Harris. Warner Brothers 9 25491–2.

"25 Minutes to Go." Johnny Cash, *Johnny Cash at Folsom Prison and San Quentin*. Columbia CG 33639.

"Unanswered Prayers." Garth Brooks, *No Fences*. Liberty c4 93886.

"Wailin' with Hank." Art Farmer Quintet. New Jazz ojc–398.

"Walking the Floor Over You." Ernest Tubb, *Ernest Tubb Collection*. sor 0049.

*Wanted: The Outlaws*. Willie Nelson, Waylon Jennings, Jessi Colter, and Tompall Glaser. rca ahki–4455.

"We Bury the Hatchet." Garth Brooks, *Ropin' the Wind*. Capitol c4 96330.

"The West Plains Explosion." Vernon Dalhart. Okeh 45215.

"When He Was Young, He Was Billed as the Next Hank Williams." Jerry Farden. Recorded Books 89110.

"White Man Singing the Blues." Merle Haggard, *Best of Country Blues*. Curb Records 77368.

"Who Did They Think He Was?" Conway Twitty, *Even Now*. mcac 10335.

"Who's Gonna Fill Their Shoes?" George Jones, *Super Hits*. Epic pet 40776.

"A Whole Lotta Hank." Hank Williams, Jr., *Strong Stuff*. Warner Brothers 60223–2.

"Wild Kentucky Skies." Marty Brown, *Wild Kentucky Skies*. mca mcad–10672.

"Would You Lay With Me (In A Field of Stone)?" Tanya Tucker, *The Greatest Hits Encore*. Capitol cdp 7 94254 2.

"The Wreck of No. 9." Bud Billings [Frank Luther]. Victor 40021; Al Craver [Vernon Dalhart]. Columbia 15121; Vernon Dalhart. Brunswick 101; Okeh 45086; Vocalion 5138.

"Wreck of the Old 97." Vernon Dalhart. Victor 19427.

"The Wreck of the 1256"/"The Roving Gambler." Vernon Dalhart [Al Craver]. Columbia 15034.

"The Wreck on the Southern Old 97." Vernon Dalhart. Edison 51361; Henry Whitter. Okeh 40015.

"You've Never Been This Far Before." Conway Twitty, *Silver Anniversary Collection*. mcad 8035.

"Young Freda Bolt." The Carter Family, *The Carter Family Country Music Hall of Fame Series*. mca mcac–10088.

"Zeb Turney's Gal"/"The Letter Edged in Black." Vernon Dalhart [Al Craver]. Columbia 15049.

—Compiled by Randolph Heard

# Notes on Contributors

MARY A. BUFWACK, who holds a Ph.D. in anthropology from Washington University, is the Executive Director of United Neighborhood Health Services in Nashville. Her book *Finding Her Voice: The Saga of Women in Country Music* (coauthored by Robert K. Oermann) appeared in 1993, and she recently served as a consultant on the documentary *The Women of Country.*

DON CUSIC, Professor of Music Business at Belmont University, is the author of seven books, including biographies of Randy Travis, Reba McEntire, and Sandi Patti, as well as *The Sound of Light: A History of Gospel Music* (1990).

CURTIS W. ELLISON is Professor and Dean of Interdisciplinary Studies, School of Interdisciplinary Studies, Western College Program, at Miami University in Ohio. He is the author of *Country Music Culture: From Hard Times to Heaven* (1995).

MARK FENSTER, Assistant Professor of Mass Communications at Shenandoah University, is currently writing a book on conspiracy theory and contemporary culture.

VIVIEN GREEN FRYD, Associate Professor of Fine Arts at Vanderbilt University, is the author of *Art and Empire: The Politics of Ethnicity in the United States Capitol, 1815–1860* (1992). Her articles have appeared in such journals as *American Art* and the *American Art Journal.*

TERESA GODDU is Assistant Professor of English at Vanderbilt University, where she teaches American and African American literature. She is the author of *Gothic America: Narrative, History, and Nation* (1997).

T. WALTER HERBERT is University Scholar and Brown Professor of English at Southwestern University in Georgetown, Texas. His most recent book is *Dearest Beloved: The Hawthornes and the Making of the American Middle-Class Family.* He is currently at work on a book about sexual violence and American manhood. The essay in this volume is taken from a project provisionally entitled "Redemptive Outlaw: Willie Nelson's Texas."

CHRISTINE KREYLING is the architecture, urban planning, and design critic for the *Nashville Scene*. National winner of the American Planning Association prize for best writing, she has contributed articles to *Boulevard, Competition, Nashville Life,* and *Architecture* magazines and coedited and contributed to *Classical Nashville* (1996). She is a member of the Congress for the New Urbanism and Urbanists of the South.

MICHAEL KUREK is Associate Professor of Composition, Blair School of Music, Vanderbilt University. He was a 1994 MacDowell Fellow in Music Composition and received the 1994 Academy Award in Music from the American Academy of Arts and Letters.

AMY SCHRAGER LANG is Professor in the Graduate Institute of Liberal Arts at Emory University. She is the author of *Prophetic Woman: Anne Hutchinson and the Problem of Dissent in the Literature of New England* and a contributor to *Journeys in the New World: Early American Women's Narratives.* She is currently completing a book on the social vocabulary of nineteenth-century American fiction.

CHARMAINE LANHAM began studies in photography at Sonoma State College and has photographed the acoustic music scene nationally for over twenty-five years. She is a bluegrass music instrumentalist and is currently completing a book of photographs chronicling bluegrass music since the 1970s.

CHRISTOPHER METRESS is Assistant Professor of English at Samford University in Birmingham, Alabama. He edited *The Critical Response to Dashiell Hammett* (1994) and is currently writing a study of Southern literature and the civil rights movement.

JOCELYN NEAL is a doctoral student in music theory at the Eastman School of Music. Her interests include rhythmic theory and twentieth-century analysis. She also competes in both ballroom and country dance contests.

TERESA ORTEGA is a freelance writer living in Schenectady, New York. Her work has appeared in *Sinister Wisdom* and *Lambda Book Report,* and she is currently completing a book, *Tall Tales of Lesbian Boyhood: Reflections on Childhood Sexuality.*

RICHARD A. PETERSON, a sociologist of culture at Vanderbilt University, is the founding chair of the Culture Section of the American Sociological Association. The coeditor (with Melton A. McLaurin) of *You Wrote My Life: Lyrical Themes in Country Music* (1992), he is also the author of *Creating Country Music: Fabricating Authenticity* (1997).

RONNIE PUGH, Head of Reference, Country Music Foundation Library and Media Center, has published *Ernest Tubb: The Texas Troubadour* (Duke University Press, 1996).

JOHN W. RUMBLE completed his doctoral work in history at Vanderbilt University and is the historian at the Country Music Foundation. He has contributed essays to the *Journal of Country Music* and prepared biographies for audio compact disc boxed-set reissues of the music of Roy Acuff and Bill Monroe for Time-Life and MCA. He is currently completing a book on Fred Rose.

DAVID SANJEK is the Archivist of Broadcast Music Inc. (BMI). He coauthored (with his father, the late Russell Sanjek) *The American Popular Music Business in the 20th Century* (1991). He has also published articles on music, film, and cultural studies, and he is currently working on a book, *Ain't Nothing Like the Real Thing: Music, Memory, Myth, and the Movies*.

CECELIA TICHI, William R. Kenan, Jr., Professor of English at Vanderbilt University, is a past president of the American Studies Association and the author of *High Lonesome: The American Culture of Country Music* (1994).

PAMELA WILSON, a doctoral candidate in media and cultural studies at the University of Wisconsin, now lives in Virginia, where she is completing her dissertation on television journalism and Native Americans in the 1950s. Her articles have appeared in the *Historical Journal of Film, Radio and Television* and in *Living Color: Race, Feminism, Television,* edited by Sasha Torres.

CHARLES K. WOLFE, Professor of English at Middle Tennessee State University, is the author of some fourteen books on country music, blues, and folk music. Most recently, he coauthored (with Kip Lornell) *The Life and Legend of Leadbelly* (1992), which won an ASCAP-Deems Taylor award. A three-time Grammy nominee, he is currently working on a study of bluegrass pioneer Bill Monroe.

# Index

Library of Congress Cataloging-in-Publication Data

Reading country music : steel guitars, opry stars, and honky-tonk
bars / Cecelia Tichi, editor.

p.   cm.

Includes essays previously published in v. 94, no. 1 (1995) of the
South Atlantic Quarterly.

Discography: p.

Includes index.

ISBN 0-8223-2156-4 (cloth : alk. paper). — ISBN 0-8223-2168-8
(paper : alk. paper)

1. Country music—History and criticism.   2. Country musicians.
I. Tichi, Cecelia.   II. South Atlantic Quarterly.

ML3524.R43   1998

781.642—dc21   97-49637   CIP   MN